FRANZ KAFKA IN CONTEXT

Franz Kafka (1883–1924) lived through one of the most turbulent periods in modern history, witnessing a world war, the dissolution of an empire and the foundation of a new nation state. But the early twentieth century was also a time of social progress and aesthetic experimentation. Kafka's novels and short stories reflect their author's keen but critical engagement with the big questions of his time, and yet often Kafka is still cast as a solitary figure with little or no connection to his age. *Franz Kafka in Context* aims to redress this perception. In thirty-five short, accessible essays, leading international scholars explore Kafka's personal and working life, his reception of art and culture, his engagement with political and social issues, and his ongoing reception and influence. Together they offer a nuanced and historically grounded image of a writer whose work continues to fascinate readers from all backgrounds.

CAROLIN DUTTLINGER is Associate Professor in German at the University of Oxford, a Fellow of Wadham College, and Co-Director of the Oxford Kafka Research Centre. An international expert on German modernism, she has been awarded numerous prizes and fellowships, including the Zvi-Meitar/Vice-Chancellor Oxford University Research Prize in the Humanities. She is the author of *Kafka and Photography* (2007) and *The Cambridge Introduction to Franz Kafka* (2013), the editor of *Franz Kafkas 'Betrachtung': Neue Lektüren* (2014) and the co-editor of *Walter Benjamins anthropologisches Denken* (2012) and *Weimar Photography in Context* (2017).

FRANZ KAFKA IN CONTEXT

EDITED BY
CAROLIN DUTTLINGER
University of Oxford

CAMBRIDGE
UNIVERSITY PRESS

CAMBRIDGE
UNIVERSITY PRESS

University Printing House, Cambridge CB2 8BS, United Kingdom

One Liberty Plaza, 20th Floor, New York, NY 10006, USA

477 Williamstown Road, Port Melbourne, VIC 3207, Australia

314-321, 3rd Floor, Plot 3, Splendor Forum, Jasola District Centre,
New Delhi - 110025, India

79 Anson Road, #06-04/06, Singapore 079906

Cambridge University Press is part of the University of Cambridge.

It furthers the University's mission by disseminating knowledge in the pursuit of
education, learning, and research at the highest international levels of excellence.

www.cambridge.org
Information on this title: www.cambridge.org/9781107085497
DOI: 10.1017/9781316084243

© Cambridge University Press 2018

First published 2018

Printed in the United Kingdom by Clays, St Ives plc

A catalogue record for this publication is available from the British Library

Library of Congress Cataloging-in-Publication data
Names: Duttlinger, Carolin, 1976– editor.
Title: Franz Kafka in context / edited by Carolin Duttlinger.
Description: New York : Cambridge University Press, 2017. | Series: Literature in context |
Includes bibliographical references and index.
Identifiers: LCCN 2017034613 | ISBN 9781107085497 (hardback)
Subjects: LCSH: Kafka, Franz, 1883–1924 – Criticism and interpretation. |
Prague (Czech Republic) – Intellectual life – History – 20th century.
Classification: LCC PT2621.A26   Z71847   2017 | DDC 833/.912–dc23 LC record
available at https://lccn.loc.gov/2017034613

ISBN 978-1-107-08549-7 Hardback

Contents

Illustrations

Notes on Contributors

MARK M. ANDERSON is Professor of German literature in the Department of Germanic Languages and Director of Deutsches Haus at Columbia University. The author of *Kafka's Clothes: Ornament and Aestheticism in the Habsburg Fin de Siècle* (1992) and editor of *Reading Kafka: Prague, Politics and the Fin de Siècle* (1989), he helped to introduce a new historical reading of Kafka. He recently edited Kafka's *The Metamorphosis* for the Norton Critical Editions series. He has also written widely on German literature from the modernist period to post-war authors such as Paul Celan, Ingeborg Bachmann, Thomas Bernhard and W. G. Sebald, and is currently working on a book about W. G. Sebald's youth.

ELIZABETH BOA is Professor Emerita of German at the University of Nottingham. Her publications on Kafka include *Kafka: Gender, Class, and Race in the Letters and Fictions* (1996); 'The Castle' in *The Cambridge Companion to Kafka* (2002); 'Karl Rossmann or the Boy who Wouldn't Grow Up' in Mary Orr and Lesley Sharpe (eds.), *From Goethe to Gide: Feminism, Aesthetics and the French and German Literary Canon* (2005); 'Figurenkonstellationen' in Manfred Engel and Bernd Auerochs (eds.), *Kafka Handbuch* (2010); 'Inside/Outside: Topographies of Self and World in Kafka's *Betrachtung*' in Carolin Duttlinger (ed.), *Kafkas Betrachtung: Neue Lektüren* (2014); and 'Observations on Time and Motion: Kafka's *Betrachtung* and the Visual Arts around 1912' in Anne Fuchs and J. J. Long (eds.), *Time in German Literature and Culture 1900–2015* (2016).

STANLEY CORNGOLD is Professor Emeritus of German and Comparative Literature at Princeton University. In 2009, with Benno Wagner and Jack Greenberg, he edited, with commentary, *Franz Kafka: The Office Writings*. In 2010, he published, with Benno Wagner, *Franz Kafka: The Ghosts in the Machine* and edited, with Ruth V. Gross, a collection of essays titled *Kafka for the Twenty-First Century*. Since then he has edited, with his translation, a Modern Library edition of Kafka's *The Metamorphosis*, translated Goethe's *The Sufferings of Young Werther* and completed an intellectual biography of the philosopher Walter Kaufmann.

MARK CORNWALL is Professor of Modern European History at the University of Southampton. He specializes in the late Habsburg Empire and twentieth-century Eastern Europe, especially the evolution of Czech, Hungarian and South Slav nationalism. His publications include *The Undermining of Austria-Hungary: The Battle for Hearts and Minds* (2000); *The Devil's Wall: The Nationalist Youth Mission of Heinz Rutha* (2012) (a study of German nationalism in the Bohemian lands); and, as editor with John Paul Newman, *Sacrifice and Rebirth: The Legacy of the Last Habsburg War* (2016). He is currently writing a book about treason in the late Habsburg monarchy.

CAROLIN DUTTLINGER is Associate Professor in German at the University of Oxford, Fellow of Wadham College Oxford and Co-Director of the Oxford Kafka Research Centre. Her research interests include German literature, thought and culture from the nineteenth century to the present; the relationship between literature, photography and visual culture; and the interplay of attention and distraction in literature and cultural history. She is the author of *Kafka and Photography* (2007) and *The Cambridge Introduction to Franz Kafka* (2013), and the editor of *Franz Kafkas 'Betrachtung': Neue Lektüren* (2014). She has also co-edited, with Johannes Birgfeld, *Curiosity in German Literature and Culture after 1700* (2009); with Ben Morgan and Anthony Phelan, *Walter Benjamins anthropologisches Denken* (2012); and with Silke Horstkotte, *Weimar Photography in Context* (2017).

MANFRED ENGEL is Professor of Modern German Literature at Saarland University and co-director of the ICLA Research-Committee 'Dream-Cultures: Cultural and Literary History of the Dream'; he was formerly Professor of German and European Literature at the FernUniversität Hagen and Taylor Chair of German Literature at the University of Oxford. His publications include *KulturPoetik: Journal for Cultural Poetics* (2000 onwards; edited with Bernard Dieterle, Monika Ritzer and Benjamin Specht); *Kafka-Handbuch* (2010; edited with Bernd Auerochs); and *Kafka und die Religion in der Moderne/Kafka, Religion, and Modernity* (2014, edited with Ritchie Robertson).

KATJA GARLOFF is Professor of German and Humanities at Reed College in Portland, Oregon. She is the author of *Words from Abroad: Trauma and Displacement in Postwar German Jewish Writers* (2005) and *Mixed Feelings: Tropes of Love in German Jewish Culture* (2016). She has published articles on authors such as Lessing, Kafka, Walser, Roth, Weiss, Celan, Adorno, Arendt, Sebald, Honigmann and Stein and is currently co-editing (with Agnes Mueller) a volume on contemporary German Jewish literature.

NICOLA GESS is Professor of German Literature at Basel University. She is the author of *Primitives Denken: Kinder, Wilde und Wahnsinnige in der literarischen Moderne (Müller, Musil, Benn, Benjamin)* (2013) and *Gewalt der Musik: Literatur und Musikkritik um 1800* (2006); she is the editor of *Literarischer Primitivismus* (2012) and the co-editor of several books, including *Primitivismus intermedial* (2015); *Barocktheater als Spektakel: Maschine, Blick und Bewegung auf der Opernbühne des Ancien Regime* (2015); and *Wissens-Ordnungen: Zu einer historischen Epistemologie der Literatur* (2014).

RUTH V. GROSS is Professor of German and head of the Department of Languages and Literatures at North Carolina State University. She is the co-editor of *Kafka for the Twenty-First Century* (2011), an author and co-editor of *A Franz Kafka Encyclopedia* (2005), and the editor of *Critical Essays on Franz Kafka* (1990). Her numerous articles on Kafka and other twentieth- century German and Austrian authors have appeared in *PMLA, Monatshefte, The Literary Review, The German Quarterly, Modern Austrian Literature, Storia della Storiografia* and *Journal of the Kafka Society of America*, among others.

MARK HARMAN, Professor of English and German at Elizabethtown College, has translated a range of works by German-language authors, including two novels by Kafka – *Amerika: The Missing Person* (2008) and *The Castle* (1998), which won the first Lois Roth Award of the Modern Language Association – and works by Rilke, Hesse and various contemporary writers. Editor and co-translator of *Robert Walser Rediscovered: Stories, Fairy-Tale Plays and Critical Responses* (1985), he has written widely about modern German and Irish literature, with special emphasis on Kafka, Joyce and Beckett. He is currently completing a volume of annotated translations of selected Kafka stories.

SILKE HORSTKOTTE is Marie Curie Research Fellow in German at the University of Warwick. Her publications include *Nachbilder: Fotografie und Gedächtnis in der deutschen Gegenwartsliteratur* (2009), *Poetiken der Gegenwart: Deutschsprachige Romane nach 2000* (2013, co-edited with

Leonhard Herrmann), *Lesen ist wie Sehen: Intermediale Zitate in Bild und Text* (2006, with Karin Leonhard), and a special issue of *Poetics Today* dedicated to 'Photography in Fiction' (spring 2008, with Nancy Pedri).

CLAYTON KOELB is the Guy B. Johnson Distinguished Professor in the Department of Germanic and Slavic Languages and Professor of English and Comparative Literature at the University of North Carolina, Chapel Hill. He is past president of the Kafka Society of America. Among his books are *Kafka's Rhetoric: The Passion of Reading* (1989), *The Revivifying Word* (2008) and *Kafka: A Guide for the Perplexed* (2010).

KATHARINA LASZLO is currently completing a D.Phil. on the representation of children and childhood in Kafka's works at the University of Oxford. Apart from Kafka, she is especially interested in the cultural history of modernism, the intersection between literature and philosophy and literary nonfiction. She also works as a freelance journalist in Berlin, writing mainly about literature for the Arts section of *Frankfurter Allgemeine Zeitung*.

J.J. LONG is Professor of German and Visual Culture at the University of Durham. He is the author of *The Novels of Thomas Bernhard* (2001) and *W. G. Sebald: Image, Archive, Modernity* (2007) and has published widely on twentieth-century German and Austrian writing, photography and the intersections between the visual and verbal media.

THOMAS MARTINEC is Lecturer in German at the University of Regensburg. He has published various articles on music in German literature (Lessing, early Romanticism, Rilke) and is currently working on a monograph on musical practices around 1900. He has also published widely on the theory of tragedy in the long eighteenth century.

BEN MORGAN is Fellow and Tutor in German at Worcester College, Associate Professor of German and Co-Convenor of the Oxford Comparative Criticism and Translation Programme at the University of Oxford. He is the author of *On Becoming God: Late Medieval Mysticism and the Modern Western Self* (2013) and articles on modernist literature, film and philosophy in the German-speaking world (Trakl, Kafka and Kierkegaard, Benjamin and Heidegger, Fritz Lang, Leni Riefenstahl, the Frankfurt School). He is also the editor, with Carolin Duttlinger and Anthony Phelan, of *Walter Benjamins anthropologisches Denken* (2012), and, with Sowon Park and Ellen Spolsky, of a Special Issue of *Poetics Today* on 'Situated Cognition and the Study of Culture' (2017).

LOTHAR MÜLLER is the editor of the features section of the *Süddeutsche Zeitung*. He taught general and comparative literature at Berlin Free University and, since 2010, he has been an Honorary Professor at the Humboldt University in Berlin. In 2013 he was awarded the Berlin Prize for Literary Criticism. He is the author of *Die kranke Seele und das Licht der Erkenntnis: Karl Philipp Moritz' Anton Reiser* (1987), *Die zweite Stimme: Vortragskunst von Goethe bis Kafka* (2007) and *White Magic: The Age of Paper* (2015).

MAREK NEKULA is a Professor at the Institute for Slavic Studies at the University of Regensburg. He participated in the creation of the Czech edition of Franz Kafka's oeuvre and the critical German edition of Franz Kafka's letters, edited by Hans-Gerd Koch. He is the author of *Franz Kafkas Sprachen* (2003), dealing with Kafka's Czech and German in their Central European context, and *Franz Kafka and his Prague Contexts* (2016), which discusses Kafka's reception in Czechoslovakia around 1963, his languages and Czech readings, as well as the reflection of language in Kafka's stories and his reading of Prague.

CLAUDIA NITSCHKE is Professor of German at Durham University. She is the author of *Utopie und Krieg bei Ludwig Achim von Arnim* (2004) and *Der öffentliche Vater: Konzeptionen paternaler Souveränität in der deutschen Literatur (1751–1921)* (2012) and of several articles on Kafka.

ANTHONY NORTHEY is Professor Emeritus at Acadia University. Over the last forty years he has been engaged in biographical research on Franz Kafka and the minor Prague literary figures Josef Adolf Bondy, Hermine Hanel and Marie Gibian. He is the author of *Kafkas Mischpoche* (1988), which also appeared in English as *Kafka's Relatives* (1991) and in four other translations. In addition to a translation of Kafka's unfinished America novel (*Lost in America*, 2010) he has written numerous articles on Kafka's life and work; his most recent one (co-authored with Eva Maria Mandl), presenting newly discovered interesting information on members of the wider family of Kafka's mother, Julie Löwy (some of them very wealthy and influential), will be published soon.

DORA OSBORNE is Lecturer in German at the University of St Andrews. She is the author of *Traces of Trauma in W. G. Sebald and Christoph Ransmayr* (2013) and editor of *Edinburgh German Yearbook* 9 (2015). Her current research looks at the role of the archive in German memory culture, and she has published articles on recent trends in memorialization as well as work by contemporary authors and visual artists.

ANTHONY PHELAN is Emeritus Fellow in German at Keble College, Oxford, where he was Professor of German Romantic Literature. He has written widely on German literature and thought from Wieland and Goethe to Benjamin and Brecht. His *Reading Heinrich Heine* appeared in 2007. His main interest is in the relation between philosophical critique and literature in modernity.

RITCHIE ROBERTSON is Taylor Professor of German at the University of Oxford. His books include *Kafka: Judaism, Politics, and Literature* (1985) and *Kafka: A Very Short Introduction* (2004). With Carolin Duttlinger and others, he is a director of the Oxford Kafka Research Centre.

LUCIA RUPRECHT is an affiliated Lecturer at the Department of German and Dutch, University of Cambridge, and a Fellow of Emmanuel College. She is the author of *Dances of the Self in Heinrich von Kleist, E. T. A. Hoffmann and Heinrich Heine* (2006, Special Citation of the de la Torre Bueno Prize), editor of *Towards an Ethics of Gesture* (*Performance Philosophy*, 2017), and co-editor of *Performance and Performativity in German Cultural Studies* (with Carolin Duttlinger and Andrew Webber, 2003), *Cultural Pleasure* (with Michael Minden, 2009) and *New German Dance Studies* (with Susan Manning, 2012). She is currently completing the manuscript of a book entitled *Gestural Imaginaries: Dance and the Culture of Gestures at the Beginning of the Twentieth Century*, under contract with Oxford University Press.

JUDITH RYAN is the Robert K. and Dale J. Weary Professor of German and Comparative Literature at Harvard University. Her long-standing interest in Kafka led to substantial involvement in the Kafka Society of America, where she was a member of the editorial board and served twice as President. Her main publications on Kafka have exlored the development of his characteristic narrative strategies and their implications for the presentation of epistemological and psychological issues in his works. A chapter on Kafka in her book *The Vanishing Subject: Early Psychology and Literary Modernism* (1991) also focuses on those issues. Her current book-length project, *Colonial Fever*, includes a chapter on Kafka's engagement with colonialism and its aftermath.

ROGER THIEL is a Research Fellow in Religious Studies at the Friedrich-Alexander University of Erlangen-Nuremberg. He is a member of the Research Group on Sacrality and Sacralisation in the Middle Ages and in Early Modern Times: Intercultural Perspectives in Europe and Asia, funded by the German Research Foundation. His current research is

devoted to sacred things and investigates the history, theory and transformation of extraordinary objects. His interdisciplinary book on Kafka,
Anarchitektur: Lektüren zur Architektur-Kritik bei Franz Kafka, was published in 2011. He has also published numerous articles on religion,
art, architecture, philosophy and literature from the seventeenth to the
twenty-first century.

EMILY T. TROSCIANKO is Research Associate in the Faculty of Medieval
and Modern Languages at the University of Oxford, and conducts
research in the cognitive and medical humanities. She also writes for
non-academic audiences, notably via her Psychology Today blog about
eating disorders, *A Hunger Artist*. Her doctoral research on the cognitive
effects of Kafka's prose was published by Routledge in 2014 as *Kafka's
Cognitive Realism*. Writing subsequently about cognitive realism and
starvation in Kafka's short story 'A Hunger Artist' helped inspire her
current project, which involves empirical and theoretical exploration of
how fiction-reading affects mental health, and vice versa.

JOHANNES TÜRK is Associate Professor of Germanic Studies and Adjunct
Professor of Comparative Literature at Indiana University Bloomington.
He also serves as director of the Institute of German Studies. He is the
author of *Die Immunität der Literatur* (2011). He co-edited, with Robert
Buch, the special issue of *Germanic Review*, *Figures and Figuration of the
(Un-)Dead*. He has published on Marcel Proust, Franz Kafka, Heinrich
von Kleist, Carl Schmitt and Thomas Mann, as well as on empathy and
on immunology. He is currently working on projects about immunity
as a political concept as well as on political emotions.

BENNO WAGNER teaches Global Studies and German Studies at Zhejiang
University, Hangzhou. His research interests include literature and/as
actor network; literature and/as digital interface; travel writing and spatial history; and political metaphors. He has published and co-edited
books on German political metaphors and on the *post histoire*, and he is
the author of numerous articles on Franz Kafka. From the mid-1990s, he
reconstructed and co-edited Franz Kafka's legal writings from Czech and
Austrian archives (*Amtliche Schriften*, 2004; *The Office Writings*, 2008).
He is currently preparing an actor network theory-based re-reading of
Kafka's work.

ANDREW J. WEBBER is Professor of Modern German and Comparative Culture at the University of Cambridge. His books include *The
European Avant-Garde, 1900–1940* (2004) and *Berlin in the Twentieth*

Century: A Cultural Topography (2008). He is the editor of the *Cambridge Companion to the Literature of Berlin* (2017) and Principal Investigator of the AHRC-funded project, 'A Digital Critical Edition of Middle-Period Works by Arthur Schnitzler'.

DANIEL WEIDNER is Professor for the Study of Culture and Religion at the Humboldt University in Berlin and Associate Director of the Centre for Literary and Cultural Research. His main areas of research are the interrelation of religion and literature, theories of secularization, the history of philology and literary theory and German-Jewish Literature. Among his publications are *Gershom Scholem: Politisches, esoterisches und historiographisches Schreiben* (2003), *Bibel und Literatur um 1800* (2011), *Sakramentale Repräsentation: Substanz, Zeichen und Präsenz in der Frühen Neuzeit* (with Stefanie Ertz and Heike Schlie, 2012). Recent English publications include 'The Rhetoric of Secularization', *New German Critique*, 120 (2014), and 'The Political Theology of Ethical Monotheism' in M. Kavka and R. Raskover (eds.), *Judaism, Liberalism, and Political Theology* (2014).

MATTHIAS ZACH is the Academic Coordinator of the Forum for Global and Transregional Studies at the University of Göttingen. He previously worked as a post-doctoral researcher at the University of Bremen's Institute for Postcolonial and Transcultural Studies. His publications include a monograph on poet-translators Yves Bonnefoy and Paul Celan as translators of Shakespeare, as well as articles on the aesthetics and politics of literary translation, on literary multilingualism and on the translation of Orientalist stereotypes.

THEODORE ZIOLKOWSKI is Class of 1900 Professor Emeritus of German and Comparative Literature and past Dean of the Graduate School at Princeton University. He has published over thirty books in the fields of German Romanticism and reception of classical antiquity in modern literature. His most recent publications are *Classicism of the Twenties: Art, Music and Literature* (2015), *The Alchemist in Literature: From Dante to the Present* (2015) and *Uses and Abuses of Moses: Literary Representations since the Enlightenment* (2016).

PETER ZUSI is Lecturer in Czech and Slovak Studies at University College London, School of Slavonic and East European Studies. His main research focus is Central European modernism, with a strong interest in avant-gardes and the relation between literature and visual arts, particularly architecture. He has published articles on various aspects of the

Czech interwar avant-garde and on figures such as Kafka, Rilke, Benjamin and Lukács. He recently edited a special issue of *Central Europe* titled 'Cultures of Bohemia in the Twentieth Century' and is currently writing a book on Kafka and Czech modernism.

Chronology

1883	3 July: Franz Kafka is born in Prague to Hermann Kafka (1852–1931) and his wife, Julie, née Löwy (1856–1934).
1885	Birth of Kafka's younger brother Georg, who dies of measles at the age of fifteen months.
1887	Birth of Kafka's younger brother Heinrich, who dies of meningitis at the age of six months.
1889	September: Kafka starts school at the Deutsche Volks- und Bürgerschule in Prague. Birth of Kafka's sister Gabriele ('Elli'; d. 1941).
1890	Birth of Kafka's sister Valerie ('Valli'; d. 1942).
1892	Birth of Kafka's sister Ottilie ('Ottla'; d. 1943).
1893	Kafka transfers to the Altstädter deutsches Gymnasium housed in the Kinsky-Palais at the Altstädter Ring.
1896	June: Kafka celebrates his Bar-Mitzvah at the Zigeuner-Synagoge in Prague; the invitations sent by Hermann Kafka refer to his son's 'confirmation'.
1897	Anti-German attacks by Czech nationalists soon extend to Jewish businesses; the Kafkas' haberdashery shop is spared.
1901	July: Kafka passes his *Abitur* (A-levels) and then goes on his first longer trip, to the German North Sea islands of Norderney and Heligoland. October: Kafka matriculates at the German-language section of the Karl-Ferdinands-Universität (Charles University) in Prague. After two weeks of studying chemistry, he changes to law; in the course of his degree he also attends seminars and lectures in philosophy, psychology, German literature, art history, Latin and Greek.
1902	In the summer Kafka and his friend Paul Kisch make plans to move to Munich to study German literature but, unlike Kisch, Kafka continues with his law degree in Prague. He meets

Max Brod (1884–1968), who will become his close friend, at a student society event. A prolific writer in his own right, Brod will later become Kafka's posthumous editor.

1906   Kafka gains his doctorate in law with the lowest pass mark and begins an internship in the Prague law courts.

1907   Kafka starts working for the Prague branch of the Trieste-based insurance company Assicurazioni Generali.

1908   Kafka moves to the state-run Arbeiter-Unfall-Versicherungs-Anstalt für das Königreich Böhmen (Workers' Accident Insurance Institute for the Kingdom of Bohemia). Eight of his short prose pieces are published in the journal *Hyperion*.

1909   September: Kafka goes on holiday with Max Brod and his brother Otto to Riva on Lake Garda. On their way home, they attend an airshow in Brescia, which will become the subject of Kafka's short text 'Die Aeroplane in Brescia' ('The Aeroplanes in Brescia').

1910   October: trip to Paris with Max and Otto Brod; Kafka returns home early because of an abscess.

1911   August–September: trip with Max Brod to Switzerland, Northern Italy and Paris. In the autumn and winter Kafka attends the performances of a Yiddish theatre troupe at the Café Savoy in Prague and befriends the actor Jizchak Löwy.

1912   June–July: trip to Weimar via Leipzig with Max Brod. In Leipzig Kafka meets Brod's publisher, Kurt Wolff, who offers him a contract for a volume of short prose. At the end of the trip Kafka spends three weeks alone at the Jungborn sanatorium in the Harz Mountains. 13 August: Kafka meets his later fiancée, the Berlin-based office clerk Felice Bauer (1887–1960), in the house of Brod's parents. September: Kafka sends his first letter to Bauer. Two days later, on 22/23 September, he writes his short story 'Das Urteil' ('The Judgement'), widely considered his breakthrough text, in a single night. September: Kafka starts working on his first novel, *Der Verschollene* (*The Man who Disappeared*). November–December: he writes *Die Verwandlung* (*The Metamorphosis*). December: Kafka's first book, the collection *Betrachtung* (*Meditation*), is published by Kurt Wolff in Leipzig.

1913   Kafka visits Felice Bauer three times in Berlin. May: *Der Heizer* (*The Stoker*), the first chapter of *The Man who Disappeared*, is published as a self-contained volume by Wolff in the

avant-garde series *Der jüngste Tag* (*The Last Judgement*).
September: Kafka attends a conference on accident prevention
in Vienna, and also looks in on the Eleventh Zionist Congress.
From Vienna he travels on to Riva (northern Italy), where he
stays in a sanatorium.

1914   1 June: Kafka and Felice Bauer get officially engaged in Berlin.
12 July: the engagement is dissolved by Bauer, who confronts
Kafka about his secret correspondence with her friend Grete
Bloch. Kafka goes on holiday with the writer Ernst Weiss in the
Danish resort of Marielyst. 1 August: Austria-Hungary declares
war on Serbia; beginning of the First World War. August: Kafka
starts writing his second novel *Der Process* (*The Trial*). October:
he takes time off work to focus on *The Trial* but writes 'In der
Strafkolonie' ('In the Penal Colony') instead.

1915   January: Kafka gives up work on *The Trial*; he meets up with
Felice Bauer for the first time since their break-up and reads her
the doorkeeper parable from *The Trial*. December: *The
Metamorphosis* is published by Wolff. The playwright Carl
Sternheim, who has been awarded the Fontane Prize for
literature, passes on the prize money to Kafka.

1916   Reconciliation with Felice Bauer. July: Kafka and Bauer spend
ten days together in the Bohemian resort Marienbad
(Mariánské Lázně). 'Das Urteil' ('The Judgement') is published
as a self-contained volume by Wolff. November 1916 – April
1917: Kafka uses a house his sister Ottla has rented in the Castle
District as a writing retreat, producing the stories that will make
up the collection *Ein Landarzt* (*A Country Doctor*).

1917   July: Kafka and Felice Bauer visit Bauer's sister Else Braun in
Budapest and renew their engagement. 12–13 and 13–14 August:
Kafka suffers two nocturnal haemorrhages, which are then
diagnosed as tubercular. September: he moves to the Bohemian
village of Zürau (Siřem) to live with his sister Ottla. December:
visit by Bauer; the engagement is dissolved.

1918   May: Kafka returns to Prague and resumes work. October: he
contracts the Spanish flu. November: he returns to work for
four days and is given leave again. He stays in a hotel in
Schelesen (Želízy).

1919   January: Kafka meets Julie Wohryzeck (1891–1944) while in
Schelesen. April: he returns to Prague and to work. September:
he gets engaged to Wohryzeck; his parents try to jeopardize the

match. October: *In der Strafkolonie* (*In the Penal Colony*) is published by Wolff.

1920   February/March: Kafka begins an intense correspondence with the married journalist and translator Milena Jesenká-Polak (1896–1944). May: *Ein Landarzt* (*A Country Doctor*) is published by Wolff. Late June/early July: Kafka spends six days with Jesenká in Vienna. July: he ends his engagement with Julie Wohryzeck. December: Kafka is granted health leave again; he stays in a sanatorium in Matliary in the Tatra Mountains until August 1921.

1921   January: Kafka ends the correspondence with Milena Jesenká. September: he returns to work but takes three further months' sick leave from October.

1922   January: Kafka's sick leave is extended again until April. He stays in a hotel in Spindlermühle (Špindlerův Mlýn) in the Tatra Mountains, where he writes his final novel, *Das Schloss* (*The Castle*). 1 July: Kafka is granted early retirement on health grounds by the Insurance Institute.

1923   July: Kafka is on holiday in Müritz on the Baltic Sea, where he meets Dora Diamant (1898–1952). September: Kafka moves to Berlin where he lives with Diamant; because of the hyper-inflation their financial circumstances are very strained.

1924   March: because of his declining health Kafka returns to Prague; he writes his final short story, 'Josefine, die Sängerin oder Das Volk der Mäuse' ('Josefine, the Singer or The Mouse People'). April: it is diagnosed that his tuberculosis has spread to the larynx. Accompanied by Dora Diamant, he moves from a sanatorium in Ortmann (Lower Austria) to a laryngological clinic in Vienna, and from there to a small sanatorium in Kierling near Klosterneuburg. 3 June: Kafka dies, with Diamant at his side. August: his collection *Ein Hungerkünstler* (*A Hunger Artist*) is published by Die Schmiede.

1925   *Der Process* (*The Trial*), edited by Max Brod, is published by Die Schmiede.

1926   *Das Schloss* (*The Castle*), edited by Brod, is published by Wolff.

1927   *Amerika*, now known by Kafka's own title, *Der Verschollene* (*The Man who Disappeared*), edited by Brod, is published by Wolff.

1939   Max Brod leaves Prague on the last train before the German invasion, taking Kafka's manuscripts with him, and reaches Palestine.

1956   Brod transfers the manuscripts (with the exception of *The Trial*) to a bank vault in Zurich.

1961   The Oxford German scholar Malcolm Pasley, with the permission of Kafka's heirs, transfers the manuscripts to the Bodleian Library Oxford.

Abbreviations and Note on the Texts

The following abbreviations are used in this book. Where a published translation is available, all quotations are referenced first to the English version and then to the German original. On occasion, translations have been tacitly modified. For works that have not been translated, the contributors have provided their own translations.

Unless otherwise stated, ellipses are editorial rather than part of the original text.

Fictional Writings

C	*The Castle*, trans. Anthea Bell (Oxford University Press, 2009)
CSS	*The Complete Stories*, ed. Nahum N. Glatzer (New York, NY: Schocken, 1976)
DL	*Drucke zu Lebzeiten*, ed. Wolf Kittler, Hans-Gerd Koch and Gerhard Neumann. Franz Kafka: Schriften, Tagebücher, Briefe: Kritische Ausgabe (Frankfurt am Main: Fischer, 1996)
DLA	*Drucke zu Lebzeiten: Apparatband*, ed. Wolf Kittler, Hans-Gerd Koch and Gerhard Neumann. Franz Kafka: Schriften, Tagebücher, Briefe: Kritische Ausgabe (Frankfurt am Main: Fischer, 1996)
HA	*A Hunger Artist and Other Stories*, trans. Joyce Crick (Oxford University Press, 2012)
M	*The Metamorphosis and Other Stories*, trans. Joyce Crick (Oxford University Press, 2009)
MD	*The Man who Disappeared (America)*, trans. Ritchie Robertson (Oxford University Press, 2012)
NSI	*Nachgelassene Schriften und Fragmente I*, ed. Malcolm Pasley. Franz Kafka: Schriften, Tagebücher, Briefe: Kritische Ausgabe (Frankfurt am Main: Fischer, 1993)

NSIA   *Nachgelassene Schriften und Fragmente I: Apparatband*, ed.
Malcolm Pasley. Franz Kafka: Schriften, Tagebücher, Briefe:
Kritische Ausgabe (Frankfurt am Main: Fischer, 1993)

NSII   *Nachgelassene Schriften und Fragmente II*, ed. Malcolm Pasley.
Franz Kafka: Schriften, Tagebücher, Briefe: Kritische Ausgabe
(Frankfurt am Main: Fischer, 1992)

NSIIA   *Nachgelassene Schriften und Fragmente II: Apparatband*, ed.
Malcolm Pasley. Franz Kafka: Schriften, Tagebücher, Briefe:
Kritische Ausgabe (Frankfurt am Main: Fischer, 1992)

ON   *The Blue Octavo Notebooks*, ed. Max Brod and trans. Ernst
Kaiser and Eithne Wilkins (Cambridge, MA: Exact Change,
1991)

P   *Der Proceß*, ed. Malcolm Pasley. Franz Kafka: Schriften,
Tagebücher, Briefe: Kritische Ausgabe (Frankfurt am Main:
Fischer, 1990)

PA   *Der Proceß: Apparatband*, ed. Malcolm Pasley. Franz Kafka:
Schriften, Tagebücher, Briefe: Kritische Ausgabe (Frankfurt
am Main: Fischer, 1990)

S   *Das Schloß*, ed. Malcolm Pasley. Franz Kafka: Schriften,
Tagebücher, Briefe: Kritische Ausgabe (Frankfurt am Main:
Fischer, 1982)

SA   *Das Schloß: Apparatband*, ed. Malcolm Pasley. Franz Kafka:
Schriften, Tagebücher, Briefe: Kritische Ausgabe (Frankfurt
am Main: Fischer, 1982)

T   *The Trial*, trans. Mike Mitchell (Oxford University Press,
2009)

V   *Der Verschollene*, ed. Jost Schillemeit. Franz Kafka: Schriften,
Tagebücher, Briefe: Kritische Ausgabe (Frankfurt am Main:
Fischer, 1983)

VA   *Der Verschollene: Apparatband*, ed. Jost Schillemeit. Franz
Kafka: Schriften, Tagebücher, Briefe: Kritische Ausgabe
(Frankfurt am Main: Fischer, 1983)

Z   *The Zürau Aphorisms*, trans. Michael Hofmann; intro. and
afterword Roberto Calasso (London: Harvill Secker, 2006)

Non-Fictional Writings

A   *Amtliche Schriften*, ed. Klaus Hermsdorf and Benno Wagner.
Franz Kafka: Schriften, Tagebücher, Briefe: Kritische Ausgabe
(Frankfurt am Main: Fischer, 2004)

AM   *Amtliche Schriften: Materialienband*, ed. Klaus Hermsdorf and
     Benno Wagner. Franz Kafka: Schriften, Tagebücher, Briefe:
     Kritische Ausgabe (Frankfurt am Main: Fischer, 2004)

B   *Briefe 1902–1924*, ed. Max Brod (Frankfurt am Main: Fischer,
     1975)

B1   *Briefe 1900–1912*, ed. Hans-Gerd Koch. Franz Kafka: Schriften,
     Tagebücher, Briefe: Kritische Ausgabe (Frankfurt am Main:
     Fischer, 1999)

B2   *Briefe 1913 – März 1914*, ed. Hans-Gerd Koch. Franz Kafka:
     Schriften, Tagebücher, Briefe: Kritische Ausgabe (Frankfurt am
     Main: Fischer, 2001)

B3   *Briefe April 1914–1917*, ed. Hans-Gerd Koch. Franz Kafka:
     Schriften, Tagebücher, Briefe: Kritische Ausgabe (Frankfurt am
     Main: Fischer, 2005)

B4   *Briefe 1918–1920*, ed. Hans-Gerd Koch. Franz Kafka: Schriften,
     Tagebücher, Briefe: Kritische Ausgabe (Frankfurt am Main:
     Fischer, 2013)

BE   *Briefe an die Eltern aus den Jahren 1922–1924*, ed. Josef Čermák
     and Martin Svatoš (Frankfurt am Main: Fischer, 1993)

BF   *Briefe an Felice und andere Korrespondenz aus der
     Verlobungszeit*, ed. Erich Heller and Jürgen Born (Frankfurt
     am Main: Fischer, 1998)

BM   *Briefe an Milena*, ed. Jürgen Born and Michael Müller,
     extended and revised edn (Frankfurt am Main: Fischer, 1999)

BOF *Briefe an Ottla und die Familie*, ed. Hartmut Binder and Klaus
     Wagenbach (Frankfurt am Main: Fischer, 1981)

D   *The Diaries of Franz Kafka, 1910–23*, ed. Max Brod (London:
     Minerva, 1992)

EFB Malcolm Pasley (ed.), *Max Brod, Franz Kafka: Eine
     Freundschaft*, vol. II: *Briefwechsel* (Frankfurt am Main: Fischer,
     1989)

EFR Malcolm Pasley (ed.), *Max Brod, Franz Kafka: Eine
     Freundschaft*, vol. I: *Reisetagebücher* (Frankfurt am Main:
     Fischer, 1987)

LF   *Letters to Felice*, ed. Erich Heller and Jürgen Born, trans. James
     Stern and Elisabeth Duckworth (London: Minerva, 1992)

LFFE *Letters to Friends, Family and Editors*, trans. Richard Winston
     and Clara Winston (Richmond: Oneworld Classics, 2011)

LM   *Letters to Milena*, ed. Willy Haas, trans. Tania Stern and James
     Stern (London: Minerva, 1992)

LOF   *Letters to Ottla and the Family*, trans. Richard Winston and Clara Winston, ed. N. N. Glatzer (New York, NY: Schocken, 1982)

O   *The Office Writings*, ed. Stanley Corngold, Jack Greenberg and Benno Wagner, trans. Eric Patton with Ruth Hein (Princeton University Press, 2008)

TB   *Tagebücher*, ed. Hans-Gerd Koch, Michael Müller and Malcolm Pasley. Franz Kafka: Schriften, Tagebücher, Briefe: Kritische Ausgabe (Frankfurt am Main: Fischer, 1990)

TBA   *Tagebücher: Apparatband*, ed. Hans-Gerd Koch, Michael Müller and Malcolm Pasley. Franz Kafka: Schriften, Tagebücher, Briefe: Kritische Ausgabe (Frankfurt am Main: Fischer, 1990)

TBK   *Tagebücher: Kommentarband*, ed. Hans-Gerd Koch, Michael Müller and Malcolm Pasley. Franz Kafka: Schriften, Tagebücher, Briefe: Kritische Ausgabe (Frankfurt am Main: Fischer, 1990)

Introduction

Carolin Duttlinger

In January 1922, Franz Kafka arrives in the spa resort of Spindlermühle in the Tatra mountains. In the advanced stages of tuberculosis, he has been granted leave from work. The remote wintry setting he encounters will be immortalized in his final novel, *Das Schloss* (*The Castle*); the thoughts he records in his diary, however, are not unique to this period of his life:

> Incapable of striking up an acquaintance with anyone, incapable of tolerating an acquaintance, fundamentally full of endless astonishment when I see a group of cheerful people . . . or indeed parents with their children; forsaken, moreover, not only here but in general, even in Prague, my 'home', and, what is more, forsaken not by people (that would not be the worst thing, I could run after them as long as I was alive), but rather by myself *vis-à-vis* people; I am fond of lovers but I cannot love; I am too far away, am banished [ich bin zu weit, bin ausgewiesen]. (29 January 1922; *D* 408/*TB* 895–6)

Kafka has a reputation as a loner, as someone almost existentially disconnected. This perception is not unfounded. Feelings of distance and isolation from his physical and social surroundings appear throughout his personal writings and are integral to his authorial self-image. The above diary entry continues, 'I get my principal nourishment from other roots in other climes, these roots too are sorry ones, but nevertheless better to sustain life [kläglich, aber doch lebensfähiger]'. Food and nourishment are recurring themes in his texts; they are a shorthand for a physical, intellectual and emotional connection to life and everything it has to offer. This is something Kafka repeatedly denies himself. Ten years earlier, he speaks of the need to 'starve' himself of 'the joys of sex, eating, drinking, philosophical reflection and above all music', arguing that 'the totality of my strengths was so slight that only collectively could they even halfway serve the purpose of my writing' (3 January 1912; *D* 163/*TB* 341). Another expression of this self-imposed asceticism can be found in a letter to Felice Bauer, where Kafka outlines his ideal mode of existence: to sit 'in the innermost room of a spacious locked cellar with my writing things and a lamp' (14/15 January 1913; *LF* 156/*B2* 40).

Passages such as these paint a consistent picture of self-imposed isolation, of a deliberate withdrawal from life and human company. What is often overlooked is their carefully constructed character. Such pronouncements, whether made to others or to himself, are part of what Reiner Stach calls Kafka's 'personal mythology'[1] – his ongoing attempts to narrate his own life story, casting events in terms of fixed patterns or trajectories. This is a coping mechanism which allows Kafka to give his life a sense of inner necessity in the face of contingency and chance.

To take this private mythology as the whole truth, however, is to fall for Kafka's rhetoric of (self-)persuasion. Only four days after the above litany about his utter isolation, he notes: 'The happiness of being with people' (2 February 1922; *D* 411/*TB* 900). This happiness points to another vital aspect of Kafka's life and character. His contemporaries describe a convivial man with a good sense of humour who deeply cared for those around him. And his writings do not speak only of isolation, but also reflect his wide and varied interests, ranging from theatre, film and the circus to gardening, rowing and aviation. Kafka took a lively interest in the cultural life of his time, in current affairs, and in history, as evidenced by his love of the biographies of writers and other historical figures. Jürgen Born's inventory of Kafka's library is an invaluable resource, for it opens up the literary and intellectual spheres in which he moved.[2] His travels took him into neighbouring European countries, but in his reading and writing he travelled much further afield.

From early on, Kafka was acutely aware of his own place within the literary tradition. In diaries and letters he mentions authors to whom he feels indebted in his own writing, singling out four nineteenth-century authors – Heinrich von Kleist, Franz Grillparzer, Gustave Flaubert and Fyodor Dostoevsky – whom he calls his 'blood-relatives' (2 September 1913; *LF* 355/*B2* 275). But he was also keenly aware of his place within modernist culture, embracing its formal and thematic innovations. Indeed, this lifelong engagement with his context extends beyond his death. The pride he took in his published books, and the fact that he corrected the proofs of his final volume, the collection *Ein Hungerkünstler* (*A Hunger Artist*), on his deathbed, underlines Kafka's (however ambivalent) commitment to the afterlife of his work.

The four sections of this volume trace Kafka's contexts in gradually expanding concentric circles. The articles in Part I, *Life and Work*, focus on his personal and professional surroundings. From his immediate and extended family and his friendships, which had a crucial impact on his development as a writer, they take us to his relationships with women, and then on to his work and illness, which shaped Kafka's adult life at different, though overlapping, stages. Kafka frequently described his post at the Arbeiter-Unfall-Versicherungs-Anstalt (Workers' Accident Insurance Institute) as a distraction from his true creative vocation, but his work also fed back into his writing. In the final years of his life, the Insurance Institute was replaced by a succession of sanatoriums and hospitals as Kafka began his seven-year battle with tuberculosis. However, to see office and sanatorium as 'other' spaces, pulling Kafka away from his writing desk, is to misunderstand the role of these and other contextual spaces. In reality, as he occasionally acknowledged to himself, such other contexts were vital for his work, for they prevented his writing from becoming inward-looking and stale. Thus Part I concludes with two articles on Kafka's literary method: on his writing strategy, which depends on parameters such as time, space and the physical tools used for this purpose; and on his style, which, for all its distinctiveness, reveals how deeply he was influenced by literary role models and predecessors.

Building on this, the articles in Part II, *Art and Literature*, explore Kafka's responses to his cultural context. As already mentioned, Kafka read widely, enjoying both contemporary texts and those written in previous centuries. In fact, for all its drive towards innovation and experimentation, modernism was a period extremely conscious of the past: of existing traditions and earlier movements, to which artists responded in different ways, either rejecting them outright or trying to build on them through new themes, forms and methods. These tensions – between a more traditional and a radically progressive model of modernism – are felt in the literature of the period, but also in the performance arts of dance, theatre and recitation, in photography and film, architecture and music. Kafka's engagement with these different contexts is underpinned by a dual focus. From current practices he tries to excavate the traces of older, sometimes archaic, traditions, which offer striking and often disconcerting glimpses into the history of human civilization.

This dual focus on the past and the present is also integral to Kafka's perception of social and political debates. Part III, *Politics, Culture and History*, opens with Kafka's home, the city of Prague, a space of centuries-old ethnic and religious conflict, before considering the impact of Czech language and literature on his writings. This geographical and linguistic setting is a constant in Kafka's life; the First World War, in contrast, marks a great rupture, radically changing the political map of Europe and spelling the end of the multi-ethnic Habsburg Empire and the foundation of the nation state of Czechoslovakia. The war also brought Kafka face-to-face with Eastern European Jewish refugees; the precarious role of Western Judaism and the foundation of a Jewish homeland in Palestine were among the burning questions of his time and personally affected many of Kafka's friends. But such debates were in turn part of a wider trend: the modernist revival of religion and spirituality, symptomatic of a search for certainty in times of rapid change. Other discourses invested with a similar, self-reflexive charge are philosophy, law – Kafka's professional discipline – and psychology and psychoanalysis. One focal point of Freud's writings is human sexuality, but debates about gender and sexuality are also integral to modernism more generally, where new models of gender identity are being negotiated. The city is *the* space for such experimentation – a cultural melting pot and crucible of social change. For all his love of nature and a simple, rural lifestyle, Kafka lived in cities all his life; he travelled to Munich, Zurich, Vienna and Paris, and he moved from Prague to inflation-torn Berlin in the last year of his life. Indeed, travel – both real and imaginary – is one of the great, recurring themes in his writings, a motif often associated with colonialist practices and the allure of the exotic. This interest in non-Western cultures manifests itself in the emergence of the disciplines of anthropology and ethnography, but forms of 'otherness' could also be found closer to home: the twentieth century was proclaimed to be the 'century of the child', and Kafka shared the period's interest in the minds and lives of children as a sphere distinct from adult life.

As the chapters in these three sections show, Kafka took a lively interest in his immediate and wider contexts, and he engaged with a wide range of cultural practices, issues and debates. His own writings add to this their own distinctive voice, often turning an established conceptual hierarchy on its head or rephrasing questions from defamiliarizing angles. These features account for his enduring appeal with readers of all kinds, from different generations and different cultural and linguistic backgrounds. No single publication could reflect Kafka's vast and extraordinarily diverse influence on academia and the arts, on social debate and common parlance, and on the ways in which we think of his times and our own, still resonantly 'modern' world. The chapters in Part IV, *Reception and Influence*, can therefore only offer a few illustrative pathways into this terrain. Kafka's earliest reception, during his lifetime and in the years after his death, is revealing, for it is shaped by an immediacy and familiarity with Kafka's own context – though the pitfalls associated with such familiarity (particularly of the personal kind) are considerable. Critical theory and deconstruction have a place in this survey because of their enduring impact on Kafka scholarship and because they showcase some of the tensions – between readings which focus on the inner workings of Kafka's texts and those which relate them to meanings and issues external to them – which have beset Kafka scholarship from the start. One possible response to such tensions is to return to first principles, by examining the ways empirical readers – particularly those new to his works – respond to his texts, though of course every such encounter is unique in its way. Examining patterns of reception, however, is important not least because these also manifest themselves in more indirect ways – in the work of Kafka's editors and translators, for instance, whose renderings are the result of an infinite number of (often very difficult) choices – choices which are complicated by the often fragmentary character of his texts. The final chapter uses the example of film and television to examine some of the more general issues that arise in creative adaptations of Kafka's works. Like the readings of Kafka that give rise to scholarship, editions and translations, creative adaptations take their departure from a specific encounter with his texts. The contexts mapped out in this volume are intended to aid Kafka's readers, making their reading encounters richer and more resonant, without detracting from the texts themselves.

NOTES

1 R. Stach, *Kafka: The Years of Insight*, trans. S. Frisch (Princeton University Press, 2015), p. 240.
2 J. Born with M. Antreter, W. John and J. Shepherd, *Kafkas Bibliothek: Ein beschreibendes Verzeichnis. Mit einem Index aller in Kafkas Schriften erwähnten Bücher, Zeitschriften und Zeitschriftenbeiträge* (Frankfurt am Main: Fischer, 1990).

PART I

Life and Work

CHAPTER I

Family

Anthony Northey

Franz Kafka's immediate family numbered only five besides him: his parents, Hermann and Julie, and his three sisters, Elli, Valli and Ottla. (Two brothers, Georg and Heinrich, died in infancy.) His wider family, however, was more extensive. Hermann Kafka had three brothers and two sisters; Julie Löwy three brothers and two half-brothers, and those of their number who had families provided Franz with altogether twenty cousins, many living in his proximity.

Although Franz Kafka's father, Hermann, was wont to mistrust mankind generally, he was open to family members and even remoter relatives. He visited siblings, in-laws, cousins and their families regularly, went on vacation with some of them and helped them in difficult times. For example, when his (half-)cousin Heinrich Kafka died in 1917, Hermann rallied support for the widow among the wealthier relatives. 'The speech that Uncle held in front of these rich people must have been marvellous' his niece Irma wrote to Franz's sister Ottla in Zürau, '"You can't take your money with you", Uncle said, "and we've all got to die. Even if you have twelve rooms, you can only sleep in one bed."'[1] Irma herself had benefited from Hermann's charitable family feeling, having been employed in his business after the death in 1911 of her father, Ludwig Kafka. And Ludwig, too, was given the chance to take over his older brother's retail business in 1886, failed and then became an insurance company employee. Hermann also managed the financial affairs of his older, widowed sister, Anna Adler, when she retired to Prague from Strakonitz in in the twenties.

In his 'Brief an den Vater' ('Letter to his Father'), Kafka suggested that marrying, founding a family, accepting, caring for and even guiding all the children who came along was the ultimate success an individual could achieve (*M* 131/*NSII* 200). Faced with the personal prospect of marriage, however, he repeatedly got cold feet and once – having urged his fiancée Felice Bauer to attend an exhibition 'Mother and Infant' in Berlin in September 1916 – he subsequently suggested that it lacked a chamber of horrors in which Hedwig, Irma Kafka's older sister, who along with her husband Karl Löw and their baby had just paid his parents a visit, could be its chief exhibit (5 October 1916; *LF* 541/*B3* 248). Twice in the father-letter Kafka mentions Hermann's reproach that he lacked a 'family feeling' (*M* 100, 121/*NSII* 144, 183), and he admitted relatives bored him (21 July 1913; *D* 225/*TB* 569). Yet boredom did not mean he was not aware of his extensive network of relatives. And if his father was to him 'the measure of all things' (*M* 104/*NSI* 151), his other relatives were the measure of at least some things, significant enough in his life that they made their way into a number of his works.

Kafka's Immediate Family

The son of a kosher butcher, Hermann Kafka was born in the *shtetl* (a predominantly Jewish eastern European small town or village) of Wossek, south-southwest of Prague. He obtained only rudimentary schooling and had to work as an itinerant peddler from the early age of ten. In his diary Kafka notes the unpleasant feeling he had when his father reminisced with his sister Julie Ehrmann about their arduous youth and how lucky the younger generation was (26 December 1911; *D* 154/*TB* 323). After completion of compulsory military service, which he always held in fond memory, Hermann Kafka settled in Prague around 1880 and with the dowry of a propitious (arranged) marriage to Julie Löwy (3 September 1882), he opened a store, and eventually a wholesale business selling fancy goods. His older brothers, Filip and Heinrich, had similar retail stores in Kolin and Leitmeritz. Hermann's notable accomplishment, however, was no match to the success of his (half-)cousins Angelus and Friedrich Kafka (the older brothers of the above-mentioned Heinrich Kafka), who founded large firms producing and distributing wine and spirits. They became standards of highest achievement, and Hermann asked Angelus to be Franz's godfather. Angelus's younger brother, Dr Moritz Kafka, became a noted Prague jurist and his son Bruno, only slightly older than Franz, a leading law professor at Prague's Charles University and socially prominent.

Julie Kafka's family was economically more advanced than her husband's; her father, a merchant, had moved the family from Podiebrad to Prague. Of her brothers, Richard Löwy had a business producing and dealing in work clothes and a family including four children; her cousin Alexander Löwy founded a brewery in the Prague suburb Košiř, became a municipal councillor there and even mayor, trumped only by his older brother Eduard, the president of the Puch Stock Company in Vienna, for decades Austria's foremost manufacturer of motorcycles and automobiles. Both Eduard's daughters married into the Austrian aristocracy.[2] The price the brothers paid for their advancement was assimilation and changing their Löwy to Lanner. The author liked to look upon his mother's family as pious and intellectual. In actual fact there were more Löwys than Kafkas who abandoned their mothers' religion, among them three of Julie's brothers: Alfred, Josef and Rudolf, the latter employed by brewer Alexander as a bookkeeper. And the Kafkas were more pious and intellectual than was hitherto thought. The unusual name of Angelus given the factory owner can be traced back to a Rabbi Angelus Kafka who lived in the Kafka-house number 30 in Wossek around 1827, strong circumstantial evidence that he was directly related. He later became district-rabbi of Pilsen (Plzeň). One of the rabbi's daughters was the mother of Prague poet/author Hugo Salus.

Kafka described his mother Julie as the 'beater in the hunt' (*M* 113/*NSII* 167), a willing tool of his father. Yet a sentence in her letter to Felice Bauer's mother, Anna, after Franz's first engagement was called off perhaps more accurately characterizes her view of a woman's power behind the throne. Referring to the possibility her son was not made for marriage because of his devotion to writing, Julie writes: 'For all that, I was counting on Felice's good sense, for I said to myself that a clever woman is able to remodel a man' (20 July 1914; *LF* 473/*BF* 613). Kafka's sisters Elli and Valli appear to have followed the usual route of female upbringing their mother had enjoyed: nannies, a governess, schooling (compulsory from age six to fourteen), which included five years of primary school and up to three years in the *Mädchen Bürgerschule* (Girls' Upper School) and possibly in Adele Schembor's private girls' school, which offered courses in foreign languages and literature.[3] Then came (probably arranged) marriages to businessmen. After helping in her father's business, the youngest sister, Ottla, however, became a worker on the farm of the family of Elli's husband, Karl Hermann in Zürau during the war and finally studied at an agricultural college. Even in marriage she broke conventional rules by choosing a Christian husband against her father's wishes.

Daughters were considered a dowry-burden; greater hope was placed in sons. In several famous Austrian (Jewish) families (Hofmannsthal, Zweig, Wittgenstein, Mahler) the fathers, or sometimes grandfathers, secured the financial footing and their sons supplied the burst of intellectually creative genius. But in an era steeped in the success of material gain, the pressure to equal or surpass the performance of the founder generation(s) was immense. Oskar, the son of Hermann Kafka's more cheerful brother Filip (in Kolin), committed suicide in September 1901 when he was not accepted at the *Kavalleriekadettenschule* (Cavalry Cadet Academy) in Mährisch Weisskirchen.

Hermann Kafka ensured that his son received a better education than he had, and expected him to excel as a jurist. Whereas some fathers nurtured cultural pursuits (Max Brod's father, for example) they hardly figured in Hermann Kafka's purview. Late in the summer of 1911 he persuaded Franz to become a partner in the Prager Asbestwerke (Prague Asbestos Works) with Elli's husband, Karl Hermann. His reasons were twofold: he hoped that Karl could fashion Franz, whose bureaucratic career seemed lacklustre, into a businessman and also that his son could keep an eye on his daughter's dowry-investment, which he, managing his own business and suffering from heart troubles, could not.

The venture, which robbed Kafka of his writing-time, soon drove him to despair. One year later, after meeting Felice Bauer, a possible marriage prospect, the two basic departure points for 'Das Urteil' ('The Judgement') came together: business success and marriage. In the novella, the father, initially waning, is suddenly restored to full antagonistic vigour when he unmasks the deception of Georg Bendemann, who is about to take over the father's business and marry Frieda Brandenfeld. He claims the failed and lonely self-exiled friend in Russia as a son after his own heart. By having Georg Bendemann, the protagonist he has just fashioned, unmasked within the story as a fiction, a fraud, the writer Kafka manages to pull the rug out from under his own feet. *Die Verwandlung* (*The Metamorphosis*) develops the theme of the misfortunes of the model son, as Gregor Samsa, previously the family's breadwinner, awakens to find himself turned into his family's misfortune and left only with the memory of when he was their self-sacrificing mainstay. These characters' self-destructive loyalty to their families reflects Kafka's own enduring ambiguity towards family life and the (masculine) roles associated with it. While he realized the value of his father's accomplishments, he was unable and unwilling to fulfil his parents' ambitions for him on both a professional and a personal level.

Adventurers and Inventors: The Wider Family

Nineteenth-century industrialization, which increased family wealth, heralded the modern age, marked by an open, ever-increasing (after 1900) internationalism running parallel to government-backed nationalism. The political socialist movement aside, it manifested itself in actors and variety acts from all over the world on the city's stages, foreign sports teams and stars and new types of sport on the field, fads and fashions from a variety

Team Laurin & Klement před odjezdem.

Toman, Vondřich, Kafka, Tuta a Podsedníček.

Figure 1 The Laurin and Klement motor-racing team before their departure for the Coupe du Monde. Oskar Kafka is third from the left. From *Sport a hry* No. 20, 21 June 1905.

of countries, and, above all, in visible daily technology in homes and on the streets from telephones to electric streetcars, to bicycles and automobiles. Oskar Kafka, the youngest son of Angelus, had been a bicycle racer of some repute in Bohemia in the late 1890s.[4] Around 1904 he graduated to motorcycles, raced in events at home and in Austria and was on the Austrian team competing for the 1905 Coupe du Monde in southern France (see Figure 1). At the same time he formed a passion for automobiles and opened an Opel-Darraqu-dealership in Prague with his racing colleague Vaclav Wondrich. The café-owner/motorist Oskar developed a penchant for fast, reckless driving, which repeatedly earned him fines, a devil may care velocity of the futurist Marinetti without his verbosity. Then, like so many other cyclists and automobile enthusiasts, Oskar (with co-owners of the Prague auto company Velox) embarked on a project to build and pilot a Blériot-model monoplane. Since the plane was built 'from scratch' it must have been started in spring of 1909.

Kafka possibly heard the news of how Oskar was spending his inheritance in café circles, or (more likely) from a disapproving Hermann Kafka. (On 30 January 1910, Oskar taxied the plane but, alas, it never flew.) Knowledge of Oskar's flight-ambitions certainly fuelled the author's enthusiasm for attending the air show in Brescia (September 1909) and the subsequent composition of 'Die Aeroplane in Brescia' ('The Aeroplanes at Brescia'), which deals with the rise of the technological middle class and was published in the *Bohemia* magazine. In it a clown-like Rougier, the slow-reading Curtiss, Mrs Rougier, a calculating businesswoman, Blériot's wife, a motherly figure, dressed too warmly for the weather, not happy if her husband does not fly, and anxious if he does – bourgeois figures all, are juxtaposed with the more sophisticated and elegant aristocracy, who on closer inspection appear withered and ugly, circulating in their own separate social bubble, deigning only to converse with a sycophantic Gabriele d'Annuzio while Giaccomo Puccini with an alcoholic's red nose looks on. In his piece, Kafka grasps the varied pace of the technical modern age (and perhaps modernism generally), oscillating between the morning's excited anticipation, the long languid stretch of boredom on a sweltering morning and afternoon while single-minded pilots and back-up-crew tinker with their planes, and finally the crowd-uniting hyper-excitement as these bourgeois rise into the sky to become (at least temporarily) heroes in the age of the new comparative: faster, further, higher, longer.

An alternative to finding fame and fortune at home was to seek it abroad. Although he himself spent most of his life in Prague, Franz Kafka retained an (adolescent's) enthusiasm for adventure and escape to far-flung countries into adulthood. His family had its share of travellers and adventurers. Julie Kafka's brothers Alfred and Josef Löwy were protégés of the engineer/entrepreneur Philippe Bunau-Varilla (1859–1940), who was instrumental in bringing about the American-built Panama Canal, and his brother Maurice (1856–1944), owner of the French newspaper *Le Matin*, both also engaged supporters of Alfred Dreyfus (1859–1935). The Löwys had been involved in the French canal effort in Panama in the early 1880s. Alfred went on to become the director of two Spanish railways owned by the Varillas and at a railway conference in Washington in 1905 even shook President Theodore Roosevelt's hand on the White House lawn and brought him greetings from Philippe Bunau-Varilla. Josef survived over ten years as an accountant for the Compagnie du Chemin de Fer du Congo in tropical Matadi and then worked shorter periods for Belgian interests (Groupe Thys) in China and Canada. Although Kafka abandoned the few lines of a Congo-story in 1917,[5] one motif gleaned from his uncles' experiences entered his work: exile in an isolated, inhospitable location. The only characteristic altered was the climate, hot to cold. Both Georg Bendemann's friend and the narrator of the fragment 'Erinnerungen an die Kaldabahn' ('Memoirs of the Kalda Railway') have retreated to frigid Russia.

No fewer than four of Kafka's paternal cousins (brothers Otto and Franz from Kolin and Emil and Victor from Leitmeritz) emigrated to the United States, the 'land of unlimited possibilities', a place for fortune hunters or a refuge for those hunted by the law. Otto Kafka was both, wanted on charges of fraud in Bohemia in 1906, and a successful businessman in New York by 1911–12. In 1909 his fourteen-year-old brother Franz joined him there (calling himself Frank). Details of the American cousins' backgrounds (family names, family photographs or Emil's tenure with Sears Roebuck) filtered through into *Der Verschollene* (*The Man who Disappeared*); but while they successfully coped with their new life, Kafka's Karl Rossmann slips ever further down the ladder. Karl's rich American uncle compares the arrival of the emigrant to America with birth (*MD* 30/V 56), ironic since Karl has already become a father, an innocent one, before he reaches American shores. His entry into an adult new world becomes a reversal of the classic *Entwicklungsroman* (novel of development).

Literary Legacies

After being diagnosed with tuberculosis and realizing that his career was coming to an end, Kafka attempted once more to explain himself and his literary ambition to his father. The circumstances surrounding Kafka's decision to dedicate his second collection of short stories, *Ein Landarzt* (*A Country Doctor*, 1920), to Hermann Kafka indicate that the book was meant as a gift for Hermann at a very important juncture in his life: his sixty-fifth birthday and retirement.[6] The collection can, among other things, be read as an attempt at looking back, and it contains various ironic or wistful references to family life on both a general and a more specific, biographical level. The assembled texts frequently thematize the relationship between generations, and the father figures featured are no longer vengeful tyrants, but helpless characters puzzled by their (literal or figurative) offspring. Two stories are set in the circus and variety theatre contexts loved by Kafka and his father and which, along with other manifestations of internationalism, had been compromised by the war. One story could even be read as a covert reference to Kafka's wider family, namely to Bruno Kafka and his newborn son, while Kafka's uncle Siegfried Löwy might be an inspiration behind the country doctor of the collection's title story.

Figure 2 Title page of the first edition of *In der Strafkolonie* (1919) with a handwritten dedication by Kafka's parents: 'Zum Andenken von unserem verstorbenen Sohn | Julie Kafka. | Prag 20.5.1926, Hermann Kafka' ('In memory of our late son').

Kafka's father reportedly took little notice of his retirement present, and so Kafka followed this up with his 'Letter to his Father'. This text – a 'letter of one hundred pages', as Kafka said to Friedrich Thieberger[7] – was Kafka's most extensive attempt to take stock of his relationship to his father and also his mother. It is at once hard-hitting and self-deprecating; in its vividness and rhetorical force, it encapsulates both the burden and the ongoing literary inspiration which stemmed from Kafka's family relations.

NOTES

1 Manuscript-photocopy of an unpublished letter in my possession.
2 *Neue Freie Presse*, no. 17180 (22 June 1912), 28. See also Eva Maria Mandl's recent blog, 'Franz Kafkas Wiener Verwandschaft', www.pratercottage.at.
3 Class Catalogues of *Volksschule* and *Mädchen Bürgerschule*, Prag Altstadt, Archiv hlavní mesta Prahy. A. K. Wagnerová, *Die Familie Kafka aus Prag: 'Im Hauptquartier des Lärms'* (Mannheim: Bollmann, 1997), p. 124. Records of the Schembor school not yet located.
4 A. Northey, 'Der Motorradrennfahrer, Automobilist und Aviatiker Oskar Kafka: Aus dem Leben eines techno-modernistischen Playboys', *Kafka-Katern, Kwartaalblad van de Nederlandse Franz Kafka-Kring*, 19, no. 1 (2011), 9–19.
5 See *ON* 7–8/*NSI* 333–334/*NSIA* 285.
6 A. Northey, 'Die Erzählsammlung *Ein Landarzt*: Kafkas persönliche Ansprache an den Vater und Kommentar zur Gesellschaft und zur Kultur im Kriege' in Daniela Uherková (ed.), *Kafka und Böhmen: Der Sammelband der Vorträge der internationalen literaturwissenschaftlichen Konferenz der Franz Kafka Gesellschaft, 2. Oktober 2006 in Prag* (Prague: Nakladatelství Franze Kafky, 2007), pp. 97–119.
7 F. Thieberger, 'Kafka und die Thiebergers' in H.-G. Koch (ed.), *'Als Kafka mir entgegen kam . . .': Erinnerungen an Franz Kafka*, new edition (Berlin: Wagenbach, 2013), p. 127.

CHAPTER 2

Friendship

Claudia Nitschke

Life

Friendships formed a central part of Kafka's life. Although he was known for keeping a certain distance from his friends, Kafka was by no means unsociable. Particularly as a younger man, he moved in various intellectual circles, frequented fashionable cafés and regularly visited Berta Fanta's famous salon (the centre of Prague's intelligentsia). Among his many acquaintances, his friendships with Felix Weltsch (1884–1964), Oskar Baum (1883–1941) and, most importantly, Max Brod (1884–1968) were formative relationships that would last a lifetime. Felix Weltsch, a librarian at Prague University, rose to prominence as the editor of the Zionist weekly newspaper *Selbstwehr* (*Self-Defence*). Oscar Baum, the blind organist and writer, son of a Jewish cloth merchant, provided the space for the young men to gather: at their meetings in his flat, the friends read and discussed their writings – a ritual Kafka had already developed with his close friend and classmate Oskar Pollak, with whom he shared a passion for literature. For Kafka, life and literature were inseparably entwined;[1] recurrent topics in his writing frequently coincide with the interests he had in common with his friends.

Kafka's idiosyncrasies created insurmountable barriers between himself and his social environment. His peculiar outlook on his bodily functions, sexuality, hygiene, and its complex psychosomatic consequences often forced him into seclusion. The particular self-scrutiny and fastidious adherence to a certain diet or complicated cleansing rituals which Brod had to endure on their mutual journeys, however, can also be seen in the context of a specific form of Jewish self-observation.[2] Kafka's life-long interest in Jewish identity not only informs his work, but also represents an intrinsic facet in many of his friendships and love relationships. It was Kafka's school friend Hugo Bergmann who introduced Kafka and his friends Brod and Weltsch (all from assimilated Western Jewish families) to the increasingly prominent Prague Zionism and to Martin Buber's Cultural Zionism. Buber (1878–1965) – not unproblematically – conceived Zionism as a creative movement positioned in opposition to the assimilated Jewish bourgeoisie of the nineteenth century, advocating the recourse to the core of Jewish existence, which for him consisted in a tight kinship community rooted in 'blood'.³ For various reasons, the intricate Western Jewish identity on which Sander Gilman elaborates in his observations on Kafka as a 'Jewish patient' (highlighting the close links between Jewishness and illness in the modernist collective imagination)⁴ was often connected to the search and desire for an alternative identity.

This desire was reflected in Kafka's friendship with Jizchak Löwy (1887–1942), an Eastern European Jew from Warsaw, whom Kafka met at the Café Savoy in Prague, where the Yiddish theatre troupe to which Löwy belonged performed in the winter of 1911/12. Kafka was a regular at these performances and made a few acquaintances among the performers, but ultimately came closest to Löwy. The actor struck Kafka as an example of uncompromised and undiluted originality, an impression not far away from Buber's notion of the creative potential of authentic, unassimilated Jewishness. Much to the dismay and astonishment of his parents (Hermann Kafka in particular perceived his own impoverished upbringing in the *shtetl* as a stigma he sought to forget and eradicate), Kafka even organized a reading in the ballroom of the Jewish town hall. The introductory speech he delivered on that occasion was dedicated to the Yiddish language and seemed tailored mainly to the scepticism and in-built aversion of an assimilated Western Jewish audience to their ill-reputed and – as they perceived it – backward Eastern European counterparts. By providing Löwy with a prominent opportunity to present Yiddish folk culture to a Westernized audience, and by openly addressing the expectations and prejudices of this very audience, Kafka boldly tackled the inherent dichotomy that dominated Western and Eastern Jewish relations. Löwy also features in Kafka's famous 'Brief an den Vater' ('Letter to his Father'), in which Kafka not only accuses his father of neglecting and suppressing his Eastern Jewish heritage, but also attacks him for calling Löwy a vermin ('Ungeziefer'). This part of the letter folds together various pertinent areas of Kafka's life, such as his Jewish identity, his friendship, his relationship with his father; the 'Ungeziefer' reference in turn ties it to his seminal literary work, *Die Verwandlung* (*The Metamorphosis*, 1912). For Kafka, Löwy – at least at first – embodied an idealized East European vitality, thus representing a counterpart to Western Jewish existence which Kafka would never stop scrutinizing and questioning.

Jewishness was also a topic that connected Kafka with Max Brod. Together they frequented the Yiddish theatre at the Café Savoy, attended Buber's lectures in 1913, and in 1915 they met Georg Langer, a member of the retinue that followed the famous Belzer Rebbe. Langer, a cabbalist, also familiarized them with Chassidism, a mystical Jewish movement founded in Poland in the eighteenth century. The encounter with Buber, especially, was an awakening for Brod, who immediately decided to put his writing in the service of Zionism. Kafka, taking stock and comparing their respective lives, consequently stated in a letter to his friend that Brod's Zionism and Brod's literature were 'one' (mid-November 1917; *LFFE* 167/*EFB* 196). Brod – somewhat more speculatively – arrived at a similar conclusion about Kafka's work: his interpretation of Kafka's writing as predominantly Jewish goes hand in hand with his attempts to force the friend to take a stand in this matter, for instance when he together with Felix Weltsch proposed him as the editor for Buber's monthly journal, *Der Jude* (*The Jew*), in 1922. Brod's dystopian novel *Das große Wagnis* (*A Big Venture*) of 1917 has been seen as a source for Kafka's *Das Schloss* (*The Castle*) and Brod himself certainly felt strongly about the analogies between the two texts. However, his reading of *The Castle* as an inventory of Jewish life characterized by otherness and hostility curtails the meaning of Kafka's fragmentary novel of 1922 which – as the intricate interconnections with his other writings show – sits in a much more multi-layered philosophical context. The way Brod approached Kafka's writings in this specific case was generally indicative of his work as a testamentary executor. In a letter of 1921 Kafka instructed Brod to burn his writings,[5] but Brod famously decided to disregard this last request; instead he became determined to secure Kafka's place in the pantheon of world literature and was also intent on retaining the prerogative of interpretation he felt entitled to as Kafka's closest friend. These aspirations gave rise to Brod's tendency to rearrange the writing and to give titles to various originally untitled pieces, which in turn led to several philological inconsistencies and de facto changes to Kafka's work. When editors started reversing the alterations in Brod's canon-building template, they also began to re-embed the separate texts into Kafka's 'Schreibstrom' (writing current), restore their original titles or, if they were lacking, eliminate Brod's titles. This endeavour also undercut Brod's homogenizing reading of his friend's work: Brod had tried to impose a specific coherence and theological structure on Kafka's texts by emphasizing their positive religiosity.

Gershom Scholem (1897–1982) reputedly expressed disbelief at the fact that Kafka had in fact chosen Brod (whom Scholem disliked) as his close friend.[6] Indeed, Brod and Kafka must have appeared as virtual antipodes (as Kafka himself declared in a letter from Zürau, in which he, in characteristic self-deprecation, cast Brod as his successful alter ego),[7] but for this reason Kafka and Brod quite naturally assumed complementary roles in their relationship, with Brod, as he himself solemnly puts it, as the suitor and Kafka as the courted friend.[8] Brod was indubitably a loyal companion and on various occasions also an essential facilitator on whom Kafka trustingly relied until his death. The journeys they had taken together before Brod got married in 1913 had brought them closer together and even sparked a literary collaboration: the novel project *Richard und Samuel* (*Richard and Samuel*) of which only one chapter was ever completed. Despite their growing apart in later years and their obvious differences, Brod would remain a fixture in Kafka's world.

Among the friends that Kafka made in later life, Robert Klopstock and Gustav Janouch exemplify another type of relationship; in particular, the friendship with the young medical student Robert Klopstock accentuated an important facet in Kafka's personality, namely his mentoring abilities, which he liked to exercise as a characteristically detached but at the same time committed and accessible interlocutor. In the same vein, Kafka also cultivated friendships with younger women, such as the eighteen-year-old Minze Eisner, whom he met in Schelesen in 1919, and the sixteen-year-old Tile Rössler, who like Dora Diamant worked for the Berlin-based *Jüdisches Volksheim* (Jewish People's Home). However, despite his crucial mentoring relationships with these and other women, they do not feature prominently as friends in his life as far as we know, which obviously has to do with external factors, such as contemporary conventions, and with the pervasiveness of ideas about gender roles around 1900, which Kafka and his friends had deeply internalized.

Janouch, an eccentric Czech high-school student who clearly thrived on Kafka's attention, later rose to fame as Kafka's biographer. His – probably largely fabricated – memoirs of his conversations with a sage and mild-mannered Kafka fed into the idolization and myth-making to which Kafka was subjected, particularly by his early readers. Klopstock, whom Kafka met in the sanatorium in High Tatras, would eventually accompany the dying writer in his last days. His devotion and attachment to his moribund friend resonate with Janouch's veneration and can be seen as an example of the profound feelings Kafka often inspired in the people around him; other friends, however, felt disappointed by his reticence. When put under pressure, Kafka did not hesitate to end relationships, as the aspiring writer and medical doctor Ernst Weiss experienced when he moved to Prague in 1916. The reasons for their estrangement are not entirely clear, but one can suspect that Weiss might have pursued Kafka too eagerly. Kafka laconically informed Felice Bauer that he had broken off his friendship with Weiss until he felt better; a half-hearted rapprochement followed in 1921 in Berlin.

Writing

While friendships provided a specific support mechanism in Kafka's life, Kafka's texts primarily problematize relations built on empathy and trust. Instead, interpersonal relationships in his works are often instrumentalized by characters, and are generally marred by betrayal, faltering or failing communication, rivalry and even (physical) struggle, as indicated by the title of one of his earliest texts, *Beschreibung eines Kampfes* (*Description of a Struggle*, 1904–10). This also applies to 'Das Urteil' ('The Judgement', 1912), a narrative that Kafka famously wrote in one creatively fruitful night. Whilst its focus rests predominantly on the conflict between the protagonist, Georg Bendemann, and his father, Georg's absent friend in Petersburg also plays a significant role. Especially at the beginning, Georg dwells at length on his friend's dire situation in Russia. However, precisely because he seems to consider his friend's feelings, he does not give him honest advice, and he also conceals his personal and professional success, which he perceives as a foil for his friend's failure. His omission of this information is mirrored by the fact that in the end the seemingly weaker friend proves to be more powerful in his mysterious alliance with the father, just as the previously frail father all of a sudden regains his physical strength and ultimately has the upper hand in their conversation.

This inversion of the power hierarchies of both family and friendship is rhetorically duplicated when the father calls the son a traitor to his friend, only to announce, ominously, that the friend is not betrayed yet. This notion of betrayal no doubt resonates with Georg's own feelings at the beginning, when he reflects on his evasive letters to the friend. The actual character of the friend is of no further importance at this point, for he arguably exists only as an (incorporeal) projection of both father and son, facilitating Georg's acceptance of his own guilt. By the time the father pronounces his death sentence, a now completely tractable Georg is all too willing to embrace it and to drown himself. This stage of destructive self-realization is not reached in close communication with the friend, but rather by competing against him and eventually admitting defeat. Substantial qualities that promote successful communication, such as recognition, mutual affection and – based on this – implicit trust, do not figure prominently in the narrative.

A similar agonistic element pervades other narratives that nominally introduce friends, such as the fragmentary first novel *Der Verschollene* (*The Man who Disappeared*), on which Kafka started working in 1912. The exceptionally friendly relationship between its protagonist, Karl Rossmann, and the young secretary, Therese, for instance, is as much a trustful sharing of intimate and painful memories as a mild competition about something as peripheral as grammatical excellence, on which the narrator dwells extensively. By contrast, Karl's thoughts and reactions to Therese's heartrending story about the death of her mother are not related in the text. Roughly a decade later, *The Castle* provides more scope for the protagonist, K., to show empathy, when his – mostly female – interlocutors recount major events in their lives. Here another facet comes to light: even in his seemingly sensitive responses the protagonist seems propelled by his own agenda, which he pursues by skilfully interrogating his acquaintances or by attempting to force them to commit to an interpretation that suits him. *The Castle* is particularly typical of these ultimately failed acts of communication, thus undercutting any proper relationship and reducing it to the strategic importance K. attributes to the various conversations. It soon becomes clear that K. subordinates the people he meets to the overarching objective (and its diverse, constantly varying sub-goals) with which he enters the village and which remains characteristically obscure throughout the novel fragment.

K.'s instrumentalization of others is anticipated in a prevalent technique used by Kafka's protagonist Josef K. in *Der Process* (*The Trial*) of 1914–15: the continuous recruitment of new helpers who more or less serve as means to an end. This specific form of utilization establishes a typical inter-subjective dynamic in Kafka's texts. It defies crucial principles of friendship in favour of strategy, either implemented by the protagonists themselves or wielded against them: while in *The Trial* and *The Castle* the protagonists prove to be proficient manipulators, Karl Rossmann in *The Man who Disappeared* subscribes to a notion of camaraderie and friendship which promptly makes him the object of exploitation, perfectly executed by his shady new friends Robinson and Delamarche. Karl's relation to the stoker whom he meets on the passage to America is, in contrast, more complicated and yet also saturated with these core themes. Kafka was sufficiently satisfied with this particular part of his fragmentary novel to publish it separately under the title *Der Heizer* (*The Stoker*) in 1913. In this chapter, Karl acts as the stoker's mentor and advocate in front of the captain, to whose authority he eventually has to bow, leaving the stoker to his fate. That the stoker just disappears at the end of the chapter 'as though [he] no longer existed' (*MD* 28/*V* 53) curiously anticipates subsequent events in the novel, with the significant change that Karl now finds himself in the role of the stoker, repeatedly accused of insubordination and then ritually expelled from his current life. In the end, abandonment and a sense of sneaking doubt prevail even in this rare instance of friendship, as Karl, disembarking from the ship, wonders whether his newfound uncle would ever be able to replace the stoker. Looking beyond Kafka's first novel, the sense of friendship and emotional closeness, which is intermittently present throughout *The Man who Disappeared*, becomes less topical in later texts.

Finally, while individual relationships are more often than not doomed to fail in Kafka's fictional world, the idea of a collective is also perceived as deeply problematic. The laws of inclusion and exclusion are often portrayed as arbitrary, as the unpublished text 'Gemeinschaft' ('Community', 1920) demonstrates with particular acuity. The five friends in this very short story, which is reminiscent of a parable, appear to be solely united by the fact that they have left the same house successively. Their otherwise peaceful lives are disturbed by a meddlesome sixth person who is then literally (with elbows) pushed away from the community (*NSII* 313). Such harsh in-group and out-group mechanisms frequently occur in Kafka's writing, as for instance in *The Castle*, where the ostracization of Barnabas's family by the village community ultimately remains just as enigmatic as the exclusion of the sixth person in 'Community'.

Relationships in Kafka's texts – between men, between men and women, between animals, between animals and men, and within and between groups – thus are predominantly defined by mutual distrust, deception, aggression, withdrawal and, finally, isolation. The most complete seclusion is presented in 'Der Bau' ('The Burrow'), a late work of 1923–4 about a mole-like creature that has created an elaborate system of underground tunnels. He frenetically perfects his burrow in order to protect himself against an ominous foe whose existence he merely seems to presume. This form of putative paranoia, answering to a calamitous yet elusive threat, the perennial struggle, and the interaction with an impalpable but fearsome enemy is more of a constant in Kafka's writing than any form of successful interpersonal communication. This finds another expression in faceless bureaucratic procedures or unapproachable, indeed unreachable, authority figures (as, for instance, in *The Trial* and *The Castle*). The concept of an intangible enemy affords an insight into underlying structures of Kafka's writing: it becomes clear that friendship presupposes an emotionally relatable alter ego capable of dialogue and commitment. This proves, however, to be a fundamentally questioned, often much longed-for, but ultimately elusive factor in Kafka's work.

NOTES

1 R. Stach, *Kafka: The Decisive Years*, trans. S. Frisch (Princeton University Press, 2013); P.-A. Alt, *Franz Kafka: Der ewige Sohn* (Munich: C. H. Beck, 2005).
2 See S. L. Gilman, *Franz Kafka: The Jewish Patient* (London: Routledge, 1995).
3 For a closer analysis of this complex term, which Buber uses in 1916 in his *Drei Reden über das Judentum* (*Three Speeches about Judaism*), see C. Battegay, *Das andere Blut: Gemeinschaft im deutsch-jüdischen Schreiben 1830–1930* (Cologne: Böhlau, 2011).
4 Gilman, *The Jewish Patient*.
5 *EFB* 365.
6 R. Stach, *Kafka: The Years of Insight*, trans. S. Frisch (Princeton University Press, 2015).
7 *EFB* 208.
8 M. Brod, *Über Franz Kafka* (Frankfurt am Main: Fischer, 1993), pp. 44–7.

CHAPTER 3

Women

Elizabeth Boa

Early on in *Der Process* (*The Trial*) Josef K. re-enacts, for Fräulein Bürstner as audience, his arrest that morning, playing the part of both accuser and accused, and so male guilt with regard to women emerges as a key theme. Three aspects of the topic 'Women' come together in this mesmerizing night scene: female characters in Kafka's fictions, women in his life and cultural images of women. This chapter will explore all three aspects and their complex interrelation in Kafka's works.[1]

Kafka began writing *The Trial* in 1914, after breaking off his first engagement to Felice Bauer (1887–1960), whose initials FB are echoed in *Fräulein Bürstner* and used throughout the manuscript of the novel as a shorthand for this character. Kafka had been writing increasingly affectionate letters to Felice's friend Grete Bloch (1892–1944), who finally told Felice about their correspondence, and Kafka was called to account by both women at a 'Gerichtshof' ('tribunal'), in a Berlin hotel (23 July 1914; *D* 293/ *TB* 658), a term which contained the core idea for *The Trial*. Long before this traumatic event, however, Kafka's engagement with Felice's photographs anticipates a key scene in the novel.[2] He bombarded Felice with letters full of questions about the images she had sent him. The transposition into words of visual details in the photos creates an eerie ambiguity: interest in the person gets deflected into interest in the image. Erotic opening to the woman was a stimulus to writing, but the activity of writing left no space for the woman: this would be the story of Kafka's relationship with Felice. In the night scene Fräulein Bürstner complains that somebody has interfered with her photographs. (She is quite right – Josef K.'s junior colleagues from the bank, mysteriously present in her room that morning, had fingered the photographs.) In depicting Fräulein Bürstner, Kafka figuratively interfered with one of Felice's photographs, transplanting it into his narrative. As he comments in a letter written on 15 December 1912: 'One hand on your hip, the other on your temple, that is life!... How supple you look! If only I had seen you dance! Have you always done gymnastics?' (15 December 1912; *LF* 216/*Bī* 333–4).

Felice's upright pose in the photo is turned by 90° in the novel: Fräulein Bürstner leans her face on one hand, her elbow resting on the cushions of the ottoman, while with the other she slowly caresses her hip. The dancing gymnast has been turned into a reclining odalisque. By 1912, Felice Bauer, a stenographer-typist by training, had advanced to a senior administrative position with the Carl Lindström Company, manufacturers of office equipment. In the discourse of the time, Felice was the epitome of the New Woman; as dancing goddess in Kafka's letter she embodies too the ideals of the *Lebensreform* (life reform) cult of the healthy natural life. But under Josef K.'s gaze, Fräulein Bürstner, a New Woman through the day, is reduced in the night-time encounter to her body: the languorous self-caress evokes Woman as a purely sexual being.

The most significant women in Kafka's life were in the main gifted and intelligent, above all his sister Ottla, of whom more later. Felice Bauer and Grete Bloch were independent women with successful careers. Milena Jesenská (1896–1944), like Felice addressee of many letters, was a journalist who wrote articles on modern city life in the 1920s, political journalism in the 1930s, and was Kafka's first translator. Her father, a Christian Czech nationalist, had her committed for some months for 'moral insanity' to try to stop her marriage in 1918 to Jewish intellectual Ernst Pollak. But freethinking, cosmopolitan Milena prevailed. In 1919, she wrote to Kafka for permission to translate *Der Heizer* (*The Stoker*) into Czech, and so began a long-distance relationship by letter. In response to a correspondent with literary interests, Kafka's letters to Milena are stylistically more highly wrought than the letters to Felice, but both sets of letters testify to deep emotional and intellectual engagement. Kafka ended the correspondence with Milena in January 1921, though a few further letters followed, the last in 1923. Kafka was by then living in Berlin with Dora Diamant (1898–1952). Born in Będzin in Poland to Orthodox Jewish parents, Dora was sent off to a religious school in Krakow when her father remarried after her mother's death, but ran away twice. Frustrated by the limitations set on women by Orthodox teaching, and despite her father's opposition, Dora came to Berlin where she trained as a teacher. When she and Kafka met in the summer of 1923, she was working in a holiday camp for refugee children in Müritz on the Baltic coast, organized by the Berlin-based *Jüdisches Volksheim* (Jewish People's Home). Kafka, who had been taking Hebrew lessons since 1917, was greatly impressed by Dora's knowledge of Hebrew.

They set up together in Berlin and Dora looked after Kafka, by then gravely ill, and remained with him until his death in 1924.

Kafka held married life to be incompatible with life as a writer. But there were other obstacles. Kafka's diaries and letters reveal a visceral horror of conjugal sex, as when he writes to Felice of how his stomach turned inside out at the sight of the used sheets on his parents' bed (19 October 1916; *LF* 525/*B3* 261). Domestic horror was intensified by disgust at (but also fascination with) an urban culture of brothels and casual encounters. He wrote to Milena of his first sexual experience, a night in a hotel room with a young shop assistant (8/9 August 1920; *LM* 130–1/*BM* 196–8). Happy next morning at the relief of bodily need, he soon left Prague for the summer. On his return, although the good-natured girl looked at him with uncomprehending eyes, he ignored her, for he could not forget a tiny repulsive gesture, a trifling obscenity she had uttered, and even years later would suddenly be shaken by desire at the memory. Kafka's account of this episode, a remarkable testimony to his trust in Milena and to his propensity for unflinching self-analysis, makes clear that the misogynistic vision of the girl as vessel of repulsive obscenities was in fact his projection; Kafka here follows Josef K. in putting himself on trial. But the letter conveys too that self-knowledge, however lucid, cannot simply banish the powerful affects of desire and disgust.

Kafka's letters to women show a lively exchange of ideas and are full of reading suggestions, but he could be condescending. In 1919 he became briefly engaged to Julie Wohryzek (1891–1944), daughter of a shoemaker and synagogue sexton. In a letter to Max Brod, Kafka praised Julie's unassuming honesty but wrote snobbishly of her cultural tastes and brash Yiddish expressions: if one wanted to classify her, she belonged to the race of shopkeepers, he suggests (6 February 1919; *LFFE* 213/*B* 252). Yet he was full of disgusted rage when his father suggested ways of satisfying sexual need without marrying such a inferior person (*NSIIA* 205); that Kafka's sexual problems began inside the family is abundantly clear from such passages in the 'Letter to his Father' ('Brief an den Vater', 1919).[3]

Generational and Social Change

Kafka's parents' generation and that of Franz and his sisters straddle a historical break between tradition and modernity in Jewish family culture. As Jana Vokecká documents, the Jewish population of Bohemia formed an 'avant-garde' in the demographic transition, typical of modernizing societies, from high to low birth rates.[4] The traditional Jewish family model was of early, virtually universal, endogamous marriage often negotiated by a matchmaker. Although the *Familiantengesetze* (Familiant Laws), introduced by the Habsburg state in Bohemia and Moravia in 1726 and abolished only in 1859, limited Jewish rights to marriage to the eldest son, the marriage rate among Jews remained higher than in the total population well into the nineteenth century. The Austrian writer and journalist Leopold von Sacher-Masoch (1836–1895) writes in 1892 of the Jews as having the liveliest intellectual life of all advanced peoples, the purest faith and the highest morality: so strong is their sense of marriage and family, he observes, that single people ('Ehelose') are a rarity.[5] But by the turn of the century the proportion of unmarried Jews in Kafka's generation was markedly higher than in the population overall. The early sketch, 'Das Unglück des Ungesellen' ('The Bachelor's Misfortune', 1911), is one of many texts in which Kafka contemplates the gloomy fate of those modern 'Ehelose' who lack a wife and household.

It takes more than statistics, of course, to forge a link between a demographic and a literary avant-garde. Key factors in the emergence of Prague's educated Jewish elite were: the shift from Yiddish to German as medium of secular education; declining religious observance and growing participation in German and Czech culture, though German remained the prime cultural medium; high Jewish participation in secondary and tertiary education, by the turn of the century ten times higher than their share of the population. Female emancipation, a key measure of socio-cultural modernization, proceeded more slowly, however. Voting rights, extended to Jewish men in 1867, were granted to women only in 1918 under the postwar constitution of Czechoslovakia. Change in girls' educational provision, albeit slower than in some Western European countries, was more advanced in Prague than elsewhere in the Habsburg monarchy. The Minerva Gymnasium, a girls' secondary school founded in 1891 by the Czech poet Eliska Krasnohorska (1847–1926), paved the way for Austrian government decrees in 1896 and 1897 granting women the right to secondary schooling and university study in the humanities. The Minerva remained into the early years of the twentieth century the only girls' school in Austria-Hungary to offer the *Abitur*, the gateway to university study and graduation. Milena Jesenská and Alice Masaryk, daughter of Czechoslovakia's first president, both attended the Minerva, which became a centre of the Czech women's movement. The first woman graduated from the Charles University in Prague in 1901 as Doctor of Philosophy, and by around 1915 there were over six hundred matriculated female university students.

New Women and Old Myths

Women's emancipation was one factor eliciting the sometimes hysterical reactions to modernization as a perceived crisis of cultural and moral values. Sigmund Freud's Oedipus story, dubious as a causal explanation, is an imaginative response to the sexual culture to which both Freud (1856–1939) and Kafka belonged. Bourgeois patriarchy in its intensified Jewish form laid down the first-born son's duty to marry, and divided womankind along ethnic and moral lines, between Jew and non-Jew and between the enclosed domestic woman and the whore. But social mobility and modern city life put ethnic separatism and double morality under huge stress. New employment opportunities for middle-class women and feminist agitation coincided with widespread urban prostitution and sexual exploitation of domestic servants. The women's movement in Prague was a largely middle-class affair, complicated by the Czech–German divide. Agitation centred on suffrage and education, with schoolteachers playing a leading role in the movement. (In *Das Schloss* (*The Castle*)), schoolteacher Gisa of the gimlet eyes and sensuous body is a tantalizingly hybrid New Woman.) In Berlin, Felice Bauer's hometown, feminist discourse was a more complex battlefield of conservative, socialist and increasingly radical tendencies. Kafka recommended Lily Braun's *Memoiren einer Sozialistin* (*Memoirs of a Socialist*, 1909/11) to Felice. Braun (1865–1916), a writer and feminist, criticized conventional marriage and argued for a more general 'feminization' of culture, a non-biological motherliness also advocated by male writers such as Georg Simmel (1858–1918).

The second engagement between Felice and Kafka was on the understanding that he would write and she would continue her professional career: there would be no children. Yet Kafka constantly urged motherliness upon Felice when she was helping out in the Jewish People's Home for refugee children from war-torn Eastern Europe. An enthusiastic postcard proclaims that he felt as if the refugee girls were his children who had belatedly acquired a mother in Felice, or as if Felice were his child and the girls her collective mother, or, in a comically Biblical self-image, as if he were the patriarch sitting at peace somewhere else as the much-needed rain poured down upon his fields (24 September 1916; *LF* 506/*B3* 233). These strange imaginings express unrealizable longings: Kafka as a latter-day Abraham or long-distance father; Felice as mother of and mothered by the girls. The fluid two-way movement of motherliness anticipates *The Castle* in de-essentializing generational identity. Kafka wrote to Felice of seeing his mother, albeit unrecognizable, in his sister Ottla (19 October

1916; *LF* 523/*B3* 261–2), while in *The Castle* the young girl she once was is still there in motherly Gardena. Nobody is nothing but a mother.

Equally, nobody is nothing but 'the sex'. Kafka knew Otto Weininger's (1880–1903) bestseller *Geschlecht und Charakter* (*Sex and Character*, 1903), which sets masculine 'character' – meaning the emergence of individuality through transcendence of 'nature', of physical, sexual urges – in opposition to a feminine submersion in the impersonal sex drive. While individuals are always a mixture of both, Weininger nonetheless holds that all women are less 'human' than any man, for they are always 'the sex'. Following conventional typology, he divides womankind into the Mother and the Whore, though the Whore, being the essence of femininity, also lurks within the Mother. Thus Weininger, like Freud, breaks the taboo which represses recognition of the Mother's sexual nature, so undoing the double morality. Radical male intellectuals, more interested in sexual freedom than social emancipation, assimilated Weininger's Whore to the *hetaera* in Johann Jakob Bachofen's (1815–1887) anthropological study *Das Mutterrecht* (*Mother Right*, 1861), in vogue in modernist circles following its republication in 1897. According to Bachofen, patriarchy was preceded by matriarchy. But before any matriarchal ordering, an original hetaerism prevailed as women, promiscuously open to any and all men, roamed swampy borderlands.

It would require an immense capacity for hypocritical blindness, quite lacking in Kafka, to equate contemporary urban prostitution with Greek temple hetaerism or Bachofen's primeval swamp women. And yet two figures in *The Trial* might suggest otherwise. The young motherly washerwoman who points the way into the slum attic where Josef K.'s first hearing takes place seems later to be helplessly submitting to sexual intercourse at the back of the room – initially like a political debating chamber, the attic is now strangely like a temple or synagogue full of bearded old men. Eerily changing space houses a nightmarish vision of a whole culture as Josef K.'s way of seeing is invaded by a mix of class, religious, ethnic and sexual guilt. Like the washerwoman's helpless sexual submission, Josef K.'s helplessness in face of what he sees – or imagines – is shameful. Weininger, himself Jewish, saw Jews as a feminine race; ostensibly Christian Josef K. here nightmarishly reverts to type. Then there is web-fingered Leni. In all Kafka's work, Leni comes closest to the sometimes decorative, sometimes luridly misogynistic images of female sexuality in the decadent art of the time. Leni embodies the mixing of different signifying systems – realism, naturalism, religious allegory, mythic allusion – that generates the many meanings of *The Trial*. Aproned housemaid, nurse or handmaiden,

promiscuous temptress, witch-like brewer of soup, little doll with protuber-
ant glassy eyes, bird-like, pecking harpy, punishing servant of the goddess of
the hunt, sadistic dominatrix: Leni is a phantasmagoria of changing images,
an amalgam of figures that threatened male phallic power at the same time
as the New Woman threatened male social power. Josef K.'s mentality, not
any actual woman, is here on trial.

Family Romance: Sisters and Mother

Although women were graduating in increasing numbers, the Faculty of
Law at Charles University remained closed to women until 1918. Compared with their brother, the lawyer, Kafka's sisters were far less well educated, in keeping with the still predominant view that woman's natural
calling was marriage and family. Kafka's sisters Elli and Valli followed the
traditional route into early marriage, quickly followed by motherhood.
But Kafka's youngest sister, Ottla, born in 1892, went her own way from
early on. Her sisters' marriages were negotiated through brokers, but Ottla
defied her father and broke with tradition to marry Josef David, a Catholic
Czech nationalist, with her brother's full support: as Kafka wrote to her,
if she could retain her self-belief to a good end, she would have achieved
more than had she married ten Jews (20 February 1919; *LOF* 37/*BOF* 69).
For Kafka, whose relations with women were otherwise so difficult, Ottla
remained throughout his life the beloved sister and alter ego: Ottla was
marrying for him too, he wrote, and he would remain single for them both
(mid-May 1920; *LOF* 49/*BOF* 88). In another letter he hailed her as 'Great
Mother' (8 October 1923; *LOF* 80/*BOF* 139). Ottla was the long-distance
mother he would have liked, as he told Felice (19 October 1916; *LF* 525/*B3*
261). Ottla and her brother shared the ideals of the *Lebensreform* movement,
which sought to repair the damage caused by industrialization and city life.
Ottla's decision to study horticulture and take up farming, mocked as non-
sense by her father, was fuelled by the same idealism as the Kibbutz movement – brother and sister dreamed of emigrating to be farmers in Palestine.
In 1917, after the diagnosis of tuberculosis ended his second engagement to
Felice, Kafka spent eight happy months with Ottla on her farm in Zürau,
a village in West Bohemia. As he wrote to Max Brod, he was living a 'good
little marriage', 'not on the basis of the usual violent high currents but of
the small windings of the low voltages' (mid-September 1917; *LFFE* 141/*B*
165).

    The erotic undertone in Kafka's feelings for his sisters, above all for Ottla,
is unmistakable. But love for a sibling-wife was saved by the incest ban from

the anguish that the prospect of actual marriage and full sexual consumma-
tion induced in him. Kafka's unfulfilled longing for maternal love, in turn,
goes back to childhood. 'Letter to his Father' was not sent to the father, but
to the mother who – protectively? – failed to pass it on and who, after reading it, returned it to her son. Yet arguably the letter did reach the person
for whom it was intended, for it analyses the intricacies of a child's jealousy
of the mother who, rather than siding with her child, sought to reconcile warring parties in the battle between father and son. Kafka accuses his
mother of constantly driving him back into the circle of his father's power.
In effect, then, love for the mother prevented the son from breaking free of
the father. Kafka's analysis of family dynamics works with inherited characteristics: energetic if brutal vitality on the Kafka side; the Löwy inheritance
of pious scholarship and depressive melancholy. Julie Kafka remembered
her maternal grandfather's book-filled study, and her great-grandfather was
a renowned Talmudic scholar and rabbi. But she was also the daughter of
a wealthy brewer, whose dowry helped Hermann Kafka, son of a village
kosher butcher, on his rise from deepest poverty to self-made businessman.
And, as was the practice among the class of traders and small manufacturers, Julie Kafka worked in the family business *for* the children, but left their
care to household servants, as the author of the 'Letter' bitterly comments.

The father of Kafka's 'Letter' sits in his armchair and rules the world. The
image follows on from the father in 'Das Urteil' ('The Judgement', 1912),
who rises up in his bed, radiant with insight, to condemn the son, and from
the father in *Die Verwandlung* (*The Metamorphosis*, 1912), who hurls the
apple that festers in the insect-son's back. But thereafter the father shrinks
or disappears from Kafka's fictions. Maternal women, by contrast, are palpable presences. In *The Castle*, powerful women like the landlady, Gardena,
motherly guardian to K.'s lover, Frieda, run village life, in contrast to puny
husbands and the largely unseen, often ridiculous male scribes, the castle
officials whose imagined power haunts village minds. In this way Kafka
obliquely satirizes patriarchal society and its nucleus, the bourgeois family:
practical matriarchal power subsists under the aegis of culturally embedded patriarchy. The Barnabas sisters are, in their different ways, greater
rebels than their brother: silent, virginal Amalia, who rejects the advances
of Secretary Sortini; promiscuous Olga, who recounts in the first person
the story of her stigmatized family. So Kafka pays oblique tribute to his
sisters in giving rebellious spirit to Amalia and sisterly voice to Olga.

Kafka is sometimes hailed as a prophet who foresaw Stalinism or the
Third Reich. Closer to the political mark is the bureaucratic (dis-)order
of the multi-national Habsburg monarchy. But he was only too aware of

persisting antisemitism even as the Jewish citizens of Prague seemed to have arrived in a new modern world. In *The Castle* the story of the Barnabas family explores how communal ganging-up transforms neighbours into pariahs. In this way *The Castle* foreshadows a terrible future. In 1941 Kafka's sisters Elli and Valli were sent to the Jewish ghetto in Łódź, where they probably died in 1942. Josef David divorced Ottla in August 1942 and shortly after she was sent to the concentration camp of Theresienstadt. In October 1943 she volunteered to accompany a group of children to Auschwitz, where she was murdered. Milena Jesenská, a cosmopolitan intellectual turned by events into a left-wing Czech patriot, died in May 1944 in Ravensbrück concentration camp. Grete Bloch was arrested in 1940 in Italy and probably died en route to Auschwitz. Felice Bauer survived, however. Married in 1919, she emigrated with her husband and their two children, first to Switzerland, then to America, where she died in 1960. Dora Diamant became a professional actress in the later 1920s, joined the Communist Party and married Lutz Lask, editor of the communist newspaper *Die Rote Fahne* (*The Red Flag*). She escaped, first from Germany then from Stalinist Russia, to England, where she died in 1952.

NOTES

1 See E. Boa, *Kafka: Gender, Class, and Race in the Letters and Fictions* (Oxford: Clarendon Press, 1996) for a longer study of the themes discussed here.
2 See C. Duttlinger, *Kafka and Photography* (Oxford University Press, 2007) on the impact of photography on Kafka's literary imagination.
3 For the full English text see www.writersmugs.com/books/books.php?book=87&.
4 J. Vokecká, *Demographic Avant-Garde: Jews in Bohemia between the Enlightenment and the Shoah* (Budapest and New York, NY: CEU Press, 2013).
5 L. von Sacher-Masoch, *Jüdisches Leben in Wort und Bild* (1892; facs. repr. Wiesbaden: Fourier, 1986), p. 17.

CHAPTER 4

Work

Benno Wagner

In June 1906, Kafka graduated with a law doctorate from the German Charles University in Prague. In October, he joined the State Criminal Court for his law apprenticeship, and one year later he took a position as a law clerk in the Prague branch of the Trieste-based Assicurazioni Generali, then already a major player on the international insurance market. On 30 July 1908, Kafka changed his career direction by joining the state-owned Arbeiter-Unfall-Versicherungs-Anstalt für das Königreich Böhmen (Workers' Accident Insurance Institute for the Kingdom of Bohemia) as an assistant law clerk. As a result of his tuberculosis, he retired on 30 June 1922, in the position of an *Obersekretär* (Senior Secretary).

These are the basic facts of a professional career that appears mediocre when compared with the posthumous impact of Kafka's work as a writer.[1] Kafka himself seems to confirm this assessment in a series of much-quoted complaints about 'the office'; however, there is at least one instance that allows for a different reading.

In the autumn of 1907, straight after joining the Assicurazioni, Kafka sounded comparatively enthusiastic about his new job when writing to Hedwig Weiler, then his girlfriend in Vienna: 'the whole business of insurance itself interests me greatly, though my present work is dreary' (8 October 1907; *LFFE* 35/*B1* 72). Very early on, the aspiring young writer was looking for explanatory models, for questions and answers, which he eventually would find in his role as an insurance expert.

Social Insurance in Austria

The German welfare state as it emerged in the late nineteenth century became a model that was emulated across Europe. Social legislation in Austria, however, had to grapple with a very different set of social and political circumstances; partly modelled on the German system, it also had a number of distinctive features. The German Chancellor, Prince Otto von

Bismarck (1815–1898), delivered his 'Kaiserliche Sozialbotschaft' ('First Imperial Message on the Social Question') on 17 November 1881, promising the working classes protection against the risks of illness, work-place accident and old age. This groundbreaking speech was followed by a second such address and a number of related speeches delivered by Kaiser Wilhelm II (1859–1941) throughout the 1880s. From 1879 onwards, the Austrian Emperor Franz Joseph (1830–1916) delivered a corresponding set of speeches, proclaiming, on 26 September 1885, extensive plans for social insurance. There were, however, three sets of differences between German and Austrian industrial accident legislation.

(1) While Bismarck, in his 'Imperial Message', had promised to 'grant to the needy the highest degree of security and support, which they are entitled to', German social insurance at first provided the workforce with only fragmentary coverage, to be extended step by step in the future. In Austria, owing to administrative as well as socio-political and ethno-political obstacles, this extension proceeded far more slowly, and it left many sectors uninsured – a situation resounding in Kafka's 'Beim Bau der chinesischen Mauer' ('At the Building of the Great Wall of China'), where the protective device of the Great Wall is flawed by numerous gaps, and where the Emperor's message to his subject never actually reaches the addressee (*NSIA* 352/*HA* 28).

(2) Industrial accident insurance in the Reich was organized by industrial associations representing specific branches of production, thus creating experts in the technical and statistical aspects of accidents connected to specific technologies. Owing to the multi-ethnic federalism of the empire, Austrian industrial insurance deviated from this functional grid of differentiation by using a spatial pattern of organization. Each Crown Land established its own accident insurance institute, thus creating an administrative structure that fostered regionally responsible dilettantes rather than technologically specialized experts – a set-up that would strengthen the role of personal, sometimes skewed, judgement in issues of technological evaluation, and thus work against a more rigorous application of standards and guidelines.

(3) The most far-reaching difference between German and Austrian social insurance, however, was grounded in the constitutional set-up of both countries. Particularly in the highly industrialized Crown Land of Bohemia, the social conflict between capital and labour constantly intersected with ethnic conflicts, most notably the struggle between Czech- and German-speakers over control in areas such as education and

administration. While industrial accident insurance translated the former conflict into a mathematically controlled distribution of risks, the clash between ethnic groups over cultural and political autonomy was beyond the grasp of statistics and probability. The nineteenth-century optimism that welfare provision and efficient administration would eliminate ethnic conflict was disproved in the last three decades of the Habsburg Empire.

Kafka's Workplace

When Kafka joined the Workers' Accident Insurance Institute in the summer of 1908, his new employer was not only practically bankrupt but also faced a severe crisis in implementing its procedures. Company owners and workers, Czechs and Germans, hesitated or refused to play the roles ascribed to them by insurance laws, each group suspecting those new regulations of working in favour of their old opponents. At the same time, the Institute's ambitious new Director, Dr Robert Marschner (1865–1934), had begun to implement sweeping reforms.[2] Between 1908 and 1918, Kafka was involved in key areas of this realignment.

A man of literature, Marschner immediately recognized the young writer's value for his 'mission impossible'. Kafka's first writing assignment concerned the above-mentioned piecemeal construction of industrial accident insurance in Austria, 'Umfang der Versicherungspflicht der Baugewerbe und der baulichen Nebengewerbe' (1908) ('On the Scope of Compulsory Insurance in the Building Trades'; *O* 54–73/*A* 107–38). Owing to an ambiguous paragraph in the basic insurance law of 1889, subsequent legislations had alternated between including and excluding workshop labour from compulsory insurance in the construction industry. While Austrian insurance experts unanimously urged full coverage of *all* construction workers, Kafka's essay used the pragmatic spirit of Marschner's reforms. After proving irrefutably the law-maker's original intention to include workshop labour in accident insurance, the essay actually advocates sticking with the latest, contrary, decision of the high court, 'if for no other reason than that [yet another change] would have introduced a new and dangerous confusion into the legal situation' (*O* 59/*A* 115). While Kafka's essay thus prioritizes the overall stability of the sector (industrial accident insurance) over one particular goal (the insurance being fully inclusive), it also pursues the latter goal. Instead of relying on legal force, the Institute sent out a letter to all construction companies, informing them about their right to cancel their workshop insurance, while explaining to them the benefits of full insurance coverage of their workers. This circular 'was supposed to function as a personal negotiation with the employer about his own particular firm, free from outside influences' (*O 65/A* 128). Written in a critical period, Kafka's report re-opens the option for enrolment at the risk of existing members deciding to leave, so as to refresh public awareness of the original purpose of accident insurance.

In the last decade of the Habsburg Empire, then, Kafka can arguably be called the (albeit anonymous) public voice of the empire's largest industrial accident insurance institute, and yet this voice did not so much represent the Institute as comment on its position as if from a slight distance, a strategy which proved useful in negotiations with employers. Three years later, in the autumn of 1911, when Marschner's reforms had set the Prague Institute firmly on the path to economic recovery, the Institute anonymously published two long articles in the influential North Bohemian *Tetschen-Bodenbacher Zeitung* to openly address the most virulent aspect of its enrolment crisis: the rampant practice among employers of manipulating the wage lists of their companies in order to reduce the overall amount of their insurance fees. Remarkably, after the first of the two articles, the journal of the employers' association, *Die Arbeit*, did not react with a wholesale rebuttal of the accusations, but dwelled instead on the unfamiliar voice entering the debate. It called the intervention 'highly remarkable', and conceded that the author 'took trouble to take an objective point of view' (see *O* 167/*AM* 183), but still assumed that he must have close connections with the Institute.

After the Institute had responded to *Die Arbeit* in a second article, Kafka noted down in his diary: 'Wrote a sophistic article for the *Tetschen-Bodenbacher Zeitung* for and against the Institute' (10 October 1911; *D* 73/*TB* 73). This remark once again highlights Kafka's particular strategy in his PR work – his use of a particular voice, and his awareness of the inner workings of the industries he was dealing with. In the two articles in question, he addresses the problem of enrolment (by pointing out that company owners withholding insurance fees were actually stealing from more honourable employers) as well as the negative perception of the insurance sector by reassuring employers of the recent dramatic turning point in the Institute's economic performance. Finally, he mobilizes the active participation of employers in the industrial accident insurance network by encouraging them to pay close attention to the Institute's annual reports, implicitly setting them up as its guardians or auditors.

Another three years later, the First World War (1914–18) would swiftly destroy what had been achieved in reforming industrial accident insurance in Bohemia. At the same time, the war would set the scene for Kafka's most comprehensive and crafty PR campaign. When in 1915 the homeland was flooded with wounded soldiers, the Vienna government established public crownland agencies for returning veterans all over the empire. In Prague, this agency was run by Kafka's Institute, while Kafka himself played a key role in the successful establishment of a psychiatric hospital for wounded veterans in the northern Bohemian village of Frankenstein. He was not only involved in a regional search for a suitable location and premises, but also wrote flyers and newspaper articles in a campaign for private and public funding.

Accident Prevention

During Kafka's time at the Institute, industrial accident prevention in Austria was in a rather deplorable state. In the autumn of 1909, various interested parties tried to use the need for better regulations to gain control over accident insurance as a whole – the unions pushing for greater bureaucratic pressure on employers to implement safety regulations, and employers responding by requiring full control of industrial accident insurance institutes as a condition for improving workplace safety. Kafka at this time attended lectures on mechanical technology at Prague Technical University. In its annual report for 1910, the Insurance Institute published his piece on 'Unfallverhütungsmaßregel bei Hobelmaschinen' ('Measures for Preventing Accidents from Wood-Planing Machines'), the first in the history of the Institute to include illustrations (*O* 109–19/*A* 194–201). By arguing for the need to replace the dangerous square cutter heads with safer round ones, Kafka masterfully uses his acquired technological expertise to shift the emphasis away from people – human error as a cause of accidents – to the machinery, thus re-aligning the apparently conflicting interests of employers and workers. While we cannot dwell on the impressive technological scrutiny and awareness of man–machine interaction displayed in this piece, the shift from human to non-human actors, and the resulting dissolution of conflicts of interest, is summarized in the text's subtitles: 'I. The round safety shaft protects perfectly [thus ensuring the workers' safety]. II. The round safety shaft is basically cheaper than the square shaft [thus serving employers' short-term interests]. III. The round safety shaft works more cheaply than the square shaft [thus serving the long-term interests of both workers and employers]' (*O* 109–19/*A* 194–201).

Not surprisingly, Kafka was also charged with drawing the big picture of Austrian accident prevention. When in September 1913 international experts met in Vienna for the Second International Congress for Rescue Service and Accident Prevention, Kafka was not only a member of the Prague Institute's delegation, but also the author of two public lectures delivered by his superiors, Robert Marschner und Eugen Pfohl, about the history and present situation of accident prevention in Austria.

Appeals against Risk Classification

Kafka's most important area of assignment, however, was located at the intersection of technology, architecture, law and statistics. To establish insurance premium levels, every firm was classified according to a system of risk percentages, expressing the insurance fees to be paid per one hundred crowns of paid wages. The *general* risk class of a company was determined by the expected level of accident compensation associated with the particular industrial branch it belonged to, and an individual firm's *particular* fee level within that risk class was determined by the technological and architectural safety level of its own operations.[3] While the latter regulation was meant to create an incentive for employers to optimize their safety standards, it also inspired the creative imagination of firm owners, who filed appeals against the technological assessment of their operations. Anticipating the wave of appeals (totalling 3,100 between 1910 and 1915) that would follow the exercise of risk classification, the Institute established a separate appeals department in March 1910 – from now on the workplace of the newly appointed law clerk Franz Kafka. His main assignment for the following three years was the writing of official statements ('Beäußerungen'), summing up the Institute's response to employers' appeals. Since Section 1 of the new industrial accident insurance law restricted compulsory insurance to machine-operated businesses, employers produced (at times quite fantastic) descriptions of their businesses, where all machinery was located in secluded or remote places, with only fractions of the workforce ever coming into contact with it. Thus the Marienbad-based boarding-house owner Norbert Hochsieder, who had equipped his facility with a modern electric Otis elevator, claimed that he was 'not using a motor in his house', and that the 'power that activates my elevator is generated in the local electricity plant, and in the house there is only a converter switch that is locked by the electricity plant and accessible only to its representatives' (*O* 195/*A* 722). Even in a subsequent version, where the technological details were corrected, the radical separation between humans and machinery remains unaltered. Now the motor is situated in the house, but it is 'always kept locked and is completely inaccessible to my employees, since it is housed under a locked cover in a room that is also kept locked and to which only the elevator operator has access' (*O* 196/*A* 223).

In this situation, Kafka's task was to re-establish a description of the actual operations in the boarding house in keeping with the statistics-based classification schedule for all industries. Therefore, the Institute's primary concern was the availability of reliable data on the insured firms' technical equipment. However, as the Institute was not legally entitled to conduct its own inspections, it had to rely on regional trade inspectorates, which served as the insurance network's cognitive organ, or 'oligopticon', a term coined by philosopher and sociologist Bruno Latour. He uses it in opposition to Michel Foucault's model of the 'panopticon', an architectural structure in which one watchman is able to observe all inmates of an institution (a prison, school or hospital) without being observed in turn. As Latour writes, 'oligoptica . . . do exactly the opposite of panoptica: they see much *too little* to feed the megalomania of the inspector or the paranoia of the inspected, but what they see, they *see it well*'.[4] The situation of Austrian industrial accident insurance, however, confirmed Latour's associated warning that 'the tiniest bug can blind oligoptica'. As the above-mentioned trade inspectors strived to establish themselves as local experts, their reports about the technical standards were often compromised, terminologically vague, and eventually threatened the whole classification process. In the summer of 1911, the Institute sent a long note of protest to the Minister of the Interior, a document that was probably written by Kafka himself. The masterfully argued memo provided a detailed analysis of linguistic and political bugs in the inspection procedures, thus putting the inspectors themselves under scrutiny (*O* no. 7/*A* no. 22).

Epilogue: After the Habsburg Empire

Practically speaking, the end of Kafka's involvement in Bohemian industrial accident insurance coincided with the end of the Habsburg Empire. In mid-October 1918, he contracted the Spanish flu and barely survived, with his health permanently compromised. On 28 October the Czechoslovak Republic was declared in Prague, on 24 December the Insurance Institute was placed under the authority of the new Ministry of Social Welfare, and Czech became the only official language. While his former superiors, Marschner and Pfohl, left the Institute, disgraced by the Czech press and political players, Kafka was promoted to the rank of Secretary and became head of the newly established *Conceptsreferat* (Drafts Department) where one staff member – Kafka himself – would supervise legal drafts of principal importance from all other departments. From now until his early retirement in July 1922, Kafka would spend no more than eighteen months in the office.

Literary Resonances

The links between Kafka's workplace and his literary work – his day-time desk in the office, and his night-time desk at home – are evident on three levels. First, many motifs and storylines in Kafka's stories and novels have been traced back to his office work. His China complex, for instance, relates technological safety issues to questions of political constitution and the role of the cultural Other in ways that echo the industrial accident insurance legislation and accident prevention in the multi-ethnic Habsburg Empire (see O 268–71/A 861–6). Der Process (The Trial), in turn, resonates with the ways in which social legislation penetrated people's lives and under-mined trust in the state and the law;[5] in Das Schloss (The Castle), finally, the administration occupies a kind of 'higher sphere' that had been reserved for religion and arts in previous centuries.[6]

Second, it can be argued that a key principle of Kafka's literary work, namely his poetics of (failed) translation, is an enriched extension of issues also addressed in his office work. Kafka's novels and stories are structured around the tension between an individual with a vital but fragile claim (a claim to justice, for instance, or to inclusion in a community) and an insti-tution with an obscure mode of operation. Whereas Kafka's institutions typically suffer from a flawed structure (like Austrian industrial accident insurance, Kafka's attic courts and castle administration display all kinds frictions and corruptions, and threaten to fall apart at any moment), the situation of the individual is far more dramatic. While industrial accident insurance required injured or mutilated workers to claim their damages in order to receive monetary compensation in proportion with previous earn-ings, Kafka's protagonists find it difficult to communicate their case in the first place, to translate their experience into the discourse of the institu-tion.[7] Because of this failure of translation, they struggle to assemble and mobilize their own support networks.

Third, taking this argument further, we can conclude that Kafka's office writings do not simply provide his literary work with one additional 'con-text', but that his literary texts are in fact an extension of his professional work. While at his office desk Kafka struggled in vain to produce the objec-tive, watertight, statistically backed reports required of him; at his home desk he continued to trace, check and evaluate risks that, by virtue of their particularity, escape mathematical calculation: on a personal level the risks faced by the bachelor, the artist and the social misfit; on a collective level, the risks generated by a society structured around an unstable set of political, cultural and ethnographic alliances and oppositions. For Kafka, the often archaic world of his fiction, a world full of strange objects, talking animals and unreadable signs, does not constitute a counter-world to his day-time struggle for modernization and transparency. Rather, he transplants the concerns of social insurance into this literary world, to trace carefully, diligently, step by step, 'with the instinct of a quadruped' (27 April 1915, *D* 338/ *TB* 740), the risks, goals and challenges of life in a world that has, in fact, never been modern.

NOTES

1 See *A* 981–96.
2 See B. Wagner, 'Kafka's Office Writings: Historical Background and Institutional Setting', in *O* 19–47: 36–8.
3 See commentary, *A* 845–7.
4 B. Latour, *Reassembling the Social: An Introduction to Actor-Network Theory* (Oxford University Press, 2005), p. 181.
5 See Wagner, 'Kafka's Office Writings', pp. 28–9.
6 See B. Wagner, 'Allogenität und Assemblage: Kafka's *Schloß* mit Blüher und Latour', *Internationales Archiv für Sozialgeschichte der Literatur*, 38, no. 1 (2013), 81–99.
7 See S. Corngold and B. Wagner, *Franz Kafka: The Ghosts in the Machine* (Evanston, IL: Northwestern Press, 2011), chapter 11.

CHAPTER 5

Health and Illness

Johannes Türk

Even before Franz Kafka was diagnosed with tuberculosis – which was, before the age of antibiotics, an incurable disease – concerns about health and illness took pride of place in his life, work and writing. Kafka's texts repeatedly describe experiences of mental and physical frailty, of injury and disease; this fixation is in turn complemented by his avid interest in the life reform movement, in dietary regimes and exercise routines, and in his frequent stays in spas and sanatoria. Kafka also grappled with questions of physical and mental health as part of his work for the Workers' Accident Insurance Institute.

The year 1917, however, marked an existential turning point. When he was first diagnosed with tuberculosis, Kafka was in the relatively privileged position of someone who was acquainted with the illness, its implications and treatments, and who was, moreover, able to afford excellent medical care. Yet from the very start, his instinctive response to his diagnosis was avoidance – a stance which would lead him to pursue treatments not at the height of contemporary medicine and to understand his illness in symbolic terms – as part of recurring patterns structuring his life. Indeed, Kafka exploited the contradictory medical interpretations of the illness with great virtuosity. Being diagnosed with tuberculosis largely freed him from the burdens of his position as a bureaucrat. His illness, then, had far-reaching implications for his writing, manifesting itself in a change of writing strategy, in his use of genre, style and themes.

Ailments and Exercise: Towards the Healthy Body

His weak health is a recurrent topic in Kafka's letters and diaries, and from an early age hypochondria, that widespread and fashionable ailment of the *fin de siècle*, was a determining factor in his self-perception. As the 'Brief an den Vater' ('Letter to his Father', 1919) suggests, weak nerves and the associated problems stemmed, at least in his father's view, from a hereditary predisposition prevalent in his mother's family, the Löwys. Dating back to his time as a student of law at Prague's Charles University, Kafka's life was characterized by an alternation between periods of illness and of convalescence. In 1905, he travelled to a sanatorium for the first time to recover from the strains of his studies. His time at Ludwig Schweinberg's sanatorium in Zuckmantel, Silesia, was the first of many stays in such institutions. Initially, though, these visits were primarily associated with social enjoyment and indeed with seduction. Mingling with 'people and womenfolk' makes Kafka feel 'rather lively', as he writes to Max Brod in 1905 (24 August 1905; *LFFE* 20/*B1* 43).

Ailments such as the furunculosis (skin abscess) he contracted during a 1910 trip to Paris, which forced him to return to Prague early, cemented Kafka's sense of his own physical weakness. On his return he describes to his travel companions Max and Otto Brod how fainting at the doctor's surgery made him feel like a girl (20 October 1910; *LFFE* 67/*B1* 127).[1] As he stresses, such effeminizing experiences of physical frailty are set to hamper his more general advancement: 'It is certain that a major obstacle to my progress is my physical condition . . . how will the weak heart that lately has troubled me so often be able to pound the blood through all the length of these legs?' (21 November 1911; *D* 124–5/*TB* 263).

Kafka turned to exercise and diet to ameliorate his condition. The early twentieth century abounded in so-called 'life reform' movements involving exercise regimes and an outdoor lifestyle as well as spiritual components such as meditation. *Turnen* (gymnastics) was an integral part of the Austrian school curriculum. As an adult Kafka followed the teachings of the Danish gymnast Jørgen Peter Müller (1866–1938), whose influential *Mit System* (*My System*, 1905) – gymnastics manual and life philosophy in one – took Europe by storm. It promised to promote individual and social well-being against the backdrop of a culture of decadence; Kafka discontinued these exercises, which he performed next to an open window, only after the outbreak of his tuberculosis.

Mark M. Anderson argues that Kafka's health regime was more than an attempt to purify the body; it was part of an asceticism which also underpinned his pared down style: 'Kafka's writing takes place in the realm of "clothing", that is, in the very temporal order of the body, material existence, suffering, and death that they strive to overcome.'[2] This is summed up in a diary entry of 3 January 1912, in which Kafka lays out a programme of abstaining from the pleasures of life for the sake of writing:

> It is easy to recognize a concentration in me of all my forces on writing. When it became clear in my organism that writing was the most productive

direction for my being to take, everything rushed in that direction and
left empty all those abilities [ließ alle Fähigkeiten leer stehen] which were
directed towards the joy of sex, eating, drinking, philosophic reflection, and
above all music. I atrophied in all these directions [Ich magerte nach all
diesen Richtungen ab]. (3 January 1912; *D* 163/*TB* 341)

This is not to say that Kafka fully identified with such life-reform movements. As Anderson points out, in spite of the 'positive tenor' of Kafka's
remarks about the nature retreat Jungborn (Saxony), which he visited in
1912, as a Jew he must have felt ill at ease in a place where guests sang
Christian hymns at open air services and walked around naked.[3]

However, visiting sanatoria continued to be integral to his recreational
routine. After his application to join the army was rejected, Kafka spent
ten days in the Sanatorium Frankenstein (Bohemia) in July 1916. This stay
in turn fed into his engagement with war veterans, among them tubercular soldiers. He frequently visited sanatoria and clinics dedicated to their
care, and was a member of a committee at the Insurance Institute oversee-
ing the purchase of the Frankenstein sanatorium, which was to be turned
into a treatment centre for veterans suffering from mental illness.[4] Kafka's
familiarity with the world of illness was thus underpinned by personal and
professional experience. As the officer in the story 'In der Strafkolonie' ('In
the Penal Colony') says of the torture machine to the visitor: 'You will have
seen a similar apparatus in private clinics' (*M* 78/*DL* 209).

Spa towns for Kafka were places of respite but also of intimacy. A 1915
trip took him and his fiancée, Felice Bauer, to Karlsbad, where he briefly
returned in April 1916. Later that year he and Felice spent what is often
considered their happiest time together in the spa town of Marienbad. It
was here that Kafka began to discover the world of Jewish spa culture,
encountering visitors from the Jewish Eastern European community.[5]

Tuberculosis: The Initial Diagnosis

When his tuberculosis erupted, Kafka was already well acquainted with
the medical details of the disease and the institutions it was treated in. By
the late 1910s, the illness was no longer associated with the romantic idea
of a heightened sensibility. As a result of urbanization and the associated
risk of contagion, it had become an endemic, incurable disease, responsible for one in four adult deaths. The medical view of tuberculosis around
1900 was based on the 'habitus phthisicus', an inherited anatomic peculiarity. In his *Handbuch der pathologischen Anatomie* (*Handbook of Pathological Anatomy*, 1842–9), Carl Rokitansky defined the main features of this

disposition as a 'compressed chest' and 'overhanging shoulders'.[6] His handbook presented a hypothetical association between tuberculosis and body
type, and contemporary medicine, as well as the influential founder of
the sanatorium movement, Hermann Brehmer (1826–1889), defined the
resulting disproportion between heart and lungs as a necessary predisposition for the disease. On the basis of anatomic similarities, the pathology
of tuberculosis was held to be continuous with the common cold and the
catarrh.

For tuberculosis sufferers, the sanatorium was the only hope of a cure.[7]
It promised to use the healing properties of elevation to act on the human
anatomy and replaced the previously used sojourn in warm, dry climates.
The sanatorium was based on the concept of an 'immune space'. Since Hermann Brehmer's 1853 dissertation on the genesis and progression of tuberculosis, high altitude was believed to provide specific immunity against
tuberculosis, citing statistical evidence for the healing properties of movement and, by consequence, elevation. Altitude was held to improve the
constitutional disproportion between an undersized heart and oversized
lungs. Stimulation of the activity of the heart through elevation, combined with a protein-rich diet, was said to help the heart muscle grow.
Places said to possess 'immunity from tuberculosis' were key to a cure. In
Germany, where in 1854 Brehmer had founded the first sanatorium in the
Silesian Görbersdorf, immunity was said to begin at an altitude of 2,000
feet, and Davos was later modelled on this first sanatorium. To 'put on pro-
tein' ('Eiweiß ansetzen') was the starting point of the treatment; Brehmer's
pupil Peter Dettweiler then added other elements, such as sun exposure.

'Constitution theories' flourished at the end of the nineteenth century,
and the concept of the 'phthitic habitus' survived well into the twentieth century. However, the understanding of tuberculosis was revolution-
alized in March 1882, when Robert Koch (1843–1910) announced that he
had identified the mycobacterium tuberculosis, known as 'tubercle bacil-
lus', as the causal agent of the disease. After the discovery of this bacterial aetiology, tuberculosis was no longer primarily perceived as an internal
organic process, but rather as an externally caused phenomenon,[8] though
this did not affect the continued influence of theories of disposition, hered-
ity and social conditions. In 1890, Koch claimed to have discovered a cure
for tuberculosis. Tuberculin, a derivate of the tuberculosis mycobacterium,
was believed to necrotize tubercular tissue. Thousands of patients travelled
to Berlin to be treated by Koch; however, the treatment proved to be a
failure and most likely even infected additional areas of the body with the
disease – and yet this did not prevent the development and prescription of

new forms of tuberculin well into the twentieth century. Kafka's diagnosis therefore occurred at a crossroads in the history of tuberculosis, when the constitution was still considered a crucial factor behind the disease, and when its bacterial aetiology, though firmly established, was not yet effective in producing a cure. In this situation, the sanatorium remained the only viable treatment option.

Illness as Symbol

Being diagnosed with tuberculosis in August 1917 was a significant turning point in Kafka's life. After repeated and severe haemorrhaging he saw the family doctor Gustaf Mühlstein on 11 August and again on the following day. The illness would shape the remainder of his life and work. In a letter to his sister Ottla, Kafka describes the haemorrhage with the help of a Czech word chosen for its onomatopoetic qualities: '*Chrleni*, I don't know whether that's the way to spell it, but it's a good expression for this bubbling up in the throat. I thought it would never stop' (29 August 1917; *LOF* 19/*B3* 308–9). The next morning, the maid of the Palais Schönborn where he was living at the time foretold his approaching end. After his diagnosis, Kafka moved back in with his parents. In the letter to Ottla, he summarizes the results of two further doctor visits:

> Three possibilities, *first*, acute cold; when the doctor said that, I contested it. Would I catch cold in August? And when I don't catch colds at all . . . *Secondly*, consumption. Which the Dr. denies for the present. Anyhow, we'll see, all inhabitants of big cities are tubercular; a catarrh of the apex of the lung (that's the phrase, the way people say piglet when they mean swine) isn't anything so bad; you inject tuberculin and all's well. *Thirdly*: this last possibility I barely hinted to him; naturally he promptly warded it off. And yet it is the only right one and also quite compatible with the second. (29 August 1917; *LOF* 19/*B3* 308–9)

With great lucidity Kaka summarizes a conversation in which Mühlstein used contemporary medical assumptions, such as the omnipresence of the mycobacterium tuberculosis and the effectiveness of tuberculin, to reassure his patient. But Kafka knew more than Mühlstein, for he did not tell his doctor that even before the haemorrhage he had had blood in his sputum.[9] This private knowledge underpinned his rejection of the doctor's first suggestion of an acute cold, a diagnosis in accord with the pathology of the time, which assumed a continuity between catarrh and tuberculosis. The second diagnostic possibility – bracketed by doubt – is the one Kafka shares. But he can only accept this diagnosis by alluding to a third explanation: his illness as the physical manifestation of a pre-existing psychological, or indeed existential, condition. As he writes in a self-addressed diary entry:

> If the infection in your lungs is only a symbol [Sinnbild], as you say, a symbol of the infection whose inflammation is called F.[elice] and whose depth is its deep justification; if this is so then the medical advice (light, air, sun, rest) is also a symbol. Lay hold of this symbol. (15 September 1917; *D* 383/*TB* 831)

Kafka's interpretation of the illness as a symbol was an attempt to vehemently ward off another possibility, suggested by his friend Felix Weltsch: namely that his illness was the result of nothing but a series of contingencies.[10] Although Kafka clearly experienced his illness as an encounter with death – in a letter to Weltsch he writes of spotting the 'Angel of Death' that Dr Mühlstein was trying to hide behind his back (22 September 1917; *LFFE* 144/*B3* 327) – he integrated it into an interpretation that did not accept the contingent reality and lent his condition a deeper reason and purpose.

Tuberculosis was confirmed in early September when Kafka, following pressure from Brod, saw Professor Gottlieb Pick, director of the Laryngological Institute at Charles University. Pick recommended a vacation in the countryside, mistakenly assuming that Kafka was unable to afford a stay at a sanatorium in Davos or Meran. But this advice suited Kafka, who 'had had enough of sanatoriums of any kind',[11] and preferred to spend his first medical leave of absence in Zürau, where his sister Ottla and her husband were working a farm.

Kafka's calm acceptance of his illness arguably conceals his surprise, indeed his shock, at the diagnosis. On 7 September 1917, he writes to Felice Bauer: 'at the age of thirty-four I should be struck down overnight, with not a single predecessor anywhere in the family – this does surprise me' (*LF* 564/*B3* 316). And to Max Brod he writes:

> In any case my attitude towards the tuberculosis today resembles that of a child clinging to the pleats of its mother's skirts. If the disease came from my mother, the image fits even better . . . I am constantly seeking an explanation for this disease, for I did not seek it. Sometimes it seems to me that my brain and my lungs came to an agreement without my knowledge. (mid-September 1917; *LFFE* 138/*B3* 319)

But the disease also released Kafka from his post at the Insurance Institute, first temporarily and then permanently, when in 1923 he was granted early retirement. He began to embrace these opportunities immediately after the diagnosis, as the fulfilment of his long-standing desire to devote himself fully to writing. Indeed, his new situation immediately manifested itself in a new approach to writing. He gave up keeping a diary, and while in Zürau started to write short, aphoristic pieces reminiscent of Kabbalistic texts. In 1917 he started to learn Hebrew, part of his growing engagement with Judaism. And yet to many among Kafka's friends, he seemed to not take the turning point of his life seriously enough.

The Final Stages

In spite of periods of weight gain and relative stability, Kafka's health was deteriorating, and he did not return to his office for more than a few months at a time. Though he spent a significant part of the remainder of his life in sanatoria, none of these offered the most modern medical facilities. During the last years of his life, worries about his dwindling financial resources at a time when high inflation further devalued his savings seem to have prevented a better choice.

His illness also shaped Kafka's (notoriously complicated) relationships with women, though this manifested itself in different ways. On 27 December 1917 Kafka ended his (second) engagement with Felice Bauer. The general medical advice at the time warned tuberculosis sufferers against intimate relationships; though his tuberculosis was not yet regarded as infectious, these guidelines supported Kafka in his determination to end the relationship. Yet his illness did not prevent him from entering into new relationships. Julie Wohryzeck, whom Kafka met in January 1919 and to whom he got engaged in the summer that year, was herself a tuberculosis sufferer. Kafka sought medical advice from his physician, Professor Pick, who deemed that he was 'physically capable of marrying only if he put on some weight'.[12] But their wedding fell through for practical rather than medical reasons,[13] and Kafka eventually left Julie Wohryzeck during an affair with Milena Pollak, née Jesenká, who was also suffering from tuberculosis. His letters to Milena, mostly written during a stay at the guesthouse Ottoburg in Meran, playfully engage with different interpretations of the shared condition and frequently speak of it in symbolic terms – a process that mirrors Kafka's own relationship to his illness.

By the time their relationship petered out in the autumn of 1920, Kafka's health had further deteriorated, and the physician of the Insurance Institute prescribed a three-month leave, which Kafka spent at a sanatorium in Matliary in the High Tatras. For the first time in his life, he saw the symptoms of tuberculosis close-up when a fellow patient invited him to look at his tubercular throat through a mirror. As Kafka writes to Brod about this encounter:

> What you see in that bed is much worse than an execution, yes, even than torturing. To be sure, we have not ourselves invented the tortures but have learned about them from diseases; no man dares to torture the way they do. (second half of January 1921; *LFFE* 253/*B* 294)

In Matliary Kafka also made a friend who would accompany him during his final months: the medical student Robert Klopstock. When Kafka started to suffer from breathing difficulties, he wrote to Brod, telling him to burn his unpublished manuscripts in the event of his death, and gave his diaries to Milena Pollak. During his subsequent spa stay, at the health resort in Spindelmühle in the Riesengebirge in January 1922, he began to write his last novel, *The Castle*.

But his condition further deteriorated, and by September 1922 doctors saw no further treatment options. In July of 1923, Kafka joined his sister Elli and her children for a vacation in the seaside resort of Müritz at the Baltic Sea. It was here that he met Dora Diamant, an orthodox Polish Jew living in Berlin and working with orphaned children. With her, Kafka decided to begin an independent life in Berlin. It was in Berlin that he wrote 'Der Bau' ('The Burrow'), a story of an animal whose increasingly futile efforts to secure his burrow – a physical extension of his self – against enemies from without and within bears a resemblance to Kafka's struggle with his illness.[14] Yet in the city, and under the additional pressure of dire poverty, Kafka's health quickly declined. Shocked by his nephew's state, his uncle, Siegfried Löwy, a doctor, convinced Kafka to leave Berlin for a sanatorium in Switzerland. The plan fell through because Kafka had no valid passport.

Instead, Kafka chose the sanatorium Wienerwald in Ortmann (Lower Austria). In March 1924, when his throat began to be affected and tuberculosis of the throat was diagnosed, Kafka went to the laryngological clinic of Professor Hayek in Vienna, where the advanced state of his illness was recorded and a pneumothorax (a disconnection of one lung) considered as a treatment option but eventually rejected in the light of his weak overall condition. At the clinic, Kafka was forced to share a room with other terminally ill patients and felt so unwell that Robert Klopstock and Dora Diamant moved him to a small private sanatorium run by Dr Hoffmann in the quiet village of Kierling near Klosterneuburg. High-ranking doctors were mobilized to visit the dying Kafka, who was still able to proofread his final book, *Ein Hungerkünstler* (*A Hunger Artist*). Other than morphine, alcohol injections into the larynx were his only treatment. On 3 June, Kafka's breathing became so laboured that he asked Klopstock for an overdose of morphine, allegedly saying to him: 'Kill me or else you're a murderer.'[15] Kafka died at around midday on 3 June 1924, with Dora Diamant by his side, and was buried at the Jewish cemetery in Straschnitz near Prague.

The final acceleration of his disease forced Kafka to abruptly abandon his life in Berlin, where he had managed, for the first time in his life, to live in a self-determined way, apart from his family. When he reached this point, we find a writer remote from the young dandy Kafka, who sought to purify his body as part of an overall programme of aesthetic asceticism. And yet Kafka's numerous sanatoria stays before and after 1917 testify to the continuities between his early years and the time of his illness. The fact that institutions he stayed in lacked the latest medical technology contributed to his decline. While he was able to face his own death with a sense of composure, Kafka *was* afraid of pain and dying, having witnessed the destruction tuberculosis could wreak in other patients. Despite and perhaps because of this, he insisted on seeing his disease primarily as a symbolic reality, expressed in the physical realm of his body; in this way, his illness became part of his ongoing project: the transformation of life into narrative.

NOTES

1 S. L. Gilman, 'Kafka und Krankheit' in B. von Jagow and O. Jahraus (eds.), *Kafka Handbuch* (Göttingen: Vandenhoeck & Ruprecht, 2008), pp. 114–20: 115.

2 M. M. Anderson, *Kafka's Clothes: Ornament and Aestheticism in the Habsburg Fin de Siècle* (Oxford: Clarendon Press, 1992), p. 5.

3 Anderson, *Kafka's Clothes*, pp. 84–8: 86.

4 R. Stach, *Kafka: The Years of Insight*, trans. S. Frisch (Princeton University Press, 2013), p. 70; *O* 44.

5 See M. Zadoff, *Next Year in Marienbad: The Lost World of Jewish Spa Culture* (University of Philadelphia Press, 2012), especially pp. 237–8.

6 S. L. Gilman, *Franz Kafka: The Jewish Patient* (New York, NY: Routledge, 1995), p. 207.

7 This paragraph summarizes J. Türk, *Die Immunität der Literatur* (Frankfurt am Main: Fischer, 2011), chapter 7.

8 C. Gradman, 'Robert Koch and the Pressures of Scientific Research: Tuberculosis and Tuberculin', *Medical History*, 45, no. 1 (2001), 1–32: 6 and 14.

9 See Stach, *The Years of Insight*, p. 189.

10 Stach, *The Years of Insight*, p. 195.

11 Stach, *The Years of Insight*, p. 192.

12 R. Stach, *Kafka: The Decisive Years*, trans. S. Frisch (Princeton University Press, 2013), p. 282.
13 See C. Duttlinger, *The Cambridge Introduction to Franz Kafka* (Cambridge University Press, 2013), p. 6.
14 See J. Türk, 'Rituals of Dying, Burrows of Anxiety in Freud, Proust and Kafka: Prolegomena to a Critical Immunology', *Germanic Review*, 82, no. 2 (2007), 141–56.
15 See Stach, *The Decisive Years*, p. 571.

CHAPTER 6

Writing

Manfred Engel

In recent years, 'writing' has become a keyword in Kafka research. Deconstructivist critics argue that Kafka's primary aim was not the creation of completed works; rather, writing, the continuous transformation of life into *Schrift* (meaning text or scripture), was for him an aim in itself – and, at the same time, the real and only subject of his texts.[1] Such claims should not remain uncontested. Though writing for Kafka was obviously better than *not* being able to write, it was definitely no substitute for the production, and indeed the publication, of finished works. Such debates aside, it is clear that Kafka developed a very original and unorthodox way of writing, which in turn had important consequences for the shape of his novels and shorter prose works. This chapter discusses the main features of Kafka's personal version of *écriture automatique* ('automatic writing' – writing which bypasses conscious control); his techniques for opening a story, continuing the writing flow and closing it; the purpose of his self-corrections; and the consequences that this mode of literary production had for Kafka's novels.

Writing in Perfection: 'The Judgement'

Kafka was notoriously critical of his own work, but there is one text that even to him appeared faultless: 'Das Urteil' ('The Judgement', 1912). Strangely enough, his main reason for approving of the narration was the way in which it had been written:

> This story 'The Judgement' I wrote at one sitting during the night of the 22nd–23rd, from ten o'clock at night to six o'clock in the morning . . . The fearful strain and joy, how the story developed before me, as if I were advancing in water. Several times during this night I carried my own weight on my back. How everything can be said, how for everything, for the strangest fancies, there waits a great fire in which they perish and rise up again . . . At two I looked at the clock for the last time. As the maid walked through the anteroom for the first time I wrote the last sentence . . . The conviction verified

that with my novel-writing I am in the shameful lowlands of writing. Only *in this way* can writing be done, only with such coherence, with such a complete opening up of the body and the soul. (23 September 1912; *D* 212–13/ *TB* 460–1)

So the narration was written in one piece, in about eight hours, continuously and spontaneously, 'like a real birth' (11 February 1913; *D* 214/*TB* 491). And it was written without a plan and quite contrary to the author's original intentions:

> When I sat down to write, after a desperately unhappy Sunday . . . I wanted to describe a war; from his window a young man should see a crowd of people approaching across the bridge, but then everything was turning beneath my hands. (3 June 1913; *LF* 296/*B2* 201–2)

The metaphors which Kafka uses to describe this writing act are very telling: 'advancing in water', 'birth', 'complete opening up of body and soul', the quasi autonomous 'development' of the story 'in front of' the author, a transforming 'fire', almost alchemistic in nature, in which even the 'strangest ideas' are 'burnt' and 'resurrected'. All this is the polar opposite to the model of a rational, pre-meditated mode of composition, which is continuously controlled and consciously organized by the author.

Why did Kafka want to write like this? Like many other modernist authors, he believed in the ability of literature and art to question our conventional ways of thinking, perceiving and acting, and to provide us with more than rational insights. If art is to achieve this goal it must be more than the creation of an individual with a limited and particular outlook. Only unpremeditated and uncontrolled writing can enable a text to 'know' more than its author. For Kafka, writing like this was an extremely dangerous task – a 'descent to the dark powers' and 'unleashing of spirits bound by nature' (5 July 1922; *LFFE* 333/*B* 384) – and a chance to be used as a mere 'instrument' by 'a higher power' (1 November 1912; *LF* 20–21/*B1* 203). It meant an 'assault on the frontiers' (16 January 1922; *D* 399/*TB* 878), an attempt to transform 'the world into the pure, the true, and the immutable' (25 September 1917; *D* 387/*TB* 838), but can also, conversely, be described as 'vanity and compulsive pleasure' – even as 'serving the devil' (5 July 1922; *LFFE* 333–4/*B* 384–5).[2]

Beginning – Writing – Ending

'The Judgement' seemed to prove that writing like this could work, that it could lead to a complete and well-composed work. This one example of seemingly effortless success stands, however, against an endless series of failures, of never completed narrations. Small wonder – for with the notion of pre-planned composition Kafka also abandoned the evolvement of a text along plotlines or character development that traditionally serves as the stabilizing backbones of narrative writing. So it is the beginning of a text alone that must build up enough 'pressure' to initiate and propel the flow of the writing stream.

Sometimes these beginnings start off from mere biographical details – the opening of 'The Judgement' (*M* 19/*DL* 43), for instance, is nothing but a slightly veiled transposition of the author's actual writing scene: Georg Bendemann, the protagonist, sees the view that Kafka saw when looking out of his window, and he is writing, just like his author. But this is merely a prelude to the unfolding of the puzzling constellation of Georg versus his distant 'friend': the opposition between himself – as a son, who stayed within the family context, found a bride, took over the family business and has thus almost succeeded in usurping the position of his father – and his friend, who 'fled' (*M* 19/*DL* 43) to Russia and has remained a bachelor and an 'old child' (*M* 19/*DL* 44). It is this constellation, whereby one person is split into two – that is to say two alternative ways of life – which acts as the creative seed as the story develops.

The all-important feature of this initial situation is a puzzling element, a deviation from familiar habits and customs, which creates a riddle, an irritating stumbling block for rational understanding. It ties a knot which is never untied – and thus keeps plaguing not only the reader but also the protagonist. Challenged by a situation which is completely alien to his previously orderly and well-adjusted life, Georg stubbornly clings to his former existence – like Gregor Samsa in *Die Verwandlung* (*The Metamorphosis*) who, though transformed into something like a giant bug, wants to continue his work as a salesman (*M* 31/*DL* 139); or like bank manager Josef K. in *Der Process* (*The Trial*) who, though inexplicably arrested and accused, tries to approach his trial like any other business transaction (*T* 90/*P* 168); or like the eponymous protagonist of 'Blumfeld, ein älterer Junggeselle' ('Blumfeld, an Elderly Bachelor'), who simply tries to ignore and conceal the two strangely alive jumping balls which suddenly turn up in his flat (*HA* 81–100/*NSI* 229–66).

Thus the fantastic inventions in Kafka's stories serve primarily to start off the writing flow and keep it going – for the initial riddle never will and never must be solved. The 'progression' of the story unfolds as *variations* of this initial situation: the protagonist's never-ending attempts to come to terms with it in ever new situations and character-constellations – and the continuous frustration of these attempts in what the critic Gerhard Neumann has called 'sliding paradoxes' (a series of 'inversions', 'distortions' and 'deflections' that change the narrative trajectory).[3] Thus the patient in 'Ein Landarzt' ('A Country Doctor') is diagnosed as perfectly healthy – and then only a moment later as fatally ill (*HA* 15–16/*DL* 256–8); the doctor's reflections on his maid Rosa turn into reflections on the patient's pink ('rosa') wound (*HA* 16–17/*DL* 257–8); the medical treatment of the patient is suddenly transformed into an ancient ritual (*HA* 16/*DL* 259).

Even more difficult than keeping the writing flow going, however, is bringing it to a satisfactory closure. Since resolving the initial problem that propels the narrative is not an option, the death of the protagonist is the most obvious choice for a convincing conclusion – and one might well say that the protagonists of 'The Judgement', *The Metamorphosis*, *The Trial*, 'Ein Traum' ('A Dream') and 'Ein Hungerkünstler' ('A Hunger Artist'), to name but a few, die for the sake of a successful ending. Merely finishing the narration's plotline is, however, not enough for Kafka. Contrary to what many critics claim, he strove for texts with an artfully closed form: for him, a novella that is 'justified' must, from the very beginning, contain 'the completed organization' (*D* 322/*TB* 711). The easiest ways to close a text whose problems remain open and unresolved are circular composition, an overarching structural pattern, or ending with a strong contrast. The first strategy can be observed in 'The Judgement', where the bridge, which was mentioned at the beginning (*M* 19/*DL* 43), becomes the setting of Georg's death – but now crossed by an 'unending stream of traffic' (*M* 28/*DL* 61); the second is used in 'A Country Doctor', where the basic topographical pattern is that of departure (setting off from home) and return, yet the return will never be completed. The third strategy can be found in *The Metamorphosis* and 'A Hunger Artist', where the death of the increasingly weak protagonists is followed by the strong, vigorous presence of the sister (*M* 75/*DL* 200) and the panther (*HA* 65/*DL* 349).

Writing Deleted: Kafka's Emendations

Compared with works by other authors, Kafka's texts contain comparatively few corrections – and most of them were made immediately, as part of the writing process. In the few instances when Kafka reworked a text or fragment more substantially, he would, quite often, start to rewrite it from the beginning as, for instance, in his only play, the fragment 'Der Gruftwächter' ('The Warden of the Tomb'; *NSI* 276–89; 290–303). Of course, these self-corrections have various reasons. The ones that are most

important for the understanding of the writing process fall mainly into
two categories: (1) the avoidance of solutions and unambiguity, and (2) the
tangling and untangling of the writing stream.

A striking example of the first category is the deletion of the final paragraph in the fragmentary *Trial*-chapter 'Das Haus' ('The Building'; *T* 182–4/
PA 345–7, see Figure 3). In a state of dream or half-sleep, Josef K. is under-
going a complete transformation, which ends his fruitless struggle against
the court:

> The light, which up to now had streamed in from behind, changed and
> was suddenly shining blindingly from the front . . . Today K. [was wear-
> ing] a new, long <, dark> suit; ~~it was~~ it was comfortingly warm and
> heavy. He knew what had happened to him, but he was so ~~conten~~ happy
> ~~with~~ about it that he did not yet want to admit it to himself.

This new state, about which K. is so happy, may well be death, but at any
rate it means a non-violent and miraculous escape from his ordeal (reminiscent of the ending of 'A Dream'; *HA* 37/*DL* 298) – and this was probably
the reason for the deletion of the passage.[4] Even some of the corrections
within the deleted passage seem to have been made to preserve ambiguity:
continuing with 'über' would have forced Kafka to specify the reason for
K.'s happiness, which 'darüber' avoids; the inserted 'dunkles' was maybe
meant to evade associations with a white shroud; and the crossed out 'es
war' would have forced Kafka to give a closer specification of K.'s transformed state.

Most of Kafka's manuscripts contain examples of this type of correc-
tion – here is another one from *The Trial*: in the last chapter K. and his
two executioners meet a policeman whom K. could ask for help. In the
manuscript he whispers into the ear of one of his companions: 'The state is
offering me its help . . . What if I transferred [hinüberspielte] the trial into
the domain of civil law. Then I might even end up defending the gentle-
men against the state' (*PA* 322). This subsequently deleted passage would
have made the categorical distinction between the 'law' under which K. is
accused and ordinary laws of state ('Staatsgesetz[e]'), between his 'court'
and the regular executive and judiciary powers of the state, too explicit –
a difference which is clearly implied in the novel and crucial for its understanding.

The second type of corrections, which I call the tangling and subsequent
untangling of the writing stream, can be easily recognized by a glance at
the manuscript. Here many emendations are accumulated in a single spot –
indicating a 'congestion' of the writing flow and Kafka's various attempts
to overcome it. These mental blocks will, quite often, happen in textual
spaces of particular semantic importance. One of these congestions occurs

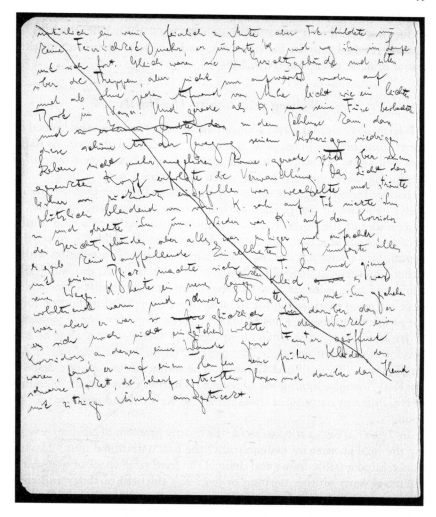

Figure 3 Page from the manuscript of *Der Process*.

towards the end of the fragmentary *Trial* chapter 'The Building', discussed above (*PA* 345), probably because Kafka found it difficult to transgress the self-imposed boundaries of his seemingly hopeless tale. Another one can be found in the manuscript of 'Forschungen eines Hundes' ('Investigations of a Dog'), when the dog tries to explain the insight which he reached at the end of his hunger experiment and his meeting with the 'Jägerhund' (*HA*

149/*NSII* 478). Put simply, the dog realizes that art is not simply opposed to life, but could well be an inspiration for life – an insight which Kafka himself reached only in his late work, and which he therefore probably found difficult to express (*NSIIA* 386–7).

Writing at its Limits: The Novels

It is fairly obvious that Kafka's 'automatic' mode of writing as embodied by the creation of 'The Judgement' was hardly suited to longer texts. As Kafka was well aware of this problem, he invented and tested new strategies of producing more extended narrations in each of his novels.

In *Der Verschollene* (*The Man who Disappeared*) Kafka used a paradigmatic structure to compensate for the missing (syntagmatic) plotline. In all episodes of the novel, Karl Rossmann is banished from a community because of an actual or apparent failure to comply with its rules; this community always has the basic structure of a family constellation with a father-, mother-, and sister-figure and Karl as the son.[5] In this way Kafka could compose a longer text by combining smaller, similar units which were far more manageable for his way of writing. Yet this did not solve the problem of closure. Thus Kafka gave up on *The Man who Disappeared* in January 1913 – only to take it up again in October 1914, after he had developed a new, more parabolic type of narration in *The Trial* and 'In der Strafkolonie' ('In the Penal Colony'). The result was the episode describing Karl Rossman joining the Oklahama Theatre. However, the blending of two different narrational styles failed and Kafka abandoned the text for good.

In *The Trial* Kafka tried to tackle the thorny problem of closure by writing the final chapter immediately after the first narrational unit.[6] Having thus created a stable frame and defined the fixed time-space of one year – the novel starts on the morning of Josef K.'s thirtieth birthday and ends on the eve of his thirty-first – Kafka merely had to fill in the middle part. For this he used the paradigmatic technique of *The Man who Disappeared*, this time, however, based on the parabolic opposition between K. in the familiar surroundings of boarding house and bank on the one hand and K. in the unfamiliar, puzzling and threatening world of the court on the other. This provided Kafka with two devices to create a sense of progression: the court-world would increasingly infiltrate K.'s familiar surroundings, and the protagonist would gradually become more and more distraught and doubtful about his innocence. Still, Kafka failed – but also succeeded in a paradoxical way: although a fragment, *The Trial* is certainly his most

'completed' long narration, which is why it became the first of his fragments to be posthumously published by Max Brod.

In his last novel, *Das Schloss* (*The Castle*), Kafka used a topographical
framework.[7] The space the protagonist K. enters by crossing a bridge is separated from the rest of the world and, like an ellipse, has two focal points:
the village and the castle. For the villagers, this polar system underpins
the self-evident unity of their daily lives, but for K. it becomes the grid
of a journey composed of starting point, path and destination: desperately
and ruthlessly he keeps striving to get into the castle. Again, closure would
have been difficult – as K. could not be allowed either to succeed or to
give up and leave the village. As in *The Trial*, the 'progress' of the novel lies
in the protagonist's gradual exploration of his new environment: getting
to know the villagers and their habits and customs, collecting information about the castle and trying to get into direct contact with its representatives. Yet this time the protagonist's reconnaissance mission dissolves
into an ever-growing multitude of storylines and life-stories, which Kafka
found increasingly difficult to integrate. In September 1922, he wrote to
Max Brod: 'I've had to abandon the Castle story, apparently for good' (*B*
413). The preceding sentence reads: 'have spent this week in not very good
spirits' – the deeply understated lamentation of an author who always struggled to write completed texts.

NOTES

1 See for instance C. Schärf, *Franz Kafka: Poetischer Text und heilige Schrift* (Göttingen: Vandenhoeck & Ruprecht, 2000) and D. Kremer, *Kafka: Die Erotik des
Schreibens* (Bodenheim: Philo, 1989), where the strange machinery in 'In der
Strafkolonie' ('In the Penal Colony') is even interpreted as a mere gigantic type-
writer, pp. 149–50.

2 Cf. M. Engel, 'Zu Kafkas Kunst- und Literaturtheorie' in M. Engel and B. Auerochs (eds.), *Kafka-Handbuch* (Stuttgart: Metzler, 2010), pp. 483–98.

3 G. Neumann, 'Umkehrung und Ablenkung: Franz Kafkas "Gleitendes Paradox"', *Deutsche Vierteljahrsschrift für Literaturwissenschaft und Geistesgeschichte*,
42 (1968), 702–44.

4 See C. Duttlinger, 'Franz Kafka, *Der Proceß*' in P. Hutchinson (ed.), *Landmarks
in the German Novel* (Oxford: Peter Lang, 2007), vol. 1, pp. 135–50

5 See M. Engel, '*Der Verschollene*' in Engel and Auerochs (eds.), *Kafka-Handbuch*,
pp. 175–91, esp. pp. 178–81.

6 See M. Engel, '*Der Process*' in Engel and Auerochs (eds.), *Kafka-Handbuch*,
pp. 192–207, esp. pp. 192–5.

7 See W. Fromm, '*Das Schloss*' in Engel and Auerochs (eds.), *Kafka-Handbuch*,
pp. 301–17, esp. pp. 301–4.

CHAPTER 7

Style

Ritchie Robertson

Universal or Regional?

Our understanding of Kafka's style has changed over the decades. Different translators have reproduced it differently, in accordance with their overall interpretation of Kafka's texts.[1] Thus his earliest translators into English, Willa and Edwin Muir, working in the 1930s, understood him as a writer of parables or parable-like narratives with a universal, ultimately religious meaning, who used a transparent style devoid of any local character. Yet some of his contemporaries regarded him as a local writer, bound to a particular place and its language. His Prague contemporary and acquaintance Franz Werfel is reported to have said in 1909, after the publication of Kafka's earliest short prose sketches: 'Beyond Tetschen-Bodenbach [a station on the frontier between Bohemia and Germany] nobody will understand Kafka.'[2] More recent readers and translators have been interested in the historical circumstances that shaped Kafka's writing and have become more alert to the distinctive flavour of his style.

Although Kafka does not, as used to be thought, write in a characteristically 'Prague German', his German has a regional colouring. It shows many grammatical features typical of the South German and Austrian language area: non-standard plurals, genders and cases after prepositions. His vocabulary is often distinctively South German, and hence offers traps for translators. When Gregor Samsa in *Die Verwandlung* (*The Metamorphosis*) pulls himself upright on a 'Kasten', it is not a 'box' (as in standard German) but a wardrobe, and he then falls onto a 'Sessel' (chair) instead of a standard 'Stuhl'. In *Der Verschollene* (*The Man who Disappeared*), Karl brings breakfast on a 'Tasse', meaning not a 'cup' but a tray. There is also occasional interference from Czech, seen in some unfamiliar idioms, though this is again a regional rather than an individual peculiarity.[3]

In the small number of texts he published during his lifetime, Kafka took pains to adjust his style to standard German norms of grammar and punctuation, though he retained regional items of vocabulary. Now that his three novels and his copious notebooks and diaries have been carefully edited from his manuscripts, however, we can see that his spontaneous writing not only had many regional features but also used punctuation suggested by the rhythms of speech rather than the strict rules of official German. For Kafka, writing was an intensely corporeal experience. After writing his 'breakthrough text', 'Das Urteil' ('The Judgement'), in a single night (22–3 September 1912), he commented: 'Only in *this* way can writing be done, only with such coherence, with such a complete opening out of the body and the soul' (23 September 1912; *D* 213/ *TB* 461). Some, especially among his most recent editors, would argue that Kafka's writing can only be fully appreciated with a facsimile of the manuscript, where the intensity of the writing experience can be gathered from the changing rhythms of the handwriting. If so, the translator is at a double remove from Kafka's original. It is improbable, however, that the stylistic purist Kafka would have liked the thought of his manuscripts going into the world uncor-rected. Even so, how far the flavour of these texts can be transported into English depends on the judgement and skill of the translator, and also on the willingness of an editor to allow the production of texts that may look unfamiliar and odd.

Stylistic Ideals and Models

While Kafka naturally wrote in a version of the language he habitually used, many features of his writing result not from local influences but from delib-erate artistic choices. Different genres dictate different styles. Thus parables and aphorisms require a concise, pithy style, whereas novellas allow more scope for elaboration, and his novels have room for extensive dialogue and long passages of abstract pseudo-reasoning in which Kafka parodies the language of bureaucracy. His own professional writings on insurance, by contrast, are strikingly clear. His lucid descriptions of dangerous industrial machinery doubtless helped him to write the technical description of the punishment-machine in 'In der Strafkolonie' ('In the Penal Colony'). Even here, Kafka adopted the stylistic ideals of economy, clarity and simplicity, and yet despite the detailed description of individual parts the machine as a whole remains curiously hard to picture.

In developing these ideals, Kafka followed a number of literary mod-els. His literary tastes were conservative. He had little interest in poetry, even less in drama. Although he occasionally read long novels (by Flaubert, Dostoevsky, Dickens), he favoured short prose fiction, diaries and autobiographical writings, especially by masters of German prose from the eighteenth and nineteenth centuries such as Johann Wolfgang von Goethe (1749–1832), Theodor Fontane (1819–1898) and Adalbert Stifter (1805–1868). Particular favourites included Johann Peter Hebel's (1760–1826) collection of prose anecdotes, *Schatzkästlein des rheinischen Hausfreundes* (*The Treasure Chest*, 1813), and the short stories and anecdotes written by Heinrich von Kleist (1777–1811) in the first decade of the nineteenth century. Of the latter he especially liked the novella *Michael Kohlhaas* (1808); in February 1913 he told Felice Bauer that he was reading *Kohlhaas* for the tenth time, 'with true piety' (9/10 February 1913; *LF* 212/*B2* 84). Kleist's complex syntax and pellucid style provided Kafka with an important model. In *Kohlhaas*, Kleist begins by presenting information in compressed form and confronting the reader with a paradox:

> About the middle of the sixteenth century there lived beside the banks of the River Havel a horse-dealer called Michael Kohlhaas, the son of a schoolmaster, who was one of the most honourable as well as one of the most terrible men of his age.[4]

Similarly, Kafka's first novel *Der Verschollene* (*The Man who Disappeared*) begins by offering the reader a lot of information in condensed form, an exact indication of place, and the seemingly casual statement of a self-contradiction – the punishment of the victim:

> As the seventeen-year-old Karl Rossmann, who had been sent to America by his poor parents because a servant-girl had seduced him and had a child by him, entered New York harbour in the already slowing ship, he saw the statue of the Goddess of Liberty, which he had been observing for some time, as though in a sudden blaze of sunlight. (*MD* 5/*V* 7)

Among contemporary writers, Kafka rejected those, especially from the Expressionist generation, who practised a highly emotional style, such as Heinrich Mann (1871–1950) and the poet Else Lasker-Schüler (1869–1945), but read avidly the understated, ironic short fiction of Thomas Mann (1875–1955), especially *Tonio Kröger* (1903). When Max Brod enthused to him about the extravagantly colourful language of a supernatural tale, Kafka replied by quoting a phrase from Hugo von Hofmannsthal's 'Das Gespräch über Gedichte' ('The Conversation about Poems', 1903): 'Der Geruch nasser Steine in einem Hausflur' (The smell of wet stones in a hallway).[5] Hofmannsthal's (1874–1929) phrase evokes a sensation in simple language; it focuses on objects, not feelings; and it has a rhythm which is quietly emphatic without being monotonous. Kafka, who read Gustave Flaubert (1821–1880) in the original French, was enraptured by a sentence from *L'Éducation sentimentale* (*Sentimental Education*, 1869): 'Elle avoua qu'elle désirait faire un tour à son bras, dans les rues' ('She admitted that she wanted to take a walk, holding his arm, through the streets'). 'What a sentence!' he wrote to Felice. 'What construction!' (16 January 1913; *LF* 186/*B2* 43). Flaubert's sentence conveys emotion of a hesitant sort ('admitted') largely by displacing it onto the simple evocation of an everyday action (walking through the streets) where intimacy ('holding his arm') is expressed with the utmost concision.

Ambiguity

Kafka goes beyond his stylistic models, however, by introducing ambiguity, which may arise from authorial mystification or from the narrative viewpoint. The description of Gregor Samsa's insect body fails to convey any object that can be visualized. His 'many legs', which are 'miserably thin' (*M* 29/*DL* 115), seem inadequate to support his heavy carapace, and his size seems to vary: by propping himself up he can reach a door-handle, implying that he is about three feet long, yet later, clinging to the wall, he is so small that his mother and sister at first fail to notice him. The castle is described in such a way as to suggest that it is not a castle at all, except to the observer who is predisposed to see it as one:

> Altogether the castle, as seen in the distance, lived up to K.'s expectations. It was neither an old knightly castle from the days of chivalry, nor a showy new structure, but an extensive complex of buildings few of them with two storeys, but many of them lower and crowded close together. If you hadn't known it was a castle you might have taken it for a small town. (*C* 11/*S* 17)

Kafka's narrative technique increases ambiguity. Events are normally filtered through the consciousness of the protagonist, though far less exclusively than Friedrich Beissner claimed in his theory of monoperspectival narration.[6] There are numerous places in *Der Process* (*The Trial*) and *Das Schloss* (*The Castle*) where an external narrator gives us information about the protagonist, or where events are reported which the protagonist cannot know about. Ambiguity arises especially at the beginning of a story, where the narrative standpoint is still uncertain. Who, for example, utters the opening sentence of *The Trial*? 'Jemand mußte Josef K. verleumdet haben, denn ohne daß er etwas Böses getan hätte, wurde er eines Morgens verhaftet' ('Someone must have been telling tales about Josef K., for one morning, without having done anything wrong, he was arrested'; *T* 5/*P* 7). Is this Josef K. asserting his innocence? If so, it is the only place where

Josef K. takes a retrospective look at his experiences. Or is it an impersonal narrator? In either case, the phrase 'etwas Böses' ('something wrong') is incongruous in a legal context, since 'böse' can mean 'childishly naughty' or, more strongly, 'evil'; it forewarns us that, as Josef K. will discover, this is no ordinary trial. The ambiguity is heightened by Kafka's use of the subjunctive mood in 'hätte', introducing a sense of uncertainty.

Reflections and conversations are rendered ambiguous by particles expressing qualifications ('allerdings', 'doch' and the like), and by the practice, shown especially by Josef K., of making a statement, then qualifying it out of existence. Thus when his landlady tells him that his arrest seems 'like something very learned', he feigns agreement, only to undermine what she is saying: 'What you just said, Frau Grubach, is by no means stupid. At least I agree with you to an extent, only I take an even harsher view of the matter, I don't see it as something learned but simply as nothing at all' (*T* 19/*P* 33–4).

Uncertainty is also suggested by Kafka's frequent use of 'seemed' and 'as if'. This may express conjectures, sometimes humorous, about the actions or motives of another character, which the protagonist can only guess at. Of the supervisor who interviews Josef K., we learn: 'it was just as possible that he had not been listening at all, for he had pressed one hand flat on the table and seemed to be comparing the length of his fingers' (*T* 14/ *P* 24). More strangely, such conjectures sometimes apply to the behaviour of the protagonist, from whose viewpoint the story is supposedly narrated. When it is said of Josef K., 'just before he reached the door he halted, as if he hadn't expected to see a door there' (*T* 26/*P* 47–8), Josef K. appears uncertain about his *own* motives. And when K. in *The Castle* suddenly speaks 'in a noticeably quiet voice' (*C* 6/*S* 9), his own viewpoint is momentarily displaced by other people's view of him.

Syntax and Word-Play

Much of Kafka's stylistic energy goes into syntax. Long sentences with many subordinate clauses build up to a final punch. He is also capable of a devastating abruptness, as when the body of the hunger artist is disposed of – '"Now clear up, let's have some order!" said the supervisor, and they buried the hunger artist along with the straw' (*HA* 65/*DL* 349). In 'Ein Landarzt' ('A Country Doctor') we find a haunting musical cadence which resists translation: 'Armer Junge, dir ist nicht zu helfen. Ich habe deine große **Wund**e aufge**fund**en, an dieser Bl**u**me in deiner Seite gehst du zugrunde' ('Poor boy, there is nothing to be done for you. I have discovered your great wound; you will be destroyed by the bloom in your side'; *HA* 16/*DL* 258). The lyricism here emphasizes the incongruous meanings and associations which the story requires us to hold together. The fatal wound is at the same time a flower: disgusting, even obscene, yet also morbidly beautiful.

Stylistic ornaments, such as metaphors and similes not drawn from the current subject-matter, are relatively rare. In 'A Country Doctor', besides the strange metaphor of the flower, we find the supernatural horses sweeping the doctor's carriage along 'like trees in a torrent' (*HA* 14/*DL* 255), inviting us to think of tree trunks being swept downstream in a flooded river, while the boy's gaping wound seems 'wide as an open-cast mine' (*HA* 16/*DL* 258). Tellingly, Josef K., kissing Fräulein Bürstner's throat, is compared to 'a thirsty animal' (*T* 26/*P* 48). Subtle word-play is relatively common, though critics disagree on particular instances. Erich Heller, in a once famous essay, sought to relate K.'s profession of land surveyor ('Landvermesser') in *The Castle* to the words 'vermessen' (audacious) and 'Vermessenheit' (hubris), but these associations only repeat what the novel makes clear anyway.[7] On the other hand, Mark Anderson has shown how important the word 'Verkehr' and its range of meanings ('traffic', 'trade', 'intercourse') were for Kafka.[8] So when the word occurs in various forms three times in 'The Judgement', we may justifiably infer that Kafka thus evokes, without ever naming, 'sexual intercourse' ('Geschlechtsverkehr') – the experience that the protagonist will never have with his fiancée because of his father's fatal intervention. In *The Metamorphosis*, Gregor mentally dismisses a fellow employee as 'ohne Rückgrat und Verstand', 'stupid and spineless' (*DL* 118/*M* 31), not quite aware that he himself, having been transformed into an invertebrate, literally lacks a spine.

Many key words are multilayered and emotionally charged. In 'The Judgement', the word 'zudecken' ('cover over') denotes both Georg's literal act of tucking up his father in bed and the metaphorical wish to deny his existence. In 'A Country Doctor', the name of the doctor's servant, Rosa, reappears with its lexical meaning 'pink' in the description of the patient's mysterious wound: 'Rose-red, in many shades, dark in the depths, growing light towards the margins' (*H* 16/*DL* 258). Here, by placing the word 'rosa' at the beginning of the sentence, Kafka ensures that it begins with an uppercase letter and thus recalls the servant's name visually as well as aurally; this allows us to infer much about the doctor's repressed sexuality and his fear of the female body. Sometimes, finally, Kafka transforms a metaphor into a literal account, as in a fragment where the word 'Schlangenfraß' (bad food, literally 'snake-food') is applied to slaves clearing the way for a giant snake (*TB* 824/*D* 380–1).

When we turn from single words to larger units such as sentences and paragraphs, we find that Kafka avoids monotony through interventions which alter the pace and tone of the narrative. For example, he uses rhetorical questions: when Gregor Samsa, emerging from his room, confronts his reinvigorated father, he asks: 'Nevertheless, nevertheless, was this still his father?' (*M* 57/*DL* 168; the original repeated word, 'Trotzdem', is shorter, pithier, and closer to the speaking voice). In the scene in the Captain's office in *The Man who Disappeared*, Kafka speeds up the tempo by breathless questions ('But everything called for haste, clarity, a precise account, yet what was the stoker doing?'; *MD* 15/*V* 27), and even an apostrophe by the narrator to the protagonist ('So hurry, Karl, make the most of the time that is left'; *MD* 19/*V* 35).

Emotional modulation sometimes comes from unexpected meditative sentences. When Josef K. and his executioners reach the quarry where they will kill him, the narrator incongruously reflects 'Everything was bathed in moonlight, with the naturalness and calm no other light possesses' (*T* 163/*P* 310). In *The Castle*, the emotionally as well as literally frozen landscape is briefly lighted by lyrical moments, such as the account of K.'s and Frieda's love-making in the unpropitious setting of the bar-room (*C* 40/*S* 68–9), and by an unexpected smile from the usually reserved Amalia: 'Amalia smiled, and that smile, although a sad one, lit up her sombre face, made her silence eloquent and her strangeness familiar. It was like the telling of a secret, a hitherto closely guarded possession that could be taken back again, but never taken back entirely' (*C* 149/*S* 265).[9]

In short texts, such as parables and aphorisms, Kafka achieves trenchancy through brevity and the absence of commentary, e.g. 'Ein Käfig ging einen Vogel suchen' ('A cage went in search of a bird'; *HA* 189/*NSII* 117). English translations are almost always wordier than Kafka's German, for he exploits to the full the capacity of German for concise expression. Narrative parables often achieve their effect through a dizzying shift of perspective at the end, seen perhaps most simply in the dialogue between a cat and a mouse, which ends abruptly: '"You just have to change direction," said the cat, and ate her up' (*HA* 186/*NSII* 343). This structural technique leads, in a more elaborate text such as 'Before the Law', to a more devastating conclusion, when the doorkeeper makes the dying supplicant realize he has wasted his whole life waiting in front of the Law: 'Nobody else could be granted entry, for this entrance was meant only for you. I shall go now and close it' (*HA* 22/*DL* 269). While many of Kafka's conclusions gesture towards a new beginning, new stories yet to come, here style, structure and content become indistinguishable.

NOTES

1 On this development, see D. Damrosch, 'Kafka Comes Home' in D. Damrosch, *What Is World Literature?* (Princeton University Press, 2003), pp. 187–205.

2 M. Brod, *Über Franz Kafka* (Frankfurt am Main: Fischer, 1974), p. 278.

3 Full detail in M. Nekula, *Franz Kafkas Sprachen* (Tübingen: Niemeyer, 2003).

4 H. von Kleist, *The Marquise of O– and Other Stories*, trans. D. Luke and N. Reeves (Harmondsworth: Penguin, 1978), p. 114.

5 Brod, *Über Franz Kafka*, p. 46, with a list of Kafka's literary likes and dislikes; see also R. Stach, *Kafka: Die frühen Jahre* (Frankfurt am Main: Fischer, 2013), p. 418. Brod misquotes; Hofmannsthal actually wrote 'Der Geruch feuchter Steine'.

6 F. Beissner, *Der Erzähler Franz Kafka: Ein Vortrag* (Stuttgart: W. Kohlhammer, 1952).

7 E. Heller, 'The World of Franz Kafka' in E. Heller, *The Disinherited Mind* (Cambridge: Bowes & Bowes, 1952), pp. 157–81: 169.

8 M. M. Anderson, *Kafka's Clothes: Ornament and Aestheticism in the Habsburg Fin de Siècle* (Oxford: Clarendon Press, 1992).

9 On lyrical moments in *The Castle*, see R. Sheppard, *On Kafka's Castle: A Study* (London: Croom Helm, 1973), pp. 94–105.

PART II

Art and Literature

CHAPTER 8

Literary Modernism

Judith Ryan

Although often seen as an 'icon' of literary modernism, Kafka has yet to be accorded a convincing position within this heterogeneous and rapidly changing movement. At different times, Kafka veered close to one or another phase of the movement, showing, for example, affinities with Aestheticism, especially in his earliest texts, written between 1904 and 1908, or commonalities with Expressionism, in his stories from 1912 to about 1919. Yet when questioned about modernism, Kafka evinced little explicit interest in the phenomenon, at least according to his friend Max Brod;[1] we do not know whether Kafka's reticence had to do with a lack of clarity about the word itself or with a desire that his writing should not simply be treated as the result of fashionable trends.

The German term used at the time was 'die Moderne' (the modern). Coined by Eugen Wolff (1863–1929) in an effort to revolutionize German literature during the late 1880s, 'die Moderne' came to have both a temporal and a formal meaning: it referred to a fairly extensive period around 1900, but also to a variety of experiments that broke away from traditional genre expectations; throughout the period itself, the term remained fairly loose and ill-defined. The English word 'modernism' retains traces of these ambiguities, referring to both the early, aesthetic phase and the more assertively avant-garde movements, many of them self-named as '-isms'.

Daniel Albright's book on modernism presents us with a telling question: 'Is there a definition of modernism that might be adequate to all the contradictions and fault lines in this vast artistic movement, or heap of artistic movements?'[2] The implicit point is well taken. Looking at the phenomenon from Kafka's vantage-point, however, we need to ask which modernist movements he knew – or rather, which he could have known, since his death in 1924 cut him off from experiencing the vast spread of Surrealism, for example, in the late 1920s (André Breton's surrealist novel, *Nadja*, appeared in 1928). Judging by his diaries and letters, the halcyon year for modernism, 1922, which saw the publication of T. S. Eliot's long poem

The Waste Land and James Joyce's experimental novel *Ulysses*, followed by Rainer Maria Rilke's *Duineser Elegien* (*Duino Elegies*) seems to have passed Kafka by. The most likely reason was the worsening of his tuberculosis, which had first been diagnosed in 1917. Spending time in sanatoria or on his sister Ottla's country farm cut him off from the close connections he had maintained with new literary developments. Writing his own texts became his main focus: in 1920 *Ein Landarzt* (*A Country Doctor*) appeared, and in 1922 he was hard at work on *Das Schloss* (*The Castle*).

Modernist Journals and Magazines

Although Kafka repeatedly stated his desire for sufficient time and solitude to write, his early work was produced within a very lively intellectual context. Together with his friend Max Brod, he was part of a literary scene sustained, on the one hand, by group meetings in Prague cafés and, on the other, by numerous small magazines that took the pulse of new kinds of writing. Some of these magazines were quite short-lived, following one another in rapid succession. Franz Blei (1871–1942), a friend of Brod and Kafka, edited a number of such literary journals; this meant that Kafka was deeply immersed in literary affairs during the early years of the century. In scholarly studies, the small literary magazines of the early twentieth century are often characterized in terms of artistic movements: some are said to belong to Aestheticism, others to Expressionism. Now that many of those journals are accessible online, it is easier to see that most of them entertained a range of different styles. As a student, Kafka had read *Der Kunstwart* (*The Guardian of Art*), one of several such productions that bore a *Jugendstil* (art nouveau) cover. Yet it also included realist and naturalist texts, as well as essays on cultural issues. Kafka soon tired of *Der Kunstwart*, but other literary journals, such as *Die Insel* (*The Island*), *Hyperion* and *Der Brenner* (produced by the Brenner-Verlag), as well as annual collections of new texts presented by leading publishing houses such as S. Fischer, kept him in touch with recent literary developments.

Readers of these journals, eager for a taste of different types of writing, enjoyed exposure to shorter texts. Some of these took the form of the prose poem, inherited from Charles Baudelaire (1821–1867) and his Symbolist successors in late-nineteenth-century France. In the early 1890s, Hugo von Hofmannsthal (1874–1929) also wrote several prose poems. From the outset, this genre had included texts that could be read as 'Minimalerzählungen' (mini-narratives).[3] The Swiss writer Robert Walser (1878–1956), bringing together elements of the journalistic sketch and the personal essay, created a form of short narrative that, while somewhat ethereal and gently playful on its surface, was also oddly knowing and subversive. Slender narrative strands, fragments of visual description, and reflective moments interacted to form a new kind of writing. Franz Blei, a gifted scout for new talent, recommended Walser to the Aestheticist journal *Die Insel*, which published some of his poems and several 'kleine Geschichten' (little stories) in 1901 and 1902. Kafka, whose pieces in *Betrachtung* (*Meditation*, published 1912) bore affinities with those of Robert Walser, developed his own characteristic style, but this still retains traces of Walser. One might compare the almost plotless 'Der Ausflug ins Gebirg' ('The Excursion into the Mountains') in *Meditation* with the more narrative (if only *ex negativo*) 'Eine kaiserliche Botschaft' ('An Imperial Message') in the volume *Ein Landarzt* (*A Country Doctor*).

Aestheticism was also the birthplace of a new frankness about sexual matters. Franz Blei's subscription-only magazines, *Amethyst* (December 1905 – November 1906) and *Opale* (1907), focused on decadent material such as poems and stories by Oscar Wilde (1854–1900) and erotic art by Aubrey Beardsley (1872–1898), along with risqué or titillating texts by other writers. While Kafka enjoyed these luxuriously produced magazines, he presented a less alluring vision in the sordid eroticism of the law courts in the attics in *Der Process* (*The Trial*) and the repugnant scene in *The Castle*, where K. and Frieda have sex amid puddles of beer on the floor.

Despite its primary focus on the erotic, *Opale* also published Carl Einstein's Expressionist novel *Bebuquin* (1917). Returning to a broader literary readership, Blei's journal *Hyperion* (1908–9), co-edited with Carl Sternheim, came much closer to gathering together a set of texts and artworks that could more properly be said to characterize the beginnings of modernism, the bolder and more strikingly experimental forms of twentieth-century literature. Usually described as Expressionist, *Hyperion* actually included a range of material, including poems, travelogues, drama and, of course, the short pieces characteristic of the period. It also published eight brief excerpts from Kafka's *Beschreibung eines Kampfes* (*Description of a Struggle*) under the title he was to give to his subsequent book, *Betrachtung* (*Meditation*). Viewing Kafka's work in this context gives us a new perspective on his relation to turn-of-the-century Aestheticism, on the one hand, and the Expressionism that was to peak in the second decade of the twentieth century. With a turn of the kaleidoscope, we see the decorative elements and fashionable *ennui* of Kafka's earliest texts in a fresh context, one that highlights sudden transitions, distortions of visual experience, and unexplained irruptions of bizarre and alien phenomena.

Kafka's Modernist Narratives

Could this new kinship with Expressionism be part of what made Kafka's story 'Das Urteil' ('The Judgement') appear to be a break-through? Consciously nor not, Kafka no doubt recognized that this narrative took its place more firmly within the framework set up by contemporary journals and publishing houses. The scenes where the father changes abruptly from a sick old man to a threatening tyrant are very much in line with Expressionist narrative practices. The dramatic gestures, bizarre claustrophobic spaces and exaggerated subjective expressions are an integral part of the Expressionist mode. The story's focus on a power struggle between two generations is also one favoured by the Expressionists. Was Kafka an Expressionist? The scholar Walter Sokel aligned Kafka's writings with the movement, even as he also recognized in Kafka a strong existential component that took the form of a 'revolt against human submission to any established reality'.[4] Yet, as others have pointed out, Kafka also developed his own style of narration that differed from the sort of Expressionism that envisaged ecstatic self-dissolution. For Kafka, this state was fundamentally impossible. In terms of modernism more generally, Kafka's texts also dash all hope for an epiphany of the type sought by James Joyce's Stephen Dedalus or Virginia Woolf's Lily Briscoe. Dashing that hope is the ultimate gesture in the parable 'Vor dem Gesetz' ('Before the Law').

Recent scholars have noted the kinship between Kafka's writing and what Walter Benjamin (1892–1940) called the 'Denkbild', a brief text that combines both image and thought.[5] This concept accurately designates what Kafka does in so many of his short texts; to my mind, it is also the most accurate designation of one of Kafka's singular innovations. Another recent category for twentieth-century short prose is what Andreas Huyssen terms the 'modernist miniature'.[6] Linking Kafka with many other contemporaries, this rubric gives a name to what had been seen during Kafka's lifetime as simply 'a new form that could not be named'.[7] Huyssen's book shows us, on the one hand, the varied functions this form fulfils in the early twentieth century. Another advantage of Huyssen's term 'modernist miniatures' is that it allows for a productive foregrounding of the visual and the role of new technologies such as moving images, photographs and films.

As for other modernist movements, we might well be able to find traces of one or another of them in Kafka's writing. Might the reflections on Josefine's song in 'Josefine, die Sängerin oder Das Volk der Mäuse' ('Josefine, the Singer or The Mouse People', 1924) allude to Dada when the mouse singer's art is compared with the common task of cracking nuts? I know of no evidence that Kafka was aware of Marcel Duchamp's *Fountain* of 1917 – a urinal signed by an invented name, R. Mutt. Dada, with its larkish exuberance, is very far from Kafka's late story, in which the possible death of the mouse singer and the consequential disappearance of her song are recounted with a poignancy that offsets the playful aspects of the narrative.

Nietzsche and Baudelaire

From today's perspective, it is sometimes difficult to see why movements that now seem so much a part of modernism failed to register, or seem to have played such a peripheral role in Kafka's literary development. We search in vain for the names of such important precursors as Charles Baudelaire and Friedrich Nietzsche in Kafka's writing, although there is other evidence, sometimes indirect, that Kafka was familiar with Baudelaire, and firmer evidence that he knew writings by Nietzsche.

What Stanley Corngold calls 'the diffuse and inexplicit presence of Nietzsche'[8] is discernible in many of Kafka's works. Like his contemporaries Rilke and Thomas Mann, Kafka clearly read Nietzsche (1844–1900). Reliable reports show that he read *Also sprach Zarathustra* (*Thus Spoke Zarathustra*) while still a student; and *Zur Genealogie der Moral* (*On the Genealogy of Morality*) was much on Kafka's mind during the middle and later phases of his work. He doubtless knew much more of Nietzsche beyond these two books. Kafka's narratives 'In der Strafkolonie' ('In the Penal Colony', written 1914) and 'Ein Bericht für eine Akademie' ('A Report for an Academy', 1917) are deeply indebted to Nietzsche's belief that no one perspective could provide access to truth, his perception of the world as in a constant state of change, his call for the establishment of a new basis for morality and his concept of human beings as a bridge between animals and the new, superior being he called the *Übermensch*. In the ape's address to a learned academy in Kafka's text, the primate's mocking attitude towards human acrobats and their assumption that trapeze acts express the pinnacle of freedom alludes to Nietzsche's figure of the tightrope walker (*Also sprach Zarathustra*, Prologue), who represents the position of man, suspended between a primitive form of existence and a higher form he is not yet ready to enter into. Throughout much of Kafka's fiction, Nietzsche's concept of the 'will to power' finds equivalents and analogies. Some of his best-known stories, such as 'The Judgement', as well as the two unfinished novels *The Trial* (written in 1914–15) and *The Castle* (mainly written in 1922) have Nietzschean underpinnings.

Whether or not Kafka read that other precursor of modernism, Baudelaire (1821–67), he certainly did know the writings of many French Symbolists, Aesthetes and Decadents who extended the poetic tradition Baudelaire had initiated. Kafka's biographer Reiner Stach describes a 'rather abstruse quality' in Kafka's early narrative *Description of a Struggle* (begun around 1904) that might fit better in a text by a 'French Decadent author like Dujardin, Huysmans, or Laforgue'.[9] Similarly, Mark Anderson argues that we should situate Kafka on the 'Franco-German cultural axis' where we have long been accustomed to position German-language writers like Hofmannsthal or Rilke.[10] Together with Max Brod, Kafka read a number of French texts, including Huysmans's novel *A rebours* (*Against the Grain*, sometimes translated as *Against Nature*, 1884) and Octave Mirbeau's *Le Jardin des supplices* (*The Torture Garden*, 1899). His friends Blei and Brod had translated Jules Laforgue. Kafka himself owned volumes of poetry by Arthur Rimbaud and Paul Verlaine, as well as a volume by Paul Claudel. And on a trip to Paris in 1910, Kafka even seems to have styled himself, with mild humour, as a *flâneur*.[11] The crueller side of decadence, by contrast, most certainly came out in the influence of Mirbeau's presentation of torture, which corresponded to what Kafka called his 'Strafphantasien' (punishment fantasies); Mirbeau's text was to become one of several tributaries that flowed into 'In the Penal Colony'.

Theories of the Mind

It is striking that Kafka never experiments with stream-of-consciousness narration, a modernist form that Edouard Dujardin claimed to have pioneered in his *Les Lauriers sont coupés* (*The Laurels have been cut*, 1887), nor does he adopt the interior monologue technique employed by his Austrian contemporary Arthur Schnitzler in his *Leutnant Gustl* (*Lieutenant Gustl*, 1901). His avoidance of these forms doubtless derives from Kafka's interest in two turn-of-the-century Austrian figures, the philosopher-psychologist Franz Brentano (1838–1917) and the physicist-philosopher Ernst Mach (1838–1916). Kafka first learned about these two thinkers from teachers at his *Gymnasium* (grammar school). Later, Kafka participated in discussions about Brentano on the café scene in Prague, first at the Café Louvre, to which Kafka and Brod belonged for a time, and then in another group created when Brod, somewhat mysteriously, wore out his welcome at the

Louvre circle. Brentano and Mach were key actors during that period in the late nineteenth century when psychology was gradually separating from philosophy. Kafka and his Prague contemporaries reflected on problems of sensory perception and how this might affect the relationship between self and world. Yet today's readers, unless they have taken a course on vision or perceptual processes in a psychology department, may not even recognize the ideas of Brentano and Mach as being part of psychology: certainly, this is not psychology of the kind we are accustomed to finding in modernist literature, where the term usually owes debts to Sigmund Freud and subsequent practitioners of psychoanalysis.

Sensory perception has important effects on the way we experience the world and ourselves. Visual and other illusions are a classic example of how hard it is to 'get behind' the phenomena we perceive. How much of the world we experience through our senses is an illusion? Is there any way to get at the truth when the mechanisms of perception constantly delude us? Such issues loom large in Kafka's early narratives, especially in *Description of a Struggle*. Perception, of course, also includes our sense of time and space. We can observe him working creatively with these categories throughout his career. Perhaps his boldest experiment with the reader's experience occurs in *The Castle*, where the distance (and difference) between the castle and the village is made visible by Barnabas, the messenger. As K. begins to learn the story of how Barnabas and his family have come to be ostracized, he is plunged into a complicated series of inset narratives. These stories seem to drone on, moving with increasing degrees of slowness. Participating in K.'s overwhelming sense of time expanding, we come close to giving up on the novel.

Brentano's and Mach's monism – their rejection of a dualist conception of conscious and unconscious mind – is another reason why Kafka did not use interior monologue or stream-of-consciousness narration. Depth psychology such as that promulgated by Freud was incompatible with their belief that everything was surface. Consciousness, relying on perception, could have areas that were more or less focused, but it had no depth. This 'flat' view of our relation to the world is crucial for understanding the two thinkers' monist approach to psychology. Brentano's concept of self, indebted to medieval scholasticism, is one in which the subject is in a constant state of construction: when we perceive an object, we at once assimilate it to our own perception and differentiate it from ourselves, thus giving rise to a phenomenological circle that moves between subject and object. In addition to this circular relation, our attention moves between focus and distraction. Kafka exemplifies this oscillation in the first chapter

of his novel *Der Verschollene* (*The Man who Disappeared*), published separately under the title *Der Heizer* (*The Stoker*) in 1913. Here, the protagonist,
Karl Rossmann, allows himself to be drawn into supporting a stoker who
claims to be oppressed by a superior; but even as Karl engages with the
stoker's story, his eyes keep straying to the small boats he can see through
the porthole bobbing up and down on the water. Following Brentano's theories, the entire scene is presented in terms of surfaces rather than depth.
Accordingly, I argue that Brentanist 'flat' philosophy should be understood
as another precursor of modernism, or perhaps in stronger terms, a 'significant alternative vision of the modern'.[12]

Kafka's attachment to psychological monism probably explains his
avoidance of narrative strategies that derived from Freudian theory,
although he knew it well, and used or even parodied it in some of his
own stories. Instead, he developed a method that became his special signature. This was the use of limited third-person narrative, in which a single character's perceptual field is presented, but not in the first person, as
would normally be the case if we had direct access to the character's sensory
impressions. The third-person pronoun creates just a touch of distance and
ambiguity, enough to hint that not everything is as it seems. Gradually, we
come to understand that the character may be deceived about what he or
she is experiencing. What used to be termed the 'einsinnig' (monoperspectival) vision[13] of Kafka's narrative fiction has come to be understood as a
strategy that allows, and even encourages, a more critical perspective on the
part of the reader. Even in some of Kafka's first-person stories, the narrator's blind spots can become apparent, as in the omission of human beings
from 'Forschungen eines Hundes' ('Investigations of a Dog', written in
1922).

Altogether, distancing strategies are characteristic of Kafka's approach
to literary modernism. He takes elements of Aestheticism and turns them
into intellectual conundrums; he deploys the grotesque effects of Expressionism without participating in its ecstatic tendencies; he is familiar with
psychoanalysis and *Tiefenpsychologie* (depth psychology) that subtend so
many forms of modernism, but draws back from them into Brentano's and
Mach's non-Freudian psychologies; and he shifts the modernist interest in
the erotic into sordid settings that bespeak a loss rather than a gain in sexual
freedom. His writing bears affinities with several forms of modernism, but
in each of these relations he takes an individual tack, usually adding some
bizarre twist that, strangely enough, does not really resolve the puzzling
situations his texts develop. That may be one of the reasons why his work
continues to be so challenging.

NOTES

1 Cited in J. Born, *Kafkas Bibliothek: Ein beschreibendes Verzeichnis*, second edition (Frankfurt am Main: Fischer, 2011), p. 236.

2 D. Albright, *Putting Modernism Together: Literature, Music, and Painting, 1872–1927* (Baltimore, MD: The Johns Hopkins University Press, 2015).

3 D. Göttsche, "'Geschichten, die keine sind": Minimalisierung und Funktionalisierung in der Kleinen Prosa um 1900' in M. Engel and R. Robertson (eds.), *Kafka und die kleine Prosa der Moderne/Kafka and Short Modernist Prose* (Würzburg: Königshausen & Neumann, 2010), pp. 19–20.

4 W. H. Sokel, *The Myth of Power and the Self: Essays on Franz Kafka* (Detroit, MI: Wayne State University Press, 2002), p. 13.

5 *The Correspondence of Walter Benjamin, 1910–1940*, ed. G. Scholem and T. W. Adorno, trans. M. R. Jacobson and E. M. Jacobson (University of Chicago Press, 1994), p. 257 (letter from Benjamin to Gershom Scholem, 22 December 1924).

6 A. Huyssen, *Miniature Metropolis: Literature in an Age of Photography and Film* (Cambridge, MA: Harvard University Press, 2015).

7 Ibid., pp. 10–11.

8 S. Corngold, *Lambent Traces: Franz Kafka* (Princeton University Press, 2004), p. 95.

9 R. Stach, *Kafka: Die frühen Jahre* (Frankfurt am Main: Fischer, 2014), p. 309.

10 M. M. Anderson, *Kafka's Clothes: Ornament and Aestheticism in the Habsburg Fin de Siècle* (Oxford: Clarendon Press, 1992), p. 23.

11 Anderson, *Kafka's Clothes*, p. 218.

12 J. Ryan, *The Vanishing Subject: Early Psychology and Literary Modernism* (Chicago University Press, 1991), p. 231 (on Kafka, see also chapter 8, pp. 100–12).

13 F. Beissner, *Der Erzähler Franz Kafka* (Frankfurt am Main: Suhrkamp, 1983), p. 57.

CHAPTER 9

Kafka's Reading

Ritchie Robertson

One of Kafka's best-known statements is: 'A book should be the axe for the frozen sea in us' (*LFFE* 16/*Bi* 36). It comes from a letter of 27 January 1904 to his friend Oskar Pollak, in which Kafka reports that he has just read all 1800 pages of Friedrich Hebbel's diaries practically at a sitting. 'I think one should only read books that bite and stab,' he tells Pollak. 'If the book we are reading doesn't wake us with a blow on the skull, then why do we read the book?' Clearly, reading was for Kafka no mere leisure pursuit but an existentially urgent activity involving exploration and self-discovery. Moreover, as a law student, and later a civil servant with literary ambitions, he had limited time for reading and had to use it well.

Kafka kept up with contemporary literature by reading periodicals. In the early 1900s he read *Der Kunstwart* (*The Guardian of Art*), a mildly conservative cultural journal which promoted the ideals of natural living that he shared, while a wider range of literature, including new texts by Thomas Mann and Hugo von Hofmannsthal, reached him in *Die neue Rundschau* (*The New Review*), Germany's leading literary periodical. From his schooldays Kafka was familiar with the Greek, Latin and German classics.[1] Although he and Max Brod read Plato in the original to keep up their Greek, ancient literature mattered little to Kafka except as a reservoir of mythical figures. He was familiar with the Bible, though not in the original languages. And he continued to read important eighteenth- and nineteenth-century writers such as Johann Wolfgang von Goethe (1749–1832), Heinrich von Kleist (1777–1811), Adalbert Stifter (1805–68) and Gottfried Keller (1819–90).

Most of Kafka's reading was prose. He seldom read lyric poetry, though he admired that of Stefan George (1868–1933) and the Romantic poems by Joseph von Eichendorff (1788–1857), 'Abschied' ('Parting'), and Justinus Kerner (1786–1862), 'Der Wanderer in der Sägemühle' ('The Wanderer in the Sawmill'); the latter, with its motif of torture, points to

Kafka's darker preoccupations (*BM* 305/*LM* 182). He loved the selection of twelfth-century Chinese poems translated by Hans Heilmann; one, about a scholar who delays joining his girlfriend in bed, seemed so apposite to his dilemma between writing and marriage that he quoted it entire in a letter to Felice (24 November 1912; *LF* 78–9/*B1* 259). In his twenties he often attended the theatre, seeing plays by Shakespeare, August Strindberg, Gerhart Hauptmann and the Czech dramatist Jaroslav Vrchlický, among others; though none aroused such enthusiasm as the comparatively amateurish Yiddish performances he attended in 1911–12.

Kafka especially admired short prose texts, such as Kleist's tales and anecdotes, the simple stories written for a semi-educated public by Johann Peter Hebel (1760–1826), the sketches and mini-narratives by the Swiss writer Robert Walser (1878–1956) and the stories of Anton Chekhov (1860–1904). 'Chekhov I love very much, sometimes quite madly', he told Milena (*LM* 185/*BM* 314). He liked to share his experience by reading stories aloud, often to his sisters; on 11 December 1913 he gave a public reading of the beginning of Kleist's *Michael Kohlhaas* (*D* 246/*TB* 610). He appreciated simplicity, concision, understatement. He rejected the sensationalism of the Gothic writer Gustav Meyrink and the 'repulsive verbiage' of Arthur Schnitzler (14/15 February 1913; *LF* 217–18/*B2* 91).[2] He often singled out sentences that he especially enjoyed, such as the opening of Thomas Mann's short story 'Ein Glück': 'Still! Wir wollen in eine Seele schauen' ('Hush! We want to look into a soul'), which he read aloud repeatedly, imitating the narrator by putting his finger to his lips.[3]

Besides fiction, Kafka loved letters, diaries and other personal writings. The Goethe texts he mentions most enthusiastically are the autobiography *Dichtung und Wahrheit* (*Poetry and Truth*, 1811) and the conversations recorded by Goethe's secretary, Johann Peter Eckermann. He owned Theodor Fontane's letters, but none of his novels, and could not remember in which novel he had once read about life in a Baltic seaside resort (obviously *Effi Briest*; March 1921; *B* 312). He loved to quote significant anecdotes from such texts, as when he reported to his Gentile lover Milena Jesenská, from Alfred Meissner's memoir of Heinrich Heine (1797–1856), a story showing that Heine's French wife did not know that he was a Jew (*LM* 40–1/*BM* 24–5). His fascination with autobiographies extended beyond those of writers. He devoured, for example, the *Memoirs of a Socialist* (1909/11) by Lily Braun, an upper-class woman who broke with her milieu to become a radical socialist and feminist and, in Kafka's view, fought her way through suffering 'like a militant angel' ('wie ein streitbarer Engel') (27 October 1920; *LFFE* 244/*B4* 363).

'Blood-Relatives' and Role Models

There were four writers whom Kafka described as his 'blood-relatives' (2 September 1913; *LF* 355/*B2* 275): Kleist, Franz Grillparzer, Gustave Flaubert and Fyodor Dostoevsky. He not only loved their fiction and personal writings but felt a close personal affinity, extending from serious to trivial matters. Of the four, only Dostoevsky had married; Flaubert and Grillparzer resolved the contradiction between art and life by remaining lifelong bachelors; Kleist committed suicide together with his lover. Kafka expressed the importance of writing by quoting from one of Flaubert's letters: 'My novel is the rock to which I cling, and I know nothing of what is happening in the world' (6 June 1912; *D* 204/*TB* 425).[4] A famous letter from Dostoevsky to his brother, describing his journey to penal servitude in Siberia, provided Kafka with the imagery of chains and surveillance that expressed his discomfort at his official engagement to Felice (29 May 1914; *D* 275/*TB* 528–9). More trivially, Kafka was pleased, when visiting Vienna in 1913, to stay in a hotel where Grillparzer had eaten lunch many decades earlier (7 September 1913; *B2* 277).

Of their fictional works, it was perhaps the novel to which Flaubert clung, *L'Éducation sentimentale* (1869), that meant most to Kafka. It centres on a young man's prolonged, obsessive and ultimately futile passion for an inaccessible married woman. Kafka read it first in German, then bought a new French edition when holidaying in Paris in 1910. He described it to Felice as 'a book that for many years has been closer to me than any but two or three people; whenever and wherever I've opened it, it has alarmed and completely absorbed me, and I have always felt like a spiritual child of this writer, albeit a poor and helpless one' (15 November 1912; *LF* 57/*B1* 237). He fantasized about reading the whole of *L'Éducation sentimentale* aloud in French to a large audience, uninterruptedly, for as many days and nights as it required (4/5 December 1912; *LF* 108/*B1* 298). Curiously, he compares the end of Flaubert's novel with that of the Pentateuch (the first five books of the Old Testament), where Moses dies without entering the Promised Land; presumably the implication is that Flaubert's hero (like Kafka himself) never enters the Promised Land of marriage. Of Flaubert's other novels, Kafka owned *Madame Bovary* (1857) and evidently also knew *Bouvard et Pécuchet* (1881), Flaubert's last and relatively weak novel, for in 1915, during a period of general depression and particular dissatisfaction with his attempts at writing, he notes (again identifying with Flaubert): 'I am writing *Bouvard and Pécuchet* very early' (9 February 1915; *D* 330/*TB* 726). He seems also to have known *Trois Contes* (*Three Stories*), for the episode in 'A

Country Doctor' where the doctor is put into the sick boy's bed reads like a parody of St Julien's encounter with the leper in the 'Légende de St Julien l'Hospitalier' ('The Legend of St Julian the Hospitaller').

The intensity with which Kafka read some books can be inferred, as in this case, from the extent to which they shaped his own writing. All three of his novels have major literary models. Kafka enjoyed Charles Dickens (1812–70), praising especially *Little Dorrit* (1857), of which he gave Felice a copy (14 December 1916; *LF* 559/*B3* 279), and in retrospect he acknowledged that with *Der Verschollene* (*The Man who Disappeared*) he had intended to write a 'Dickens novel' based specifically on *David Copperfield* (1850) (8 October 1917; *D* 388/*TB* 941). Karl Rossmann's journey through America clearly recalls David's journey on foot to find refuge with his aunt; Karl's employment as a lift-boy corresponds to David's work in the blacking factory, Mack to Steerforth, and so on. However, the vitality that Kafka admired in Dickens also produced shockingly weak passages, from which Kafka's relative lack of creative energy fortunately kept him free.

If *The Man who Disappeared* is a Dickens novel, *Der Process* (*The Trial*) is a Dostoevsky novel. Kafka owned *The Brothers Karamazov* (1880) and *Crime and Punishment* (1866), and according to Brod he also liked *A Raw Youth* (1875). *Crime and Punishment* is the subject of a long passage in a letter to his sister Ottla (presupposing that she has read the novel too) where Kafka focuses on the curiously intimate relationship between Raskolnikov and the investigating judge who suspects him of murder (mid-March 1919; *LOF* 40/*B4* 81–2). Kafka notes that the judge ('Untersuchungsrichter', the same term as in *The Trial*), having talked familiarly with Raskolnikov, almost loves him, but only 'almost', for he still accuses his suspect of the crime. This recalls the frighteningly ambiguous relationship that Josef K. has to the Court, which professes to treat him with the utmost consideration but in fact wears him down and finally puts him to death.

Das Schloss (*The Castle*), finally, is a Strindberg novel. The Swedish dramatist and novelist August Strindberg (1849–1912) was hugely popular in early twentieth-century Germany and helped to inspire Expressionist drama. Kafka was fascinated by his turbulent personal life, with a succession of disastrous marriages, which found expression in such plays as *The Father* (1887) and in many novels. Although Kafka saw *The Father* on stage, he read mainly the novels, particularly *By the Open Sea* (1890). Here the protagonist is a cerebral scientist who settles on an island near Stockholm and falls in love with a young woman whose natural vitality complements and sustains his intellectuality. Like all Strindberg's female characters, however, she proves destructive, abandoning the hero for another man and leaving him to a lonely death. Here we have the basic pattern of *The Castle*, where a hyper-rational man (a land surveyor, used to mathematics) enters a remote community and takes up with a local woman (Frieda) in an ultimately destructive relationship.[5] We have also a tragic (albeit dated) view of the relation between the sexes which was widely shared by male Central European intellectuals in the early twentieth century.

Beyond the Canon

The texts that lodged in Kafka's imagination firmly enough to shape his writings were not always canonical, however. He sometimes read pornography. Leopold von Sacher-Masoch's *Venus im Pelz* (*Venus in Furs*, 1870) left traces both in *The Man who Disappeared* and in *Die Verwandlung* (*The Metamorphosis*), where Gregor shares the name which Sacher-Masoch's protagonist Severin is compelled to assume by the sadistic dominatrix. Kafka's Gregor even has, opposite his bed, a picture of a lady in furs, which he has cut out of a fashion magazine. The gruesome story by the decadent French writer Octave Mirbeau, *Le Jardin des supplices* (*The Torture Garden*, 1899), helped to inspire the punctilious description of the torture machine in 'In der Strafkolonie' ('In the Penal Colony'). Kafka's morbid fascination with torture is abundantly plain from his diaries. In 1920, admittedly with self-punishing exaggeration, he wrote to Milena: 'Yes, torturing is extremely important to me, I'm preoccupied with nothing but being tortured and torturing' (*LM* 172/*BM* 290).

Kafka also went in for more light-hearted reading. He enjoyed travel narratives, such as Arthur Holitscher's book *Amerika heute und morgen* (*America Today and Tomorrow*, 1912), which provided him with ample material for *The Man who Disappeared*, and the magazine *Über Land und Meer* (*Over Land and Sea*). His favourite reading included a series of cheap paperbacks intended for boys called *Schaffsteins Grüne Bändchen* (*Schaffstein's Little Green Books*), including historical narratives, adventures in the German colonies and accounts of exploration. He particularly liked *Der Zuckerbaron* (*The Sugar Baron*, 1914) whose protagonist, beginning his colonial career as a land surveyor, may have suggested a motif for *The Castle*.[6] The variety of Kafka's reading is conveyed by his diary entry of 23 December 1921, which records that he has 'again' been reading *Náš Skautík*, the journal of the Czech Boy Scout movement, and Tolstoy's *The Death of Ivan Ilyich* (*D* 398/*TB* 876).

Since Kafka is so often seen as a writer with a profound religious and/or philosophical message, one might expect to find him immersed in serious reading. Certainly, around 1900, he read some of the mystical and quasi-philosophical works that were then fashionable. On summer evenings in 1900 he read Nietzsche's *Zarathustra* (1883–91) aloud to a young woman in the village of Roztok. In November 1903 he tells Oskar Pollak that he is reading the medieval mystic Meister Eckhart and the nineteenth-century psycho-physicist Gustav Fechner (9 November 1903; *LFFE* 10/*Br* 29). Thereafter his leisure reading was largely literary. Søren Kierkegaard (1813–55), whose philosophy Max Brod claimed was crucial to understanding Kafka's fiction, figures in Kafka's diary in 1913, but with *Buch des Richters* (*The Book of the Judge*), a selection from the journals. Kafka was interested in the personal rather than the philosophical content, finding clear analogies between Kierkegaard's troubled relationship with Regine Olsen and his own with Felice Bauer. 'He confirms me like a friend', he wrote (21 August 1913; *D* 230/*TB* 578).

A turning-point came when Kafka, excited by the Yiddish performances by a theatrical troupe from Galicia, began to explore Jewish history and culture. His diary contains extensive excerpts from a history of Yiddish literature recently published in French. He read Heinrich Graetz's *History of the Jews* (1853–75), a standard historical source for assimilated and secularized Jews' and gradually assembled a small collection of books on the religious history of Judaism. Though he still resisted Brod's attempts to recruit him for Zionism, he explored the culture of the Eastern Jews, especially through collections of legends and folk-tales. The Hasidic tales recounted by Martin Buber (1878–1965) appealed to him less because of the mannered style that Buber initially adopted (but toned down in later editions).

Philosophical and Religious Texts

Another turning-point in Kafka's reading habits followed his diagnosis as tubercular in 1917. Convalescing in the country, he resolved, as he told Brod in December, to become 'clear about the last things'.[7] His reflections produced the series of notes now often known as the Zürau aphorisms. Now at last we find an engagement with Kierkegaard's philosophical and religious writings. In October 1917 Kafka wrote to his friend Oskar Baum that he knows only *Fear and Trembling* (1843), but after a visit from Baum he moved on to *Either-Or* (1843) and was disappointed. He associates *Either-Or* with some recent books by Martin Buber and with the work of the idiosyncratic Christian writer Rudolf Kassner: 'They are books that . . . can be read only by having a touch of real superiority to them. But as it is, their loathsomeness grows by the minute' (January 1918; *LFFE* 190/*B4* 22). What prompted this strong statement?

A concrete objection that Kafka makes to Kierkegaard is that he writes with too much *Geist* (wit, ingenuity), and this quality lifts him too high above the earth which ordinary people inhabit:

> He has too much *Geist*, he travels with his *Geist* as though in a magic carriage high above the earth, even where there are no paths. And cannot discover for himself that there are no paths. Thus his humble request for people to follow him becomes tyrannical, and his honest belief that he is 'on the way' becomes arrogance. (*NSII* 105)

Writing to Brod, Kafka complains that although in life Kierkegaard got on well with ordinary people, he loses sight of them in his writing 'and paints this monstrous Abraham in the clouds' (mid-March 1918; *LFFE* 200/*B4* 31). Reacting against Kierkegaard's spiritual elitism, Kafka, in a letter of June 1921 to Robert Klopstock, imagines another Abraham, one who by contrast was so humble that he could not believe the divine summons was meant for him, or too preoccupied with everyday affairs to be able to drop everything and take his son to be sacrificed (June 1921; *LFFE* 285/*B* 333).

More congenial than Kierkegaard, because more down-to-earth, were the late diaries of Tolstoy and the autobiography of the eighteenth-century philosopher Salomon Maimon (1753–1800), who made his way from Lithuania to Enlightenment Berlin and whose life-story Kafka described as 'an extremely harsh self-portrayal of a man running as though haunted between Eastern and Western Jewry' (December 1917; *LFFE* 173/*B3* 371). He valued Maimon's autobiography too because it contained a handy summary of the philosophy of the great medieval Jewish thinker Maimonides (*c.* 1135–1204). Kafka in his later years read much to instruct himself, close to beginner's level, in the history of religion. He had already read such works of comparative religion as Gustav Roskoff's *Geschichte des Teufels* (*History of the Devil*, 1869) and Nathan Söderblom's *Das Werden des Gottesglaubens* (*The Development of Theism*, 1914), both with much intriguing information about the religious beliefs of primitive people. Late in his life, certainly no earlier than 1921, he acquired a large collection of popular studies, often written by distinguished theologians, mainly on Old Testament topics, but including also one on Gnosticism. He may have acquired them only after he moved to Berlin late in 1923 and began studying at the Hochschule für die Wissenschaft des Judentums (College for Jewish Studies).[8]

Did Kafka's reading in philosophy extend beyond Plato, Nietzsche and Kierkegaard? It has sometimes been claimed that he thought only in images and had no head for abstract thought. But he was a trained lawyer, and *The Trial* parodies legal reasoning at great length. Kafka showed his capacity for minute and abstract argument in commenting on a philosophical treatise by Brod.[9] When he and Brod first met, Brod was giving a lecture to fellow-students on Arthur Schopenhauer (1788–1860), in which he criticized Nietzsche; Kafka leapt to Nietzsche's defence, and their argument led to a lifelong friendship. But there is no explicit engagement with Nietzsche, or with Schopenhauer, in Kafka's writings, though many traces especially of Schopenhauer can be found. Thus the theme of 'the indestructible' in the Zürau aphorisms seems to come from Schopenhauer's chapter 'On Death and its Relation to the Indestructibility of our Essence' in *Die Welt als Wille und Vorstellung* (*The World as Will and Representation*, 1818); the image of the inaccessible castle has a striking antecedent in Schopenhauer; and the theme of inevitable guilt in *The Trial* and 'In the Penal Colony' has also been traced to Schopenhauer.[10] If Kafka's acquaintance with philosophy was limited, it was through disinclination, not intellectual incapacity.

Reading for Kafka was no mere amusement but a form of self-discovery. His tastes were individual, with no deference to canons of 'high' literature and much sympathy for the 'low' and ephemeral. Biographical texts let him explore experiences analogous to his own. Historical, religious and philosophical texts corresponded to his own changing existential needs. Above all, the great novels he admired provided templates which helped his own fiction to attain originality.

NOTES

1 Kafka's school reading is summarized in K. Wagenbach, *Franz Kafka: Eine Biographie seiner Jugend, 1883–1912* (Bern: Francke, 1958), pp. 56–8.
2 Many of Kafka's literary likes and dislikes are listed by M. Brod, *Über Franz Kafka* (Frankfurt am Main: Fischer, 1974), p. 46. See also P.-A. Alt, *Franz Kafka: Der ewige Sohn* (Munich: Beck, 2005), pp. 138–45.
3 Brod, *Über Franz Kafka*, p. 295.
4 From Flaubert's letter to George Sand, 9 September 1868.
5 See R. Robertson, 'Kafka und die skandinavische Moderne' in M. Engel and D. Lamping (eds.), *Franz Kafka und die Weltliteratur* (Göttingen: Vandenhoeck & Ruprecht, 2006), pp. 144–65.
6 See J. Zilcosky, *Kafka's Travels: Exoticism, Colonialism, and the Traffic of Writing* (Basingstoke and New York: Palgrave Macmillan, 2003).
7 Brod, *Über Franz Kafka*, p. 147.

 8 These books are listed in Wagenbach, *Franz Kafka*, pp. 262–3. In J. Born's
   otherwise invaluable *Kafkas Bibliothek: Ein beschreibendes Verzeichnis* (Frankfurt am Main: Fischer, 1990) they are listed individually, not as a collection, so
   one cannot gather when Kafka acquired them. Hence Alt, *Franz Kafka: Der
   ewige Sohn*, p. 582, following Born, gives a misleading impression of Kafka's
   reading.
 9 M. Brod, *Der Prager Kreis* (Stuttgart: Kohlhammer, 1966), pp. 110–12.
10 See T. J. Reed, 'Kafka und Schopenhauer: Philosophisches Denken und
   dichterisches Bild', *Euphorion*, 59 (1965), 160–72; Søren Fauth, '"Die Schuld
   ist immer zweifellos": Schopenhauersche Soteriologie und Gnosis in Kafkas
   Erzählung "In der Strafkolonie"', *Deutsche Vierteljahrsschrift für Literaturwissenschaft und Geistesgeschichte*, 83 (2009), 262–86.

CHAPTER 10

Gesture

Lucia Ruprecht

In his 1934 essay 'Franz Kafka: On the Tenth Anniversary of His Death', Walter Benjamin (1892–1940) famously claims that Kafka's entire body of work constituted 'a code of gestures which surely had no definite symbolic meaning for the author from the outset'.[1] The decoding of Kafka's gestural universe proves indeed impossible. Yet it is set within a context of abundant practical and theoretical engagements with gesture. Gestures are a prominent means of representation at the beginning of the twentieth century.

Béla Balázs's 1924 treatise *Visible Man or the Culture of Film* celebrates silent film's ability to revive the 'long-forgotten language of gestures and facial expressions',[2] painters like Oskar Kokoschka (1886–1980) portray hands that 'express emotion through eye-catching gestures',[3] and the dancer and choreographer Vaslav Nijinsky (1889–1950) reclaims expression for dance by 'bringing it back to the simple gesture', as Jacques Rivière writes in his review of the 1913 production of *Le Sacre du printemps*, which Nijinsky created alongside composer Igor Stravinsky (1882–1971) and painter and archaeologist Nicholas Roerich (1874–1947).[4] Thinkers such as the art historian Aby Warburg (1866–1929), the physiologist and psychologist Wilhelm Wundt (1832–1920) and the philosopher Ludwig Klages (1872–1956) contribute to this turn towards the gestural from a range of theoretical and political perspectives. Together, they participate in forming what is considered, here, a multifaceted *gestural imaginary*: a cultural imaginary that constitutes itself in gestural form, reflecting upon the period's fascination with gestures as a semiotic system and mode of expression.

Kafka's writings give ample evidence of the fact that the author possessed an eye for gesture, and that he acquired mastery in his literary engagements with embodiment in close observation of social gesturing in private and public contexts. As his diaries show, he also studied aesthetic registers of gesture in non-textual art forms, above all the Yiddish theatre, which employed gesture in a prominent way.[5] What are the principal practices and theories of gesture around 1900, and how does Kafka relate to them?

Gesture between Health and Pathology, Authenticity and Code

The vocabulary of recovery and return that we find in the above-cited quotations by Balázs and Rivière characterizes a substantial part of the discourse on gesture at the beginning of the twentieth century. The assumption of gestural decline and reanimation grants gesture a primordial status, more originary than, if not opposed to, discursive language. Many theoretical discourses and artistic endeavours shared the belief in a natural tie between gesture, authentic experience and healing or salvation. Especially in the emerging field of *Ausdruckstanz* (dance of expression), gestural choreographies were invested with an almost religious significance. The laws of human gesture were placed in relation to the cosmic laws of the universe.[6]

This correspondence not only added a collective dimension to the promotion of fresh dancerly aesthetics that drew their energy from the individual human body, it also bestowed on the physical body a metaphysical aura. As technology increasingly dominated everyday life, gestural education and expression were meant to restore impoverished human beings who had lost touch with their natural bodily constitution. Benjamin calls this form of deprivation 'poverty of experience', and links it to the psychological and physical effects of the First World War.[7] Kafka's *Office Writings* include descriptions of 'nervous men who shake and jerk in the streets' (*O* 340/*A* 499), returning soldiers whose physical conduct was visibly marked by war trauma, and who therefore needed special medical care – for which Kafka was campaigning. But his civilians too show signs of physiological affliction. In *Der Process* (*The Trial*), Kaminer, junior employee at Josef K.'s bank, displays an 'intolerable smile caused by a chronic muscular spasm' (*T* 15/*P* 27), and is unable 'to control his tedious fidgetiness' (*T* 23/*P* 41).

A programme of gestural training or healing also motivated the first theories of film, most notably the writings of Balázs. Balázs opens *Visible Man* with one of the most urgent discussions of gestural crisis that can be found in early-twentieth-century cultural criticism. Overburdening the new medium with utopian potential, the gestural aesthetic of silent film is endowed with the promise of cultural renewal. For Balázs, it is language, the 'culture of the word', consolidated by the 'advent of printing', that has drawn attention away from the body: 'It is a law of nature that any organ that falls into disuse degenerates and atrophies. In the culture of words our bodies were not fully used and have lost their expressiveness in consequence. This is why they have become clumsy, primitive, stupid and barbaric.'

Film, in Balázs, is to revive the 'long-forgotten language of gestures and facial expressions', which he considers 'the visual corollary of human souls immediately made flesh'. Balázs entrusts cinema with a prophetic social mission: '*Man will become visible once again.*'[8] In Russia, Soviet film director Lev Kuleshov (1899–1970) and theatre director Vsevolod Meyerhold (1874–1940) draw on the body as an instrument of 'experimentation for future social transformation and for understanding a new commonality'.[9] They create 'laboratories' of new gesture, training bodies that could compete with technology's versatility and speed.[10]

A different kind of training accompanies the new forms of dance in Western society. Instead of matching the machinic, dance rejected the latter's alienating impact. 'For a number of decades', Rudolf von Laban (1879–1958) writes in his 1920 treatise *The Dancer's World*, 'our culture has been witnessing a movement which strives towards bodily healing and bodily cultivation by promoting sports, gymnastics and dance'. People were meant to free themselves from 'the pathological distortions brought about by the poisons of the soul', so that 'the call for dance', in Laban's view, constituted a 'call for recovery'.[11] Kafka's interest in physical education is well documented. Yet his own investments in physical training also made him acutely aware of the ideologies of able-bodiedness that were attached to this training, and he challenged them in his writings. The most striking examples of the 'recovered body' in Kafka are thus not human, but animal bodies, such as the 'young panther' that takes over the cage of the deceased 'hunger artist', 'equipped nearly to bursting with all the necessaries' (*HA* 65/*DL* 349).

Not all examples of the new cultivation of the body gave an impression of health, however. The advanced and unusual aesthetic of dance sometimes elicited ambivalent critical responses. Dance's inaugural moment of gestural renewal, Nijinsky's above-mentioned choreography of *Le Sacre du printemps*, was widely considered the product of a pathological imagination; other performances at German dance conventions were compared to what was conceived as the gestural spasm of Expressionist film. Expressionist literature too charted excessive gestural behaviour, with Alfred Döblin's short story 'Die Ermordung einer Butterblume' ('The Murder of a Buttercup', 1903–5) as perhaps the most memorable example; and visual artists, especially Expressionists like Kokoschka and Egon Schiele, focused on the depiction of distorted gestures as genuine elements of their new aesthetic.[12] The emphasis around 1900 on gesture's association with health and authenticity must be seen, then, as only one side of a preoccupation whose other side bore a heavier and more problematic charge. Modernist aesthetics also included a sustained engagement with pathological gesticulation, which was associated with dysfunctional physiological reflexes or compulsive psycho-physical automatisms.

The above-cited examples of the shell-shocked and the dexterous body in Kafka show that his interest in the gestural was embedded in this historical context. Yet when Benjamin describes Kafka's work as a 'code of gestures', he acknowledges that Kafka was not in the first instance concerned with questions of authentic, healthy or indeed pathological expression. Rather, Benjamin zooms in on Kafka's obsession with codified forms of attire and conduct. Gesture, in this perspective, is part of conventional vocabularies of behaviour, of outward-directed, strategic modes of expression, or 'cool conduct'.[13] The sociologist and anthropologist Helmuth Plessner's 1924 anti-expressive – and anti-Expressionist – essay 'Grenzen der Gemeinschaft' ('The Limits of Community') approaches gesture in relation to this context. Plessner calls for a 'spirit of tact, restraint, goodness, and ease', pitting this spirit against the 'cramped faces of today's humanity', which distort themselves by displaying exaggerated, formless behaviour in the attempt to display tortured emotions.[14] Expressionism's powerful cultural revaluation of subjectivity was of course not as oblivious to form as Plessner suggests. On the contrary, it produced its own gestural codifications. Thus the film critic Lotte Eisner describes stereotyped forms of gesturing in Expressionist film,[15] while Benjamin speaks of Expressionism's 'clenched fist in papier-mâché', of a reproducible gesture of revolution.[16] As will be shown in the following, Kafka's gestures register this often paradoxical closeness, but also the problematic tension between the subjectivity of expression and the generality of the code.

Kafka's Gestures

Kafka records many scenes of gestural conduct in his diaries. Often these gestures are coded in terms of gender and relate to the adjustments in behaviour that are demanded by social hierarchies. In his Paris travel diary he describes a man and two women in a hotel lobby; the man's 'arm continually trembled as if at any moment he intended to put it out and escort the ladies through the centre of the crowd' (September 1911; *D* 456/ *TB* 1000). A few pages later we read about the less formal etiquette of the brothel visit – where a gap-toothed girl was 'anxious lest I should forget and take off my hat' (*D* 459/ *TB* 1007). Kafka's diary accounts of social gesture take notice of moments where codes of conduct draw special attention to themselves. Conventional gestures are not naturally enacted – or avoided – but affected by a specific kind of stress that bears on the potential of social automatisms to fall out of kilter at any moment.

The gestures described in Kafka's literary texts elaborate such types of estrangement. They often defamiliarize traditional manners and conventions altogether. They belong to a new, unknown code. Like the pockets and buckles covering the suit of Franz, one of the guards in *The Trial*, this gestural code is best characterized as a semiotic system which is 'probably significant, but incomprehensible' (*T* 8/*P* 13). Its strategic social value remains as doubtful as its meaning. Gestures in Kafka are sometimes accompanied by apparently self-evident explanations that presuppose a convention where there is none. Thus in *Der Verschollene* (*The Man who Disappeared*), Karl Rossmann is 'lowering his face before the stoker and slapping his trouser-seams as a sign that all hope was gone' (*MD* 16/*V* 29). More often, however, the underlying script to which the gestural vocabulary presumably refers is not spelled out at all.

Rule-guided communication or conduct is not being rejected in principle; yet the content of the rules remains unknown. Kafka's gestures can hardly be accessed by a Brechtian logic of social *gestus*, that is. *Gestus* stands for the socially embedded habitual behaviour of people; in this sense, it is readable and gives access to their position in social hierarchies. When framing his discussion of Kafka in Brechtian terms, Benjamin makes sure to indicate the limits of this framework: 'Kafka could understand things only in the form of a *gestus*, and this *gestus* which he did not understand constitutes the cloudy part of the parables.'[17] Benjamin's essay 'Programm eines proletarischen Kindertheaters' ('Programme for a Proletarian Children's Theatre', 1929) addresses gestures in a manner that better seems to fit Kafka's approach. Here Benjamin argues that a child's gesture does not belong to the social world of adults, but should be considered 'a signal from another world, in which the child lives and commands'.[18]

Kafka's gestures, then, might be taken as signals from a personal imaginary in which the author experiments with narrative voices and agents, as in his first book, *Betrachtung* (*Meditation*); from inaccessible worlds of power, as in *The Trial* and *Das Schloss* (*The Castle*); or from the outside world of social interaction, where they sometimes tell about an event by re-performing it, as in his diaries. Kafka describes his gestural signals with a precision of detail that urges the reader to acknowledge their deliberate nature.

As we have seen in the example from *The Man who Disappeared*, his early works abound with such accuracy; *Meditation* too can be considered an archive of carefully described idiosyncratic gestures. This clarity

of gestural appearance seems to be the inverse function of the 'cloudi-
ness' of gestural meaning. Why should there be a connection between
rubbing one's fingertips together and the undoing of shame, as in 'Entlarvung eines Bauernfängers' ('Unmasking a Confidence-Man'; *M* 7/*DL*
16)? Why is the running of the little finger across the eyebrows the 'characteristic gesture' of someone paralysed by misery, as in 'Entschlüsse'
('Decisions'; *M* 8/*DL* 19)? *Meditation* is concerned, above all, with the
ostentatiousness of gestural performance and the way these gestures travel
across the eighteen short pieces that make up the volume. Benjamin
speaks of Kafka's attempt to derive meaning from his code of gestures 'in
ever-changing contexts and experimental groupings'.[19] The gestural reiterations and correspondences that can be traced in *Meditation* confirm
Benjamin's observation. The rubbing-together of fingertips in 'Unmasking a Confidence-Man' recurs, with a slight variation, in 'Unglücklich-
sein' ('Unhappiness'), where the child scrapes her fingertips against a wall
(*M* 16/*DL* 35); the confidence-man makes a sound like 'teeth snapping
together' (*M* 6/*DL* 14) while the small businessman 'speaks through his
teeth' (*M* 10/*DL* 23, modified translation); and so on. But to attribute
meaning to these evolving gestures remains challenging. What they indicate is a slipperiness of identity in the early prose, producing embodied narrative voices and protagonists who cannot be separated from each
other.[20]

The later works assign gestures more clearly to specific protagonists, but
they also develop the doubling and multiplication of gestures to powerful
effect, particularly in the shape of a gestural standing-in for someone else.
Kafka's post as legal secretary in the Arbeiter-Unfall-Versicherungs-Anstalt
(Workers' Accident Insurance Institute) involved the right of signature even
in cases where he was not the actual author of a document. Recent research
has suggested a more general logic of agency by proxy in Kafka's works,
eroding 'parts of the distinction between Kafka's legal-administrative and
literary-aesthetic writing'.[21]

This logic of the proxy is performed to perfection by the two most
prominent gestural agents of the later works, the assistants Artur and
Jeremias in *The Castle*. If the proxy situation is defined by speaking in the
name of someone or something else, most likely an official or an institution, Artur and Jeremias personify this process. Apart from Jeremias's
monologue towards the end of the novel, which occurs once he has been
separated from his double, Artur, the assistants do not say much, at least
not in direct speech; but they gesture constantly, and they do so, as we

later learn, in the name of Klamm, the castle official whom K. is trying to reach. However, they also do so in the name of each other. Of
twin-like appearance, they are treated by K. like a single man, that is,
like each other's exchangeable proxies. They do not only carry out the
same tasks, they also enact either the same, or at least complementary gestures. These gestures are in turn graceful, childish, endearing and annoy-
ing; they are slapsticks performed for pure entertainment, as Jeremias tells
K. after his dismissal from the latter's services. Thus when K. first meets
the messenger Barnabas, his assistants are taking turn rising 'as if from the
depths' behind the man's shoulders, then bobbing 'quickly down again
with a slight whistle imitating the wind, as if alarmed by the sight of
K.' (*C* 108/*S* 191). The 'outward eagerness' (*C* 21/*S* 35) that fuels these
two casts doubt on the genuineness of their performance. They are actors
portraying the role of assistants, and more often than not they overdo
their task. Rather than gesturing 'at first hand', they are performing a cultural record of gestural vocabulary that encompasses more standard elements, like saluting (*C* 18/*S* 31), and more playful ones, like the bobbing up-and-down quoted above. As such, they seem not quite human;
their 'jaunty bearing' gives the impression 'as if their joints were galvanized' (*C* 204/*S* 366), but when tired they seem 'not being properly alive'
(*C* 207/*S* 371).

Benjamin places Kafka's assistant figures outside the paternal spell of the
family circle and other hierarchies, attributing to them a particular kind of
hope that relies on their detachment from the authoritarian dynamic of
oedipal structures.[22] Imitating a repertoire of cultural conduct, Artur and
Jeremias derive their energy from a quasi-technological type of replication,
rather than from biological reproduction. We do not know who their parents are, or whether they have any parents at all; and they do not have
children. The assistants embody a principle that Kafka portrays in its most
parodical essence in the two little celluloid balls that follow (or 'assist') the
bachelor Blumfeld. Kafka's gestural agents do not express their soul. They
perform – jokingly and yet strangely mechanically – in the name of a code
whose underlying script remains beyond our reach.

In Kafka, then, gestures are not authentic or natural; they rarely give
direct access to lived experience. Instead, they are 'second-hand' gestures;
they function as performed record of the way in which life is not lived but
(re-)enacted. In this sense, Kafka's account of the staging of an accident on
a Paris street on 11 September 1911 might serve as blueprint for his literary
engagement with the gestural. The owner of a motor-car which has just

collided with a tricycle delivers a pantomimic simulation of the crash after the event under the eyes of a quickly forming crowd:

> He sees the tricycle cutting across his path, detaches his right hand, and gesticulates back and forth in warning to it, a worried expression on his face – what motor-car could apply its brakes in time in so short a distance? Will the tricycle understand this and give the motor-car the right of way? No, it is too late; his left hand ceases its warning motions, both hands join together for the collision, his knees bend to watch the last moment. It has happened, and the bent, motionless tricycle standing there can now assist in the description. (*D* 462–3/ *TB* 1013)

If the diary account reports how someone gestures towards a road accident, it is presented in a way that suggests this gesturing-towards as the main object of attention.²³ Kafka's literary gestures thus highlight themselves, playfully, painfully or enigmatically. They are set within a multi-faceted historical context that arises in both discourse and practice. The diary account remains exceptional here, as it employs gesture for mimetically recalling an event that is easily accessible. More often than not, however, the events that are presumably alluded to in Kafka's gesturality indeed seem to stem from agents in 'another world', whose reasoning is not ours. What makes this author's gestural negotiations unique, therefore, is the fact that they are reflective of a body which behaves according to codes of conduct whose foundations remain inaccessible. Through its evocation of an unexplained necessity, Kafka's ingeniously idiosyncratic approach to gesturality formulates a thought-provoking contribution to gestural thinking at the beginning of the twentieth century.

NOTES

1 W. Benjamin, 'Franz Kafka: On the Tenth Anniversary of His Death' in M. W. Jennings, H. Eiland and G. Smith (eds.), R. Livingstone (trans.), *Walter Benjamin: Selected Writings*, 4 vols. (Cambridge, MA: The Belknap Press of Harvard University Press, 2002–6), vol. ii.2, pp. 794–818: 801.
2 B. Balázs, 'Visible Man or the Culture of Film' in E. Carter (ed.), *Béla Balázs: Early Film Theory* (New York: Berghahn, 2011), pp. 1–90: 10.
3 E. R. Kandel, *The Age of Insight: The Quest to Understand the Unconscious in Art, Mind, and Brain, from Vienna 1900 to the Present* (New York: Random House, 2012), p. 153.
4 J. Rivière, 'Le Sacre du printemps' in B. A. Price (ed. and trans.), *The Ideal Reader: Selected Essays by Jacques Rivière* (New York: Meridian Books, 1960), pp. 125–47: 139.
5 See E. T. Beck, *Kafka and the Yiddish Theater: Its Impact on his Work* (Madison, WI: University of Wisconsin Press, 1971).

6 See R. v. Laban, *Die Welt des Tänzers: Fünf Gedankenreigen* (Stuttgart: Walter Seifert, 1920).

7 W. Benjamin, 'Experience and Poverty' in Jennings, Eiland and Smith (eds.), *Walter Benjamin: Selected Writings*, vol. ii.2, pp. 731–6: 732; see also J. Zilcosky, '"Samsa war Reisender": Trains, Trauma, and the Unreadable Body' in S. Corngold and R. V. Gross (eds.), *Kafka for the Twenty-First Century* (Rochester, NY: Camden House, 2011), pp. 179–206.

8 Balázs, 'Visible Man or the Culture of Film', pp. 10–11.

9 B. Kunst, 'Dance and Work: The Aesthetic and Political Potential of Dance' in N. Klein and S. Noeth (eds.), *Emerging Bodies: The Performance of World-making in Dance and Choreography* (Bielefeld: Transcript, 2011), pp. 47–59: 53.

10 See O. Bulgakowa, *The Factory of Gestures: Body Language in Film*, DVD (PPMedia and Stanford Humanities Lab, 2008).

11 Laban, *Die Welt des Tänzers*, pp. 137–8, 135, 178.

12 See G. Blackshaw, 'The Pathological Body: Modernist Strategising in Egon Schiele's Self-Portraiture', *Oxford Art Journal*, 30, no. 3 (2007), 377–401.

13 See H. Lethen, *Cool Conduct: The Culture of Distance in Weimar Germany* (Berkeley, CA: University of California Press, 2002); for a historical approach to gestural codes from the perspective of art history, see A. Warburg, *The Renewal of Pagan Antiquity: Contributions to the Cultural History of the European Renaissance* (Los Angeles, CA: Getty Research Institute for the History of Art and the Humanities, 1999).

14 H. Plessner, *The Limits of Community: A Critique of Social Radicalism* (Amherst, NY: Humanity Books, 1999), p. 194.

15 See L. Eisner, *The Haunted Screen: Expressionism in the German Cinema and the Influence of Max Reinhardt* (London: Thames and Hudson, 1969), p. 144.

16 W. Benjamin, 'Left-Wing Melancholy' in Jennings, Eiland and Smith (eds.), *Walter Benjamin: Selected Writings*, vol. ii.2, pp. 423–7: 424.

17 Benjamin, 'Franz Kafka', p. 808.

18 W. Benjamin, 'Program for a Proletarian Children's Theater' in Jennings, Eiland and Smith (eds.), *Walter Benjamin: Selected Writings*, vol. ii.1, pp. 201–6: 203–4.

19 Benjamin, 'Franz Kafka', p. 801.

20 See L. Ruprecht, 'Anfangsszenen von Autorschaft in Kafkas *Betrachtung*' in C. Duttlinger (ed.), *Kafkas 'Betrachtung': Neue Lektüren* (Freiburg: Rombach, 2014), pp. 37–55.

21 D. Densky, 'Proxies in Kafka: *Konzipist* FK and *Prokurist* Josef K.' in Corngold and Gross (eds.), *Kafka for the Twenty-First Century*, p. 132.

22 Benjamin, 'Franz Kafka', p. 798.

23 The diary account also shows how Kafka's texts gesture towards other, non-literary discourses, such as the legal and bureaucratic ones which are anticipated in the performance of the car owner who prepares for the arrival of a policeman; see B. Wagner, 'The Calm of Writing: Kafka's Poetics of Accident', in S. Corngold and B. Wagner (eds.), *Franz Kafka: The Ghosts in the Machine* (Evanston, IL: Northwestern University Press, 2011), pp. 177–202: 257, note 7.

CHAPTER 11

Performance and Recitation

Lothar Müller

Recitation in Modernism: The Example of Ludwig Hardt

In 1924, shortly after Franz Kafka's death, Max Brod gave Ludwig Hardt's *Vortragsbuch* (*Recitation Book*, 1924) to Kafka's nephew. He added a dedication: 'to Felix Hermann, in memory of his Bar Mitzvah ceremony – and of his immortal uncle Franz Kafka'. The book is an anthology of poetry and short prose from early Romanticism to Modernism, but it is also a self-portrait of the reciter Ludwig Hardt (1886–1947) – an overview over his repertoire, addressed to potential audiences. The book contains short endorsements of Hardt's art by Thomas Mann (1875–1955), Herbert Eulenberg (1876–1949) and Erwin Loewenson (1888–1963) as well as Else Lasker-Schüler's poem 'Ludwig Hardt'. An appendix lists recitation programmes which Hardt could be hired to perform, including 'Heine – Baudelaire – Wedekind', 'idylls and fairy tales' and 'mixed programmes'.[1] After 1920, Hardt also included nine texts by Kafka in his repertoire, taken from the collections *Betrachtung* (*Meditation*, 1912) and *Ein Landarzt* (*A Country Doctor*, 1920). In the *Recitation Book* Kafka's texts are juxtaposed with short prose by Robert Walser (1878–1956) and poems by Georg Heym (1887–1912).

Born 1886 in East Frisia, Hardt was educated as an actor at the Hochschule für dramatische Kunst (Academy of Dramatic Art) in Berlin. Because of his diminutive stature, his repertoire of dramatic roles was limited, and thus he began to specialize in recitation. From 1905 onwards he began to tour, and by 1920 had become one of the best-known reciters in the German-speaking countries.

For Kafka's literary career, Hardt's significance is comparable to that of his publisher Kurt Wolff. Hardt's recitations meant that Kafka's short prose became known through channels other than the printed book. Hardt's recitation of Kafka's works in the 'Meistersaal' in Berlin on 9 March 1921 was the first of many such events, and during Kafka's lifetime his texts may well have reached more listeners than readers. One of these listeners was Thomas Mann. In August 1921, he notes in his diary: 'For tea with L. Hardt, who read prose by a Prague author, Kafka, to me, strange enough [merkwürdig genug]'. Mann then read Kafka, presumably the *Landarzt* (*Country Doctor*) collection, 'recommended to me by the reciter Hardt', and declared himself 'rather interested' in the texts.[2]

Soon thereafter, in October 1921, Kafka got to know Hardt in person during his two-week stay in Prague. Performing at the Mozarteum and at the commodity exchange, Hardt also performed texts by Kafka, who in turn sent him a letter requesting that he read Kleist's 'Anekdote aus dem letzten preußischen Kriege' ('Anecdote from the last Prussian War', 1810). This text was one of a selection of short prose works that Kafka regularly read to his sisters.[3]

Ludwig Hardt made his career combining voice and book, an association which dates back to early Romanticism. While literature in this period became increasingly associated with printed matter, reciting literature at private, semi-public and public readings was a vital part of intellectual life. Indeed, it was precisely the alliance of silent reading and public performance which shaped the rise of the spoken word in the eighteenth century. This dynamic alliance of voice and book was not based on the illusion of a voice without a written text. Thus Goethe (1749–1832) distinguished explicitly between recitation and declamation, the latter more or less bound to stage performances.

> By recitation is understood such a lecture, as it might be performed without a passionate rising of the voice, even though not without a change of tone between cool and quiet and most excited speech, finding itself in the middle. The listener is always aware that there is a third object.[4]

This third object is the book, from which the reciter recites even when he puts the book aside and performs from memory.

In the nineteenth century, recitation was professionalized as it became tied to the institutions of the theatre and the concert hall. By the early twentieth century, actors such as Josef Kainz (1858–1910) and Alexander Moissi (1879–1935) went on tour without ensembles or directors, while poets such as Detlev von Liliencron and Richard Dehmel were travelling propagandists for their work. Publishing houses and bookstores discovered author readings as a marketing instrument. Karl Kraus (1874–1936), editor of the magazine *Die Fackel* (*The Torch*), frequently performed in Vienna, Berlin, Prague and Budapest, where he was known for his Shakespeare cycles and his readings of his own poetry and journalism. Kafka was in the audience when Kraus read his essay 'Heine und die Folgen' ('Heine and the Consequences') in the Hotel Central in Prague on 15 March 1911.[5]

Kafka as Listener and Reciter

Kafka's career as an author and reader is closely entwined with his role as a listener and reciter. The debating societies, lecture halls and theatres he frequented as a student were part of his education and of the literary infrastructure within which he became an author. Kafka enjoyed reading his own and others' texts out loud – in private, to family and friends, but sometimes also in public. He met his close friend Max Brod in the Lese- und Redehalle der deutschen Studenten in Prag (Reading and Discussion Hall of German Students in Prague, established 1848) where Brod had given a lecture on Schopenhauer. Two years later, in autumn 1904, Brod introduced Kafka to the musician and budding actor Oskar Baum. Their meeting led to the group of friends developing rituals for reading out loud, alternating between texts such as Flaubert's *La Tentation de St. Antoine* (*The Temptation of Saint Anthony*, 1874) and their own unpublished manuscripts. Around 1909–10, Kafka began to absorb the technique of recitation, turning his voice into a stage voice, copying models of recitation he saw in contemporaries such as Brod and Franz Werfel and professional reciters such as Emil Milan. Kafka's recitation practice started in his family. He read to his sisters from Plato, Grillparzer and Mörike and his own texts, and then developed his voice among his friends, to whom he read rarely, but emphatically. Finally he ventured to recite in public. On 11 December 1913, Kafka read from Kleist's novella *Michael Kohlhaas* (1810) at a public reading in Prague, but afterwards subjected himself to a scathing, but humorous, review:

> In Toynbee Hall read the beginning of *Michael Kohlhaas*. Complete and utter fiasco. Badly chosen, badly presented, finally swam senseless around in the text. Model audience. Very small boys in the front row. One of them tries to overcome his innocent boredom by carefully throwing his cap on the floor and then carefully picking it up, and then again, over and over. Since he is too small to accomplish this from his seat, he has to keep sliding off the chair a little. Read wildly and badly and carelessly and unintelligibly. (*D* 246/ *TB* 610–11)

Kafka's account shows a text exposing the reciter's weaknesses. The reverse scenario, of a recitation revealing a text's deficiencies, occurred when in early November 1911 Max Brod, with the author's approval, read from Kafka's Paris travel diary to their joint friends. Kafka comments:

> one sentence comes marching up with so rough a start that the entire story falls into sulky amazement; a sleepy imitation of Max (reproaches muffled – stirred up) seesaws in, sometimes it looks like a dancing course during its first quarter hour. (5 November 1911; *D* 105/ *TB* 226–7)

Ideally, though, writing and reading form a harmonious whole:

> If I were ever able to write something large and whole [ein größeres Ganzes], well shaped from beginning to end, then the story would never be able to detach itself from me completely, and it would be possible for me calmly and with open eyes, as a blood relation of a healthy story, to hear it read, but as it is every little piece of the story runs around homeless and drives me away from itself in the opposite direction. (5 November 1911; *D* 105/ *TB* 226–7)

Kafka would later use the metaphor of blood relations to describe his bond to Dostoyevsky, Kleist, Grillparzer and Flaubert. But here, the metaphor stands for the ideal of the author's relationship to a text of his own from which he had already inwardly distanced himself. The one example in Kafka's oeuvre where the success of writing produces an entire cascade of equally successful recitations is 'Das Urteil' ('The Judgement'), written eruptively in the night of 22–3 September 1912. In his diary, Kafka described the story's creation in quasi-mythological terms, as primal, a scene at the end of which the reciter is born out of the author. For, having finished the story at daybreak, Kafka immediately went on to read it to his sisters: 'As the maid walked through the ante-room for the first time I wrote the last sentence. Turning out the light and the light of day . . . The trembling entrance into my sisters' room. Reading aloud' (23 September 1912; *D* 213/ *TB* 460–1).

He then went on to read 'The Judgement' to Brod a few days later, on 6 October 1912; when he read it to his friends the Weltsch family, in February 1913, he used the proofs sent by the literary magazine *Arkadia*, where the story was about to be published. Finally, 'The Judgement' was also the text Kafka read at an author evening hosted by the Herder Society in the Prague Erzherzog Stephan Hotel on 4 December 1912. It was Kafka's first ever public reading of his own literary work. If its creation constituted a primal scene of writing, then his letter to Felice Bauer, written immediately after the public reading, features a primal scene of reading out loud:

> Frankly, dearest, I simply adore reading aloud; bellowing into the audience's expectant and attentive ear warms the cockles of the poor heart . . . Nothing,

you know, gives the body greater satisfaction than ordering people about, or at least believing in one's ability to do so. As a child . . . I used to enjoy dreaming of reading aloud to a large, crowded hall (though equipped with somewhat greater strength of heart, voice, and intellect than I had at the time) the whole *Education sentimentale* in one sitting, for as many days and nights as it required, in French of course (oh dear, my accent!), and making the walls reverberate. (4/5 December 1912; *LF* 108/*B1* 298)

By wanting to read out Flaubert's entire *Education sentimentale* (1869), Kafka wants to impregnate himself with the texts written by his great role models. He must have known that Flaubert put his own texts through rigorous tests by reading them in a very loud voice; Kafka's letters and diaries are full of descriptions of his own physical weakness, including that of his voice. Thus Kafka started rehearsing to strengthen his voice.

Another outlet for Kafka's appetite for public performance was his story 'In der Strafkolonie' ('In the Penal Colony', 1914). On 2 December 1914, he first recited the text in the home of Franz Werfel's parents. He then performed again, this time in public, at an event which was part of the series of 'Evenings for new literature' in the Munich 'Neue Kunst' gallery, held on 10 November 1916, and hosted by the bookseller and gallerist Hans Goltz. Other authors featured in this series included Salomo Friedländer (1871–1946), Else Lasker-Schüler (1869–1945), Alfred Wolfenstein (1883–1945) and Theodor Däubler (1876–1934).

As his letters to Felice Bauer show, Kafka had been very keen to accept Goltz's invitation, but also concerned about the possibility of failure. In order to get the event past the censors, Goltz gave it the title 'Tropische Münchhausiade' ('Tropical Münchhausen tales'). Kafka's text, featuring horrific scenes of torture and execution, stirred up a lot of controversy and the author, after digesting the mostly scathing reviews, called his Munich appearance 'really a huge failure'.

As author readings and voice artists such as Ludwig Hardt gained in popularity, newspapers and magazines began to review such events. Thus the Zionist magazine *Selbstwehr* (*Self-Defence*), which Kafka read regularly, featured a section 'From the Lecture Hall'. Though Kafka never published any such reviews, his journals and letters contain various passages that are reminiscent of this genre. For Kafka obviously not only attended readings by authors he valued but also attended such events to study the patterns which made them a success or failure. Writer Bernhard Kellermann's reading in the Prague German Casino on 27 November 1910 is an example of the latter, with a disastrous combination of deficient performance skills and clumsy time management. As Kafka writes,

> because of the boring manner of the reading, the people, despite the story's cheap suspense, kept leaving one by one with as much zeal as if someone were reading next door. When, after the first third of the story, he drank a little mineral water, a whole crowd of people left. He was frightened. 'It is almost finished', he lied outright. When he was finished everyone stood up; there was some applause that sounded as though there were one person in the midst of all the people standing up who had remained seated and was clapping by himself. (27 November 1910; *D* 28/ *TB* 127–8)

Kellermann (1879–1951), like Kafka himself, was untrained as a public speaker, quite unlike the many actor-reciters who toured Germany and Austria in the early twentieth century. One of these was the Austrian actor Alexander Moissi, a star of Max Reinhardt's Deutsches Theater in Berlin, whom Kafka saw at the Prague Rudolfinum on 28 February 1912. Moissi was a charismatic reciter, performing self-devised programmes from 1911 onwards. Of Italian-Albanian background, he was hailed as a melodious and musical speaker.

The programme included Goethe's 'Prometheus' poem, Richard Beer-Hofmann's 'Schlaflied für Mirjam' ('Lullaby for Miriam') and Hugo von Hofmannsthal's poetic obituary of the actor Josef Kainz, who had died two years earlier. Kainz had been Moissi's mentor; in fact, Goethe's 'Prometheus' had featured prominently in his own solo performances. The Rudolfinum was the size of a concert hall and gave Moissi scope to project his theatre-inflected voice; Kafka's diary contains a vivid account of his reading (3 March 1912; *D* 190/ *TB* 393–5). At first Moissi sat silently, with a book on his lap, but then began to read with an almost supernatural intensity: 'Not a word is lost, nor is there the whisper of an echo, instead everything grows gradually larger as though the voice, already occupied with something else, continued to exercise a direct after-effect; it grows stronger after the initial impetus and swallows us up.' But Kafka is rather critical of Moissi's 'unashamed tricks and surprises at which one must look down at the floor and which one would never use oneself: singing individual verses at the very beginning, for instance, [Beer-Hofmann's] "Sleep Miriam, my child"; wandering around of the voice in the melody'. Kafka critically draws attention to Moissi's musical intonation, his singing voice, which takes on a life of its own, obscuring the musicality of the poem itself: 'Despite the fact that so many melodies were to be heard, that the voice seemed as controlled as a light boat in the water, the melody of the verses could really not be heard.'

Kafka and the Theatre

Most of Kafka's notes on recitation date from the years 1910–12, the time when he also became increasingly visible as a public literary figure. But this time also saw Kafka taking a particular interest in the theatre. In February 1912, he attended Frank Wedekind's *Erdgeist* (*Earth Spirit*) at its premiere at the Neues Deutsches Theater in Prague, and in May Max Reinhardt's Prague production of Hofmannsthal's *Jedermann* (*Everyman*), a guest performance of the Deutsches Theater Berlin. During a trip to Paris in October 1910, he attended a dramatization of the Goncourt brothers' novel *Manette Salomon* (1867). In early December 1910, he saw Schnitzler's *Anatol* (1893) while in Berlin, followed, within only a couple of days, by Molière's *Le Mariage forcé* (*The Forced Marriage*, 1664), Shakespeare's *Comedy of Errors* (1594) and Max Reinhardt's production of *Hamlet*, starring Albert Bassermann and Gertrud Eysoldt as Ophelia.

But it is another theatrical tradition that really captured Kafka's imagination. From October 1911 until spring 1912 he attended more than twenty performances given by a Lemberg-based Yiddish theatre troupe, whose most prominent member was the actor and reciter Jizchak Löwy (1887–1942). Having first performed rather unsuccessfully in the Hotel Central, the group then moved to the Café Savoy, whose stage was closer to the vaudeville tradition.[6] Kafka's encounters with the Lemberg theatre troupe act as a gateway not only to Yiddish theatre and Yiddish poetry but also to Eastern European Jewish culture. His sensitivity for linguistic differences and regionalisms, a regular feature of his diaries, is particularly apparent in his diary passages on these performances, where Yiddish theatre is primarily characterized as an aural phenomenon. Though Judaism is commonly regarded as a book-based religion and culture, Yiddish theatre, and the Yiddish language more generally, are marked by a pronounced *distance* from the written word, setting it apart from the Hebrew language of the synagogue. Kafka's diary notes emphasize this, not least when they draw on the gestural element of Yiddish theatre, which is in turn a model for his own expressive prose.[7] But there is another line which connects Kafka's encounter with the Lemberg theatre troupe to his own writing, namely the role or figure of the impresario. This was a role which Kafka adopted on 12 February 1912 when he introduced a recitation evening given by Jizchak Löwy in the banquet hall of the Jewish Council Hall in Prague. Löwy was more than an actor; he was the narrator of his own biography, a translator from Hebrew and an ambassador for Eastern European Jewish culture and the Yiddish language. Kafka introduced his friend's performance by giving a brief lecture on the Yiddish language.

As his diary shows, Kafka prepared himself for his lecture with enormous energy, but also with doubt and feelings of insecurity. In part, these concerns focused on the seemingly paradoxical approach he pursued in his talk, where he was asking his Western Jewish audience to open their ears to Yiddish, while at the same time rejecting the possibility that this Eastern European Jewish culture and its language could ever become assimilated into the audience's own, Western cultural sphere. But Kafka was also worried by the prospect of the lecture itself. In his diary account, the Western Jewish impresario, introducing his Eastern Jewish protégé through a refined, thoroughly elaborated talk, is standing next to the author Kafka, who is presenting his own case with a strong voice:

> Joy in Löwy and confidence in him, proud, unearthly consciousness during my lecture (coolness in the presence of the audience, only the lack of practice kept me from using enthusiastic gestures freely), strong voice, effortless memory, recognition, but above all the power with which I loudly, decisively, determinedly, faultlessly, irresistibly, with clear eyes, almost casually, put down the impudence of the three town hall porters and gave them, instead of the twelve kronen they demanded, only six kronen, and even these with a grand air. In all this are revealed powers to which I would gladly entrust myself if they would remain. (My parents were not there.)
> (25 February 1912; *D* 181–2/*TB* 378–9)

Irrespective of its melancholy conclusion, Kafka's diary account betrays a palpable sense of pride in his own, 'strong' voice. It underlines his desire to harness the sphere of recitation for his own burgeoning authorship, using the ephemeral phenomenon of the human voice to complement, transmit and enhance the more enduring medium of the written text.

NOTES

1 L. Hardt, *Vortragsbuch: Die Hauptstücke aus seinen Programmen nebst Darstellungen seiner Vortragskunst sowie etliche Glossen von ihm selbst* (Hamburg: Enoch, 1924), pp. 423ff.

2 T. Mann, *Tagebücher 1918–1921*, ed. I. Jens und P. de Mendelssohn. (Frankfurt am Main: Fischer, 1980), vol. 1, pp. 542 and 547.

3 *EFB* 468, note 2.

4   J. W. Goethe, *Regeln für Schauspieler* in Weimarer Ausgabe (Weimar: Böhlau, 1901), div. I, vol. XL, pp. 144–5.

5   *Franz Kafka: Eine Chronik*, compiled by R. Hermes, W. John, H.-G. Koch and A. Widera (Berlin: Wagenbach, 1999), p. 64.

6   L. Müller, 'Die Unruhe eines Westjuden: Franz Kafka, das jiddische Theater und die Unübersetzbarkeit des Jargons', *brücken: Germanistisches Jahrbuch Tschechien–Slowakei*, 15 (2007), 149–80; G. Massino, *Franz Kafka, Löwy und das jiddische Theater* (Frankfurt am Main and Basel: Stroemfeld/Nexus, 2007).

7   E. Torton Beck, *Kafka and the Yiddish Theatre: Its Impact on his Work* (Madison, WI: University of Wisconsin Press, 1971).

CHAPTER 12

Film

Silke Horstkotte

The 1910s, the decade during which Kafka wrote the bulk of his oeuvre, were a decisive period in media history when the new medium film broke free of its co-existence with other forms of optical spectacle and established itself as the leading mass medium of modernist culture. Kafka's writing coincides with, and is shaped by, a threshold era during which the cinema was institutionalized, a commercial film industry established, and cinematic modes of production and reception were formed which we still know today. This rapid development of an independent film language, of narrative forms, performance settings and commercial structures happened between the first presentation of the cinématographe by the brothers Lumière in 1895 and about 1917. From the end of the First World War until the 1960s, in turn, commercial cinema as a universally understood system of visual representation changed very little, with one exception: the introduction of sound film in 1928–9 privileged a realistic film aesthetic that was more in line with spectators' everyday reality than had been the case in silent film, leading to different forms of immersion. It is therefore in the specific context of silent film and of the media culture surrounding it that Kafka's engagement with film needs to be situated.

Kafka actively followed the development of early film and frequently visited the cinema. In his comprehensive study *Kafka Goes to the Movies*, the actor Hanns Zischler was the first to take stock of the many films that Kafka had seen, and literary scholars such as Carolin Duttlinger and Peter-André Alt have since followed Zischler in describing Kafka as a media-savvy man of his time.[1] In his autobiographical writings, Kafka took notes on a number of films, and he expressed an ongoing interest in the cinema. Yet Kafka's literary works exhibit a curious distance from the cinema. No direct reference is made to film in his narrative fiction, and the scattered references to the cinema in his early diaries never coalesce into a consistent statement, while his later texts seem to lose interest in the cinema altogether. And unlike his friend Max Brod, Kafka never attempted writing *for* the

cinema. The importance of film as a context for Kafka lies in this ambivalence between an almost reluctant fascination on the part of Kafka the
spectator, and the critical distance displayed by Kafka the diarist. It is the
ambivalence of someone who was extremely aware of the processes of modernization, urbanization and acceleration which were rapidly transforming
the world in which he was living, and who recognized the catalysing role
that the cinema played in these processes; however, Kafka's anxiety about
the fragmentation of vision in the cinema would ultimately lead him to
disregard film as a model for literary production.

Film in the Early Twentieth Century: Spectacle and Immersion

In the history of film, each type of cinema has implied a specific model
of spectatorship predicated on the relation between a physically present
audience and the projected images on the screen. Just as literature presupposes specific properties of the printed book, so film depends on a cinematic space that is both physical and discursive, where film and spectator encounter each other. In the early 1900s, films had been shown in
fairgrounds, cabarets, music halls and other multi-purpose public settings.
They were part of a mixed programme of attractions designed to surprise
and awe, entertain and divert audiences. The films shown in these settings
were very short, lasting at most a couple of minutes. They often documented so-called 'actualities' as for instance the arrival of a train or a factory workers' strike. At the time of its invention, film, the camera and its
projector were seen first as the technological consequences of a diverse set
of scientific and pseudo-scientific practices often directed at entertaining
a mass public, and these short films were not so much meant to *represent*
something as to show what only film could show – even to show *that* film
could show something. Early cinema is therefore often called a cinema of
showing or, in the memorable phrase of film historian Tom Gunning, a
'cinema of attraction'.[2]

Besides non-fictional documentaries, however, there also existed fictional short films, often with fantastic subjects such as Georges Meliès's
famous *Le Voyage dans la Lune* (*Journey to the Moon*, 1902). It is this fictional
and narrative format that was to sow the seeds for film's coming of age in the
1910s. During this decade, film length increased dramatically from the early
short films to full-length feature films, which developed media-specific new
forms of narration and an independent sense of fictionality. Film historians distinguish between four phases, based on film length, in the development of early silent film in the German-speaking countries: (1) very

short films after 1895; (2) short film programmes after the establishment of stationary cinemas ('nickelodeons') in 1905–6; (3) the introduction of narrative long films as part of mixed short- and long-film programmes shown in larger, more established cinemas from around 1910–11; and finally (4) narrative feature films filling an entire programme after the end of the First World War. Within only ten years, the cinema of showing had morphed into a cinema of telling, and the tales it told were fictional.

This development of a 'cinema of narrative integration'[3] was not merely a question of form, as it went along with massive changes in the way that film was shown and viewed, the locales that were used and the audiences who visited them. Across Europe, large and glamorous film 'palaces' opened, and reputable stage actors made their first appearance on the screen, attracting a well-off and educated audience. In Prague, the brothers Ponrepo had operated the first nickelodeon since 1907, showing a mixed programme of short films interspersed with magic tricks they performed themselves. This model was quickly replaced, however, by a number of sumptuously decorated movie theatres which had opened by 1914, of which one, the Bio Lucerna, is still in use today. Max Brod mentioned that he and Kafka often visited these cinemas, especially the Orient. Here silent and immobile spectators were placed at a significantly greater distance from the screen than had been the case in the early nickelodeons. The nickelodeon and its predecessors had produced a mobile and multi-sensory viewing experience that often overwhelmed and elated spectators. The new cinema architecture, in contrast, was based on a sharp distinction between screen space and auditorium space, constructing a uniform and homogeneous perspective for spectators irrespective of their precise position in the auditorium.

Together with other factors, especially the lack of an independent sound track and the complete darkening of the cinema, this spatial set-up led to a passive and contemplative mode of reception whereby an embodied viewing experience was suppressed in favour of an imaginary immersion into the cinematic illusion. The cinema constituted a cultural space with a wholly unprecedented quality of experience, producing a trance-like state of daydreaming. To facilitate this dreamlike immersion, many culturally important and aesthetically ambitious silent films of the period had fantastic plots – for instance *Der Andere* (*The Other*; directed by Max Mack, 1913) or *Der Student von Prag* (*The Student of Prague*; directed by Stellan Rye, 1913). Other factors including the use of sound contributed to the otherworldly quality of early film. For although it did not possess an independent sound track, silent film was almost never really silent. Films were accompanied by live or recorded music and initially also often 'explained' by a narrator. Moreover, films were not exclusively black and white, as around 80 per cent of films were dyed, hand-coloured or stencilled. Even though the early cinema immobilized the spectator and focused on just one sense, it also freed the other senses, producing not solely an optical but a multi-sensory environment. Reception records from the silent film era often emphasize the tactile and auditive dimension of cinematic spectatorship, which were less explicitly subsumed to a dominance of the visual than they are today. Perception in the cinema, then, was never completely passive, as several factors worked together to activate the spectator's imagination.

The cinema did not so much gather an audience that already existed than build and shape individual spectators into an audience so that they returned regularly and made the cinema a focal point of their spare time. In this respect it was the first technical medium to explicitly address a mass audience whose bodies and senses were collectively subjected to a calculated regulation of affects, marking the beginning of twentieth-century mass culture. The movie theatres of the 1910s particularly attracted the new social class of salaried employees, to which Kafka also belonged – a group which regularly had significant amounts of spare time at its disposal and the disposable income to spend on such entertainment. In public discourse, political pamphlets and newspaper articles, anxieties raised by these social changes combined with misgivings about the cultural status of film, culminating in the heated 'cinema debate' of 1913, in which cultural conservatives and public health officials denounced the cinema as a place of loose morals, a meeting point for petty criminals and a breeding ground for bacteria.[4] Reacting against charges of moral depravity and aesthetic inferiority, intellectuals who had paid their first visit to the cinema when films with ambitious screenplays and well-known stage actors were shown in newly opened movie palaces defended film as an innovative medium and called for a more constructive literary response.

Film and Literature

Initially, many contributions to the cinema debate had seen cinema as a rival to the theatre, but it was on literature that the new medium had the largest influence during the 1910s and 20s. This influence was threefold. First, many intellectuals wrote *about* the cinema in their contributions to the cinema debate, in film reviews (the first independent film review appeared in 1913) and in the form of an emerging film theory, for instance

Emilie Altenloh's *Zur Soziologie des Kino* (*On the Sociology of the Cinema*, 1914) or Hugo Münsterberg's *The Photoplay* (1916). Second, literary authors began writing *for* the cinema, producing scenarios and screenplays. Third, authors began to develop new forms of writing inspired by the cinema, such as the poems collected in the anthology *Der selige Kintopp* (*The Blessed Cinema*, 1913–14), which experimented with a cinematic style. In 1913, the critic and journalist Kurt Pinthus invited a group of Expressionist writers to contribute samples of this new writing to a *Kinobuch* (*Cinema Book*). Thirteen authors responded to Pinthus's call for contributions, among them Max Brod, who engaged with the aesthetic possibilities of film in order to present his vision of a cinema of the future – a cinema of intense psychological interiority. Kafka, however, did not contribute to the collection, although he surely must have known about it through Brod if not from Pinthus directly. This is perhaps surprising given his fascination with the cinema, but also symptomatic of his indirect, often circuitous approach to film and its literary relevance.

'The onlookers go rigid when the train goes past' ('Die Zuschauer erstarren, wenn der Zug vorbeifährt'; *D* 9/ *TB* 9). Thus reads the very first sentence of Kafka's surviving diary. We do not know what event prompted Kafka to make this observation. However, the reference to spectators seems to point towards a cinematic context and has led Hanns Zischler and the scholars who have followed him to read the sentence as a remark about the movies. We can only speculate whether the sentence relates to the famous episode – now cast into doubt by some film historians – where an audience fled the nickelodeon in terror as a train, filmed by the Lumières, drew into the station of La Ciotat (southern France). What is certain is that Kafka's sentence deals with an overwhelming visual perception and with the writer's uncertainty about how to physically react to this experience.

Kafka does not simply describe cinematic experience, as many of his contemporaries had done, but contrasts it with a second observation, this time about writing, and thus turns the experience of film into a means of reflecting on his own writing process. His second sentence reads, '"If he should forever ahsk me." The *ah*, released from the sentence, flew off like a ball on the meadow' ('"Wenn er mich immer frägt" das ä losgelöst vom Satz flog dahin wie ein Ball auf der Wiese'; *D* 9/ *TB* 9). Here, the reconditioning of human perception in the cinema is transposed onto the level of writing, using the experience of speed, which was associated with the cinema as well as with modern modes of transportation, as a way of envisaging new modes of literary production.

Kafka's early works frequently reference speed and acceleration, a common theme in literary modernism when the experience of railway and automobile travel was increasingly simulated by the technical media and thereby detached from immediate physical sensation. Film, which developed in close conjunction with a more general modernization of human perception, takes up the topic of speedy movement by showing traffic scenes and car chases while also contributing to the formation of a new, faster perception. This new cinematic experience was in turn embedded in the modern city, where shop-window displays, billboard advertisements and news columns had to be swiftly deciphered as pedestrians negotiated the urban traffic. Film fascinated Kafka precisely for its capacity to alter and expand human perception, yet its velocity appeared to him to pose a threat both to the form of writing that he practised and to the subjectivity of the writer.[5] However, his reaction to film is never specific to the medium, but forms part of a larger attempt to re-imagine literary writing in the age of acceleration and *flânerie*, fashion and consumption.

Among Kafka's early texts, the prose miniatures of *Betrachtung* (*Meditation*, 1912) and the fragmentary novel *Der Verschollene* (*The Man who Disappeared*, 1912–14) are particularly rich in descriptions of urban traffic and transportation. Although they make no direct reference to the cinema, these texts often seem to cite film scenes or to simulate cinematic tracking shots, transposing the movement of the depicted scene onto the mode of its description – a daring technique at a time when the film camera was still largely stationary. The depiction of the American city in *The Man who Disappeared*, the importance of travel and movement, and the use of exaggerated mimics and gestures typical of silent film acting are particularly suggestive of a cinematic context. If it is read as an indirect commentary on the cinema, however, the novel's conclusions are deeply critical. Bit by bit, its protagonist, Karl Rossmann, loses all his belongings, his social identity and, finally, even his name before disappearing into the American West.

So does the dream world of the cinema lead to a loss of critical subjectivity? This danger was certainly discussed by many of Kafka's contemporaries. In his *Nachlaß zu Lebzeiten* (*Posthumous Papers of a Living Author*, 1936), Robert Musil compared cinematic spectatorship to gazing through a looking glass, arguing that the fragmentation of vision and its isolation of details led to a loss of human form. Building on insights from empirical psychology, Musil came to the conclusion that the cinema changed human vision profoundly and that this also necessitated a new literary conception of subjectivity. Kafka appears to arrive at a similar judgement when noting his emotional reaction to a cinema visit, writing in an abbreviated style of description that he was in the process of developing in his diaries:

> Was at the cinema. Cried. 'Lolotte'. The good minister. The little bicycle. The reconciliation of the parents. Boundless entertainment. Before it, a sad film, 'The Accident on the Dock', after it, the gay 'Alone at Last'. Am entirely empty and insensible, the passing tram has more living feeling. (20 November 1913; *D* 238/ *TB* 595)

The same kind of short verbless sentences that are used to record the film's plot are here employed when describing the numbness and emptiness of the spectator as he emerges from the dark cinema into the urban traffic. The hypnotism of the cinema appears to pose a grave danger to the creative imagination of its spectator.

Like Musil, Kafka drew comparisons with older optical technologies in charting the consequences of cinematic spectatorship for literary writing. In his travel diary of 1911, he describes a business trip to the industrial town of Friedland in northern Bohemia. Searching for entertainment and distraction, Kafka had chanced upon an establishment with which he was familiar from his youth: the *Kaiserpanorama* (Imperial Paronama). An optical apparatus originating in the nineteenth century, the *Kaiserpanorama* consisted of a revolving rotunda similar to a peep show that presented the spectator with a series of stereoscopic views, often of landscapes and tourist attractions. Kafka's diary entry contrasts this outdated institution to the cinema, coming to a conclusion that at first seems to favour the *Kaiser-panorama*: 'The pictures more alive than in the cinema because they offer the eye all the repose of reality. The cinema communicates the restlessness of its motion to the things pictured in it; the repose of the gaze would seem to be more important' (January/February 1911; *D* 430/ *TB* 937).

Faced with the alternative between the velocity of the cinema and the demands it made on human perception on the one hand, and the reduced speed of the *Kaiserpanorama* on the other, Kafka opts for the latter. This is also a decision for the demands of human perception over the realism of representation: the cinema is judged to adequately represent a modern speed culture ('the restlessness of its motion'), but the *Kaiserpanorama* corresponds more closely to the human gaze. However, Kafka's diary entry does not end with this conclusion, but formulates a utopian synthesis between the two media: 'Why can't they combine the cinema and stereoscope in this way?' (January/February 1911; *D* 430/ *TB* 937). In light of this vision, the miniatures in Kafka's first book, *Meditation*, can be read as experimenting with a mobile – yet not too speedy – subject position and with a writing style that places itself in between cinema and *Kaiserpanorama*, or else in between the active spectatorship of the cinema of attraction and the more passive, dreamlike reception of the narrative cinema. Indeed, the composition of *Meditation* resembles the serial programming of the cinema of attraction, and its stories contain many typical scenes from the early movies. Yet these are never seen on the screen, but only in the dreams and visions of characters and narrators – a mental film which bypasses the alternative between cinema and *Kaiserpanorama*, paving the way for Kafka's dreamlike later texts.

NOTES

1 H. Zischler, *Kafka goes to the Movies*, trans. S. H. Gillespie (University of Chicago Press, 2003); C. Duttlinger, *Kafka and Photography* (Oxford University Press, 2007); P.-A. Alt, *Kafka und der Film: Über kinematographisches Erzählen* (Munich: C. H. Beck, 2009).
2 See Gunning's groundbreaking article for the important distinction between 'cinema of attraction' and 'cinema of narrative integration': 'The Cinema of Attraction: Early Film, Its Spectator, and the Avantgarde' in T. Elsaesser (ed.), *Early Cinema: Space, Frame, Narrative* (London: BFI Publishing, 1990), pp. 229–35.
3 Gunning, 'The Cinema of Attraction', p. 232.
4 Original sources are collected in J. Schweinitz, *Prolog vor dem Film: Nachdenken über ein neues Medium 1909–1914* (Leipzig: Reclam, 1992).
5 Duttlinger, *Kafka and Photography*, pp. 33–61.

CHAPTER 13

Photography

J. J. Long

Before Kafka

On 27 January 1839, a report on the invention of the daguerreotype was published in the German-language Prague newspaper *Bohemia*. In the same year a Prague physics professor, Ferdinand Hessler (1803–65), published instructions for preparing daguerreotypes in a yearbook for trade and science, and was himself the first producer of daguerreotypes in Bohemia.[1] Vilém Horn had opened the first permanent photographic portrait studio in what is now Wenceslas Square in Prague in 1840. He went on to found the first German-language photographic periodical, *Photographisches Journal*, which was launched in 1854, and set up the first photographic supplies business in Europe.[2] Prague scientists also made major contributions to photographic processes: Jakub Husník developed the collotype process in the 1860s, and Karl Klič perfected the photogravure process in 1878. By the time of Franz Kafka's birth in 1883, his home city had become a major international photographic centre, and the business of photography flourished: portrait studios abounded, exhibitions were frequent and there was a lively trade in landscape prints, albums and postcards.

The *Kaiserpanorama*

Kafka's engagement with photography was dominated by vernacular forms: postcards, newspapers, studio portraits, cinema stills, stereoscopic views and holiday snaps. Kafka's diary description of a visit to the *Kaiserpanorama* (Imperial Paronama) in the north Bohemian town of Friedland crystallizes the key questions that emerge throughout his writings on photography. The *Kaiserpanorama* was a form of popular entertainment consisting of a cylindrical wooden column, some five metres in diameter and accommodating up to twenty-five viewing stations. A spectator seated at one of these could observe a changing display of fifty stereoscopic views. As

Carolin Duttlinger points out, the *Kaiserpanorama* involved a combination of discipline and spectacle: the body of the observer was fixed in space, his or her eyes pressed to the brass eye-pieces of the viewing station. At the same time, the individual nature of viewing and the slow replacement of one image by the next allowed for contemplation of the image that was not entirely determined by the apparatus. Duttlinger also notes that the *Kaiserpanorama* involved multi-sensory perception: the show Kafka describes was accompanied by music from a kind of mechanical organ called an Ariston, while the three-dimensional nature of stereoscopic viewing enhanced the haptic dimensions of visual experience.[3]

Central to the *Kaiserpanorama*'s appeal was travel: viewers could experience faraway places from their fixed location, as Kafka himself noted in a postcard to Max Brod: 'I went to the Imperial Panorama and saw Brescia, Mantua, and Cremona' (2 February 1911; *LFFE* 71/*Br* 132). In naming these three northern Italian cities, Kafka refers back to a visit made by Brod to the *Kaiserpanorama* in Prague just a month before Kafka writes his postcard. In his diary, Brod mentions the same three cities, which were known to both writers from their trip to Italy in 1909.[4] In mentioning the *Kaiserpanorama*, then, Kafka reinforces a friendship by evoking shared and multi-layered memories that combine the experiences of travel and of commodified representations of distant scenes. Spectacle, travel, the role of the haptic in visual perception, the perpetuation of affective ties and the mnemonic resources of the photograph are recurrent themes in Kafka's engagement with photography.

Kafka and the Postcard

Austria was the first country in the world to introduce postcards. An article by Viennese economics professor Erich Hermann, 'On a new kind of postal correspondence', appeared in the Viennese daily *Neue Freie Presse* on 26 January 1869.[5] Hermann's argument is predominantly economic: postcards would rationalize correspondence. But he also suggests that the elaborate formality of letter-writing would give way to a new, telegraphic communication style. The Austro-Hungarian postal service quickly implemented Hermann's proposals: postcards were introduced on 1 October 1869, and within a month sales had reached one-and-a-half million.[6] By 1895, picture postcards bearing the legend 'Gruß aus...' or 'Greetings from...' had become both popular and ubiquitous. By the end of the nineteenth century, buying and sending postcards from tourist destinations had become a Europe-wide craze, especially in the German-speaking world.[7] While some early commentators lamented the fact that authentic and unmediated experience had become impossible in the age of the picture postcard,[8] recent scholars of visual culture have recognized that postcards do not necessarily function in this way.[9] The key thing is what people *do with* postcards, and how they function within the practice of everyday life.

Almost all of Kafka's postcards were sent while he was travelling. Not only holiday resorts and tourist destinations, but numerous little provincial Bohemian towns had their own postcards, as did hotels, restaurants, even sanatoria. Kafka's correspondence ostensibly corroborates the fear that even the most trivial of objects had become commodified by means of photographic representation: no matter how insignificant a place, its image is offered for sale. But it also shows how mass-produced commercial objects can become the vehicle for constructions of intimacy, evocations of presence and occasions for reflection on the nature of postcard correspondence itself.

Comparison with Kafka's letters shows that he modified his writing style on postcards: he uses shorter sentences, sporadically neglects German punctuation rules and truncates syntax. Indeed, there are occasions where the picture on the postcard partially or completely removes the need for the written word, while in other cases text and image enter into creative new configurations. Some early Kafka postcards have no message at all beyond a signature. A postcard sent to his sister Elli from the Baltic island resort of Norderney on 24 August 1901 shows a tranquil seascape, and bears the printed caption 'Greetings from Norderney/After the storm' ('Gruß aus Nordeney/Nach dem Sturm'). It is signed, simply, 'Franz' on the picture side (*B1* 10). The signature establishes Kafka's presence at the site depicted, proclaiming 'I was here.' Language is used not to convey information, but phatically, for social or emotive purposes. Here, the signature complements the printed greeting in order to reinforce an intimate bond.

Linked to this is Kafka's tendency to make the photographic image the subject of his correspondence. As Esther Milne argues, picture postcards operate within an economy of immediacy: 'The picture . . . encourages the idea that sender and recipient share the same view.'[10] Kafka at times invokes, at times undermines this assumption. In a postcard to his sister Ottla from Weimar on 3 July 1912, he writes: 'Dear Ottla, Of course I am writing to you too, and how gladly. And am sending you the beautiful house of Frau von Stein, where last night we sat for a long time on the rim of the well' (*LOF* 6/*B1* 156). Charlotte von Stein's house is one of the best-known tourist landmarks in Weimar, and the postcard reproduces a conventional tourist sight. But Kafka appropriates this anonymous, mass-produced object in order to create a sense of intimacy at a distance. It is telling that he talks about the image as if it were the thing itself rather than a representation, thereby implying that Ottla can partake of the presence of the object and see it as Kafka did.

And yet there are also moments where this assumption of shared viewing is vertiginously undercut. On 20 December 1909, Kafka sends Ottla a postcard depicting the grand synagogue in Pilsen (*LOF* 3/*Bi* 114; image 463). The same day, though, he sends another postcard, this time an aerial view of Pilsen's Kopecky Promenade, with the synagogue prominent but now visible as part of a larger urban ensemble: 'You mustn't think that the synagogue is the centre of Pilsen, as one might deduce from my previous cards' (*Bi* 115). Through this succession of postcards, Kafka questions photographic referentiality, highlighting instead the capacity of photography to convey entirely misleading impressions. But he also undermines the assumption that the sender and recipient of the postcard have the same view of the object, asserting the primacy of his own, embodied, experience of place over its representation, while also ironically commenting on the status of Jewish sites in Pilsen. As a writer of picture postcards, then, Kafka was adept at turning mass-produced images into highly individual tokens of presence and intimacy, while self-reflexively drawing attention to the limits of this process.

The Social Life of Photographs

By stressing questions of intimacy and presence, my focus has been less on what photographs *depict* than on what they *do*, the work they perform within social life. This performative function of photography is nowhere more evident than in Kafka's long-distance relationship with Felice Bauer. On 20 September 1912, Kafka writes to her for the first time, re-introducing himself after the couple's first meeting on 13 August 1912.

> My name is Franz Kafka, and I am the person who greeted you for the first time that evening at Director Brod's in Prague, the one who subsequently handed you across the table, one by one, photographs of the Thalia trip, and who finally, with the very hand now striking the keys, held your hand, the one which confirmed a promise to accompany him next year to Palestine. (*LF* 13/*Bi* 170)

In a subsequent letter of 27 October 1912, he includes a lengthy description of the evening, in which the photographs played a central role: 'Handing round the Thalia photographs made for a very pleasant diversion . . . You took looking at the pictures very seriously, and glanced up only when Otto gave some explanation or I handed you another picture' (27 October 1912; *LF* 24/*B1* 193). The term 'Thalia photographs' refers to Kafka and Brod's sojourn in Weimar the previous month, as part of a 'Thalia Tour' run by the Austrian Lloyd travel company.[11] This episode inaugurates a correspondence that involves the frequent exchange and interpretation of photographs; as Duttlinger notes, Kafka develops a fetishistic obsession with these images, and his response to them oscillates between eroticism and melancholia.[12] But in terms of the photographic context in which Kafka lived and wrote, the social life of photographs is as important as their psychosexual aspects.

The content of the Thalia images is irrelevant in this exchange; the photographs are important because they facilitate a particular kind of sociability. Passing photographs of one's travels from hand to hand while talking about them was, until recently, common in the West, and remains so in the developing world.[13] It demonstrates the imbrication of vision, orality and tactility in the everyday practice of viewing photographs. Seeing, touching and speaking about images facilitate the expression and experience of an interpretive community and thereby constitute the social group. In his letters, Kafka repeatedly emphasizes photography's role in the development and consolidation of social bonds.

Kafka's first letter to Felice, for example, links the handling of photographs to the holding of Felice's hand to the typing of the letter in a complex relay that invokes the haptic in order to create a sense of corporeal presence across time and distance. As Kafka's correspondence with Felice progresses, he repeatedly foregrounds the capacity of photographs to evoke the absent body less as visual representations than as tactile material objects. Kafka carries a photograph of Felice as a little girl in his breast pocket on a business journey to Kratzau, calling her a 'charming little companion' (25 November 1912; *LF* 84/*B1* 267), and later carries Felice's adult portrait around in his hand (26 December 1912; *LF* 151/*B1* 362). He kisses a photograph of Felice (as he frequently also does with her letters), and puckers his mouth in anticipation of the next photograph (25/26 December 1912; *LF* 150/*B1* 361). He compares the emergence of a photograph from its envelope with the eventual descent of Felice herself from a train, as if rehearsing the moment of face-to-face meeting in paper form (2/3 December 1912; *LF* 103/*B1* 293), and takes a photograph of Felice to bed with him (15 December 1912; *LF* 128/*B1* 333). The theme of hands emerges again when Kafka receives a letter with a photograph from Felice during his sister Valli's wedding. 'I felt', he writes, 'as though you were squeezing my hand' (12/13

January 1913; *LF* 182/*B2* 37). Throughout the courtship of Felice, then, it is not just the content but the materiality of the image that is significant: photography's status as a technology of presence relies in part on the way photos are carried, touched, and kissed, which constitutes the social life of the image.

Photographs in Fiction

Mass-produced images from illustrated publications provided Kafka with source material for several of his fictions.[14] The specific mode of Kafka's engagement with photographic publications in his writing was facilitated by advances in printing technologies developed around the time of his birth. The reproduction of photographs in newspapers and printed books had been made possible by the development of the half-tone process, a form of photomechanical etching that allowed photographic images to be printed on the same block as moveable type. This led to the expansion of the illustrated periodical press and the possibility of cheap photographically illustrated books, such as Arthur Holitscher's 1911 travelogue *Amerika: Heute und Morgen* (*America: Today and Tomorrow*), which provided Kafka with material for *Der Verschollene* (*The Man who Disappeared*).

But photographs are important beyond their status as source material. Within Kafka's texts, photographs – snapshots as well as studio portraits – are looked at, handled, lost, exchanged and discussed. They crystallize central questions of identity, intimacy, desire and power as well as articulating historically specific conditions of bourgeois Jewish life.

Studio portraits from late-nineteenth- and early-twentieth-century Prague are generally indistinguishable from studio portraits made elsewhere in Europe at the time: there was widespread standardization in terms of props and pose, testifying to the increasing homogenization of the ways in which bourgeois identity was imagined and represented.[15] The many extant photographs of Kafka and his family, as well as the family photographs described in his writings, are entirely typical of the bourgeois portraits of the age. Karl Rossmann describes a photograph of his parents in which his mother has sunk into an armchair while his father stands erect, one hand on the chair, one clenched in a fist placed on an illustrated book on a decorative table (*MD* 69/*V* 134). The conventional markers of bourgeois photographic identity are fully apparent: the gender hierarchy implied by the standing man and seated woman, the domestic interior signified by the armchair and occasional table, the book as a symbol of education, and the static hand positions that signal the subordination of the body to the mind (even if the father's fist suggests that this subordination is achieved through an effort of will). This kind of domestic portraiture constituted a means of regulating conduct and reproducing ideologies of class, gender and kinship.

The images in *The Man who Disappeared* foreground photography's role in sustaining these ideologies at a time of increasing mobility: in Kafka's America, a country populated by exiled Europeans, family photography becomes a symbolic surrogate for the geographically dispersed, extended family. In Karl Rossmann's case, this symbolic function is threatened by the loss or theft of the only photograph he has of his parents (*MD* 85–6/ *V* 166–9), which contributes to Rossmann's increasing sense of powerlessness and disorientation.

Looking at some photographs in the salon of the head cook in the Hotel Occidental, Rossmann's eye is caught by a portrait of a soldier, which, like the other photographs on display, he assumes to be of European origin. It is a 'picture of a young soldier who had put his cap on a small table and was standing to attention with his wild black hair and was filled with proud but suppressed laughter' (*MD* 90/ *V* 177). A soldier portrait is also prominent in *Die Verwandlung* (*The Metamorphosis*): as Gregor Samsa, the recently metamorphosed insectoid protagonist, looks out of his bedroom across the family living room, he sees a photograph of himself 'from his time in the reserve hung on the wall, showing him as a lieutenant' ('aus seiner Militärzeit, die ihn als Leutnant darstellte'; *M* 39/*DL* 134–5). The immediate context of these images is the role of the Habsburg military in the closing years of the empire. By the time Kafka came to compose *The Man who Disappeared* (written 1912–14) and *The Metamorphosis* (written 1912, published 1915), nationalist movements within Austria-Hungary were exerting increasing centrifugal pressure on the Habsburg 'state of many nations'. Throughout this time, the Common Army, so-called to distinguish it from the Hungarian *Honvéd* and the Austrian *Landwehr*, remained a supra-national bastion of loyalty to the Emperor, in which nationalist sentiment and ethnic animosity were largely absent. Two aspects of this are particularly relevant to Kafka. The first is that the Common Army was positively receptive to Jewish soldiers, and did not tolerate the expression of antisemitic views.[16] While Jews were underrepresented in the regular army, they were massively overrepresented in the Reserve Officer corps, and it is perhaps telling that in an early draft of *The Metamorphosis* (and in the published translation), the photograph is said to depict Gregor as a 'reserve lieutenant' (*DLA* 212). The second is that although the proportion of Czechs in the Common Army was less than in the population overall, they were by far the best-represented national group after Germans and Hungarians.

Figure 4 Fairground novelty photograph of Kafka with (left to right): Albert Ehrenstein, Otto Pick and Lise Kaznelson, Vienna Prater, 1913.

In the work of a German-speaking Czech-Jewish writer in the late-Habsburg era, then, descriptions of soldier photographs dramatize not only the role of social convention in identity-formation but also questions of national, ethnic and religious identities. The ceremonial identity presented in military portraits constitutes a compensation for the fact that genuine popular adherence to the empire was waning. Arguably such portraits are also markers of successful Jewish assimilation, but this is not untroubled. For Gregor's metamorphosis can be seen as a literalization of the antisemitic metaphor of the unassimilated Jew as vermin ('Ungeziefer'). Gregor's gazing at his own soldier portrait thus suggests that the values of national loyalty and cultural assimilation represented by military service are no protection against the immediate and seemingly arbitrary transformation back into verminhood.

After Kafka

One of the best-known photographs of Kafka is a novelty photograph taken at the Prater pleasure park in Vienna (see Figure 4). It shows Kafka, Otto Pick, Alfred Ehrenstein and Lise Kaznelson. Kafka and his companions are seated behind a painted aeroplane flying over Vienna's *Riesenrad* (giant

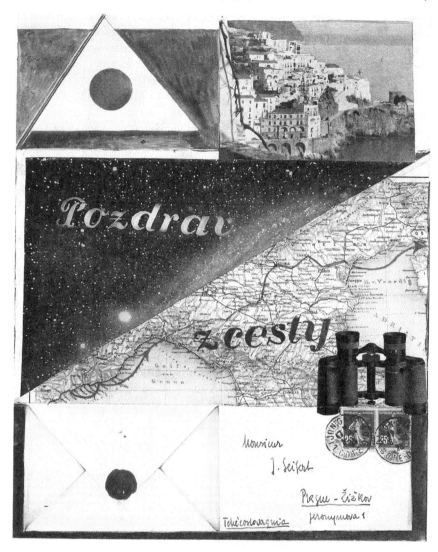

Figure 5 Karel Teige, *Greetings from a Journey* (1923).

Ferris wheel). On the face of it, this is merely a conventional, kitschy product of the entertainment industry. But its self-evidently constructed and
artificial nature presages the montage techniques that became the signature of the interwar photographic avant-garde.

While Kafka's writings betray no interest in art photography, the Czech avant-garde was fascinated by many of the same themes that characterize Kafka's engagement with the medium, the difference being that they engaged *visually* with popular photographic culture, self-reflexively deploying its own visual forms to comment on the salient features of European modernity. In the interwar period, photomontages by members of the avant-garde Devětsil group deployed maps, envelopes, photographs, prints and postcard-style text in a disjunctive, dynamic way, as exemplified by two montages produced in the final years of Kafka's life: Karel Teige's *Greetings from a Journey* (1923; see Figure 5) and Jindřich Štyrský's *Souvenir* (1924). These are ostensibly far removed from the photographs Kafka uses, describes and discusses. But Kafka and the Devětsil group share an understanding of the centrality of photography to questions of travel, memory, communication and the construction of intimacy at a distance. Kafka's engagement with photography may not have been radical, but it was entirely of its time.

NOTES

1 *Jahrbuch für Fabrikanten und Gewerbetreibende, Physiker, Chemiker, Techniker, Pharmacenten, Oekonomen u.s.w.* (Prague: Vereine zur Ermunterung des Gewerbsgeistes in Böhmen, 1840 [1839]).

2 On early Czech photography, see R. Skopec, 'Bohemia, Moravia and Slovakia', *History of Photography*, 2 (1978), 141–53, P. Tausk, 'Josef Sudek: His Life and Work', *History of Photography*, 6 (1982), 29–58, and www.schaufler.cz.

3 C. Duttlinger, *Kafka and Photography* (Oxford University Press, 2007), pp. 55, 58.

4 See the commentary to the letter of 2 February 1911; *B1* 481.

5 E. H[erman]n, 'Über eine neue Art der Corresondenz mittels der Post', *Neue Freie Presse*, 26 January 1869.

6 See R. Carline, *Pictures in the Post: The Story of the Picture Postcard and its Place in the History of Popular Art* (London: Gordon Fraser, 1971), p. 37 and F. Staff, *The Picture Postcard and its Origins* (London: Lutterworth, 1979), pp. 45–6.

7 See Carline, *Pictures in the Post*, p. 40; Staff, *The Picture Postcard*, pp. 57–60.

8 Staff, *The Picture Postcard*, p. 79.

9 D. Crouch and N. Lübbren, 'Introduction' in D. Crouch and N. Lübbren (eds.), *Visual Culture and Tourism* (Oxford: Berg, 2003), pp. 1–21: 11; E. Milne, *Letters, Postcards, Email: Technologies of Presence* (New York: Routledge, 2010), pp. 115–34; C. M. Geary and V.-L. Webb, 'Introduction: Views on Postcards' in C. M. Geary and V.-L. Webb (eds.), *Delivering Views: Distant Cultures in Early Postcards* (Washington, DC: Smithsonian Institution Press, 1998), pp. 1–12: 4.

10 Milne, *Letters, Postcards, Email*, p. 110.

11 See the commentary to the letter of 20 September 1912; *B1* 522.

12 Duttlinger, *Kafka and Photography*, pp. 125–72.

13 For an introduction to the issues raised in this paragraph, see E. Edwards, 'Thinking Photography beyond the Visual?' in J. J. Long, A. Noble and E. Welch (eds.), *Photography: Theoretical Snapshots* (Abingdon: Routledge, 2009), pp. 31–48.

14 See Duttlinger, *Kafka and Photography*, pp. 112, 212–13, 233. Duttlinger also identifies the probable photographic prototypes for the ekphrastic evocations of Rossmann's family (pp. 88, 91) and the Nature Theatre of Oklahoma (p. 97).

15 On studios, see H. Baden Pritchard, *The Photographic Studios of Europe* (London: Piper and Carter, 1882).

16 M. Berger, *Eisernes Kreuz, Doppeladler, Davidstern: Juden in deutschen und öster-reichischen Armeen: Der Militärdienst jüdischer Soldaten durch zwei Jahrhunderte* (Berlin: trafo, 2010–13), pp. 107–12.

CHAPTER 14

Music

Thomas Martinec

Music plays a vital role in many of Kafka's texts throughout his literary career. In *Die Verwandlung* (*The Metamorphosis*, 1912), Gregor's sister playing the violin marks the turning point of the narrative, for it causes the encounter of the three lodgers with the beetle, which ultimately makes Gregor's parents decide to get rid of him (*M* 65–9/*DL* 183–93). In the story 'Ein Landarzt' ('A Country Doctor', 1917) the eponymous protagonist is confronted with his own death sentence, performed as 'an utterly simple melody' by a school choir (*HA* 16 /*DL* 259). Karl Rossmann in *Der Verschollene* (*The Man who Disappeared*, 1912–14) plays the piano several times in the novel, and in *Der Process* (*The Trial*, 1914–15) K. wonders why the priest's sermon in the cathedral is not introduced by the church organ (*T* 149/*P* 284). Indeed, the close and precarious relationship between music and silence is also the theme of three later texts: 'Das Schweigen der Sirenen' ('The Silence of the Sirens', 1917), a radical rewriting of Homer's myth about the destructive power of the sirens' song in *The Odyssey*; 'Forschungen eines Hundes' ('Investigations of a Dog', 1922), where the dog narrator's 'research' is triggered by a disturbing musical experience; and 'Josefine, die Sängerin oder Das Volk der Mäuse' ('Josefine, the Singer or The Mouse People', 1924), which explores the (unanswerable) question of whether Josefine is a true musician or merely whistles like an ordinary mouse.

Musical Aesthetics from the Eighteenth to the Twentieth Century: Transcendence and Anxiety

Kafka's texts repeatedly present music as something close to the protagonists' hearts and yet radically, disturbingly alien; as both mysteriously inaccessible and overwhelmingly immediate. In this they echo various discourses on music and musical experience from the late eighteenth century onwards, most of which also have literary implications. In his *Herzensergießungen eines kunstliebenden Klosterbruders* (*Confessions from the*

Heart of an Art-Loving Friar, 1787) and *Phantasien über die Kunst, für Fre-
unde der Kunst* (*Fantasies on Art for Friends of Art*, 1799), two core texts
of early German Romanticism, Wilhelm Heinrich Wackenroder (1773–98)
developed a concept that later was to be named 'absolute music'.[1] The idea
was that music creates an intimate link to areas that were hard to capture
with words, in other words emotions and transcendental spheres, because
unlike literature, music does not have to *describe* these areas with words
that always fall short of the objects they refer to; instead we can feel love,
anger, fear, etc. by listening to music, because its aesthetic means are able
to express all this in an immediate manner. The same holds true for transcendence: according to the concept of 'absolute music', a symphony, for
instance, gives listeners emotional insight into and access to divine spheres
by letting them experience what cannot be described.

Being linked to the 'absolute', music even becomes a new religion, a
'Kunstreligion'. In nineteenth-century philosophy, the unique status of
music was reflected by Schopenhauer's idea that music is the only immediate articulation of the 'will', whereas all other ways of aesthetic expression
can only imitate objects that are generated by this will; as he puts it, the
world is 'embodied music' (*Die Welt als Wille und Vorstellung*/ *The World as
Will and Representation*, 1818).

But the great power ascribed to music in nineteenth-century aesthetics
and philosophy also led to a significant degree of anxiety, for the overwhelming effect of music was seen to pose a threat to the listener. Wackenroder describes the power of music as an act of violence to which the listener
must surrender, for the soul is incapable of resisting its sensual temptations.
Thus the listener is trapped: elevation and surrender are but two sides of
the same coin.[2] The above-mentioned episode of Ulysses and the sirens in
Homer's *Odyssey* is an ancient example of this fear that was to become a key
concern in German Romanticism. Later in the century Friedrich Nietzsche
(1844–1900) gave the overwhelming effect of music, which he describes as
Dionysian power, a more positive turn. In *Die Geburt der Tragödie aus dem
Geiste der Musik* (*The Birth of Tragedy from the Spirit of Music*, 1872) he
identifies the enthusiastic and overwhelming power of music as the origin
of Attic tragedy and laments its loss through the emphasis on reason in the
course of the philosophical development.

The Birth of Tragedy also demonstrates that the power of music played an
important role in literary discourse; after all, Nietzsche refers to music in
order to discuss a literary genre. Independent of this highly philosophical
approach, literary aesthetics had always featured an interest in music, not
least because language contains a musical dimension in that sound, rhythm

and melody are important qualities of poetic language. In early Romanticism, this interest in the musical dimension of the text was intensified, as writers were keen to benefit from the potentials of 'absolute music' by emphasizing the musical dimension of literature. Romantic texts are full of music, songs, musicians and musical instruments, and euphony ('Wohlklang') of the text plays an important role. Later in the century, Richard Wagner (1813–83) continued to make the boundaries between literature and music even more permeable: in *Oper und Drama* (1852), for instance, he discusses his concept of the total work of art ('Gesamtkunstwerk'), in which literature and music (as well as other disciplines) form one great unity.

In Kafka's lifetime, musical aesthetics underwent a radical change, marked by an attempt to free music from its most fundamental formal features and conventions. In his *Entwurf zu einer neuen Ästhetik der Tonkunst* (*Sketch of a New Aesthetic of Music*, 1907), Ferruccio Busoni (1866–1924) distinguishes between 'real' music and 'musical art' ('Tonkunst'). The latter he regards as marred by dogmatism, both on the technical side of composition and with regard to what constitutes musicality more generally (that is to say the ability to play an instrument, to understand harmonics, etc.). In contrast to these traditional notions, Busoni argues for a new kind of music able to capture 'eternal harmony'. To that end he seeks to extend the means of musical expression even further than composers such as Gustav Mahler (1860–1911) and Anton Bruckner (1824–96): rhythmical and harmonical patterns are being extended, silence is becoming very important (before, during and after a piece of music) and the basic distinction between sound as periodical movement and noise as a non-periodical one is questioned. Arnold Schönberg's (1874–1951) twelve-tone-music and the composers of the Second Vienna School (Schönberg, Alban Berg, Anton Webern and others) formed the first peak of a development aimed at reinventing the aesthetic foundations of music.

Yet music is also debated within a very different, cultural-anthropological context. At its core lies the question of both Jewish identity and antisemitism. Music plays an important role in religious and secular traditions of Judaism. Since the fifteenth century, klezmer music has been a vital component of various Jewish festivities. At the same time, Jews found themselves confronted with the antisemitic stereotype that they lacked musicality. In his notorious treatise *Das Judenthum in der Musik* (*Judaism in Music*, 1850), Richard Wagner attacks the sound of Jewish speech as intolerably jumbled and almost incomprehensible, in order to then conclude: 'Now, if the aforesaid qualities of his dialect make the Jew almost incapable of giving artistic enunciation to his feelings and beholdings through *talk*, for such an enunciation through *song* his aptitudes must needs be infinitely smaller.'³

Kafka and Music: Distance and Encounter

Kafka's personal attitude towards music forms an important context of music in his texts. Kafka was, by his own admission, completely unmusical. After his visit to a concert in which works by Johannes Brahms (1833–97) were performed, he noted in his diary: 'The essence of my unmusicalness consists in my inability to enjoy music connectedly, it only now and then has an effect on me, and how seldom it is a musical one' (13 December 1911; *D* 176/ *TB* 291). A few months later, Kafka sent a poem to Felice Bauer that had been sung several times by a choir during his stay in a sanatorium. After briefly commenting on the text, Kafka goes on: 'If only I could keep the tune in my head, but I have no memory for music' (17/18 November 1912; *LF* 48/ *Br* 243). In retrospect, Max Brod confirms that his best friend 'was lacking a genuine musical talent... Kafka did not play any instrument... I would sometimes drag him to concerts, but I soon gave up since the impressions they made on him were of a purely visual nature.'⁴

The striking significance of music in Kafka's texts demonstrates that his unmusical predisposition cannot simply be regarded as a mere absence of music. Instead, Kafka felt urged to take a stand in a discursive environment in which music was highly significant in many ways. Thus he employs musical incompetence to justify his exclusive focus on writing:

> When it became clear in my organism that writing was the most productive direction for my being to take, everything rushed in that direction and left empty all those abilities which were directed toward the joys of sex, eating, drinking, philosophical reflection and above all music. (3 January 1912; *D* 211/ *TB* 341)⁵

With regard to musical performances, Kafka was aware of the overwhelming effect they can have: 'The natural effect of music on me is to circumscribe me with a wall, and its only constant influence on me is that, confined in this way, I am different from what I am when free' (13 December 1911; *D* 176/ *TB* 291). It is also worth mentioning that Kafka was extremely sensitive to noise.⁶ In a famous letter to his friend Felix Weltsch in November 1917, he describes a night in which his sleep was disturbed by the noise of mice: 'What a terribly silent, noisy people this is' (*LFFE* 168/ *B3* 365). Kafka's distance to music and noise is counterbalanced by various encounters with music. Together with Max Brod, Kafka visited some thirty performances of the Yiddish theatre in the winter of 1911–12, in which music was performed as well; here Kafka believed to have found the more authentic kind of Judaism his parents had not passed on to him.[7] But he also encountered the ambivalence of music in his reading of Franz Grill-parzer's novella *Der arme Spielmann* (*The Poor Fiddler*, 1848). This is a tale about an old man who has dedicated his entire life to playing the violin after the woman he loved had married another man; however, although the fiddler seems to find some kind of fulfilment in his playing, the tunes he produces are completely dissonant and terrible to listen to.

Kafka's Texts: Music and Silence

Kafka's literary texts echo both the author's own attitude and the discourses on music and musical experience outlined above. To begin with, music is shown to lead to a higher level of life, inaccessible to reasonable investi-gation. When Gregor Samsa is listening to his sister playing the violin, he wonders: 'Was he a beast, that music should move him like this? He felt as if the way to the unknown nourishment he longed for was being revealed' (*M* 66/*DL* 185). The implication that one has to be an animal in order to be deeply moved by music suggests that music functions as a 'pure' lan-guage, unspoiled by cultural convention; thus it is also able to point to the 'unknown nourishment' as something close to the 'absolute'. This idea is taken up later in 'Forschungen eines Hundes' ('Investigations of a Dog', 1922), in which animals are again presented as having an intimate connec-tion to music. The narrator comments on his recollection of the seven dogs performing an ecstatic dance: 'At the time I still knew almost nothing of the musicality granted solely to the tribe of dogs' (*HA* 123/*NSII* 428). As in the Romantic tradition, this musicality turns out to be unexplainable: although the experience with the seven dogs leads the 'Forscherhund' to dedicate his entire life to analysing and explaining the behaviour of his race, he ultimately proves to be unable to fulfil his task.

As one of Kafka's most important texts on music, 'Forschungen' also illustrates yet another aspect of the musical discourse since early Romanticism. The overwhelming power of music triggers two contrast-ing responses. On the one hand, the listener responds to this power with desire and feels elevated by it. In this capacity, music can have a benefi-cial effect on the listener. When the 'Forscherhund' is almost starving, it is musical ecstasy that saves his life: 'And I was, really, completely beside myself. In normal circumstances I would have been gravely ill, incapable of moving, but I couldn't resist the melody' (*HA* 150/*NSII* 479). On the other hand, however, musical power also triggers the listener's fear of losing himself, and demonstrates his ultimate helplessness in this situation. While the 'Forscherhund' is contemplating his observation of the seven young dogs,

> the music suddenly gained the upper hand, practically seized hold of you, drew you away from these real little dogs, and, wholly against your will, hackles rising and struggling with all your might, howling as if you were being hurt, you could give your mind to nothing but the music coming from all sides, from the heights, from the depths, from everywhere, music surrounding, overwhelming, crushing the listener to a point beyond destroying him, music still so near that it was already far away, almost inaudibly sounding its fanfares still. (*HA* 124/*NSII* 429)

This is an excellent example of musical violence and the listener's helplessness in the face of it. There is no chance of resisting the power of music; the listener turns out to be a victim. What makes his helplessness even worse is the fact that the music has no source that could be removed in order to end its effect; instead, music takes on a life of its own, sounding from all directions at once. Music appears as an independent force that generates itself in order to eliminate both the musicians and the listener. In other words, the power to point to the 'absolute' also turns music into an absolute power.

'Josefine, the Singer or The Mouse People' centres on a question that echoes a key concern of musical aesthetics in the early twentieth century: does Josefine sing or whistle, in other words, does she produce musical sounds or natural noises? However, unlike Busoni, Schönberg and others, who explored ways of overcoming traditional boundaries of music, Kafka's narrator leaves this question unanswered by offering a circular argument, which structures the entire text.[8] It starts with an emphasis on singing ('Anyway, it is not just piping that she produces'; *HA* 66/*DL* 362), turns into 'evidence against her song' (*HA* 72/*DL* 362) ('of course it is piping'; *HA* 74/*DL* 367), then suggests that Josefine, who at this point disappears, did actually sing ('She herself is withdrawing from her song'; *HA* 78/*DL* 376), before returning to its starting point again: 'Was her real piping truly any louder and livelier than our memory of it will be?' (*HA* 80/*DL* 376). To sing, or not to sing, that is the (unanswered) question. While the aesthetic status of Josefine's performances remains undecided throughout the text, yet another important aspect of musical aesthetics around 1900 enters the scene: silence. 'To us the sweetest music is the silence of peace' (*HA* 65/*DL* 350), the narrator explains, and when he contemplates the reason for the listeners' response to Josefine's performances, silence rather than singing appears as one option: 'Is it her singing that transports us, or rather perhaps the solemn silence surrounding that thin little voice?' (*HA* 67–8/*DL* 354).

The uncertainty of musical boundaries can be found in many of Kafka's texts. Although music always affects the listener strongly, the means to achieve this effect are often situated at the extreme ends of the sound spectrum, not in the well-tempered middle-part of traditional aesthetics. Kafka's listener becomes overwhelmed either by complete silence or by extreme noise. In 'The Silence of the Sirens' Kafka rewrites the famous episode of the *Odyssey* by ascribing much more power to silence than to the Sirens' singing: 'Yet the Sirens have an even more terrible weapon than their song, namely their silence. Though this has never yet happened, it is imaginable that someone might save themselves from their song, but never from their falling silent' (*NSII* 40).

While in this short piece singing and silence are seen as opposites, the 'Forscherhund' finds music *within* silence: 'They didn't talk, they didn't sing, they were generally silent, almost doggedly so, yet by their magic they conjured up music out of empty space. All was music' (*HA* 123/*NSII* 428). At the opposite end of the sound spectrum, listeners find themselves confronted with extreme noise. Towards the end of *The Man who Disappeared*, Brunelda is introduced as a former singer who is only yelling these days (*MD* 161/*V* 318–19), and noisy trumpets are shown to suppress human voices in a mass rally (*MD* 166/*V* 326–7). Likewise, in *Das Schloss* (*The Castle*; 'Amalia's secret', chapter 17) the fire brigade is given special trumpets for its annual folk festival, which shock people by generating maximum noise with a minimum of breath: 'Hearing that noise, you'd have thought the Turks were upon us, and no one could get used to it. We all jumped every time the trumpets sounded' (*C* 167/*S* 299).

Kafka also presents music in its capacity to establish a community and by the same token to exclude an individual from this community. This exclusion stems either from a lack of musical competence or from unique musicality. The former affects Gregor Samsa's sister: after she has played the violin for a while, the lodgers withdraw from her: 'It really seemed more than obvious that they were disappointed in their assumption that they were to hear some beautiful or entertaining violin-playing' (*M* 66/*DL* 185). Similarly, the 'Forscherhund' finds himself locked out of the community of seven dogs as he is not part of their musical trance: 'But they behaved – I couldn't, couldn't understand it! – as if I weren't there, dogs who don't answer to another dog's call!' (*HA* 125/*NSII* 431).

Josefine the singer, on the other hand, faces the reverse problem: she is excluded because of her musicality. 'Josefine, the Singer or The Mouse People', then, is an exploration of the relationship between the artist and the community, for the text circles around the question of how Josefine's singing is perceived by the mouse people: 'there is plenty of enthusiasm and applause, but she has long ago learnt to do without real understanding, as she sees it' (*HA* 68/*DL* 355). While the mice are enthusiastic about Josefine's singing, the artist feels herself misunderstood; because of her music she is welcomed by the community, but for the same reason cannot be part of it. The exploration of Josefine's singing also echoes the antisemitic stereotype of the unmusical Jew. It is present in the underlying sense that, because of their nature, mice cannot sing: while Josefine is described as 'this nothing of a voice' (*HA* 72/*DL* 362), a key feature of the mouse people is 'our unmusicality' (*HA* 73/*DL* 365). Although antisemitic exclusion does not operate *within* the narrative, as both Josefine and the mouse people are members of the same 'species', the notion that an entire people and their artist are unmusical clearly refers to stereotypes outside the text.

In Kafka's texts, music can be a disturbing noise, a longed for silence, or both; it is able to violently overwhelm involuntary listeners, or to lead them to a hidden dimension of reality. Music serves as a means of exclusion and humiliation, but it can also create a sense of community. All of these functions echo various discourses about music and musical experiences as well as Kafka's personal take on music and his extreme sensitivity to noise. In some ways, Kafka's music resembles K.'s castle: it may be less physical as it is built of rhythm and sound, but in this quality it also denies access; and yet it can be felt as a force both powerful and ultimately unfathomable.

NOTES

1 C. Dahlhaus, *Die Idee der absoluten Musik* (Kassel: Bärenreiter, 1978).
2 See C. Caduff, 'Der gottverlorene Ton: Musik in Texten von Kleist, Kafka und Anne Duden' in R. Sorg and B. Würffel (eds.), *Gott und Götze in der Literatur der Moderne* (Munich: Fink, 1999), pp. 245–57: 247.
3 R. Wagner, 'Judaism in Music' (1850)', second extended edition 1869, in R. Wagner, *Judaism in Music and other Essays*, trans. W. A. Ellis (University of Nebraska Press, 1995), p. 86.
4 M. Brod, *Über Franz Kafka* (Frankfurt am Main: Fischer, 1974), p. 103.
5 Max Brod confirms this idea by suggesting that Kafka, 'as if as a compensation for his particular gift of musical literary composition, lacked any genuine musical talent' (*Über Franz Kafka*, p. 103).

6 See J. Daiber, *Kafka und der Lärm: Klanglandschaften der frühen Moderne* (Münster: Mentis, 2015).

7 See G. Lauer, 'Judentum/Zionismus' in M. Engel and B. Auerochs (eds.), *Kafka-Handbuch* (Stuttgart: Metzler, 2010), pp. 50–8: 51; F. Lilienfeld, *Die Musik der Juden Osteuropas: Lomir ale singen*, second edition (Zurich: Chronos, 2008), p. 75.

8 See C. Lubkoll, 'Dies ist kein Pfeifen: Musik und Negation in Franz Kafkas Erzählung "Josefine, die Sängerin oder Das Volk der Mäuse"', *Deutsche Vierteljahrsschrift für Literaturwissenschaft und Geistesgeschichte*, 66 (1992), 748–64: 760.

CHAPTER 15

Architecture

Roger Thiel

Within Franz Kafka's literary universe, architecture is a central theme, which underpins his writings from the beginning right to the very end – from the early story 'Kinder auf der Landstraße' ('Children on the Highway', written in 1903–4), to 'Der Bau' ('The Burrow', 1923–4), one of his last, unfinished, texts. Architecture occurs in his novels, short stories and fragments as well as his notebooks, diaries and letters, where it is more than a theme, for it often takes on a self-reflective dimension, reflecting the architecture, the narrative structure and the composition of the text. Indeed, many different kinds of architectonic agglomeration, structures and details serve as organizing principles and poetological devices: cities, squares, palaces, cathedrals; walls, towers, pits; staircases, stairs, windows, doors, gates, attics, roofs; galleries, bridges, streets – to name but a few. In addition, the symbolic qualities of architecture play an important role. Kafka does not evoke all these structures, details and (symbolic) qualities to conceptualize the positive aspects of architecture but to scrutinize and criticize them, to ironize and finally reveal the negative implications that were suppressed or unconscious in the history of architecture.

To demonstrate what architecture is, how it works and how it dominates Kafka's texts, I shall point to some of its important historical and theoretical markings. Architecture is the medium that – in the first architectural theory of the Occident, Vitruvius' *De architectura libri decem* (*Ten Books on Architecture*, around 15 BC) – was destined to embody and represent the principles of commodity, firmness and delight via the triad of *utilitas*, *firmitas* and *venustas*. These symbolic and metaphysical qualities that were attributed to architecture, and that were meant to be realized, embodied, in actual buildings, were discussed and adapted across history, from the Renaissance (Leon Battista Alberti (1404–72) and Andrea Palladio (1508–80)) to the twentieth century, but they were also – as in Kafka's case – challenged and revoked. The reason why this idealist notion of architecture could last all the way into modernity testifies to its adaptability but also its theological foundation: as God was the creator of the world, satisfied with his creation, the architect is his counterpart on earth. As Ludwig Wittgenstein (1889–1951) wrote, 'Architecture immortalizes and glorifies something. Hence there can be no architecture where there is nothing to glorify.'[1] How this glorification works has been shown by the philosopher Heiner Mühlmann in his theory about the emergence of cultures.[2] Kafka's texts, however, relate to Wittgenstein's second claim. They demonstrate, for instance, why towers cannot be built, bridges give way and buildings cannot provide shelter. Mühlmann's socio-biological theory revitalizes the (ancient) rhetorical topos of *decorum* used by Leon Battista Alberti. *Decorum* is a collective term for 'projection', 'ornament' and 'symbolic adhesion'. The paradigmatic site for such projections is architecture. Like rhetorical figures, which add to the semantic dimension of language, purely ornamental columns and pillars and symbolic representations, e.g. on friezes, are added to the essential tectonic elements of architecture.

Going beyond the symbolic qualities of architecture and its realization of metaphysical ideas, the sociologist Dirk Baecker has sought to define the 'leading thought' of architecture through five core concepts: space, function, form, construction and, last but not least, event.[3] Its most fundamental purpose, however, is what Baecker calls 'shielding' ('Abschirmung'), the delineation of inside and outside.

Architectural Discourses around 1900

In exploring the intricate links between architecture and text in Kafka's writings, these considerations are as central as the theoretical discourses on architecture around 1900 to which Kafka's texts either implicitly or explicitly allude. After 1900, it was the re-evaluation of space that captured architects' attention. New conceptions of architectural space emerged between 1914 and 1922, involving such notions as the addition, division and crossover of space.[4] This radical re-evaluation of architectural space was based on three developments in the nineteenth and early twentieth centuries. The revolutionary new technique of steel construction resulted in the lightness of the steel/iron skeleton; opposing this development, however, German architect Gottfried Semper (1803–79) favoured the wall for 'Raumesabtheilung' (the division of space) and as a screen for 'symbolic adhesion'.[5] Against the emphasis on functional engineering in iron- and steel-skeleton architecture, he highlighted the common etymological origin of 'Wand' (wall) and 'Gewand' (robe, garment). Finally, in his treatise *Ornament und Verbrechen* (*Ornament and Crime*, 1908) architect and theorist Adolf Loos (1870–1933) demanded that the wall be freed and 'cleansed' of all ornament, thus becoming a clean slate or *tabula rasa*.

Reading Kafka's texts, one detects not only that he was familiar with these positions, but moreover that they figure as the foundation or back-drop for his textual expeditions. Indeed, construction is a key term in Kafka's texts, where it oscillates between a figurative and a literal archi-tectural meaning. On 19 January 1913 he writes in his diary: 'Everything appears to me to be an artificial construction' (*D* 237/ *TB* 594) and on 21 November 1913: 'I am on the hunt for constructions' (*D* 239/ *TB* 597). But Kafka's constructions are never successful, and so he notes on the same day: 'Miserable observation which again is certainly the result of some-thing artificially constructed whose lower end is swinging in emptiness somewhere' (*D* 238/ *TB* 596). Semper had predicted the failure of the 'pro-visional arrangements' of the steel skeletons, while Viennese *fin de siècle* architect, theorist and city planner Otto Wagner singled out the functional building style for its beauty in his 1896 book *Die Baukunst unserer Zeit* (*Architecture of Our Time*). This is echoed by architectural writer Adolf Behne in his 1926 essay 'Der moderne Zweckbau' ('The Modernist Func-tional Building'), though his main emphasis is on the permanence of any building.

Transitions: Kafka's Walls and Bridges

As a writer who was almost obsessively interested in issues of (textual) construction, Kafka is particularly drawn to one particular example of functional architecture: the bridge. The beginning of his short story 'The Bridge' ('Die Brücke', 1916/17) reads: 'I was stiff and cold; I was a bridge; I lay across an abyss' (*HA* 183/*NSI* 304–5). The second part of this sentence represents the connecting device that a bridge is. This odd phenomenon of a narrator, or subject, who is at the same time an inanimate object is expressed by a grammatical peculiarity: this first-person is written in the past tense (the German imperfect tense), and therefore the narrator is speaking from beyond the events of the text. The bridge's fate is inscribed in its very fact or purpose: 'once a bridge is put up, it cannot stop being a bridge without falling down' (*HA* 183/*NSI* 304–5). As a consequence, this anthropomorphised structure, by dint of its very hybridity, has to be destroyed: 'I was plunging down, and I was already being torn apart and pierced by the sharpened pebbles' (*HA* 183/*NSI* 304–5). Far from being a 'building of permanence' (Behne) and as such obeying the ancient imper-ative of *firmitas*, the construction is ruled by the law of transience.

The bridge is just one example of Kafka's love of all kinds of crossings and transitional structures. Doors, stairs and staircases, as for instance in 'Vor dem Gesetz' ('Before the Law', 1914), 'Der neue Advokat' ('The New Advocate', 1917) and 'Die Sorge des Hausvaters' ('Odradek, or Cares of a Householder', 1917), are worth mentioning here as well as walls, which are featured in 'Eine kaiserliche Botschaft' ('A Message from the Emperor') and 'Beim Bau der chinesischen Mauer' ('At the Building of the Great Wall of China', both 1917). Walls are not only the earliest sacred buildings and serve the purpose of 'shielding' ('Abschirmung'), they also belong to the six central elements in Vitruvius' and Alberti's architectural theories.[6] Two texts featuring walls – one well-known, one lesser known – demonstrate Kafka's usage of Semper's, Loos's and Mies's wall and space theories – and how he deconstructs them.

On 21 July 1913 Kafka describes in his diary an architectural scene even more disturbing than 'The Bridge'. It consists of a single sentence:

> To be pulled in through the ground-floor window of a house by a rope tied around one's neck and to be yanked up, bloody and ragged, through all ceilings, furniture, walls, and attics, as if by a person who is paying no attention, until the empty noose, dropping the last fragment of me when it breaks through the roof tiles, is seen on the roof. (*D* 224/ *TB* 567–8)

This scene could be read as a more extreme, destructive version of the following description of the Castle's tower in *Das Schloss* (*The Castle*, 1922):

> It was as if some melancholy inhabitant of the place, who should really have stayed locked up in the most remote room in the house, had broke through the roof and was standing erect to show himself to the world. (*C* 11/*S* 18)

For Gottfried Semper, architecture has its origin in the proto-architectural category of clothing ('Bekleidung'). It originates from here and develops into a 'metabolism' (literally: 'Stoffwechsel', a concept Semper adopted from the chemist Jakob Moleschott). As Semper argues, 'the origins of architecture, text and clothing are the same'.[7] Illustrating his argument, he adopted a philological method – one of the major discourses of the nineteenth century – to examine the Indo-European roots of words. Kafka seems to share this idea. His one-sentence text demonstrates not only the interconnection between walls, ceilings, roof tiles and roof, all of which serve as shelter, but also the close but problematic connection between skin and house;[8] architectural constructions designed to shelter have an inherently destructive potential that leads to ruins and death.

Deconstruction and Failure

Wherever Kafka uses architecture in his texts, the process of building, the creation of shelter and shielding, is accompanied by its counterpart, destruction or 'Abbau'.[9] Nobody has described the intriguing role of architecture in Kafka's work more brilliantly than Walter Benjamin (1892–1940). In his notes for a book project on Kafka, Benjamin writes: 'No human art appears as deeply compromised as the art of building in Kafka. None is more essential and none makes perplexity more perceptible.'[10]

The first text mentioned by Benjamin, the fragment 'At the Building of the Great Wall of China', is not about a conventional human dwelling but about a much grander project: the eponymous wall, which serves as both border and sacred building. The history of this wall is intertwined with that of a much older structure. The text features a scholar's book ('Gelehrtenbuch'), which explores the Biblical Tower of Babel. Its author discovered that it was on account of the weakness of its foundations that the building failed, and was bound to fail (*HA* 104/*NSI* 343); 'only the Great Wall would for the first time in human history create a secure foundation for the Tower of Babel. So, first the Wall and then the Tower' (*HA* 104/*NSI* 343). The wall is intended to provide 'a defence for centuries' (*HA* 101/*NSI* 339), yet in fact it is 'not only unfit to be a defence – the structure itself is in constant danger' (*HA* 101/*NSI* 338). Even after decades of building work, the wall exists only in fragments separated by gaps and is thus unable to contain and protect. As the narrator concludes, such a building project – which was moreover meant to serve as a foundation for a tower – 'could only be meant as an intellectual concept' (*HA* 104/*NSI* 343).

And, indeed, there are examples in the theory and practice of architecture which could well have been an inspiration for this and other Kafka texts. After the wall was released from the 'carpets' (Semper) and the ornaments of their *decorum* by Loos,[11] the wall between inside and outside became porous because of the use of glass as, for instance, in the buildings by Walter Gropius (1883–1969) and the glasshouse by Bruno Taut displayed at the *Werkbund* exhibition in 1914. Glass could open up a house wall, breaking down the boundary between inside and outside and completely changing the experience and perception of a building. The main concept here was intensity, which was closely connected to the notion of emptiness. In 1908, the theorist of perception August Endell wrote: 'The most powerful aspect is not form but its inversion: space, emptiness . . . the motions of this emptiness.'[12] Endell was highly esteemed by pioneering modernist architect Ludwig Mies van der Rohe (1886–1969); emptiness,

intensity and the re-evaluation of space in relation to 'negative space' –
thus Bauhaus architect, painter and theorist Siegfried Ebeling[13] – all fed
into Mies's own pared-down architecture, his ideal of a 'space without qualities', where building becomes a 'spiritual decision'.[14]

In Kafka's 'At the Building of the Great Wall of China', the failure of the
horizontal building (the wall) in turn causes the failure of the vertical structure (the tower). In 'Das Stadtwappen' ('The City Coat of Arms', 1920),
the narration is devoted to the *failure* of building the tower. The narrative
trajectory of 'At the Building of the Great Wall of China' leads from the
wall to the tower, while in 'The City Coat of Arms' it goes from the tower
to the 'city for the workmen' (*CSS* 477/*NSII* 319), another vertical project
comparable to the great wall. The reason for giving up the tower project
is that 'the second or third generation had already recognized the sense-
lessness of building a heaven-reaching tower', and hence 'they troubled less
about the tower than the construction of a city for the workmen' (*CSS*
477/*NSII* 319). But this urban development project will not be successful
either because

> all the legends and songs that came to birth in that city are filled with longing
> for a prophesied day when the city would be destroyed by five successive
> blows from a gigantic fist. It is for that reason too that the city has a closed
> fist on its coat of arms. (*CSS* 477/*NSII* 323)

The fist – a detail in the Prague coat of arms – is often used as an
apotropaion, a magical device intended to shield against evil, but in Kafka's
story it foreshadows the destruction of the city. In fact, the prospect of
destruction is in itself destructive: 'the time was spent not only in conflict;
the town was embellished in the intervals, and this unfortunately enough
evoked fresh envy and fresh conflict' (*CSS* 477/*NSII* 319). This sentence
contains, in condensed form, a theory about the generation of human
culture.

Community and Culture

For Heiner Mühlmann, all cultures originate from a period of stress or
terror (war or revolution, for instance), which unites a community in its
attempt to overcome it. In the retrospective evaluation of this process, a culture reflects on its values – and therefore on itself. The emergence of culture
is the result of what Mühlmann calls 'maximal stress cooperation' (MSC),
whereas its subsequent evaluation takes place in the relaxation phase and
with the help of *decorum*.

Kafka's texts not only anticipate Mühlmann's model but invert it. Living in dysfunctional communities characterized by failed communication and abandoned building projects, his narrators long for the ultimate crisis – ultimate destruction – yet Kafka's radical events cut off any possibility of cooperation in the face of destruction and hence the possibility of a subsequent evaluation. In this respect, they pursue a 'negative' model of *decorum* – the longing for an ultimate crisis that does not allow a culture to develop or retain a sense of the future, for virtually all of Kafka's communities and societies are cast under the sign of negativity and impending destruction.

Kafka's late unfinished text 'Der Bau' ('The Burrow', 1923/4) is set underground, in 'an entirely self-contained subterranean enclosure'.[15] Kafka was attracted by subterranean structures as a counterpoint to walls and towers; as he writes in his notebook, 'we are digging the pit of Babel' (*NSII* 484). In architectural theories from antiquity to the Renaissance, architecture as place of action was connected with the most common purpose of architecture: happiness, which is the sum of all virtues in the actions of men. For architects like Alberti, Palladio or Michelangelo, happiness was connected to three other concepts: permanence (*firmitas*), dignity (*dignitas*) and appropriateness (*decorum/aptum*). These aspects underpinned the ultimate purpose of any building: providing a life without danger and with dignity for its inhabitants.[16] Once again, Kafka's texts both echo and defy this purpose. His subterranean burrow, a labyrinth made up of 'a crazy little zigzag system of passages' (*HA* 158/*NSII* 586), is designed to cause vertigo and confusion rather than happiness, dignity or safety. And yet, although the burrow causes its inhabitant endless anxiety, it is designed to provide shelter in an anticipated 'deadly struggle' (*HA* 161/*NSII* 592).

Kafka's burrow prefigures the bunker, arguably the most 'advanced' architectural structure of the late twentieth century. American architect Peter Eisenman, like Freud, Benjamin and Kafka before him, associates architecture with the uncanny, with suppression and anxiety. His buildings and writings plead for 'an architecture that embraces the instabilities and dislocations that are today in fact the truth, not merely a dream of a lost truth ... In fact, it is this truth of instability which has been repressed.'[17] For Eisenman, then, buildings should not provide an (illusory) sense of safety but should rather enable an 'unmediated confrontation with an existential anxiety'.[18] Kafka does the same in 'The Burrow', whose subterranean structure transforms happiness into doubt and despair; dignity into anxiety; *firmitas* into *infirmitas*.

Wherever Kafka thematizes architecture, he demonstrates that, to echo Wittgenstein, there is nothing to build and hence 'nothing to glorify', eroding architecture's age-old promise of permanence and human happiness. Kafka's buildings underline the failure which is inherent in every built entity. Throughout his works, then, architecture embodies what he calls the 'constructing destruction of the world' ('aufbauende Zerstörung der Welt'; *NSII* 105).

NOTES

1 L. Wittgenstein, *Culture and Value* (University of Chicago Press, 1980), p. 69.

2 H. Mühlmann, *The Nature of Cultures: A Blueprint for a Theory of Culture Genetics* (Heidelberg: Springer, 1996).

3 D. Baecker, 'Die Dekonstruktion der Schachtel: Innen und Außen in der Architektur' in N. Luhmann, F. D. Bunsen and D. Baecker (eds.), *Unbeobachtbare Welt: Über Kunst und Architektur* (Bielefeld: Cordula Haux, 1990), pp. 67–104.

4 C. Feldtkeller, *Der architektonische Raum: Eine Fiktion* (Brunswick and Wiesbaden: Birkhäuser, 1989), p. 146. The German terms read 'Raumaddition', 'Raumdivision', 'Raumdurchdringung', 'Raumverklammerung', 'Raumverschachtelung', 'Raumverschlingung', 'Raumverschneidung' and 'Raumverschränkung'.

5 G. Semper, *Der Stil in den technischen und tektonischen Künsten, oder praktische Aesthetik*, 2 vols. (Frankfurt am Main: Verlag für Kunst und Wissenschaft, 1860; Munich: Bruckmann, 1863).

6 See L. B. Alberti, *Zehn Bücher über die Baukunst*, ed. M. Theuer (Darmstadt: Wissenschaftliche Buchgesellschaft, 1975), p. 21.

7 Semper, *Der Stil*, vol. I, p. 227.

8 See C. Benthien, *Skin: On the Cultural Border Between Self and World* (New York, NY: Columbia University Press, 2004).

9 T. W. Adorno, 'Aufzeichnungen zu Kafka' in *Prismen: Kulturkritik und Gesellschaft* (Frankfurt am Main: Suhrkamp, 1955), pp. 302–42: 312–13.

10 W. Benjamin, *Gesammelte Schriften*, ed. R. Tiedemann and H. Schweppenhäuser (Frankfurt am Main: Suhrkamp, 1972–89), vol. II, p. 1188.

11 Kafka went to a lecture by Loos. On 26 March 1911 he writes in his diary: 'früher Vortrag Loos und Kraus' (*D* 45/*TB* 159).

12 A. Endell, *Die Schönheit der großen Stadt* (Stuttgart: Strecker und Schröder, 1908), p. 51.

13 S. Ebeling, *Der Raum als Membran* (Dessau: Bauhaus, 1926); this little pamphlet was written in 1923.

14 F. Neumeyer, *Mies van der Rohe – Das kunstlose Wort: Gedanken zur Baukunst* (Berlin: Siedler, 1986), p. 231.

15 H. Sussman, 'The All-Embracing Metaphor: Reflections on Kafka's "The Burrow"', *Glyph*, 1 (1977), 100–13: 100.

16 H. Mühlmann, *Ästhetische Theorie der Renaissance: Leon Battista Alberti* (Bonn: Habelt, 1981), p. 23.
17 P. Eisenman, 'Misreading Peter Eisenman', in P. Eisenman, *Eisenman Inside Out: Selected Writings 1963–1988* (New Haven, CT: Yale University Press, 2004), pp. 208–25: 212.
18 Ibid.

PART III
Politics, Culture, History

CHAPTER 16

Prague: History and Culture

Marek Nekula

Franz Kafka is closely connected with Prague biographically, culturally and in his writings. The role of Prague and its different contexts for the narrative of Kafka's life and the interpretation of his work was strongly emphasized at the milestone Liblice conference in 1963, which tried to explore Kafka from 'the Prague perspective', and this perspective continues to underpin Kafka scholarship.[1] Prague for Kafka was a shorthand for a life of engrained habit;[2] as he writes to Felice Bauer in February 1916:

> If you, Felice, are in any way to blame for our common misfortune . . . it is for your insistence on keeping me in Prague, although you ought to have realized that it was precisely the office and Prague that would lead to my – thus our – eventual ruin . . . we went to buy furniture in Berlin for an official in Prague. Heavy furniture which looked as if, once in position, it could never be removed. Its very solidity is what you appreciated most. The sideboard in particular – a perfect tombstone, or the memorial to the life of a Prague official – oppressed me profoundly. If during our visit to the furniture store a funeral bell had begun tolling in the distance, it wouldn't have been inappropriate. (*LF* 462/*B3* 152–3)

These sentiments have a long history. Over a decade earlier, in 1902, Kafka writes to his school friend Oskar Pollak:

> Prague doesn't let go. Either one of us. This old crone has claws. One has to yield, or else. We would have to set fire to it on two sides, at the Vyšehrad and at the Castle Hill, then it would be possible for us to get away. (20 December 1902; *LFFE* 5–6/*B1* 17)

By referencing the Castle and Vyšehrad Hills, Kafka evokes the conflicting symbols of the Czech–German struggle for ethno-national equality in Bohemia and the associated rule over Prague territory – a struggle of little concern to the area's Jewish population.

The Medieval and Early Modern Period

The erstwhile seat of the Přemyslid royal dynasty, the Castle Hill became a symbol of the Habsburg rule over Bohemia, which lasted for nearly four centuries, from 1526 until 1918. In a letter written in Czech to Růžena Hejná, who worked as a maid in the house in the Golden Lane rented by his sister Ottla, Kafka referred to the Castle Hill in a 'German' manner as *císařský hrad* ('Emperor's Castle') (October 1917; *B3* 341). The cathedral scene in *Der Process* (*The Trial*) evokes the gothic St Vitus's Cathedral on the Castle Hill.

The Vyšehrad hill, located on the other side of the river Vltava (Moldau), is another Prague landmark. Encouraged by the forged 'early Medieval' Czech 'Green Mountain' manuscript (printed in 1818), the Czech public believed the Vyšehrad (High Castle) to be older than the Castle Hill, and Prague to have been founded by the Slavonic princess Libuše, in fulfilment of her vision experienced on Vyšehrad hill. Because of this myth, it was seen as the heart of the Old Slavonic territory and became a symbol of the Slavonic origin of Prague and the Bohemian state in the nineteenth century. From the 1860s onwards, the Vyšehrad cemetery was transformed into a Czech national cemetery; in the 1890s a 'Czech Christian Pantheon' – symbolically excluding both Christian Germans and Jews – was built and inaugurated at the funeral of the Czech writer Julius Zeyer in 1901.

Ethno-national conflicts in Prague and surrounding Bohemia came to a head in the nineteenth and the early twentieth centuries, but bilingual and non-bilingual speakers of German, Czech, Latin and other languages had lived in Prague for centuries. The thirteenth century saw a major wave of immigration by German-speaking people into Prague and other Bohemian, Moravian and Silesian cities as well as into the previously uninhabited mountainous regions along the country's borders. Jewish people had lived in the Prague area from the tenth century onwards, but they were mostly ignored in the ensuing struggles between Czech- and German-speakers for political and cultural dominance.

In the fifteenth century, the Hussite reformation movement, named after Jan Hus (*c.* 1369–1415) who was inspired by John Wycliffe and preached in Czech, led to the isolation of Prague and the Kingdom of Bohemia from the rest of the Catholic Holy Roman Empire. In the nineteenth century, Hus, who was called the 'John the Baptist' of the Lutheran reformation, later became a figurehead of the Czech national 'reawakening'; he featured prominently in the school curriculum studied by Kafka, Max Brod, Franz Werfel and other Prague German authors.

The Bohemian kingdom embraced the Lutheran reformation, and although the Catholic Ferdinand of Habsburg was elected king in 1526, the Bohemian Protestant nobles were powerful enough to protect the relative political and religious autonomy of Bohemian lands in the context of the Habsburg Holy Roman Empire. Rudolf II even made Prague the capital of his empire in 1583, and made it possible for the Jewish quarter to develop and prosper – shaped by the philanthropist and Jewish mayor Mordecai Maisel (1528–1601) and Rabbi Judah Loew ben Bezalel (*c.* 1525–1609), widely known as the Maharal (an abbreviation of *Moreinu Ha-Rav Loew*, 'Our Teacher, Rabbi Loew'). According to legend, he created the Golem, an animated figure made from clay, to defend the Prague ghetto against antisemitic attacks. The legend was published in a collection of Jewish tales in 1847; in 1914 it was turned into a world-famous novel by the Austrian writer Gustav Meyrink and adapted for film by Paul Wegener in 1920.

After an uprising of Protestant nobles (which in turn triggered the Thirty Years War) was defeated at the Battle of the White Mountain near Prague in 1620, Bohemia became a mere province of the Habsburg Empire and was ruled from Vienna. The Protestant elite and many ordinary Protestants left Prague and Bohemia; the Catholic population was in turn enlarged by newcomers from Austria, Bavaria, Italy and Spain. During this time, a giant armoured fist with sword was added to the Prague coat of arms to honour its resistance against Swedish troops in 1648 – a motif which Kafka evokes in his story 'Das Stadtwappen' ('The City Coat of Arms'; *CSS* 434/*NSII* 323).

The cultural shift from Czech to German was reinforced by reforms of schooling and the administrative system in the eighteenth century. By 1800, Prague – in 1784 the earlier more separate towns of Castle Hill and the Lesser Town as well as the Old and New Town were administratively unified – could be called a German city, and German remained the dominant language at least until the census of 1857.

The Nineteenth and Early Twentieth Centuries: Czech Expansion and Modernization

In the nineteenth century Prague changed profoundly. In 1850 the erstwhile Jewish quarter (formed in the thirteenth century), now called *Josefov* or *Josephstadt* (Joseph's Town), became incorporated into the city, and the external city walls were demolished in several stages. Industrialization triggered a wave of migration from the Czech-speaking countryside into the city, which saw a rapid increase in the proportion of Czech-speakers. From the 1840s onwards activists of the Czech national movement started to mobilize large swathes of the Czech-speaking population behind an ethno-nationalist agenda.

The urban public space reflected these changes. In 1861 the Czech National Party won the majority in the city and turned Prague into a centre of Czech cultural and political life. German street names were complemented and later replaced by Czech names, and Czech national monuments were erected across the city. The first one, set up in 1863, was dedicated to Václav Hanka (editor of some forged manuscripts of thirteenth- and fourteenth-century Bohemian poems 'discovered' in 1817). In the 1890s, statues of Libuše, Přemysl and other mythical heroes from Slavonic history were installed on Palacký Bridge, followed in 1915 by the monument to Jan Hus in the inner city. After Prague became the capital city of Czechoslovakia in 1918, monuments associated with the Habsburg rule, for example the monuments to Emperor and King Franz I (1850) and to Marshall Radetzky (1858), were removed from the public space.

The notion of art and literature divided along ethno-national lines seemed obsolete and obstructive to many Czech and German authors and artists working in Prague around 1900. In his story 'Der Jäger Gracchus' ('The Hunter Gracchus', 1917), Kafka describes the 'vivid' shadow cast by a (national) monument on the newspaper in the hands of a reader sitting under that monument. Written during the First World War, the story can be understood as a critical response to national discourses in the public sphere. In a letter to Max Brod written five years later, Kafka expresses his dislike of such monuments: 'It is a wanton and senseless impoverishment of Prague and Bohemia that mediocre stuff like Šaloun's *Hus* or wretched stuff like Sucharda's Palacký are erected with all honours' (30 July 1922; *LFFE* 347/*B* 400–1).

In the second half of the nineteenth century, the predominantly Czech-speaking suburbs became incorporated into the inner city. Between 1890 and 1910 the Czech-speaking population grew from 213,000 to 405,000, while the German-speaking population fell from 39,000 to 33,000. As Prague grew, there were plans for the reconstruction of the city to ensure better sanitation. Most of these plans were never realized, but a slum clearance project predominantly affecting the Jewish quarter was carried out from 1895 onwards. The 'Gypsy' Synagogue, which was attended by the Kafka family, was demolished in the process, and the family subsequently worshipped at the Spanish Synagogue, rebuilt in the Moorish style in 1882–3.

Hartmut Binder has connected the bridge in 'Das Urteil' ('The Judgement', 1912, published 1913) with the Svatopluk Čech Bridge, which was built on the top of part of the former Jewish ghetto between 1905 and 1908 and which stood in front of the apartment of Kafka's family at the time he wrote this story.[3] Kafka wrote this story after his 'Jewish rebirth', initiated by visits to the performances of the travelling Yiddish theatre in 1911–12. In the 1930s, Pavel Eisner argued that it was the continuing 'triple ghetto' of the religious, social and national (linguistic) isolation of rich Prague German Jews that gave 'Prague German Literature' its distinctive voice.[4] But this simple and memorable image does not fit the private bilingual spaces in which Franz grew up, or his understanding of cultural life (Kafka visited both the German and the Czech 'National' Theatres), or the 'international' intellectual networks created by modern authors and artists in Prague since the 1890s who were actively in contact with Paris and the German-speaking cities.

Language Conflict and Antisemitism

The public sphere in Bohemia and Prague infected by ethno-national discourse nevertheless changed not only in terms of the character of urban space, but also in the form of its institutions. From 1880, rival German and Czech school associations in Bohemia were trying, respectively, to preserve the German schools and to expand the network of Czech schools that supported ethno-national education in subjects like national history or national language and literature. In 1882 Prague University (founded in 1348 by Charles IV) was finally divided into Czech and German parts – Kafka studied law from 1901 in the German one, where he also attended lectures on German literature given by August Sauer. All these institutional changes reflected the shift from the ideal of an individual Czech–German bilingualism to the ethno-national division of Bohemian society in parallel educational systems and other institutions.

Before 1918, Czech was rarely offered as a subject at German schools in the border areas of Bohemia and Moravia or in the Bohemian and Moravian cities dominated by Germans. The German schools in Prague pursued a different approach. From the end of the nineteenth century onwards, German schools in Prague offered Czech as an optional subject, in response to the dominance of Czech in the city. Born into a bilingual Czech and

German Jewish merchant family who counted Czech- and German-speakers among their customers, Kafka was able to cultivate his Czech at the primary and secondary German schools he attended, where he also obtained a solid education in Czech literature, as is clearly visible in his writings, for instance in the 'Schema zur Charakteristik kleiner Literaturen' ('Character Sketch of Small Literatures') formulated in his diary on 16 October und 17 December 1911 (*TB* 93 and 397–8). One of the Czech authors read and discussed in the optional Czech course was Božena Němcová. Resonances of her novel *Babička* (*The Grandmother*) can be discerned in Kafka's novel *Das Schloss* (*The Castle*).

The organization of Bohemian society along the Czech–German language border enforced by public institutions was also reflected in the 'Doppelsprachigkeit' (language parallelism) of administration. In 1880 Czech was granted equal status to German in external communications of the state administration with the general public. In 1897 the Badeni reform aimed to make Czech equal to German in internal communications as well, but this was blocked after protests by the German population in Bohemia and obstructionism by German and Hungarian deputies in the *Reichsrat* (Imperial Council). This in turn provoked riots by Czech nationalists in Prague and other Bohemian cities, which ended in attacks on Jewish merchants and businesses, particularly in Prague.

In August 1911, Kafka and Max Brod travelled through Switzerland. In his diary, Kafka sums up Brod's comments on the complex linguistic landscape of Switzerland, comparing it to the language conflict in Prague and Bohemian public institutions: 'Max: Scrambling languages together as the solution for national difficulties; the chauvinist would be at his wits' end' (*EFB* 78). Kafka, from 1908 until 1922 an official of the Arbeiter-Unfall-Versicherungs-Anstalt (Workers' Accident Insurance Institute) in Prague, was confronted with this Czech–German language conflict in public institutions both during the Habsburg years, when a division of the Institute along linguistic lines was being considered, and after 1918, when Prague became the capital city of the newly founded Czechoslovakia and Czech the first official language in his place of work. Kafka's literary texts, such as 'The City Coat of Arms' (1920), reflect the author's experience of Czech–German linguistic conflict, but also of antisemitism. In a letter to Milena Jesenská written in November 1920, Kafka recalls antisemitic phrases as evidence of a more general antisemitic atmosphere: 'I've spent all afternoon in the streets, wallowing in the Jew-baiting. "Prašivé plemeno" – "filthy rabble" I heard someone call the Jews the other day' (*LM* 169–70/*B4* 370).

The Jewish Population: Acculturation, Integration and Disintegration

The segregation of Jews in Bohemia and Prague started to change with Joseph II's emancipatory legislation, supported by the Jewish Enlightenment or *Haskalah*, which emerged from the 1780s onwards. German began to be taught in Jewish schools and was used by Jewish traders; the Bohemian Jews outside the cities adopted Czech as well. In Austria, Jewish emancipation was enshrined in the constitutions of 1849 and 1867. From the 1850s onwards, Bohemian Jews were moving to Prague and Plzeň (Pilsen). As they acculturated to their German- or Czech-speaking environment, the use of Yiddish (and Hebrew) in everyday communication declined.

In turn-of-the-century Prague, the vast majority of the Jewish population spoke German as their first language. In 1900, 91 per cent of Jewish children in Prague attended German schools; at the census in 1890 and 1900, about half of those who declared German as their first language in Prague were Jewish.[5] German speakers in Prague were a politically liberal group made up of intellectuals, officials, merchants, industrialists, landed gentry or nobility; they tended to be wealthier than the Czech-speaking majority of the population.[6]

In Prague, Jews were well integrated into the German community and played an active part in the cultural life of the city. In German-speaking parts of the Bohemian borderlands as well as among Czech-speaking residents in Prague, however, reactions to Jewish emancipation were more critical and even hostile. Thus in 1869 the Czech journalist and poet Jan Neruda published an antisemitic pamphlet *Pro strach židovský* (*For Jewish Fear*) in the *Národní listy* (*National Gazette*), the press organ of the Young Czech wing of the National Party.[7]

The situation was also changing for Czech-speaking Jews who lived in the countryside; one of them was Kafka's father Hermann, born in Osek near Strakonice. From the 1860s onwards, many Jews moved to small Czech-speaking Bohemian towns (Kafka's mother was born in the town of Poděbrady), sympathized with the Czech national movement and established their own organizations, such as the Spolek českých akademiků židů (Czech-Jewish Students' Association) founded in 1876. Following a second wave of migration of Czech-speaking Jews to Prague or Plzeň (Pilsen) in the 1880s, the Czech-Jewish movement became more prominent in these cities. In 1883, the association Or Tomid (Eternal Light) was founded in Prague, promoting Czech as the language to be used in the synagogue. In contrast to the integration of the German-speaking Jews into Prague German organizations, however, Czech-speaking Jews continued to be marginalized by the Czech national movement. And yet the number of Jews in Bohemia who declared Czech as their everyday language grew from one third in 1880 to 50 per cent within a decade, while the number of Jews in Prague who claimed to be German-speakers fell from 74 per cent in 1890 to 45 per cent in 1900.

One obvious factor in this development was the local migration of Czech-speaking or Czech-German bilingual Jews – such as Kafka's parents – to Prague from the 1870s onwards. However, this statistical shift cannot be explained by migration alone. For Jewish citizens who in the census declared Czech to be their everyday language, this was also a way of showing Czech national loyalty in the face of growing nationalism and antisemitism in Prague. This antisemitism was manifest for example in the anti-Jewish riots in 1897 or in the public hysteria surrounding the trial of Leopold Hilsner for 'ritual murder' in 1899.

The Zionist Response

An antisemitic agenda was increasingly characteristic of German student organizations in Prague; many of these students came from the Bohemian borderlands. The year 1891 saw the establishment of the 'Aryan' student organization Germania – Verein deutscher Hochschüler (Germania – German Students' Association), while Jewish students remained organized in the Lese- und Redehalle der deutschen Studenten in Prag (Reading and Discussion Hall of German Students in Prague, established 1848). In 1893, Russian students in Prague founded an orthodox Jewish student association called Makabäa.

In 1899 Bar Kochba, a student association with a Zionist orientation was established. In 1903–4 it was led by Kafka's schoolmate and friend Hugo Bergmann, who emigrated to Palestine in 1920, where he founded the Jewish National Library in Jerusalem and later became rector of the Hebrew University. The Zionist movement around Bar Kochba sought to put Western, assimilated Jews back in touch with their Jewish heritage. It drew particular inspiration from Martin Buber's notion of cultural Zionism, and hosted a series of talks by Buber in Prague. From 1907, the Zionist weekly *Selbstwehr* (*Self-Defence*) was published in Prague. From 1919 to 1938 it was run by Kafka's friend Felix Weltsch; Kafka regularly read it during and after the First World War.

Crossing Literary Fields

It might seem that Prague was insurmountably divided along national and religious lines, and that German-speaking Jews in particular were ultimately excluded from both Czech and German culture, experiencing a sense of cultural and linguistic isolation. Yet this bleak picture is exaggerated. While ethno-national and antisemitic narratives were picked up by nationalist politicians, there were many pro-Jewish counter-narratives. More importantly, Prague's rich literary and cultural life crossed nationalist, linguistic and religious borders, with public halls such as the Mozarteum but also cafés such as the Union, the Arco and the Louvre acting as hubs of discussion and encounter.

As Peter Zusi demonstrates in his article in this volume, Kafka was familiar with classic Czech and contemporary Czech literature, which he read either in the original or in translation. Kafka probably knew some Czech writers, such as Fráňa Šrámek (1877–1952), personally, also thanks to Max Brod, one of the most important mediators between Czech and German culture. Brod helped to bring Leoš Janáček (1854–1928) and Jaroslav Hašek (1883–1923) to prominence; together with fellow writers such as Otto Pick and Jaroslav Kvapil, he helped to create transnational networks which linked Prague to Paris, Vienna, Leipzig and Berlin.

Such open-minded contact between modernist artists and authors across linguistic and national borders was also vital for Kafka, whose texts were translated into Czech by Milena Jesenká and other translators during his lifetime. They appeared in publications of the Czech Left and of the Catholic group Dobré dílo (Good Work) in the 1920s and 1930s. Cultural and linguistic exchange was also supported by Prague Zionists, who developed a specific form of Neo-Bohemianism. Indeed, the conception of a cultural and political 'binationalism' was a distinct contribution by Prague Zionists such as Hugo Bergmann to the foundation of the Israeli nation state, which was conceived as binational: Jewish and Arab.[8] Resonances of these Zionist debates can be found in Kafka's literary texts, such as 'Schakale und Araber' ('Jackals and Arabs', 1917).

In December 1923, Kafka wrote a letter in Czech from inflation-ravaged Berlin to his sister Ottla and her Christian husband, Josef David. As he remarks, 'postage is already as expensive as it is at home' – with the Czech words 'u nás' ('bei uns', at home) meaning Prague (*LOF* 88/*BOF* 151). Although he bemoaned the grip that Prague had on him and his contemporaries, Kafka remained mentally and emotionally bound to the city and its unique culture throughout his life.

NOTES

1 M. Nekula, *Franz Kafka and his Prague Contexts: Studies in Language and Literature* (Prague: Karolinum, 2016), p. 13–36.

2 J. Čermák, 'Kafka und Prag' in W. Koschmal, M. Nekula and J. Rogall (eds.), *Deutsche und Tschechen: Geschichte – Kultur – Politik* (Munich: Beck, 2001), pp. 217–35.

3 H. Binder, *Kafkas Welt: Eine Lebenschronik in Bildern* (Reinbek: Rowohlt, 2008), p. 425.

4 P. Eisner, 'Německá literatura na půdě ČSR od r. 1848 do našich dnů' ('German literature on Czechoslovak territory from 1848 to the present') in *Československá vlastivěda* (Encyclopaedic Information on Czechoslovakia), vol. VII: *Písemnictví* (Literature) (Prague: Sfinx, 1933), pp. 325–77.

5 G. B. Cohen, *The Politics of Ethnic Survival: Germans in Prague 1861–1914* (Princeton University Press, 1981), p. 224.

6 K. Čapková, *Czechs, Germans, Jews? National Identity and the Jews of Bohemia* (New York: Berghahn Books, 2012), p. 69.

7 See *Judaica Bohemiae*, 46, no. 2 (2011).

8 See D. Shumsky, *Zweisprachigkeit und binationale Idee: Der Prager Zionismus 1900–1930* (Göttingen: Vandenhoeck & Ruprecht, 2012).

CHAPTER 17

Czech Language and Literature

Peter Zusi

Recent years have seen a certain tendency to refer to Kafka as a 'Czech' author – a curious designation for a writer whose literary works, without exception, are composed in German. As the preceding chapter describes, Kafka indeed lived most of his life in a city where Czech language and society gradually came to predominate over the German-speaking minority, and Kafka – a native German-speaker – adapted deftly to this changing social landscape.

Referring to Kafka as Czech, however, is inaccurate, explicable perhaps only as an attempt to counterbalance a contrasting simplification of his complicated biography: the marked tendency within Kafka scholarship to investigate his work exclusively in the context of German, Austrian or Prague-German literary history. The Czech socio-cultural impulses that surrounded Kafka in his native Prague have primarily figured in Kafka scholarship through sociological sketches portraying ethnic animosity, lack of communication and, at times, open violence between the two largest linguistic communities in the city. These historical realities have given rise to the persistent image of a 'dividing wall' between the Czech- and German-speaking inhabitants of Prague, with the two populations reading different newspapers, attending separate cultural institutions and congregating in segregated social venues. This image of mutual indifference or antagonism has often made the question of Kafka's relation to Czech language and culture appear peripheral.

Yet confronting the perplexing blend of proximity and distance, familiarity and resentment which characterized inter-linguistic and inter-cultural contact in Kafka's Prague is a necessary challenge. Kafka himself (as well as many of his closest friends, such as Max Brod) actively defied the ethnic and cultural barriers characterizing early twentieth-century Prague by associating with Czech writers, following Czech cultural periodicals and attending Czech theatre presentations. Yet even Kafka's references to Czech culture show moments of striking intimacy surrounded by prominent

159

silence. Any discussion of the significance of Czech language and literature for Kafka, therefore, must acknowledge both the intimacy and the silence.

Kafka's Czech Proficiency

Kafka spoke Czech quite fluently, but was not wholly bilingual. Kafka's family spoke German amongst themselves, though his parents and siblings all spoke Czech to varying degrees as well. (Kafka's youngest sister eventually married a Czech, and their family became effectively Czech-speaking.) Kafka's mother appears to have been less fluent than his father, who grew up in a south Bohemian village which was largely Czech-speaking, and in later life Hermann Kafka routinely spoke Czech with employees, and often with customers, at his shop (and he did not hesitate to use the Czech form of his name, 'Heřman', when it seemed commercially tactful).

Czech-speaking domestics and governesses were a consistent feature of Kafka's childhood and were probably the most important source of his early acquisition of the language. As a young man Kafka's proficiency in Czech was such that he was on occasion called upon to undertake sensitive negotiations in Czech with disgruntled employees of his father's shop. After the establishment of the Czechoslovak Republic in 1918, Kafka's employer, the Arbeiter-Unfall-Versicherungs-Anstalt (Workers' Accident Insurance Institute), changed its language of operation to Czech, and many German-speaking employees were made redundant or gave notice of their own accord; Kafka, however, was not only able to retain his job but indeed continued to gain promotions in the Czech-speaking environment.

In his correspondence with the Czech author Milena Jesenská (1896–1944) – one of the most famous epistolary romances in world literature – Kafka insisted that Jesenská write to him in Czech, claiming that 'German is my mother-tongue . . . but Czech feels to me far more intimate' (*LM* 26/*BM* 17). In his comments on the Czech translations Jesenská was producing of some of his work at the time, Kafka responded to the nuances of her Czech with subtlety and sensitivity. Jesenská's Czech translation of Kafka's story 'Der Heizer' ('The Stoker') appeared in the 22 April 1920 issue of the left-wing cultural journal *Kmen*. This was the first translation of Kafka's work into any language. Jesenská's translations of stories from Kafka's *Betrachtung* (*Meditation*) and of his 'Bericht für eine Akademie' ('Report to an Academy') appeared in the course of 1920, and her version of 'Das Urteil' ('The Judgement') was published in 1923. Kafka's own letters to Jesenská were in German, to be sure, and indeed even when he wrote business correspondence in Czech Kafka often asked his Czech brother-in-law to proofread for him, probably from awareness of the social and professional sensitivities of language-use at the time. Yet this insecurity also reflects the exorbitant self-criticism of a writer desiring utter command over every nuance in his written expression: Kafka could not write in Czech at the level of a Franz Kafka, but that is a demanding standard indeed.

Kafka and the Czech Cultural Environment

Kafka's knowledge of Czech literature and culture is less widely known, although this was a major component of 'the very air that Kafka breathed'.[1] During his school years, Kafka – who attended exclusively German-language schools both at primary level and at the *Gymnasium* – chose to receive instruction in Czech that went well beyond the requirements stipulated by the curriculum and well beyond mere language instruction. His classes exposed him to an impressive overview of Czech history and classical Czech literature: ancient Czech myths from, among other sources, the so-called 'Forged Manuscripts' (purported to be medieval but in fact nineteenth-century falsifications), extracts from the seventeenth-century philosopher Jan Amos Komenský (1592–1670), texts by major representatives of the Czech National Revival (such as Jan Kollár, František Ladislav Čelakovský and František Palacký), Czech Romanticism (such as Karel Hynek Mácha, Karel Jaromír Erben and Božena Němcová) and even near-contemporary Czech authors (such as Jan Neruda, Karolína Světlá, Jaroslav Vrchlický, Julius Zeyer, Svatopluk Čech and Alois Jirásek).

Remarkably, given the social tensions of the period, the German-language *Gymnasium* Kafka attended used the same anthologies of Czech literary and historical texts used in Czech schools; students were thus presented with 'an extremely detailed chronological exposition of the Czech National Revival in its various phases'.[2] Kafka received excellent grades in these classes and demonstrably drew on these educational foundations later in life, such as in his famous diary entry on 'small literatures' or through his continuing interest in Božena Němcová's (1820–62) novels and correspondence.

Beyond this formal education Kafka continued throughout adulthood to read original works of Czech literature as well as Czech translations of French or English texts, to subscribe to or at least occasionally peruse a broad and eclectic range of Czech cultural periodicals, to follow current events in Czech politics, and to maintain acquaintances with a number of Czech authors (such as the brothers Jiří and František Langer, Fráňa Šrámek or Michal Mareš). Several of Kafka's closest friends, including Max Brod, were proficient in both languages and took an active interest in supporting cultural contacts among Czech- and German-language writers and artists. Thus, for example, Kafka was certainly familiar with the work of the most significant poet of Czech Symbolism, Otokar Březina (1868–1929), as Kafka's own publishing house, Kurt Wolff Verlag, published several volumes of Březina's poetry in translations by Otto Pick, Emil Saudek and Franz Werfel, whom Kafka knew.

These facts are isolated, but that they add up to more than the parts is revealed by an episode Kafka relates in a letter to Jesenská, which says much about his intuitive awareness of contemporary Czech literature. Discussing an issue of the sharply left-wing Czech cultural journal *Kmen* he had perused[3] – the same journal in which Jesenská's translation of his story 'Der Heizer' ('The Stoker') had recently appeared – Kafka relates that the 'first good piece of original work' he read there was a story by a writer named Vladislav Vančura, 'or something like that' (*BM*, 228). Kafka had the name quite right, and the writer well pegged: while at that time Vančura (1891–1942) was barely known, he would emerge over the next few years as one of the most original and significant voices of Czech modernist prose.

Kafka and Contemporary Czech Authors: Beyond the Anxiety of Influence?

Such evidence of Kafka's conversancy with Czech culture, however, is distinctly tempered by the gaps that surround it. Kafka never mentioned even in passing, for example, the work of the great Czech-Jewish modernist Richard Weiner (1883–1937), even though Weiner was represented in Franz Pfemfert's anthology of *Jüngste tschechische Lyrik* (*Recent Czech Lyric Poetry*, 1916), to which several of Kafka's friends provided translations (in fact, Kafka may himself have assisted on some of these). Yet if there is any contemporary Czech author in whom one would expect Kafka to have taken an interest, surely it is Weiner, who 'in origin, in the social environment in which he grew up and lived, in his understanding of the world, in his aesthetic views, and in depth of talent' was closest to Kafka of any contemporary Czech author.[4]

Weiner came from a bourgeois, bilingual Jewish family background, and addressed in his work themes startlingly similar to Kafka's. Weiner's story 'Ruce' ('Hands', 1918) can illustrate this affinity. A young man named Vít arrives at the house of a young woman named Marie. A servant tells him that Marie already has a visitor, but Vít brushes this off, declaring confidently that as an old friend of the family he is always welcome. Entering the parlour he finds Marie with Dr Sykora, whom he has never met but knows to be Marie's fiancé, an engagement entered into after only a brief acquaintance. Awkward silence makes clear that Vít has interrupted a quarrel between the couple; indeed, it turns out that they have just cancelled their engagement. Vít settles into the role of neutral mediator, assuming a fatherly tone and inquiring what possible reason there could be for this. The couple inform him sharply that *he* is to blame.

The body of the story serves to transform this seemingly preposterous accusation, this unspecified guilt, from absurdity into actuality. Gradually, a subliminal reality that Vít – trusted family friend – in fact desires Marie, that this desire is reciprocated, and that they both harbour selfish satisfaction seeing the unfortunate Dr Sykora destroyed by jealousy, becomes an irresistible dynamic. Whether this reflects the release of previously repressed feelings or the spontaneous generation of a new, alternative reality is unclear. As unconscious supplants conscious reality, the characters' hand gestures become the true agents of the narrative. But, as with Kafka, the unconscious does not drive the story in the direction of psychological parable; rather it provides a frame that makes startling and irrational developments appear logical and realistic. Vaguely defined guilt, the fragility of identities, latent sadism simmering under the surface of human interactions, the force of gestural language, and a blurred boundary between consciousness and the unconscious represent distinctly Kafkan moments in Weiner's story.

Another Czech author critics have compared to Kafka, yet about whom Kafka himself remained silent, is Jaroslav Hašek (1883–1923). Hašek's masterpiece, *Osudy dobrého vojáka Švejka za světové války* (*The Adventures of the Good Soldier Švejk during the World War*, 1921–3), is often described as a picaresque novel, and the comic manner in which the dim or arguably deceptive title figure manages, paradoxically, to undermine belligerent authorities through mindless subordination to them seems at first to have little in common with the stubborn, despairing struggles depicted in Kafka's major fictions. Yet critics have noted a shared concern with the absurdity and inhumanity of the hyper-rationalized world: both Kafka and Hašek transform recognizably late-Habsburg bureaucratic machinery into a cipher for alienated modern life.

Different though they are, Kafka's and Hašek's protagonists manoeuvre amongst endless obstacles and relentless menace; indeed, no less a figure than Walter Benjamin noted that 'K. has rightly been compared with the

Good Soldier Švejk: the one is astonished at everything; the other at nothing.'[5] For many years the Kafka–Hašek comparison was fuelled by conjectures that the two authors might have met, or at least been present in
the same room, during meetings of a Czech anarchist group in Prague in
the years before the First World War, which seemed to confirm an underlying affinity between them. These speculations are now discredited. The
early fame of Hašek's *Švejk* was due in no small measure to the efforts of
Max Brod, who wrote an enthusiastic review of an early theatre adaptation
of scenes from the novel, compared Hašek to Cervantes and Rabelais and
(after Kafka's death) collaborated on a German-language stage adaptation
of *Švejk* that enjoyed considerable success in Berlin in the late twenties.[6]
Kafka's silence in this case, therefore, is conspicuous.

Ironically, one of the few claims one might plausibly venture of direct
influence of a work of Czech literature on Kafka is one of the most surprising, as it relates to Božena Němcová's (1820–62) *Babička* (*Grandmother*,
1855) – a sentimental-realist novel presenting a largely idealized portrayal
of Czech village life. Kafka's deep enthusiasm for the work is documented,
and several critics have followed Brod's lead in identifying certain episodes
from *Babička* as an impulse to plot strands in *Das Schloss* (*The Castle*).[7]
That Kafka appears to have been captivated by this narrative world dia-
metrically opposed to his own, that is, one based on harmony and reconciliation rather than hostility and alienation, has puzzled critics, and it has
proved difficult to derive much significance from Brod's inferences beyond
simply stating that in *The Castle*, 'Kafka inverts – and subverts – the idealized relations between the village and the manor house that obtain in
Němcová's novel.'[8]

Babička, however, is not so relentlessly idealizing as such a claim implies,
and is in fact shot through with elegiac or even ominous elements: the
episodes narrating the Grandmother's difficult life in the past, for example,
and especially the sub-plot of mad Viktorka, a girl from the village who
was seduced and then abandoned. Viktorka kills her infant child and then
in self-punishment denies herself the forgiveness of the community and
shuns all human society, living like a frightened animal in the forest outside
the village. Němcová's novel thus puts its own idealizing moments into
question, and it is highly plausible that this tension is part of what drew
Kafka to the work.

Here lies the conundrum in assessing Kafka's relationship to Czech literature. Kafka lavishly praised the writing of Němcová, but ignored the
work of Weiner. Kafka and Brod shared a strong interest in Nietzsche,
but remained indifferent to the brilliant and eccentric Ladislav Klíma's

(1878–1928) dramatic responses to Nietzsche's philosophy. Kafka possessed the militantly anti-German *Slezské písně* (*Silesian Songs*) by the Moravian poet Petr Bezruč (1867–1958) in German translation, but he read *The Autobiography of Benjamin Franklin* in Czech.[9] Do such facts yield a coherent picture? The names from Czech culture one might reasonably expect to have been significant for Kafka are often absent from the documents of his life, while, conversely, the names that assume importance are not necessarily what one would anticipate. And in Kafka's only sustained statement relating to Czech literature, his diary entry on 'small literatures', there are absolutely no names at all: the 'small' literatures of Czech and Yiddish serve Kafka merely as icons of a particular relation between writer and community which he feels is inaccessible to him, a relation characterized by intimacy and mutual sustenance, but that presupposes a 'lack of significant talents' (25 December 1911; *D* 149/ *TB* 314). Kafka reflects here on 'Czech literature', not on Czech writers. Moreover, most of those reflections, portraying Czech literature as a tool for community-formation and ignoring developments towards literary modernism, were long out of date and 'do not apply to the period around 1900', as Kafka would have known well.[10]

The final twist in this discussion is that literary relevance to Kafka can appear even in cases where the 'dividing wall' image mentioned at the outset does indeed seem to apply. The example of Viktor Dyk (1877–1931) is a case in point. Dyk was not only one of the most prominent Czech authors contemporary with Kafka but was also an energetic activist for Czech independence and, after the establishment of an independent state, became a senator and prominent figure of the far right. While Dyk's version of Czech nationalism has its complexities, it was certainly strident – strident enough to land him in prison for treason during the First World War. While in prison, Dyk wrote perhaps his most famous poem, 'Země mluví' ('The Earth Speaks', 1918), which has often been taken as an emblematic literary statement of territorializing nationalism. His most famous prose work, *Krysař* (*The Ratcatcher*, 1911), is a re-working of the legend of the Pied-Piper of Hamelin. What is striking, however, is how the title figure – with whom the author clearly identifies, though not uncritically – represents an archetypal outsider, without fixed abode and indeed without a name. (The first words we hear the Ratcatcher speak are 'I have no name. I am nobody. I am less than nobody. I am a ratcatcher.')[11] Like K. in *The Castle*, the Ratcatcher has intruded upon a closed community that regards him with suspicion (indeed, the stolid citizens of Hamelin attempt to renege on their contract with the Ratcatcher on the grounds that, as he has no name, his identity as signatory to the contract cannot be proven).

The Ratcatcher is more powerful than K.: he successfully takes revenge, but at the cost of his life, since he, too, is lured by his own song into the abyss. Yet the exploration of outsiderhood, the critical view towards inward-looking communities and the recognition of uncertain identity as reflective of the modern condition – themes often associated in Kafka biographies with his status as German-speaking Prague Jew – are central to this novella by a nationalist Czech author as well.

NOTES

1 M. Nekula, *Franz Kafka and his Prague Contexts* (Prague: Karolinum, 2016), p. 160. The following account draws heavily on the details Nekula provides in this fundamental study.

2 Nekula, *Franz Kafka and his Prague Contexts*, pp. 145–50: 148. See also pp. 151–95 of Nekula's study.

3 The Czech word *Kmen* is a loan-translation of the German *Stamm*, retaining the literal meaning of tree-trunk and the metaphorical meaning of tribe or group of people.

4 F. Kautman, 'Franz Kafka und die tschechische Literatur' in E. Goldstücker, F. Kautmann and P. Reimann (eds.), *Franz Kafka aus Prager Sicht* (Berlin: Voltaire Verlag, 1966), pp. 44–77: 66.

5 W. Benjamin, 'Franz Kafka: On the Tenth Anniversary of His Death' in M. W. Jennings, H. Eiland and G. Smith (eds.), R. Livingstone (trans.), *Walter Benjamin: Selected Writings* (Cambridge, MA: Harvard University Press, 1999), vol. II, pp. 794–816: 814. Translation modified.

6 See G. Vassogne, *Max Brod in Prag: Identität und Vermittlung* (Tübingen: Niemeyer, 2009), pp. 205–13.

7 See M. Brod, *Über Franz Kafka* (Frankfurt am Main: Suhrkamp, 1974), pp. 371–4.

8 A. Thomas, *Prague Palimpsest: Writing, Memory, and the City* (University of Chicago Press, 2010), p. 98.

9 For details on Franklin, see Nekula, *Franz Kafka and his Prague Contexts*, p. 158; and J. Born, *Kafkas Bibliothek: Ein beschreibendes Verzeichnis* (Frankfurt am Main: Suhrkamp, 1990), p. 169. Bezruč's *Slezské písně* appeared in multiple, slightly diverging editions in the first decades of the twentieth century, and Rudolf Fuch's German translation (with a foreword by Franz Werfel) was published in 1917.

10 G. von Bassermann-Jordan, 'Franz Kafka, die "kleine Litteratur" und das Tschechische', *Internationales Archiv für Sozialgeschichte der deutschen Literatur*, 35, no. 2 (2010), 98–121: 120.

11 V. Dyk, *The Ratcatcher*, trans. R. Kostovski (Washington, DC: Plamen Press, 2014), p. 1.

CHAPTER 18

The First World War

Mark Cornwall

In his autobiography, Max Brod noted the sweetness of existence before 1914. The First World War then changed everything as a generation ignorant of war was brutally swamped by events.[1] Nobody could avoid the hostilities and this included Kafka, for although his writings imply detachment they also reveal how the conflict invaded his everyday life. In April 1915, when travelling by train from Prague to Vienna, he sensed that what united the passengers in his carriage was the war experience. Later, at Budapest railway station, he witnessed an old couple tearfully bidding each other farewell and noted down, 'Even this wretched little happiness . . . is destroyed by the war' (27 April 1915; *D* 336/ *TB* 735–7). And yet in exploring Kafka's war we nevertheless encounter his ambivalence, for while he was repelled by its power to manipulate individual lives, he consistently felt drawn out of his personal sense of isolation to play some part in the European drama.

Insecurities and Opportunities

Although many historians have studied the Habsburg monarchy's last war, there are few who focus on the region of Bohemia where Kafka spent most of those four years. In late July 1914, when Austria-Hungary declared war on Serbia, the administration of Bohemia was in an extraordinary situation owing to Czech and German nationalist intransigence. A year earlier the provincial assembly based in Prague had been adjourned, replaced by a committee that ruled by decree; in March 1914 the Austrian prime minister also adjourned indefinitely the parliament in Vienna. In both cases the fraught Czech–German relationship in Bohemia had been largely responsible for disrupting Austria's political machinery. Thus by 1914, Bohemia's future was uncertain, but in place already was a framework for ruling the province in an authoritarian manner.

The start of hostilities solidified this rule by decree, as everyday life became harnessed to the war effort. By August 1914, emergency measures were introduced across the Habsburg Empire, allowing the Prague military command to intervene and often trump the more conciliatory stance of the Bohemian civilian administration. In order to quell or pre-empt dissent, the military played a decisive role in suspending 'subversive' meetings, censoring the press and arbitrarily interning those who transgressed their interpretation of patriotism. It seems unlikely that Kafka knew of such arrests when he started to write *Der Process* (*The Trial*), although hints about state vigilance were already appearing in the daily press. From September, however, the removal of political suspects became ever more marked; by January 1915, 950 were in prison in Bohemia for 'political offences'. This was followed in May by the seizure of the Czech leader Karel Kramář (1860–1937), who was taken to Vienna and subjected to a six-month treason trial. Kafka, despite his relative interest in politics, makes no mention of this dramatic turn of events, a lacuna even more notable since in 1916 his friend Max Brod was called as a witness for the defence in the Kramář trial; Brod thereafter always felt he was the subject of state surveillance.[2]

Yet Kafka, returning to Prague from Berlin in late July 1914 preoccupied by his break-up with Felice Bauer, could not be ignorant of how freedom of information was being curtailed in Austria-Hungary, with the banning of forty-six newspapers by the end of the year. Censorship scarred all newspapers, German or Czech, forcing editors to parrot an official narrative of the war with minimal independent comment. But for Kafka the postal censorship was the most frustrating: a 'capricious mail service', which interrupted the ties to his fiancée in Berlin, causing letters to disappear or to be delayed extensively. He even had nightmares about the subject (19 August, 15 and 30 September 1916; *LF* 522, 531, 538/*B3* 206, 225, 242). The war therefore constantly impinged on and disrupted daily routines and communications, yet in the safety of Prague, Kafka might sometimes have asked himself if he was really suffering because of the war. Certainly the city, humming with military arrivals and departures, gave him no peace for writing and forced him regularly to move apartments. Although according to Brod, he was 'often and gladly alone',[3] he complained that 'silence avoids me as water on the beach avoids stranded fish' (4 April 1915 and 8 September 1916; *LF* 489, 525/*B3* 127, 217). His primary objective was also sabotaged by his office work at the Workers' Accident Insurance Institute. The call-up, from which he was exempted because of his reserved occupation, not only created staff shortages; it brought new challenges from factory accidents caused by inadequate supervision of the wartime machinery.

Despite these curbs on freedom, the war offered a chance to participate in a collective adventure, where many discovered personal fulfilment away from a humdrum existence. One of Kafka's biographers suggests the mixture of 'risk' and 'security' that occurred when a civilian donned uniform.[4] Some felt immediately at one with the euphoria of 1914, as was clear in early August when Kafka himself watched a march-past of artillery in Prague, the flowers thrown by onlookers, and their superficial cries of 'hurrah' or 'nazdar'. Underneath this facade, the 'spirit of 1914' was more complex, since the turmoil could stimulate both hopes and fears.

This ambiguity was present in Kafka, at once repelled and enticed by the surge of events. He abhorred the patriotic parades and passionately 'hated' those going off to fight (6 August 1914; *D* 301–2/ *TB* 546–7). But he also felt envy, like many exempted or unfit men who sensed that a meaningful, energetic existence might elude them. Later, in April 1915, he would answer his own question about suffering, writing to Felice, 'I mostly suffer from the war because I myself am taking no part in it' (4 April 1915; *LF* 489/*B3* 127). Three times he would try to enlist, noting in May 1916: 'I will stick to the following: I want to join the army, to give in to a wish I've suppressed for two years' (11 May 1916; *D* 361/ *TB* 786). Whether this stance exemplified risk or security, can we really term it, as do some Kafka scholars, 'remarkable pacifism'?[5] For Kafka certainly desired some kind of war 'immersion' away from the boredom of Prague and an unfulfilling job.[6] It moved him particularly in the early period of hostilities, when the tormenting thoughts of war devoured him from every direction (13 September 1914; *D* 314/ *TB* 677). And even as late as 1918, after a period of convalescence, he did not balk at the fact that his exemption from military service might expire (28 January 1918; *LFFE* 194/*B* 229).

Indeed, Kafka, despite what some commentators suggest, showed a certain conventional allegiance to the Habsburg monarchy's colossal struggle. He expressed his alarm at Serbia's defeat of Austrian forces, his hope for success on the battlefield, his expectation too that Germany would win (September/December 1914; *D* 314, 322/*TB* 677, 710).[7] As early as September 1914, the long lists of casualties were appearing in the press (a million by the end of the year). Kafka's first real understanding of the calamity probably came in November, when his brother-in-law personally recounted the horror of fighting in the front-line. Personal losses like his old friend Oskar Pollak (killed on the Italian front in June 1915) probably compounded his sense of isolation from real events. Some who were left on the home front – mainly women – interpreted their stoicism as 'wartime sacrifice' and engaged actively in 'patriotic' humanitarian aid. Here to a degree fits

Kafka's brief help with Jewish refugees in 1914, or his commitment from 1916 to shell-shocked soldiers. The war was providing new opportunities but also highlighting new insecurities, and individuals were forced to acclimatize. A broader question, however, was the fate of the Habsburg Empire, something that Kafka occasionally pondered.[8] As the war continued, the question loomed of how the monarchy's pre-war environment might be changing and, specifically in unstable Bohemia, what form the transformation might take.

Kafka's Patriotism

Historians have often suggested that while Germans vocally backed the war, and Jews too were wholly patriotic, most Czechs were wholly unsympathetic. The stereotyping emerged quickly, but it is a categorization that requires blurring. Apart from querying the very idea of ordinary civilians' nationalist commitment, we should note how the Habsburg monarchy's legitimacy weakened in tandem with a deterioration of social conditions. 'Disloyalty' seemed most strident in the political sphere, but it can be measured too at a grassroots level via Kafka's own behaviour.

Concerning the actions of Bohemian politicians, the German–Czech stereotypes had some validity from the outset. In September 1914 all German Bohemian politicians had declared their full loyalty to the Habsburg cause. Within a year this patriotism had both aggressive and defensive dimensions, for under cover of wartime the beleaguered German position was being shored up against a perceived Czech nationalist advance. Buoyed up by the military successes of spring 1915, the German Bohemian leaders set out a 'German course', to finally implement their dream since 1882 of territorially dividing Bohemia along national lines and ensuring that German would always overrule Czech there as the state language. This gradually gained the support of the Austrian government.

In contrast, Czech wartime politics was characterized from the start by opportunism towards Vienna, continuing with at least a veneer of cooperation until late 1917. Although Prague's Czech city council always offered public homage to the emperor, most Czech leaders were wary about any open commitment. When the war went well for Austria they tended towards cooperation (so-called 'activism') with Vienna, but no compromise was possible with the German nationalists as their radical agenda took shape. On the political level, therefore, there was only a superficial armistice between Czechs and Germans, aided by the absence of any political forum for venting complaints in Prague or Vienna.

In terms of everyday patriotism, if those identifying with Czech culture often showed less support for Austria's war, ordinary Czechs' treacherous stance was vastly exaggerated both by their opponents and by retrospective Czech nationalist memoirs. Kafka's own behaviour matches thousands of other Bohemian civilians in wishing to play some role in the war, often at a tangent to official patriotism but sometimes verging upon it. One example was over public subscription to war bonds, supported by Kafka's own bosses at the Insurance Institute. The authorities viewed the public response to such campaigns as a measure of commitment to Austrian victory. While Czech speculation was relatively weak, there was some German-Jewish enthusiasm, implying a confidence in Austrian victory. Kafka's behaviour in November 1915 is suggestive. He excitedly considered buying up two thousand crowns' worth of bonds but noted: 'There was nothing in my head save my doubts about the war bonds which didn't cease plaguing me.' His uncertainty may have been over the financial outcome, but this cannot be divorced from his conscious mental investment in the war. Characteristically, he then channelled this temporary excitement – 'I felt myself directly involved in the war' – into the idea of writing: 'I felt myself up to it, wanted nothing save the opportunity to write' (5 November 1915; *D* 351/*TB* 771).

The insecurity faced by war veterans is a further touchstone for measuring Kafka's perspective. From mid-1915 his Insurance Institute was entrusted with managing aid to disabled veterans across Bohemia; through this Kafka became involved in campaigns to fundraise and create a special psychiatric hospital for 'German Bohemia', which opened in 1917 near Rumburg (Rumburk) in northern Bohemia. His office writings reveal empathy with the veterans and how they 'shattered their future for our pleasant continued existence'; his public appeals in local newspapers like the *Rumburger Zeitung* to 'patriotism' also contained a twist, dwelling on the humanitarian communal purpose rather than referencing any collective wartime sacrifice (*O* 339, 347/*A* 498, 507). Yet this work was not wholly anational and perhaps affirmed his underlying sympathy with the German cause. Essentially it was a campaign for German-Bohemian veterans – not Czechs; it could easily mesh with the openly nationalist approach of Heinrich Rauchberg, his former law professor at Prague University who was also involved in this welfare initiative.[9]

In Bohemia the war therefore tested each adult's allegiance, demanding some patriotic engagement. Many Jews may have felt a 'tripartite identity' – loyalty to Austria, to German (or Czech) culture, and to Judaism[10] – but Kafka's own self-identification fits this categorization only loosely. In March 1917, with evident social distress across the empire, he still displayed

Austrian sympathies to one patriot who petitioned him, but was reluctant to go further and become an 'activist' for the Austrian cause.[11] Later, at the end of the year, he rejected contributing to the patriotic journal *Donauland*, not so much because he opposed Austria or the war, but because of its distortion of reality – 'an unmitigated lie' as he put it (17 December 1917; *LFFE* 179/*B* 210). Its uplifting propaganda was clearly at odds with life on the home front, where war weariness stimulated by the food crisis was steadily undermining the state's legitimacy.

Social Disintegration

It is true that Bohemia's 'food basket' was far better than elsewhere, and rural localities managed to hoard supplies as Kafka found when, from September 1917, he convalesced from tuberculosis in the village of Zürau (Siřem) (22 September 1917; *LFFE* 143, 149/*B* 168, 175).[12] Yet all this was relative, since rationing and the first urban food demonstrations had begun in spring 1915. By December 1915 half of Prague's bakeries had closed because of lack of flour; by 1916 potatoes were sold only by special dispensation. By 1918 a more violent note was injected as protestors across Bohemia voiced nationalist grievances as well.

The food shortages had also contributed early to a rising xenophobia, for blame was attributed not just to profiteers but to those considered traitors to state security. German nationalists attacked 'Czech hoarders' who were supposedly stopping the provisioning of the German borderlands. More obvious scapegoats were the mass of Jewish refugees, pushed out of Galicia by the advancing Russian armies and flooding Bohemia from late 1914. By late 1915, 57,000 were present in Bohemia, rising to 72,000 by 1917. Kafka himself, like some of Prague's Jewish leadership, was disconcerted by these arrivals; when convalescing at Marienbad in July 1916, his description of one leading Hasidic rabbi as a Sultan betrays a sense of both humour and detachment (*LFFE* 120–3/*B* 142–5). Yet he was also intrigued by these eastern Jewish refugees, who seemed to offer a reassuringly broad Jewish *Gemeinschaft* (community) as a countermodel to gentile homogeneity. Far less is known about Kafka's own experience of wartime antisemitism, not just in Prague, but during his stay, from the autumn of 1917, in Zürau near the German antisemitic bastion of Saaz (Žatec). There may be a hint in a dream he records, where the German Jewish writer Franz Werfel is abused as a 'proletarian Turk', the ultimate outsider to Austrian identity (19 September 1917; *D* 384–5/ *TB* 835). But generally Kafka seems to have escaped antisemitic excesses, like the Prague food riots of March 1918,

when he was still in Zürau. His personal experience was probably confined
to his workplace, when he applied for a salary rise (*O* 220–1). Though most
colleagues identified him as German, antisemitic discrimination had certainly increased by late 1917: as he told Brod, the Institute was now 'closed
to Jews' (13 November 1917; *LFFE* 165/*B* 194).

It was in spring 1917, when socio-economic and national tensions in
Bohemia were converging, that he composed the unfinished story 'Beim
Bau der chinesischen Mauer' ('At the Building of the Great Wall of China'),
which explores problems of social-national cohesion with a remote emperor
ruling in the background. In the real world under the new Habsburg
emperor Karl, the Viennese centre was demonstrably losing control over its
home front. Karl's 'constitutional regime' of 1917 meant laxer censorship,
an amnesty for Czech political prisoners like Kramář and the reconven-
ing of the Austrian parliament as a forum for public debate. To the army's
dismay, a public discourse was reinstated just as war-weariness and strikes
were mounting in Bohemia.

When the Austrian parliament met in May 1917, there was no secret
about the incompatible agendas of the Czech and German nationalist
camps, both hoping for governmental support while keeping one eye on the
course of hostilities. In the final months of the war, the 'German course'
of dividing Bohemia in two was materializing, and the justice ministry
moved to create a new German judicial district of Trautenau (Trutnov). It
was a gesture wholly provocative to the Czechs; Kafka would later link
it to the monarchy's imminent disintegration.[13] Yet he remained silent
about the equally antagonistic Czech agenda. From May 1917, after Vienna
had snubbed their demands for Czech–Slovak unity, Czech parliamentary
deputies moved en masse into opposition and waited to see how the Habsburg Empire would fare in the war. In this closing nationalist vice of 1918,
any Bohemian Jews might have felt trapped, for Jewish allegiance was eclectic. Whether they were Austrian patriots, Zionists thirsting for cultural
autonomy or nationally indifferent like Kafka – in each case, Jewish 'outsiders' were suspect to the nationalists whose rhetoric was dominating the
public discourse.

As Kafka's short story 'Ein altes Blatt' ('An Ancient Manuscript', 1917)
shows, violence easily erupts when social crisis produces rising insecurity.
By 1918 Kafka was clearly aware of the food demonstrations in Rumburg
and the major military revolt occurring there in May, for he visited the town
that summer. But if he sensed something of the empire's disintegration,
he reacted mainly by contemplating the ideal types of community that
might emerge constructively out of imminent destruction.[14] Biographers

therefore often suggest that Kafka had no real interest in the turbulent events at home and abroad. Certainly he did not immediately witness the collapse of the Habsburg monarchy in October, for he was confined to bed with Spanish influenza.

Yet from the fragmentary evidence, it is clear he was observing and talking about the military conflict with Max Brod. He noted the accelerating movement abroad – the conquest of Palestine and the Bolshevik revolution (mid-September and 24 November 1917; *LFFE* 142, 170/*B* 167, 200). At the end of 1917 he dreamt about the Austrians' fight on the Italian front after their dramatic break-through at Caporetto and was relieved that efficient German soldiers finally intervened to produce victory (10 November 1917; *D* 389–90/*TB* 843–4). On the Bohemian home front too, he occasionally twitched the curtains in 1918 to observe the mounting national-social tensions. They even invaded the Insurance Institute, where German employees opposed the idea of a Czech director; and the incident over the Trautenau judicial district hints at his aversion to German Bohemian national chauvinism. When the empire had disappeared, in December 1918, he read the memoirs of the German-Bohemian poet Alfred Meissner (1822–85) about the 1848 revolution, observing the relevance of that nationalist turmoil to what had just taken place (*LFFE* 209/*B* 247).

The story of Bohemia in the Great War is one where thousands of individuals tried to pursue an ordinary life while realizing that their world was being irrevocably transformed. Kafka, in sharing this experience, noted perceptively that 'all human misery' was concentrated in the conflict (*O* 339/*A* 498). While by nature deeply introspective and preoccupied with his personal and literary concerns, he could not avoid being drawn into the war trauma and was then ambivalent about how to behave. The image emerging from the sources is that of an 'engaged outsider', a loner amidst the turmoil, sometimes challenging convention but often also sharing in the conventional behaviour of his fellow Bohemians.

NOTES

1 M. Brod, *Streitbares Leben: Autobiographie* (Munich: Kindler, 1960), pp. 117–19.
2 Brod, *Streitbares Leben*, pp. 148–50.
3 M. Brod, *Franz Kafka: Eine Biographie* (New York: Schocken Books, 1946), p. 189.
4 E. Pawel, *The Nightmare of Reason: A Life of Franz Kafka* (London: Collins Harvill, 1988), p. 340.
5 See *O* 354.

6 R. Robertson, *Kafka: Judaism, Politics and Literature* (Oxford: Clarendon Press, 1985), pp. 131–2.

7 Brod, *Streitbares Leben*, p. 135.

8 Robertson, *Kafka: Judaism, Politics and Literature*, p. 137.

9 See *O* 344–5.

10 See M. Rozenblit, *Reconstructing National Identity: The Jews of Habsburg Austria during World War I* (Oxford University Press, 2001), p. 23.

11 R. Hayman, *K: A Biography of Kafka* (London: Weidenfeld and Nicholson, 1981), p. 218.

12 When Kafka stayed in Turnau (Turnov) in September 1918, his hotel could still supply meat and eggs but no vegetables, milk or butter (*LFFE* 206/*B* 244).

13 Robertson, *Kafka: Judaism, Politics and Literature*, p. 137.

14 See Robertson, *Kafka: Judaism, Politics and Literature*, pp. 138, 188–90.

CHAPTER 19

Travel, Colonialism and Exoticism

Matthias Zach

Travel, colonialism and exoticism have featured prominently in recent scholarship on Kafka's life and work. Whilst some postcolonial interpretations assign rather too unequivocal a meaning to Kafka's polysemic texts, many studies highlight important new contexts for Kafka's work, underlining his keen interest in issues of race, nationalism and colonialism. Such studies have explored Kafka's enthusiasm for colonial adventure stories and travelogues; his use, or subversion, of colonial setting and Orientalist clichés; his coded critique of ethnographic exhibitions, which paraded people of non-Western origin in front of a European audience; and his reaction to the widespread depiction of Central and Eastern European culture as backward or inferior.[1] Kafka's writings, then, both reflect and actively critique colonial and imperial structures, presenting the familiar as foreign and the foreign as familiar. Space plays a central role in this undertaking.

Spatial Politics

Travel, colonialism and exoticism are discrete yet interconnected paradigms; among other things, all three are ways of negotiating and appropriating space. Exoticism involves the stereotypical semantic characterization of 'other' spaces and their inhabitants; travel is a physical and imaginary exploration of space, in a constant mutual readjustment of preconceived opinion and new impressions; and colonialism, spurred on by the imaginary and physical surveying and mapping of space, and based on economic, technological and military superiority, is inextricably linked to the violent appropriation of foreign territories.

The attempt and, more often, the failure to appropriate a place or space is a strikingly frequent feature of Kafka's texts. Moreover, on different levels ranging from the very big to the very small, the appropriation of space plays a central role in Kafka's life. The military conquest or political 'acquisition' of foreign territory was an intrinsic part of politics in Kafka's lifetime, both in Europe and beyond. But space, and different ways of relating to it, also played an important role for Kafka in his day-to-day life. This includes a deeply ambivalent attachment to his home town of Prague and the inter-relation between his different domiciles and his writing process (the fam-ily home, the apartment in the Alchimistengasse, etc.). Kafka's repeated involvement in horticulture and agriculture is also important in this con-text, for instance through his gardening work in the Dvorský nursery and the Pomologisches Institut (Institute of Pomology) near Prague or the interest he took in his sister Ottla's attempt to establish a farm in Zürau and in Minze Eisner's education in the Israelitische Gartenbauschule (Israelite School of Horticulture) in Ahlem.

The relationship between such practices and colonialism (and, in fact, Zionism) is of course not direct, but it is not merely etymological either – the Latin *colonia* designates a farm or settlement. Indeed, agriculture and other (physical or imaginary) appropriations of space are, along with mil-itary conquest and administrative control, central aspects of colonialism and imperialism.

In her influential introduction to colonialism and postcolonialism, Ania Loomba proposes the distinction between 'colonization as the take over [sic] of territory, appropriation of material resources, exploitation of labour and interference with political and cultural structures of another terri-tory or nation, and imperialism as a global system'. 'Thus', Loomba adds, 'the imperial country is the "metropole" from which power flows, and the colony or neo-colony is the place which it penetrates and controls'.[2] Although much postcolonial research has examined the ways in which, in actual fact, the distribution of power in colonial settings is much less clear-cut, Loomba's heuristic dichotomy is useful here because it helps point out the ambivalence of the position from which Kafka writes. While the multi-ethnic Austro-Hungarian Empire did not have overseas colonies – which is why, in a kind of rhetorical compensation, Bosnia and Herzegovina were sometimes referred to as 'our colonies' (see Kafka's letter to Felice Bauer of 27 October 1912; *LF* 23/*Br* 192) – its position on the European conti-nent was highly ambiguous: it was both part of Western European politics and culture and part of a different, Eastern European tradition that was aligned with cultural otherness through mechanisms which closely parallel the stereotypical description of non-European and, in particular, 'Oriental' nations and cultures.[3]

The inextricable links between different forms of domination, and between different ways of preparing and carrying out the appropriation of a given territory, have been underlined by postcolonial research in the wake of Edward Said's foundational *Orientalism* (1978) and *Culture and Imperialism* (1993). Famously, Said focuses on emblematic texts like Joseph Conrad's *Heart of Darkness* (1899) and argues that such texts 'illuminat[e] the special mix of power, ideological energy, and practical attitude characterizing European imperialism'.[4] In a sense, Said draws out the implications of the well-known statement by Conrad's narrator, who declares that the 'conquest of the earth, which mostly means the taking it away from those who have a different complexion or slightly flatter noses than ourselves' is 'redeem[ed]' by 'the idea only'.[5] In Said's view, therefore, *Heart of Darkness* 'is extraordinarily caught up in, is indeed an organic part of, the "scramble for Africa" that was contemporary with Conrad's composition'[6] and exemplifies the way in which the European novel, down to the level of its very form, is closely linked to the history of Western imperialism:

> Without empire . . . there is no European novel as we know it, and indeed if we study the impulses giving rise to it, we shall see the far from accidental convergence between the patterns of narrative authority constitutive of the novel on the one hand, and, on the other, a complex ideological configuration underlying the tendency to imperialism.[7]

Whether or not one agrees with W. H. Auden's verdict on Kafka according to which 'there is no modern writer who stands so firmly and directly in the European tradition',[8] Kafka has certainly been an avid reader of Dickens, Flaubert and a number of other authors who have contributed to building the 'patterns of narrative authority' which Said describes. This also helps to point out the fact that, in terms of colonial temporality, Kafka writes at a relatively late moment: whilst the world is still very much structured by colonial domination at the beginning of the twentieth century, the era of the greatest European colonial expansion is already over by the time he composes his texts.

Kafka's Spaces

Both explicitly and implicitly, Kafka responds to these spatial and temporal ambivalences. Some of his best-known texts – 'In der Strafkolonie' ('In the Penal Colony'), 'Ein Bericht für eine Akademie' ('A Report to an Academy') – directly evoke colonial settings. And although the number of texts that refer explicitly to a colonial situation is, after all, relatively small, the spatial structure of a number of other texts suggests postcolonial readings.[9]

More generally, their spatial structure is among the most striking features of Kafka's texts, many of which are set in a kind of *terre vague* that disorients both characters and reader. Thresholds often play a crucial role. More often than not, Kafka's protagonists are outsiders unable to enter a particular space, who are ejected from a space that used to be theirs, or who cannot make a space their own: examples include the protagonist of 'Vor dem Gesetz' ('Before the Law'), Gregor, turned into 'some sort of insect' (Susan Bernofsky's translation of Kafka's 'ungeheures Ungeziefer') at the beginning of *Die Verwandlung* (*The Metamorphosis*), or the land surveyor in *The Castle*. Conversely, the space of a character is often taken over by an intruder, for example at the beginning of *Der Process* (*The Trial*) or at the end of *The Metamorphosis*, or the threat of invasion pervades a text in its entirety, as is the case in 'Der Bau' ('The Burrow'). Over and over again, Kafka's characters attempt to appropriate a space for themselves, and/or they suffer the appropriation of their own territory by others. Kafka's texts, then, negotiate possibilities of locating oneself, of taking over space and of having one's space taken over. Whilst, in Conrad's narrative, the 'conquest of the earth' is shown in all its brutality but is finally successful, in most of Kafka's texts, the protagonists end up with no space to call their own.

'Der neue Advokat' ('The New Advocate'), the first text in the collection *A Country Doctor*, represents a particularly telling example of the ambivalent role that processes of spatial appropriation play in Kafka's work.[10] The advocate Dr Bucephalus is introduced as the former 'battle-charger' ('Streitroß') of Alexander the Great. Instead of going to war and conquering foreign lands, however, Bucephalus now impresses onlookers by quickly hastening up the steps to the courthouse and is entirely content with immersing himself in the study of the law books. At first, the text establishes an opposition between the current moment and the era of the 'great Alexander':

> With astonishing insight they say to themselves that under the present social order Bucephalus is in a difficult situation, so for that reason as well as for his significance in world history, at the very least he deserves some concessions to be made. Today – it cannot be denied – an Alexander the Great does not exist [gibt es keinen großen Alexander]. (*HA* 12/*DL* 251)

While the phrase 'große[r] Alexander' refers to a heroic past, the purported admiration for Alexander and his times (and, thus, for the colonialist 'conquest of the earth') is multiply refracted. Firstly, Kafka makes Bucephalus, rather than Alexander himself, the protagonist (if it is indeed appropriate to speak of a protagonist in the case of this text). Secondly, the opposition between present ('the present social order', 'Today') and past ('the time when he was Alexander of Macedon's battle-charger') is subverted through a conflation of different temporal levels; thus, at the end of the text Bucephalus is said to be reading his law books 'far from the tumult of Alexander's battle'. Finally, the violent conquest of land epitomized by Alexander is itself depicted in ambivalent terms:

> True, there are plenty who know how to murder [Zu morden verstehen zwar manche]; and there is no lack of skill [Geschicklichkeit] in using a lance to strike a friend across the banqueting-table; and for many Macedonia is too restricted, making them curse Philip, the father – but no one, no one can lead an army toward India [niemand, niemand kann nach Indien führen]. (*HA* 12/*DL* 251–2)

Again, the passage merges past and present ('for many Macedonia *is* too restricted'), and it betrays an ambivalent attitude towards leadership: on the one hand, the 'qualities' named at the beginning ('plenty who know how to murder'; 'using a lance to strike a friend across the banqueting-table', an allusion to an episode from the life of Alexander), which appear to be necessary either to lead oneself or to follow a leader, are hardly positive ones (although terms such as 'verstehen' and 'Geschicklichkeit' may suggest otherwise); on the other hand, the syntax of the phrase as well as the repetition of the indefinite pronoun 'no one' clearly gives a positive connotation to the role of the leader. This positive connotation is equally present as the passage continues:

> Even in those days the gates of India were inaccessible, but the royal sword pointed towards where they lay [aber ihre Richtung war durch das Königsschwert bezeichnet]. Nowadays the gates have shifted in a very different direction, further and higher; no one points the way; there are many bearing swords, but only to wave them about; and the gaze ready to follow them is bewildered. (*HA* 12/*DL* 252)

Ritchie Robertson has underlined the religious dimension of this passage, arguing that 'the emphasis on leadership rather than warfare...makes Alexander resemble a national leader who can guide his people out of captivity' and calls this 'a suggestion of Moses'.[11] At the same time, though, there is a clear emphasis on real-world power politics and military conquest (perhaps somewhat stronger in an earlier version of the text, where Kafka writes 'Alexanderschwert' instead of 'Königsschwert'). Robertson, who points out the superimposition of different temporal levels in Kafka's text, also highlights this military dimension by pointing out the parallels between Alexander and Napoleon:

> Kafka practises another kind of superimposition which causes other historical figures to loom up behind Alexander. Now that there is no Alexander, we are told, 'niemand, niemand kann nach Indien führen'... this recalls Kafka's fascination with Napoleon, who also planned to conquer India.[12]

In his desire for conquest, Napoleon, with whom Kafka has indeed had a long-standing fascination,[13] embodies both the profound implication of the arts and sciences in the violent appropriation of foreign territories – the scientific expedition accompanying Napoleon's campaign in Egypt is probably the most famous example of the collusion of political, military and scientific interests – and the close interconnectedness of European and colonial struggles over territory. Thus Robertson's very useful notion of 'superimposition' is illuminating not only with respect to individuals such as Alexander, Napoleon and Moses, but also with respect to different geographical and political spaces, and the reference to India in this story may be read both literally (when Kafka wrote 'The New Advocate' in early 1917, the British Raj was still going strong) and as referring to other conquered spaces, in colonial and other contexts.

Beyond Colonialism

More generally, then, both the repeated attempts to conquer or appropriate space and the repeated failure of such undertakings, which can be found in many Kafka texts, need to be seen within the context of the time. They reflect the ambivalent position of an author from the multi-ethnic Austro-Hungarian Empire writing at a moment when the most aggressive period of European colonial expansion was already over and when anti-colonial movements were, albeit slowly, gaining ground (in India, for instance, Gandhi was successfully organizing non-violent farmers' protests in 1917). Thus texts such as 'The New Advocate' betray both a reluctant fascination with the model of empire and a sense of the ultimate untenability of colonial domination.

Finally, though, the notion of superimposition applies here too. Clearly, the colonial contexts of Kafka's life and work are inseparable from the territorial conflicts in Europe – the two Balkan Wars of 1912 and 1913 and the First World War, which resulted in the break-up of the Habsburg Empire and the redrawing of the map of Europe and its colonies. Another important reference point is the Zionist project, itself closely intertwined with the history of European nationalism and colonialism as well as European anti-semitism. The appropriation of space, a complex and persistent theme in Kafka's texts, thus has to be understood against the backdrop of geopolitics on a global scale. In their ambivalent stance towards expansionist ambitions, which are the subject of both fascination and critique, Kafka's narratives reflect the similarly precarious climate of their time. They call for a postcolonial perspective able to draw both their forward-looking vision and their inevitable blind spots.

NOTES

1 For recent bibliographical information concerning postcolonial work on Kafka (as well as a reading of 'Jackals and Arabs') see A. Dunker, 'Kolonialismus in der Literatur des 20. Jahrhunderts' in G. Dürbeck and A. Dunker (eds.), *Postkoloniale Germanistik: Bestandsaufnahme, theoretische Perspektiven, Lektüren* (Bielefeld: Aisthesis, 2014), pp. 271–327 (pp. 289–98 on Kafka), and G. Dürbeck, 'Bibliographie: Postkoloniale Studien in der Germanistik' in Dürbeck and Dunker (eds.), *Postkoloniale Germanistik*, pp. 579–651 (pp. 628–30 on Kafka).

2 A. Loomba, *Colonialism/Postcolonialism* (London: Routledge, 1998), pp. 6–7.

3 See I.-K. Patrut, 'Kafkas "Poetik des Anderen", kolonialer Diskurs und postkolonialer Kanon in Europa' in H. Uerlings and I.-K. Patrut (eds.), *Postkolonialismus und Kanon* (Bielefeld: Aisthesis, 2012), pp. 261–88.

4 E. W. Said, *Culture and Imperialism* (London: Chatto & Windus, 1993), p. 81.

5 J. Conrad, 'Heart of Darkness' [1902] in J. Conrad, *Heart of Darkness and Other Tales* (Oxford University Press, 2002), p. 107.

6 Said, *Culture and Imperialism*, p. 80.

7 Ibid., p. 82.

8 W. H. Auden, 'The Wandering Jew' in W. H. Auden, *Prose and Travel Books in Prose and Verse*, 2 vols. (Princeton University Press, 2002), vol. II, p. 110.

9 See for instance Wilko Steffen's interpretation of *Das Schloss* (*The Castle*), which makes use of Mary Louise Pratt's notion of the 'contact zone' as a space of imperial encounter. W. Steffens, *Schreiben im 'Grenzland zwischen Einsamkeit und Gemeinschaft': Franz Kafkas 'Schloß' als 'Contact Zone'* (Bielefeld: Aisthesis, 2012).

10 For a detailed reading, see R. Reuss, 'Franz Kafka: "Der neue Advokat"' in E. Locher and I. Schiffermüller (eds.), *Franz Kafka: Ein Landarzt. Interpretationen* (Bozen: Edition Sturzflüge/Innsbruck: StudienVerlag, 2004), pp. 9–20.

11 R. Robertson, *Kafka: Judaism, Politics, and Literature* (Oxford: Clarendon Press, 1985), pp. 139.

12 Robertson, *Kafka: Judaism, Politics, and Literature*, pp. 138–9.

13 See H. Binder, 'Kafka und Napoleon' in U. Gaier and W. Volke (eds.), *Festschrift für Friedrich Beissner* (Bebenhausen: Rotsch, 1974), pp. 38–66, and Robertson, *Kafka: Judaism, Politics, and Literature*, pp. 132–4.

CHAPTER 20

Law

Theodore Ziolkowski

The titles of Kafka's works, especially those written during the years 1912–14, suggest his fascination with law: 'Das Urteil' ('The Judgement'), 'In der Strafkolonie' ('In the Penal Colony'), 'Vor dem Gesetz' ('Before the Law'), *Der Process* (*The Trial*), to cite only the most conspicuous ones. His literary language teems with legal terms: in the penultimate paragraph of 'The Judgement' the father 'condemns' his son ('ich verurteile dich') to death by drowning. The novel features a vocabulary of legal terms – judge ('Richter'), court ('Gericht'), judgement ('Urteil'), law ('Gesetz'), advocate ('Advokat'), among others – that occur literally dozens of times.[1] The title itself – *Der Process* – designates the entire legal proceeding beginning with an inquisitorial investigation that may or may not culminate in an indictment and trial.

The famous opening sentence of the novel – 'Someone must have been telling tales about Josef K., for one morning, without having done anything wrong, he was arrested' (*T* 5/*P* 7) – contains two technical terms drawn from the Austrian Criminal Code of 1852.[2] The word 'Verleumdung' (translated as 'telling tales') is the legal designation for slander (§§209–10), a crime punishable by imprisonment from one to five years: Josef K. assumes that someone has reported him ('verleumdet') to the authorities because of an imputed crime. The term 'Böses' ('evil' or 'malicious', here translated as 'wrong') occurs in the opening paragraphs of the Austrian code (§§1–2) to define crime: any deed carried out with 'evil or malicious intent' ('böser Vorsatz'). The novel contains as well numerous allusions to specific laws. When the arresting guards, for instance, joke that K. 'admits he doesn't know the law and at the same time claims he's innocent' (*T* 9/*P* 15), they are simply stating a principle set forth at the outset in the Austrian

Criminal Code (§3): 'No one can claim innocence on the basis of ignorance of the existing criminal law.'[3]

Kafka's Knowledge of the Law

Kafka employs all these terms and procedures with the precision to be expected from a writer trained in law. To be sure, it was never his ambition to be a practising attorney. When he entered the (German-speaking) Ferdinand Karl University of Prague in 1901, he initially toyed with majors in chemistry as well as German literature and art history. But by the beginning of his third semester he had committed himself to a degree in law, the Dr jur. (*Doctor juris*), which in effect amounted to the ticket of admission to careers in business, banking, industry, government and various other occupations.

The legal curriculum of the period focused more on the history and theory of law than on its practical aspects.[4] During the first four semesters the students were exposed primarily to the history of both Roman and German law as well as to ecclesiastical jurisprudence. In addition, law students were required to attend at least two courses in the Faculty of Philosophy. (Kafka chose 'Practical Philosophy' and 'Basic Questions of Descriptive Psychology'.) In the summer of 1903 Kafka passed the intermediate examination on the history of law 'with good success'. The second half of the curriculum was devoted to more immediate subjects: political science ('Staatslehre') as well as the Österreichisches Allgemeines Bürgerliches Gesetzbuch (Austrian Civil Law Code) and its procedures. During his last three semesters Kafka attended lectures by the well-known criminologist Hans Gross on criminal law, criminal proceedings and the philosophy of law. Meanwhile, all these issues provided a lively topic of conversation at the gatherings of the Philosophers' Club at the Café Louvre that Kafka attended twice a week with his friends.

To attain a degree in law students did not submit a dissertation but were required to pass three oral examinations. Kafka adequately passed the first of these – on civil law, trade law and laws of exchange – in November 1905, but four months later, as the result of poor preparation, he barely made it through the second: on Austrian constitutional law, international law and political economics. (Ironically, given his subsequent career, Kafka was notably weak in such subjects as public finance and economic policy.) His performance in the last of the exams – on Roman, Canon and German law – was graded as 'satisfactory'. On 18 June 1906, therefore, he received his degree in the ceremonious commencement celebration.

Kafka's Experience as a Lawyer

Kafka spent the year after his graduation at the Provincial Court in Prague, where he absolved the internship prescribed for law students who planned to enter government service, but because of his less than sterling academic record, as well as his Jewish background, the job hunt did not go smoothly. In October 1907, through family connections, he obtained a position with the Prague branch of the Italian international insurance company Assicurazioni Generali, which specialized in transportation insurance on land and sea as well as life insurance. Writing rapturously to a friend that 'the whole world of insurance itself interests me greatly' (8 October 1907; *LFFE* 35/*B1* 72), he entertained grand hopes of adventurous postings to the company's foreign offices, but his poor preparation restricted him to dreary office work in Prague on transportation policies.

In the spring of 1908, after unsuccessful attempts to find employment in the postal service and other government positions, he attended evening courses at the Prague Commercial Academy on workers' insurance, which qualified him for a position as law clerk with the Arbeiter-Unfall-Versicherungs-Anstalt (Workers' Accident Insurance Institute) for the Kingdom of Bohemia in Prague, which he assumed in July 1908, again with the help of personal connections, and where he remained until his early retirement in 1922. During his years with that semi-governmental establishment Kafka's outstanding performance enabled him to move smoothly through the ranks, becoming director of the appeals department and vice-secretary. In that capacity he wrote a number of incisive briefs on such matters as compulsory insurance for the building trades, accident prevention from wood-planing machines and in quarries, and hospitals for war veterans.[5]

His practical experience with the law familiarized Kafka with the legal vocabulary and routines that, as noted above, inform his works and that have been frequently cited by Kafka scholars. Beyond that, his insurance investigations often provided him with background for his stories. His extensive 1914 report on quarries, for instance, which is accompanied by photographs, sets the stage for the final scene of *The Trial*, where Josef K. is murdered in a quarry.[6] And as Kafka knew, his own Institute was originally located in rented rooms on the fourth floor of an apartment house in Prague – a setting that precisely anticipates the mysterious Court to which Josef K. is summoned in that novel.[7] However, vocabulary and practice, which are readily obvious, constitute only one aspect of Kafka's interest in law and its pronounced influence on his literary work. Equally significant, though less frequently noted, is his concern with the history and theory of law.

The Twentieth-Century Legal Controversy

In the early twentieth century Europe witnessed the greatest crisis in the philosophy of law since the codification controversy surrounding the Code Napoléon (1804) and the Prussian legal code a century earlier (1794), when three different conceptions of law were competing for authority: the long-established tradition of Roman law with its inherent tendency toward codification; the philosophy of natural law with its claim to reason and order; and the practice of customary law with its appeal to familiarity. In a widely circulated lecture of 1907 the eminent philosopher of law Georg Jellinek (1851–1911) spoke of the contemporary Battle of the Old and the New Law as yet another stage in a perennial struggle going back to Aeschylus's *Eumenides*.[8]

Nineteenth-century judicial thinking in continental Europe was largely dominated by a legal positivism that denied the existence of absolute standards of right and wrong or the relevance of moral norms of good and evil, focusing its attention instead on the rational analysis of existing systems of law. This positivism eventually reached its radical extreme in the so-called Pure Law theory, according to which the law is autonomous and self-contained, a formal pattern of pure logic distinct from political and social ideology. The excesses of legal positivism inevitably produced a counter-reaction in the form of sociological approaches that sought to understand the law as an expression of society and its values and rejected pure rationalism in favour of a realism grounded in experience. Thus the German scholar Rudolf von Jhering concluded his *Der Geist des römischen Rechts* (*The Spirit of Roman Law*, 1852–65) with the statement that 'Life does not exist for concepts, but the concepts exist for life' – a statement echoed in the United States by Oliver Wendell Holmes in the opening paragraph of his classic work *The Common Law* (1881): 'The life of the law has not been logic: it has been experience.' This tendency reached its extreme in the so-called Free Law school, which argued that the particular circumstances in any given case were more important than written legal norms and that the judge should feel free to ignore positive law altogether, or to complement it, by applying his sense of right and wrong to the realities of the case before him.

This new way of thinking was accompanied by the development of modern criminal psychology, in which Austria was a leader – a circumstance exemplified by the interest of Sigmund Freud (1856–1939) and other Viennese psychiatrists in the criminal mind.[9] These thinkers were opposed to the classical school that prevailed in the German legal system, a system based on the assumption, stemming from Immanuel Kant's *Metaphysik der Sitten* (*Metaphysics of Morals*, 1797), that criminals are people who have decided of their own volition to break the law; therefore they deserve the punishment specified for their crime, a punishment they were able to foresee. Kafka's professor Hans Gross, known as the father of criminal psychology, wrote the standard work on the subject, his *Criminalpsychologie* of 1897, in which he argued that psychology has a major role to play in the understanding of any criminal proceeding: not just the mental state of the criminal but also the psychology of the judge, experts, witnesses, jury – in short, of every agent in the judicial process.

Lawyers in the German tradition were trained to look at the criminal act and the facts of the case. Characteristically, the German penal code of 1871 begins with the definition of offences – felonies, misdemeanours and so forth – and their penalties. Kafka and his contemporaries in the Austro-Hungarian Empire, in contrast, were taught to concentrate more on the criminal and his intent. The Austrian code of 1852 opens with a paragraph defining crime according to the inner criterion of 'evil intent': the 'Böses' mentioned in the opening sentence of *The Trial* – a concept that does not occur in the German criminal code. It goes on to explain (§8), 'To have a crime it is not necessary that the deed be actually carried out.' This attitude accounts for the Law's accusation of Josef K. for crimes of which he is allegedly unaware.

Given its obvious implications for the public at large, the dispute between the two legal codes predictably aroused broad interest in the Austro-Hungarian Empire and inspired a significant literary response. Between 1902 and 1907 the influential Viennese writer Karl Kraus (1874–1936) published in his one-man journal *Die Fackel* (*The Torch*) forty-one articles indicting the antiquated Austro-Hungarian legal system and arguing for the decriminalization of all behaviour that is not socially harmful. The popular Austrian novelist Karl Emil Franzos (1848–1904) paid homage to Jhering's highly consequential pamphlet *Der Kampf um's Recht* (*The Struggle for Right*, 1872) in the title of his best-known novel *Ein Kampf ums Recht* (*A Struggle for Right*, 1882), in which a rural judge is so profoundly offended by an injustice perpetrated on his community that he takes to the mountains with a band of renegades as 'the great avenger'. In Robert Musil's grand panorama of Viennese society in the year 1913, *Der Mann ohne Eigenschaften* (*The Man without Qualities*, 1930–43), the protagonist's father becomes a member of the commission appointed by the Ministry of Justice to revise the criminal law code in light of recent developments with particular attention to the legal response to insanity. In *Der Abituriententag* (*The Class Reunion*, 1928) the Prague author Franz Werfel depicted the personal dilemma of the examining magistrate in his investigation of a man accused of murdering a prostitute. Werfel's typically Austrian emphasis on the preliminary investigation emerges vividly when it is contrasted with the German literary preference for the later stages of the proceedings, which is strikingly evident in Leonhard Frank's *Die Ursache* (*The Cause*, 1916) and Ricarda Huch's *Der Fall Deruga* (*The Deruga Case*, 1917). In both novels, which deal respectively with cases of murder and euthanasia in pre-1914 Germany, the focus is on the accused, not the investigators, and the scene is restricted almost entirely to the courtroom.

Two Systems of Law

Another factor came into play in the Austro-Hungarian Empire. It has often been noted that *The Trial* is based on a duality of legal systems implied by 'the laws' with which Josef K. is familiar and 'the Law' to which he is summoned. More rarely discussed, however, are the historical factors underlying this opposition. Unlike the universities in the recently unified German Empire, whose code of criminal law dated back only to 1871 and whose thoroughly modern constitution had taken effect as recently as 1900, universities in the Habsburg Empire still expected their students to have a comprehensive grounding in the Roman law upon which Austro-Hungarian law was essentially based: the effective Criminal Code of 1852 went back to the *Constitutio Criminalis Theresiana* of 1768.

Accordingly Kafka, as we have seen, spent most of his first two years studying Roman civil law and canon law along with the history of German and Austrian law. He was therefore fully aware of the parallel existence in history of dual legal systems such as Roman civil law and canon law, which functioned side by side effectively throughout centuries of European history. This awareness plays a role in several of his works. His story 'In the Penal Colony' depends for its alienating effect on the fact that the explorer comes from a European country governed by a legal system utterly different from the one in force on the penal island he is visiting. In *The Trial*, Josef K. is caught between the constitutional state of 'the laws', in which he lives and works, and the utterly distinct jurisdiction of 'the Law', which operates according to rules that are never clearly set down and specified. Kafka, living and working in Prague, located midway between Berlin and

Vienna, was in the perfect intermediate position from which to view the conflict between the systems of German and Austro-Hungarian law and between the theories of 'pure' and 'free' law.

His literary work of course amounts to far more than a satirical response to the legal controversies in *fin-de-siècle* Europe, or a potpourri of parodied legal terminology. *The Trial* constitutes among other things a compelling statement about the nature of human guilt and responsibility – our tendency to deny the guilt into which we are inevitably plunged by existence and our reluctance to accept responsibility for the consequences of our actions. The occurrence in the first sentence of the term 'Böses' introduces into his novel a moral universe absent from the 'purer' German law. This guilt need not be understood in any narrowly legal sense; it can be read as theological, metaphysical, existential, or social guilt. Yet without Kafka's training as a lawyer and his awareness of the contemporary legal controversy between Pure Law and Free Law he would have been unable to portray Josef K.'s dilemma in a similarly compelling fashion.

Kafka's preoccupation with the law reached its apex in the judicially focused works of the period from 1912 to 1914: the terms and perplexities of the law figured prominently in the mind of the young writer who had only recently completed his law studies. But the law also featured in later stories such as 'Der neue Advokat' ('The New Advocate', 1917) and 'Zur Frage der Gesetze' ('On the Question of the Law', 1920). Kafka's often frustrating dealings with statutes and bureaucratic procedures, his first-hand experience with the devious methods of businessmen eager to avoid the costs of properly insuring their workers, and indeed his confrontation with the consequences of the First World War, when scores of injured soldiers descended on the Insurance Institute, gave a new impetus to his imagination. As a result, in his later works – 'Beim Bau der chinesischen Mauer' ('At the Building of the Great Wall of China', 1917), *Das Schloss* (*The Castle*, 1922), 'Der Bau' ('The Burrow', 1923–4) – his attention shifted increasingly from the legal controversies that dominated the pre-war scene to the horrors of modern bureaucracy that we associate today with the adjective 'Kafkaesque'.

NOTES

1 See W. Speidel (ed.), *Complete Contextual Concordance to Franz Kafka, 'Der Prozess'* (Leeds: Maney, 1978).
2 For a full discussion see T. Ziolkowski, *The Mirror of Justice: Literary Reflections of Legal Crises* (Princeton University Press, 1997), pp. 226–40.

3 The Italian philosopher Giorgio Agamben, apparently unaware of the more immediate source, has recently sought to demonstrate that Kafka's representation of slander as well as the 'K.' in the protagonist's name are based on ancient Roman law. See G. Agamben, 'K.', in his *Nudities*, trans. D. Kishik and S. Pedatella (Stanford University Press, 2010), pp. 20–36.

4 The record of Kafka's university studies is summarized in detail in H. Binder (ed.), *Kafka-Handbuch in zwei Bänden* (Stuttgart: Alfred Kröner, 1979), vol. I, pp. 259–332.

5 See K. Hermsdorf (ed.), *Franz Kafka: Amtliche Schriften* (Berlin: Akademie-Verlag, 1984) and S. Corngold, J. Greenberg and B. Wagner (eds.), *Franz Kafka: The Office Writings* (Princeton University Press, 2009).

6 See the discussion of these photographs in C. Duttlinger, *Kafka and Photography* (Oxford University Press, 2007), pp. 173–205, esp. pp. 201–5.

7 B. Wagner, 'Kafka's Office Writings: Historical Background and Institutional Setting', in Corngold, Greenberg and Wagner (eds.), *Franz Kafka: The Office Writings*, pp. 19–48: 29.

8 G. Jellinek, 'Der Kampf des alten mit dem neuen Recht', in his *Ausgewählte Schriften und Reden* (Berlin: Häring, 1911), vol. II, pp. 392–427.

9 See, for instance, S. Freud's 'Psychoanalytische Bemerkungen über einen autobiographisch beschriebenen Fall von Paranoia (Dementia Paranoides)' (1910), in the *Studienausgabe* of his works, A. Mitscherlich et al. (eds.) (Frankfurt am Main: Fischer, 1973), vol. VII, pp. 133–203 and E. Bleuler, *Dementia Praecox, oder Gruppe der Schizophrenien* (Leipzig and Vienna: Deuticke, 1911).

CHAPTER 21

Philosophy

Ben Morgan

'I don't know Kant', Kafka wrote to Felice Bauer in October 1917 (*LF* 569/*B3* 350). His statement can serve as a warning to readers not to expect philosophical models behind Kafka's writings, in spite of all the interest they have subsequently sparked in twentieth-century thinkers.[1] For the generations writing immediately before and after 1800 (Friedrich Schiller and Johann Wolfgang von Goethe, Friedrich Hölderlin, Novalis and Heinrich von Kleist, and even Heinrich Heine) such a statement would have been inconceivable. But the status of the author of the *Kritik der reinen Vernunft* (*Critique of Pure Reason*, 1781/87) had changed by the turn of the twentieth century. In Robert Musil's novel of troubled adolescence *Die Verwirrungen des Zöglings Törleß* (*The Confusions of Young Törless*, 1906), the luminous authority of Immanuel Kant in middle-class homes was a subject for irony, despite, or perhaps because of, the neo-Kantian revival of Hermann Cohen (1842–1918) and Ernst Cassirer (1874–1945).

In any case, Kafka was not an avid reader of philosophy; the books he recommends in letters are literary: Flaubert's *Sentimental Education* (15 November 1912; *LF* 57–8/*B1* 237), Kleist's *Michael Kohlhaas* (9/10 February 1913; *LF* 212/*B2* 84), Goethe's *Die Leiden des jungen Werthers* (*The Sorrows of Young Werther*, 13/14 March 1913; *LF* 250/*B2* 133); or biographical. When his friend Felix Weltsch expresses an interest in the writings of the medieval Jewish philosopher Moses Maimonides (*c.* 1135–1204), Kafka recommends that he accompany this study with a reading of the autobiography of the eighteenth-century Enlightenment figure Salomon Maimon (*c.* 1753–1800) because of the way it portrays an individual caught between Western and Eastern forms of Judaism (30 November 1917; *LFFE* 173/*B3* 371). Moreover, in the same letter that he suggests tempering philosophical argument with the concrete details of an individual life, he also asks Felix Weltsch to order a copy of Augustine's *Confessions* (AD 397–400) for him (*LFFE* 173/*B3* 371): it is an individual life that catches Kafka's attention, more than a philosophical argument.

The major exception to this rule is the Danish proto-existentialist thinker Søren Kierkegaard (1813–55) whose thought, when Kafka first encountered it in 1913, seemed directly to echo his own circumstances, causing him to note in his diary: 'He bears me out like a friend' (21 August 1913; *D* 230/*TB* 578). Philosophy and life seem to him briefly to be united. This chapter will explore and contextualize Kafka's intense engagement with Kierkegaard. In order to understand the terms of the encounter, we need to look first at Kafka's relation to the wider intellectual currents of the early twentieth century.

Philosophical Affinities in Context

Kafka did not know Kant, but he was not entirely ignorant of philosophy. From the age of nineteen, he went occasionally to meetings in the Café Louvre in Prague to discuss the work of the Aristotelian and proto-phenomenologist Franz Brentano (1838–1917) (*B1* 397). In his diaries Kafka mentions reading Plato's *Republic* in July 1912 (15 July 1912; *D* 481/*TB* 1047), and in a letter to Felice in September 1916 he tells of reading Plato to his sister Ottla (10 September 1916; *LF* 526/*B3* 219). Max Brod recalled that what particularly interested him and Kafka when they read Plato together, struggling with the original Greek, was the lively presentation of the Sophists' intellectual acrobatics and Plato's (or Socrates's) irony.[2] Nor was Plato the only classical philosopher Kafka read. As a twenty-year-old, he wrote to his friend Oskar Pollak that he believed himself unable to live without the writings of the Roman Emperor Marcus Aurelius (AD 121–180) for they encouraged him to be a self-controlled, strong and upright human being (10/11 January 1904; *LFFE* 14/*B1* 33).

These traces of philosophical reading suggest a broad education and intellectual curiosity. Another comment in a letter to Oskar Pollak conveys a more precise sense of Kafka's philosophical affinities. On 8 November 1903, he writes to Pollak that he is reading, amongst other things, 'Eckehart. Some books are like a key to the unknown rooms of one's own castle' (*LFFE* 10/*B1* 29). In 1903 two rival translations into modern German of writings by the Dominican mystic, Meister Eckhart (1260–1328), were published, one by Gustav Landauer and the other by Herman Büttner. Given his spelling of the Dominican's name ('Eckehart') it seems likely that Kafka read the Büttner version.[3] But both editions had similar aims. Landauer's translation hoped to present a 'living' Eckhart, rather than a monument from the past, reading his texts as evidence of a radical pantheism which pushes beyond Church dogma and makes no claims about the soul. Büttner's foreword similarly emphasizes how Eckhart writes with a directness that breaks out of the scholastic milieu in which the friar wrote.[4]

Interest in Eckhart in the period is part of a wider search for forms of spiritual life unconstrained by the beliefs and restrictions associated with institutionalized religion. Two of the publishing ventures that contributed to this process are well represented in Kafka's library. The Diederichs Verlag, which was responsible for Büttner's Eckhart edition, also published the versions of Tolstoy and Plato that Kafka owned, as well the *Gesamtausgabe* or complete edition of Kierkegaard's writing that paved the way for the increasing attention paid to his work in the German-speaking world of the early twentieth century. Kafka's own library includes the Diederichs editions of *The Concept of Anxiety* (1844), *Stages on Life's Way* (1845) and *Sickness unto Death* (1849).[5]

Diederichs saw the Kierkegaard edition as an effort by his publishing house to address the spiritual dilemmas of the modern world. A comparable aim motivated the journal *Der Brenner* that was the other major vehicle for Kierkegaard in German translation between 1914 and 1923. In addition to Kierkegaard, the journal, and in particular one of its major contributors, Carl Dallago, mixed Nietzsche, Jesus, Dostoevsky and the Daoist philosophy of Laozi to produce an eclectic, post-religious spirituality that was combined with a commitment to modernist poetic experimentation as represented by the journal's major poetic discovery, Georg Trakl (1887–1914). What the Diederichs Verlag and the *Brenner* share is an interest in articulating models of human life in a secular world where philosophical, theological and literary vocabularies are not strictly separated. Kafka's work belongs in this milieu, although it never settles on a single position.

This wider intellectual context of post-religious experimentation helps to explain the traces of influence of the work of Arthur Schopenhauer (1788–1860) and Friedrich Nietzsche (1844–1900) that critics have noted in Kafka's work, despite the paucity of direct evidence of Kafka's reading. The parallels may arise from common concerns as much as from Kafka's detailed study of the texts, as we can see in the case of Nietzsche. The remnants of Kafka's library include a 1904 copy of *Also sprach Zarathustra* (*Thus Spoke Zarathustra*, 1883–91), but it is annotated in someone else's hand; we know that Kafka read the book as a teenager in the summer of 1900.[6] Direct evidence for a fuller study of Nietzsche does not exist. Nevertheless, critics have found parallels between Kafka's stories, such as 'In der Strafkolonie' ('In the Penal Colony', 1914) and 'Ein Landarzt' ('A Country Doctor', 1917), on the one hand, and Nietzsche's discussions of punishment in *Zur Genealogie der Moral* (*On the Genealogy of Morals*, 1887) and his demythologizing attitude to embodied human existence in *Menschliches, Allzumenschliches* (*Human, All Too Human*, 1878) and later texts, on the other.[7] But the striking similarities do not require direct influence to explain them once we acknowledge the intellectual climate in which Kafka wrote. Parallels can be caused by shared assumptions and working methods as much as by direct reading. Focusing on common intellectual habits and projects shifts our focus away from purported intellectual lineages to the question of literature's engagement with a wider practical context: with wider ways of living of which reading will only be a part.

Kafka's own writing habits endorse such a reading, as we can see in a letter of 1921 in which he adapts Schopenhauer to his purposes rather than directly quoting him. Kafka owned nine of the twelve volumes of Schopenhauer's complete works (only two of which show intermittent pencil markings).[8] Reiner Stach suggests that Schopenhauer might have been part of Kafka's voracious reading while he was convalescing in Zürau in the winter of 1917–18 (alongside his continued commitment to learning modern Hebrew; Kafka's philosophical interests were always accompanied by other concerns, such as his critical engagement with early Zionism).[9] Explicit traces of this philosophical encounter do not appear until the 1920s. In a letter to Max Brod of June 1921, Kafka compares the attitudes of the Viennese journalist and critic Karl Kraus (1874–1936) to those of Schopenhauer. Both share bleak analyses of the world they live in but nonetheless evince a certain personal cheerfulness (*LFFE* 287–8/*B* 337).

As we saw with the figure of Marcus Aurelius, and with the Kierkegaard Kafka read in 1913, his concern here is with universal human predicaments rather than with theoretical ideas. Kafka's comment does not require a detailed knowledge of Schopenhauer's texts so much as a vaguer sense of an intellectual affinity. In a letter to Minze Eisner from the same year this is made even clearer. Here Schopenhauer's philosophy is paraphrased in a way adapted to Kafka's argument: the world looks beautiful if we approach it only as an object of aesthetic perception, but life requires that we ourselves live through every detail of every moment of our own existence, turning distanced aesthetic appreciation into a continuous struggle (June 1921; *LFFE* 267/*B* 310). The point is not whether this is an accurate summary of Schopenhauer (Born suggests Kafka is paraphrasing ideas from the first two books of *Die Welt als Wille und Vorstellung* (*The World as Will and Representation*, 1818–19)),[10] but rather that a philosopher is invoked to explain the more important question of what, from a first-person perspective, it feels like to live through our own lives. The practice of living trumps theoretical speculation.

In an article on Kierkegaard published in an issue of *Der Brenner* that Kafka owned, Theodor Haecker made the same point in relation to the Danish thinker: Kierkegaard's philosophy is the record of a lived reaction to life and it demands from the reader a similarly engaged response, not just abstract reiterations of central ideas.[11] Kafka's response to Kierkegaard can be read as just such a lived engagement.

Modalities of Faith

Kafka's first reading of Kierkegaard in 1913 concentrates on the selection from his diaries published in 1905.[12] He notes the parallels between Kierkegaard's life and his own, as he struggles with the commitment of his betrothal to Felice Bauer: Kierkegaard similarly chose a life of writing over a marriage to Regine Olsen (21 August 1913; *D* 231/ *TB* 579). As Kafka thinks more about Kierkegaard, however, his attitude becomes more distanced. By the time of his more detailed study of the Danish thinker in 1917 and 1918, a fascinated but critical attitude has replaced the identification of 1913.

Kafka was not alone in turning to Kierkegaard in 1917/18. The sales figures for the Diederichs edition of Kierkegaard significantly increased from 1917 onwards.[13] The search for new vocabularies that could replace the habits of thought of Wilhelmine and Habsburg societies was intensifying. Kafka's being diagnosed with tuberculosis and his retreat to Zürau are among the personal reasons for his philosophical and spiritual meditations at this period; but the particular form they take fits the wider pattern of a culture reeling from the shock of the First World War, and the interrogation that this demanded of values and patterns of thought.

Kafka's letters of 1918 tell us that he read *Either/Or* (1843), *Fear and Trembling* (1843), *Repetition* (1843) as well as an account of Kierkegaard's relationship to Regine Olsen published by Insel. He also ordered *Stages on Life's Way* (1845). A diary entry from 1922 records that he later re-read parts of *Either/Or* (18 December 1922; *D* 423/*TB* 925), and a letter written in June 1921 to the young medical student Robert Klopstock, to be discussed in more detail below, betrays a continuing re-thinking of Kierkegaardian themes (*LFFE* 284–6/*B* 332–4). While the reading of Eckhart, Nietzsche and Schopenhauer did not leave many direct traces, Kafka's study of Kierkegaard can be traced in his letters and notebooks and evidently affected him in a way comparable to Flaubert's *Sentimental Education*, albeit starting at a later point in Kafka's life.

The Kierkegaardian figure to whom he returns most often is Abraham. Kierkegaard's *Fear and Trembling*, a book written pseudonymously in the character of Johannes de Silentio, takes Abraham as the paradigm of the leap of faith. The demand that he sacrifice Isaac is monstrous and nonsensical: it cannot be justifed by the idea that he will get something in return. Abraham's faith is not translatable into the terms of an existing vocabulary. Indeed, it cannot be spoken about, because to speak about it is to appeal to the universal, and so once again to position and make sense of the monstrous deed.[14] 'Faith itself cannot be mediated into the universal, for thereby it is cancelled. Faith is this paradox, and the single individual simply cannot make himself understandable to anyone.'[15] The 'knight of faith' is Johannes de Silentio's name for the individual who can take on the burden of this incommunicable commitment. An admirable figure, in his determination and his steadfastness, but Johannes himself admits that he would not have the courage to act as Abraham did.[16]

Kafka questions both the inexplicable sense of calling and the incommunicable nature of faith. He is aware that Kierkegaard's texts, written in the voices of the various pseudonyms, are self-consciously hyperbolic: the books, he writes to Brod, are pseudonymous to their core – rhetorical strategies even where they seem most confessional (26/27 March 1918; *LFFE* 202/*B3* 34). What they want to present, they know they cannot: the relation of the individual to God, which lies beyond all evaluation. For this reason they must turn against a world that is incapable of revealing divinity. However, for Kafka, this means Kierkegaard's texts 'rape' the world (*LFFE* 203/*B3* 35). In contrast to Kierkegaard, in the notebooks of 1918 Kafka suggests it is impossible not to have faith: it is synonymous with being alive. The more difficult task is to come to terms with this predicament: to work one's way through to an acknowledgement of the underlying 'yes' of one's life (*NSII* 102). What this involves, amongst other things, is a form of humility, a willingness to mistrust one's own sense of importance.

Kafka's alternative to the knight of faith is explored most fully in the first letter he wrote to Robert Klopstock in June 1921. The letter starts with Kafka saying he has never been an unbeliever, rather his head is always full of questions. To demonstrate his point he gives three possible accounts of Abraham: the first Abraham cannot answer God's call because the household needs him, and the household must come first, for how is a man to have a son, and indeed a knife to sacrifice him with, if he has not looked after the household (*LFFE* 285/*B* 333)? The second Abraham extends this thought experiment: is he only prevaricating, keeping his face focused on the task in hand because he is scared to look up and see Mount Moriah (*LFFE* 285/*B* 333)? The third Abraham would be willing to do what God asks, but how can he be sure that God has called him? Is not answering the call a ridiculous presumption (*LFFE* 285–6/*B* 333–4)?

Kierkegaard uses the pseudonym to communicate to his reader a hyperbolic thought experiment: incommunicable faith. Kafka's Abrahams are similarly perplexing: there is no meta-ethic to adjudicate between the different versions Kafka explores. But the texts' modes of address are very different. Kierkegaard hopes indirectly to provoke his readers into making an existential commitment he cannot spell out more directly for fear of pre-empting what the readers must discover for themselves. Kafka's communicative strategies are more inclusive: the letter makes it clear that he is continuing a conversation he has already begun with Klopstock. Moreover, his options do not assume that individual experience will be privileged: it is possible that Abraham is prevaricating, but the commitment to the household, and the cautiousness about claiming to be called, keep the search for the underlying 'yes' firmly in the realm of the social.

Perhaps Kafka, by his example, helps us to be better readers of Kierkegaard: encouraging us to return to his texts to re-discover the enabling, pedagogical project in all its tensions.[17] But, in contrast to Kierkegaard's invocation of an ineffable God who is qualitatively distinct from the human world, Kafka's communication is grounded in shared human experiences: a visceral awareness of others that insists on acknowledgement, even though, as the story 'Eine kleine Frau' ('A Little Woman', 1923–4) dramatizes, the appropriate vocabulary often eludes narrators and characters alike.

But not always. For instance, Kafka's narrator in *Das Schloss* (*The Castle*, 1922) at one point uses a positive account of human interaction for a powerful simile. When K. steps into the sleigh that he believes is waiting for Klamm and sniffs the brandy, its smell is as sweet and flattering, 'as hearing praise and kind words from someone you love, and you don't know why, nor do you want to know, you are just happy to hear the beloved person uttering them' (*C* 92/*S* 164). The simile suggests communication below the level of the words themselves, as the imagined speaker listens to the tone and the genre of the words without attending to the details of the occasion. The figures in Kafka's texts may rarely enjoy positive versions of such attunement. But, in this simile, its possibility accompanies failure as the promise of a different interaction.

Max Brod read *The Castle* as a response to *Fear and Trembling*.[18] We don't have to follow him in reading castle officials as representatives of heaven, or the castle as an emblem of divine grace. As we have seen, Kafka's relation to philosophical texts was both less direct and more grounded in lived experience. Instead, the promise of human interaction that we find in his choice of simile, but also in his intellectually exploratory letter to Klopstock and indeed in the very fact of his writing, reminds us that his intellectual projects shared with Kierkegaard's an attention to the process of philosophizing, and the awareness that a reading cannot simply repeat what the text says. But in responding to Kierkegaard, Kafka also returned his readers to a world of palpable, embodied interaction: a shy vindication of human vulnerability.

NOTES

1 For the responses of Walter Benjamin, Theodor Adorno and Jacques Derrida to Kafka's writings, see the chapters on 'Critical Theory' and 'Deconstruction' in Part IV of this volume: 'Reception and Influence'.

2 J. Born, *Kafkas Bibliothek: Ein beschreibendes Verzeichnis* (Frankfurt am Main: Fischer, 1990), p. 120.

3 G. Landauer (ed.), *Meister Eckharts mystische Schriften* (Berlin: Karl Schnabel, 1903). H. Büttner (ed.), *Meister Eckeharts Schriften und Predigten*, 2 vols. (Leipzig: Diederichs, 1903), vol. I. The editors of the critical edition of the letters suggest Landauer's edition without further explanation (*B1* 402).

4 Büttner, *Meister Eckeharts Schriften und Predigten*, p. x. Landauer sketches his version of Eckhart in his introduction. Landauer, *Meister Eckharts mystische Schriften*, pp. 5–7.

5 Born, *Kafkas Bibliothek*, pp. 114–16; for details of Kafka's Diederichs editions of Plato and Tolstoy, see pp. 50–3 and 119–20.

6 Born, *Kafkas Bibliothek*, p. 119; P. Bridgwater, *Kafka and Nietzsche* (Bonn: Bouvier, 1974), p. 10.

7 D. Oschmann, 'Philosophie' in M. Engel and B. Auerochs (eds.), *Kafka Handbuch: Leben – Werk – Wirkung* (Stuttgart: Metzler, 2010), pp. 59–64: 60–1.

8 Born, *Kafkas Bibliothek*, pp. 128–30.

9 R. Stach, *Kafka: Die Jahre der Erkenntnis* (Frankfurt am Main: Fischer, 2008), p. 259.

10 Born, *Kafkas Bibliothek*, p. 128.

11 T. Haecker, 'F. Blei und Kierkegaard', *Der Brenner*, 5, no. 10 (1914), 457–65: 463.

12 S. Kierkegaard, *Buch des Richters: Seine Tagebücher 1833–1855*, ed. H. Gottsched (Leipzig: Eugen Diederichs, 1905).

13 Sales figures can be found in I. Heidler, *Der Verleger Eugen Diederichs und seine Welt (1896–1930)* (Wiesbaden: Harrassowitz, 1998), pp. 281–3.

14 S. Kierkegaard, *Fear and Trembling* in H. V. Hong and E. H. Hong (eds.), *Kierkegaard's Writings* (Princeton University Press, 1983), vol. VI, p. 60.

15 Ibid., p. 71.

16 Ibid., pp. 75 and 120.

17 For Kierkegaard's engagement with everyday life, see J. Bukdahl, *Søren Kierkegaard and the Common Man*, trans. B. H. Kirmmse (Grand Rapids, MI: Eerdmans, 2001).

18 J. Born, *Franz Kafka: Kritik und Rezeption 1924–1938* (Frankfurt am Main: Fischer, 1983), pp. 148–9.

CHAPTER 22

Religion

Daniel Weidner

Kafka wrote in an epoch characterized by heightened interest in religious matters, and he was in turn read from a religious perspective from early on. Max Brod (1884–1968), his closest friend, first editor and biographer, described Kafka as a quasi-religious 'sage', whose writings proclaim a moral doctrine; other early readers read Kafka as expressing the discontent and fear produced by the modern, disenchanted world. Although such 'existential' readings fell into disrepute in the 1970s and 80s, Kafka's texts have recently become a focus again for readers who are interested particularly in the Jewish tradition, but also in the role of the secular in modernity.

Against the backdrop of a general 'return' of religion to the forefront of public and academic debate, Kafka's writings have gained a new urgency and now belong to a set of core texts frequently referenced in such discussions. As in other contexts, Kafka seems to challenge fixed assumptions about ourselves – be it our religious identity, the religious history of our current, supposedly secular culture, or the religion of other cultures, which is often perceived as threatening or uncanny. To understand Kafka's relationship to religion, we need to sketch out, first, the general religious context of his time; second, the more specific theological debates among Christians and Jews; and third, the sense of disenchantment and a general loss of religion, which concerned Kafka's contemporaries and is still of paramount importance for us today.

Religious Renewal Around 1900

At the beginning of the twentieth century, religion regained a new social and cultural significance. In the course of the nineteenth century, religion had rapidly lost its social power and symbolical force, having been marginalized by science and technology, by nationalism and the emerging modern society. However, at the height of this development, religion became an issue again. It is not without irony that two of its fiercest nineteenth-century critics, Karl Marx (1818–83) and Friedrich Nietzsche (1844–1900), became the founders of all-encompassing worldviews (*Weltanschauungen*) with distinctively religious traits, making universal, existential pronouncements which combined elements of both metaphysics and ethics. In fact, this emergence of secular *Weltanschauungen* represents an important turning point in the history of modernity, at a moment when a general sense of optimism and an orientation towards the future began to lose plausibility. At the turn of the twentieth century, there was a widespread sense that progress could not be sustained or, indeed, that civilization inevitably led to a certain discontent. The *fin-de-siècle* generation looked eagerly for a new sense of orientation, a quest that culminated in the First World War. Its outbreak was widely perceived as the spiritual awakening of a culture that had become all too 'materialistic'; later on, as the extreme cruelty of modern warfare became apparent, the war was interpreted as yet another, cataclysmic sign of the inherently negative, catastrophic, nature of modernity.

The search for a new *Weltanschauung* proved highly fruitful within the realm of religion. Alongside the established churches and new, decidedly modern forms of confessional piety, a wide range of new religions or quasi-religious worldviews emerged, which combined traditional forms and symbols with modern techniques and modes of communication. At the margins of Christian culture, a renewed interest in mysticism and heterodox piety became prominent, as evidenced by a popular book series published by Eugen Diederichs, which included such authors as the medieval mystic Meister Eckhart (1260–1328) and the Jewish philosopher Martin Buber (1878–1965). 'Eastern' spirituality fascinated readers in texts by Russian authors such as Lev Tolstoy (1828–1910) and Fyodor Dostoevsky (1821–81), in Buddhism, or in the Chassidic Jewish folk tales that Martin Buber promoted in several collections. Beyond this, movements such as spiritism, theosophy and anthroposophy found an eager audience for their teachings, which blended different traditions, as well as for their new rituals such as the spiritist séance, which combines basic features of religious anthropology – the contact with the deceased – with elements of modern science.

Even modern science itself became a kind of *Weltanschauung*, most prominently among the followers of Charles Darwin's theory of evolution and of the German physiologist Ernst Haeckel (1843–1919). Haeckel was the author of the bestselling *Die Welträthsel* (*The Riddle of the Universe*, 1899) and the founder of the 'federation of monists', a lobby group for modern secular education which doubled as a quasi church of science. Other groups included Nietzscheans, Wagnerians and socialists, proponents of

Lebensreform, a back-to-nature lifestyle, and of vegetarianism. Many of these movements overlapped with each other, and they fed into various youth movements that developed in the early twentieth century in reaction against the 'saturated' and stale lifestyle of bourgeois society.

A large part of these movements can be termed 'aesthetic' in a wider sense, since they tended to transfer religious dogma or scientific concepts into a more open, syncretistic language or symbolism. More specifically, art itself could be the subject of a *Weltanschauung*, as epitomized by Aestheticism, a prominent movement of the *fin de siècle*. Nietzsche, arguably the most influential thinker in this context, had claimed that after the decline of religion and metaphysics the world could be conceived of only in aesthetic terms. As a result, art and poetry were often invested with strong religious overtones, as when the poet Rainer Maria Rilke (1875–1926), in reference to the medieval prayer book, called one of his poetry collections *Das Stunden-Buch* (*The Book of Hours*, 1905), or when Symbolist poet Stefan George (1868–1933) makes frequent references to a mythology of a coming god and organizes his disciples in a self-contained 'circle', which exhibits all the features of a sect.

Like most young intellectuals of this time, Kafka had some interest in these new forms of spirituality. Raised in an assimilated Jewish family, he did not show a particular interest in traditional religion in his youth but regarded his religious education as rather superficial. As an adult, he would blame his father for his materialism and his neglect of his own Jewish roots. His father might have himself had a sense of these roots, 'but it was too little to be handed down to the child' (*M* 124/*NSII* 188–9). Since in Judaism in particular, religious identity is handed down from father to son, Kafka's struggles with his own religious identity essentially contributed to the deeply problematic image of his father as depicted in 'Brief an den Vater' ('Letter to his Father') and elsewhere.

And yet Kafka's religious interests were in fact rather diverse. In 1909 he took part in a spiritist séance and in 1911 he visited Rudolf Steiner (1861–1925), the charismatic founder of anthroposophy; in 1909 he heard Martin Buber give a speech in which he called upon modern, Western Jews to turn back to their roots and to Chassidic piety in particular; as an encounter with Judaism, however, Kafka was more impressed by the performances of a Yiddish theatre troupe from Lemberg (Lviv), which he enthusiastically attended in the winter of 1911–12. Within the wider artistic context of Kafka's life and writing, the movement of Expressionism had strongly religious overtones. In 1911 Kafka's friend, the Prague-born writer Franz Werfel (1890–1945), published his collection of Expressionist poetry called *Der*

Weltfreund (*The Friend of the World*, 1911), which used a heightened pathos addressing 'man' or 'the creature' in a new, urgent tone that sought to overcome cultural barriers and stale literary conventions. Though cataclysmic in its results, the First World War seemed to answer early Expressionism's call for a new age, which had been proclaimed using a mix of religious symbolism; this prepared the ground for a 'messianic' brand of philosophy that was characteristic of the interwar period, as in the writings of Ernst Bloch (1885–1977) and Walter Benjamin (1892–1940).

Jewish and Christian Theologies

The religious revival around 1900 also affected the established churches and their theologies. In 1900 the Lutheran theologian Adolf von Harnack (1851–1930) published *Das Wesen des Christentums* (*The Essence of Christianity*), a series of popular lectures which posit the teaching of Jesus as a cornerstone of modern culture. Harnack, a professor of church history and an influential bourgeois-liberal politician, embodied the fusion of Protestantism with cultural and academic achievement that had dominated the nineteenth century, fuelling the quasi-religious connotations of concepts such as nation, *Bildung* (education) and *Wissenschaft* (research, encompassing both the sciences and the humanities) in the German-speaking context. However, cracks were appearing in this notion of 'cultural Protestantism'. One the one hand, Christian thinkers like Søren Kierkegaard (1813–55) questioned the alleged synthesis of Christianity and culture; following them, after the First World War the 'dialectical theology' of Karl Barth (1886–1968), Rudolf Bultmann (1884–1976) and others would question the liberal optimism of cultural Protestantism, stressing instead the hidden nature of God in relation to man. On the other hand, Harnack was criticized by Leo Baeck (1873–1956), the chief rabbi of Berlin, for drawing an intentionally distorted picture of an archaic Judaism to make Jesus appear all the more modern. A certain hegemony of Protestantism, which had determined German religious debates in the nineteenth century, was thus being questioned from both within and without.

Prague, a multi-ethnic and multi-religious city with a strong and long-standing Jewish community, was the place of particularly intense discussions on the nature of religion and the relationship of different religions to each other. A number of Kafka's closest friends wrote essays on religion – works which are not properly systematic, let alone dogmatic, but represent an intellectual take on religious matters. Thus Kafka's school friend Hugo Bergmann (1883–1975) argued in his 1913 essay that in Judaism, the basic religious duty, the 'Heiligung des Namens' ('Sanctification of the Name'), is a form of 'moral action' for the community. In his *Heidentum, Christentum, Judentum (Paganism, Judaism, Christianity*, 1921), Max Brod distinguished paganism, which does not resist evil at all, from Christianity, which tries to mend all evil, and from Judaism, which resists concrete evil, e.g. in social matters, but also accepts the 'essential' evil that is a necessary part of human existence. Brod later applied these ideas to Kafka, whom he saw primarily as an ethical teacher: accepting the tragic moments of life, Kafka had continuously searched for the right way of life in a true community. Hans Joachim Schoeps, Brod's co-editor of Kafka's writings, read Kafka differently, namely in terms of a more straightforward dialectical theology, according to which Kafka's world is determined by radical doubt and the absence of any form of redemption. His interpretation is a precursor of the existentialist readings that would become prominent after the Second World War.

Both Brod and Schoeps based their analysis not merely on Kafka's fiction, but on a series of aphorisms that Kafka wrote, particularly during his stay in Zürau in 1917. During this time Kafka read Talmudic texts as well as the works of Kierkegaard and tried to undertake an existential self-analysis in which religious questions played a central role. Referring to a vast array of both Jewish and Christian motifs, Kafka wrote about concepts such as truth, good and evil, grace, transcendence, sin and especially primal sin, and the final judgement.

Owing to their elliptical nature, these aphorisms are difficult to interpret and do not form a coherent doctrine; rather, they have an experimental character. For example, Kafka repeatedly reflects on 'the indestructible', which seems to represent a realm of transcendence: 'Man cannot live without a permanent trust in something indestructible within himself, though both the indestructible element and the trust may remain permanently hidden from him. One of the ways in which this hiddenness can express itself is through faith in a personal god' (*Z* 50/*NSII* 124). However, in a way that is typical of Kafka's writings more generally, this idea is then transformed into a dialectical paradox: 'Faith means: to liberate that which is indestructible within oneself, or, more correctly: to liberate oneself, or, more correctly: to be indestructible, or, more correctly: to be' ('Glauben heißt: das Unzerstörbare in sich befreien oder richtiger: sich befreien oder richtiger: unzerstörbar sein oder richtiger: sein'; *NSII* 55). Like many of his contemporaries, particularly those working within the realm of dialectical theology, Kafka's preferred rhetorical figure is the paradox; as Gerhard Neumann has argued, however, Kafka's paradoxes do not remain stable but begin to 'slide' – that is, to change or evolve, thus baffling our understanding not just once but continuously.[1] Indeed, Kafka often structured his aphorisms using literary devices typical of his writing more generally. Thus he might present them as dialogues, as in the following example:

> 'It cannot be claimed that we are lacking in belief. The mere fact of our being alive is an inexhaustible font of belief.'

> 'The fact of our being alive a font of belief? But what else can we do but live?'

> 'It's in that "what else" that the immense force of belief resides: it is the exclusion that gives it its form.' (*Z* 108/*NSII* 139–40)

Here, the concluding identification of life with faith is presented as the solution to a problem that is hard to understand. Elsewhere, Kafka turns abstract concepts and arguments into little theatrical scenes, parables or miniature stories. Thus the cryptic statement 'There is a destination but no path ['Weg'] there; what we refer to as path is hesitation' (*Z* 26/*NSII* 118) is elsewhere elaborated on as follows: 'The true path [Weg] leads along a rope, not a rope suspended way up in the air, but rather only just above the ground. It seems more like a tripwire than a tightrope' (*Z* 3/*NSII* 113). The abstract reflection about the difficulty of ethical action (the 'true path') is expressed through an image which displaces the original question and makes us think of it differently. Kafka not only reflects on religious problems but rewrites them in unsettling ways, thus questioning our assumptions about both religious tradition and ourselves.

Religion and Secular Modernity

Though hugely influential, the religious interpretation of Kafka's works by critics such as Max Brod was not universally accepted. Contemporary thinkers such as Walter Benjamin argued that it was far too simple to reduce Kafka's writing to a religious 'message', for he was concerned not only with the religious tradition but also with modern life, and with the relation between the two. What Kafka's writings show us, according to Benjamin, is that modern life is only seemingly rational but actually full of the relics of a pre-rational, mythical age, which is embodied by the strange creatures that populate Kafka's texts. The underlying questions – what happens to a world which has lost its religion foundation, and what happens to religion after it is deposed as that unquestioned foundation – were fiercely debated among Kafka's contemporaries. Ever since Nietzsche's proclamation that

'God is dead', the quest for new ideologies or belief systems to fill this void
was accompanied by a debate about the secularization of modern society.
The sociologist Max Weber (1864–1920) described the 'disenchantment' of
the modern world, arguing that a Protestant religious ethic had been transformed into the secular ethic of professional labour; in a similar vein the
political theorist Carl Schmitt (1888–1985) claimed that the fundamental
political concepts of the West were actually secularized theological concepts, but he also stressed that this foundation was in turn on the verge of
being lost in the modern mass democracies. Modern society is thus determined by a cultural afterlife of religion whose ideas and practices continue
to have an effect, albeit in refigured, distorted ways.

Kafka was well aware of these developments for they underpinned the
progressive dissolution of traditional religious practices in his own immediate family. Indeed, this dissolution of living religious rituals is repeatedly
described in his narratives. In the short story 'Der Landarzt' ('The Country Doctor', 1917), the villagers who used to call the priest now call the
eponymous doctor, but he is unable to live up to the expectations of his
audience, thus exposing the fundamental crisis of institutions new and old
in the modern age. The story not only narrates this crisis but expresses it
by its very fractured form, which is full of gaps and uncertainties. In *Der
Process* (*The Trial*, 1914–15), one of the key chapters is set in the dark and
empty cathedral, where Josef K. is waiting for an Italian business partner to
show him some of the sights. Instead, he meets the prison chaplain, who
engages K. in a conversation and, in response to K. protesting his innocence, recounts the famous parable about the man from the country, who
wants to enter the 'law' but is precluded from doing so by the doorkeeper.

Read as a religious parable, the connotations of the law as a transcendent,
sublime entity seem obvious; however, as the ensuing discussion between
K. and the priest reveals, it is difficult to derive a precise meaning from the
law's inaccessibility, let alone from the law itself. Thus it remains ambiguous whether the sublime law is just an awkward ideology brought forward
by the prison chaplain or whether it enshrines a truth that K. merely is
unable to understand. Moreover, the discussion between K. and the chaplain, being modelled on the exegetical discussions of the Talmudic sages,
doubles the hermeneutical problem, since the unwillingness or inability of
the man to enter the law seems to mirror K.'s failure to understand the
parable. Therefore, when the priest insists (in a gesture of resignation?)
that 'what is written is unchanging, and opinions are often just an expression of despair at that' (*T* 153/*P* 298), for K. the 'simple story had become
misshapen' (*T* 155/*P* 303), and he leaves the cathedral without any sense of

illumination. Their discussion underlines the fundamental ambiguity of the law in *The Trial*: is it a political or an ethical, even a religious, category? Is it lost or just barred? Does it actually exist or is it a mere fiction, and what would 'fiction' mean in this context? Read in a religious light, the parable and its interpretation can reflect a more general modern experience, where these and similar questions remain unanswered in a cultural context that is determined by the modern subject's yearning for and simultaneous resistance against religion.

The parable of the doorkeeper has provoked numerous, indeed countless, interpretations and has become one of the core texts to embody our modern, secular world. In his letters to Walter Benjamin dating from the 1930s, the Jewish historian Gershom Scholem (1897–1982) argued that Kafka depicts a world full of the remnants and 'ruins' of religion, a world in which the 'law' is still valid but has lost its meaning, a state that Scholem called the 'nothingness of revelation' ('Nichts der Offenbarung') situated on the border of religion and nihilism.[2] Similarly, the Italian philosopher Giorgio Agamben (b. 1942) reads Kafka as expressing a fundamental crisis of *political* legitimacy which characterizes modern societies, where 'the law' has become nothing but an empty form of domination: its promise of liberation, even revelation, 'bans' the modern subject, that is, it arrests him and holds him under its spell, just as the promise of the law bans the man in Kafka's parable, rooting him to his spot until eventually he dies in front of it (*T* 155/*P* 294–5).[3] Again, Agamben's interpretation highlights that Kafka's texts not only reflect the religious context of modernity but also defamiliarize the concepts and ideas we use when thinking about religion. Whether we belong to a particular confession or identify with a secular modernity, reading Kafka is likely to unsettle the certainty of our convictions.

NOTES

1 G. Neumann, 'Umkehrung und Ablenkung: Franz Kafkas "gleitendes Paradox"', *Deutsche Vierteljahrsschrift für Literaturwissenschaft und Geistesgeschichte*, 42 (1968), 702–44; reprinted in H. Politzer (ed.), *Franz Kafka* (Darmstadt: Wissenschaftliche Buchgesellschaft, 1973), pp. 459–515.
2 *The Correspondence of Walter Benjamin and Gershom Scholem 1932–1940*, ed. G. Scholem, trans. G. Smith and A. Lefevere (Cambridge, MA: Harvard University Press, 1992), pp. 126–7.
3 G. Agamben, *Homo Sacer: Sovereign Power and Bare Life* (Stanford University Press, 1998), p. 51.

CHAPTER 23

Judaism and Zionism

Katja Garloff

Franz Kafka belonged to a generation of Prague Jews who questioned the bourgeois-liberal model of assimilation to which their parents had sub-scribed more or less uncritically. For the parent generation, assimilation to German culture had not been entirely a matter of choice – the Habsburg rulers had tried to homogenize the diverse populations in the empire, for instance, by requiring Jews to adopt German surnames and use the German language in Jewish schools – but it had created new social and economic opportunities that many welcomed. Kafka's generation was more aware of the precarious in-between position in which assimilated Prague Jews found themselves. On the one hand, most ethnic Germans never fully accepted them, but rather perpetuated antisemitic prejudice that, after the rise of political and racial antisemitism during the second half of the nineteenth century, changed in character but not in strength. On the other hand, their strong identification with German culture rendered the Jews suspicious in the eyes of many Czechs, who since the beginning of the Habsburg rule in the seventeenth century had developed their own nationalist movement and fought for greater political and cultural autonomy.

Kafka's 'Brief an den Vater' ('Letter to his Father', 1919) offers a socio-psychological portrayal of this generation of Jews who were suspended between different ethnicities, cultures and religions. Kafka suggests that his father was unable to transform his vaguely felt attachment to Judaism into a meaningful heritage or any other form of empowerment, which is one of the reasons why the child Kafka could experience religion only as empty ritual and rote learning. Hermann Kafka's ambivalent relationship to Judaism caused him to react strongly negatively when his adult son even-tually became interested in things Jewish:

> Because I was the mediator, Judaism became abominable to you, Judaic scriptures unreadable; they 'disgusted you' . . . your 'disgust' . . . could only mean that unconsciously you acknowledged the weakness of your Judaism

208

and of my Jewish upbringing, had absolutely no wish to be reminded of it, and responded to any reminder with open hatred. (*M* 126/*NSI* 191)

Throughout his adult life, Kafka went through phases of intense interest in things Jewish and developed alternatives to the bourgeois-liberal model of assimilation while nonetheless retaining a sense of critical distance from this tradition.

Yiddish Culture

The first surge of interest in Jewish culture Kafka experienced coincided with what is often described as the beginning of his 'mature' writings. In the autumn and winter of 1911–12, just a few months before he wrote 'Das Urteil' ('The Judgement', 1912), Kafka attended a number of Yiddish theatre performances staged by a Galician Jewish troupe in the Café Savoy in Prague. He befriended the actors, especially the lead actor, Jizchak Löwy (1887–1942), and recorded detailed impressions of the performances in his diary. He was mesmerized by the expressive physicality, lively gestures, intense emotions and familial warmth he found on the stage. He describes how the first performance he visited inspired in him a sense of Jewish communality, to which he reacted with nervous excitement: 'Some songs, the expression "yiddische kinderlach", some of this woman's acting (who, on the stage, because she is a Jew, draws us listeners to her because we are Jews, without any longing for or curiosity about Christians) made my cheeks tremble' (5 October 1911; *D* 65/ *TB* 59). For Kafka, Yiddish theatre promised first and foremost the possibility of cultural authenticity and a sense of community for deracinated Western Jews. He also took note of aspects he considered less attractive – and at times seemed repulsed by the poverty, crowdedness and dirt he saw – but he interpreted those as further signs of the authenticity of Yiddish theatre and the Eastern European Jewish world from which it hailed.

Dan Miron has argued that Kafka misconstrued much of what he saw and heard. According to Miron, Kafka did not recognize the modernity of Yiddish theatre, which is both a product and a vehicle of secular humanism and in many ways departs from the *halakha*, that is the body of religious laws that traditionally governed most aspects of Jewish life. Rather than acknowledge the secular character of Yiddish theatre, Kafka 'insisted on seeing [it] as a direct continuation of the traditional ghetto culture'.[1] This was certainly true for the first few performances, which led Kafka to idealize Yiddish theatre as a point of origin and a source of his own sense of

Jewish identity. However, Kafka also began to perceive Yiddish language and culture as a centrifugal and potentially destabilizing force.

Yiddish literature is one of the examples of what Kafka called, in a famous diary entry, a 'minor literature'. Because of its minority status and adherent sense of its own precarious position, a minor literature is subject to constant change, comparable to the 'keeping of a diary by a nation' (25 December 1911; *D* 148/ *TB* 313). Kafka's 'Introductory Speech on the Yiddish Language', which he delivered in 1912 during an evening of poetry readings by Jizchak Löwy, further develops this idea. In his speech, Kafka depicts Yiddish as a quintessentially diasporic language that continuously absorbs words from other languages without ever creating a stable semantic or grammatical system. The rhetoric of the speech is intended to have both centripetal and centrifugal effects on its audience. On the one hand, it is a performance meant to draw Kafka's audience – assimilated, German-speaking Jews whom he could not expect to understand or appreciate Yiddish – into the kind of community he believed to have found among Eastern European Jews. On the other hand, Kafka imparts to his listeners a contradictory message: he first tells them that they *can* understand Yiddish (because it derives from Middle High German) and then that they *cannot* understand Yiddish (because it resists translation into German). Ironically, Kafka attempts to draw his listeners into a community by highlighting the psychological split within them – a split between a sense of familiarity as well as distance towards the Yiddish tradition.[2] Indeed, the speech dramatizes and interrogates Jewish communality in a way that is also characteristic of Kafka's literary works.

Prague Zionism

One place to look for answers to the fraught question of Jewish collective identity is Zionism, in which Kafka showed a lifelong interest. He never formally joined a Zionist organization but followed the debates about Jewish national identity and participated in them in many ways. In 1910, introduced by his friend and former schoolmate Hugo Bergmann (1883–1975), he began to attend the events of the *Bar Kochba*, the Zionist association of Jewish students in Prague. From 1911 until his death, Kafka regularly read the Prague Zionist journal *Selbstwehr* (*Self-Defence*), which reviewed or published several of his short prose texts. He also read Martin Buber's (1878–1965) journal *Der Jude* (*The Jew*) from its first appearance in 1916, and in 1917 contributed two pieces, 'Schakale und Araber' ('Jackals and Arabs', 1917) and 'Ein Bericht für eine Akademie' ('A Report to an Academy', 1917).

His enthusiastic reading of such books as Heinrich Graetz's *Volkstümliche Geschichte der Juden* (*History of the Jews*, 1888) and Simon Dubnow's *Neueste Geschichte des jüdischen Volkes* (*The Newest History of the Jewish People*, 1920) round out the picture of his deep interest in the collective experience of the Jews. During the First World War, he showed interest in the practical programmes of Zionism, including charitable work with Jewish refugees from Eastern Europe. From 1917 onwards, he intermittently took Hebrew lessons and contemplated moving to Palestine – in particular towards the end of his life, in 1923, though the rapid progression of his tuberculosis made this plan impossible. All of these activities have led friends of Kafka such as Max Brod (1884–1968) and Felix Weltsch (1884–1964) to regard and describe him as a fellow Zionist, though this label has been contested by others and indeed by Kafka himself.

Prague Zionism did not promote a monolithic ideology or endorse a clear agenda but is best characterized as a cultural or spiritual Zionism. Originally formulated by the Hebrew essayist Ahad Ha'am (1856–1927), cultural Zionism aimed at the establishment of a Jewish spiritual centre in Palestine. The goal was not necessarily the founding of a political state but the revitalization of Jewish culture, which would then propagate from Palestine to the diaspora. These ideas found their way to Prague via Martin Buber, who between 1909 and 1911 delivered his famous 'Three Speeches on Judaism' for the Bar Kochba organization. The speeches, which electrified the young Zionists of Prague, rely on highly metaphorical language. In the first speech, Buber appeals to the modern Jew to reconnect to the 'community of his blood'.[3] Blood is here a metaphor for Jewish interiority, spirituality and continuity rather than a racial concept – and it is up to the individual Jew to make a choice and embrace this common ground. In his impassioned call for a Jewish cultural renaissance, Buber never defines the basis of Jewish collectivity much further than this. Another sign of the non-dogmatic character of Prague Zionism is the relatively harmonious coexistence of different factions, for instance, the respective supporters of Yiddish and Hebrew as the main Jewish language. Whereas political Zionists such as Theodor Herzl (1860–1904) and Max Nordau (1849–1923) disdained Yiddish as a stunted ghetto language, the Bar Kochba promoted the study of Hebrew and also sponsored presentations on and of Yiddish literature – such as the one introduced by Franz Kafka in 1912.

It is not easy to sum up Kafka's attitude towards Zionism. In his letters and diaries, he makes contradictory statements, expressing sympathy for the Zionist movement yet rejecting the label 'Zionist' (as he would challenge all such labels). Moreover, his literary texts are resistant to Zionist interpretations because they contain virtually no explicit references to Jews and Judaism – in stark contrast to the preoccupation with such matters in his diaries and letters. If anything, Kafka engages with Zionist concerns in an indirect and parabolic manner that gives his literary texts an irreducible multivalence and multidirectionality. The two stories he published in Buber's *Der Jude* are a case in point. 'A Report to an Academy', in which an African ape claims to have found a 'way out' of captivity by imitating his human captors, has frequently been read as a Zionist critique of Western Jewish assimilation. However, the ape's transformation can equally well allude to other adaptive processes, including evolution, civilization, colonialism – and even to the Zionist attempt to turn the Jews into a nation like all other nations. 'Jackals and Arabs', which evokes Jewish religious ideas and practices such as messianic hope, ritual bathing and kosher butchering, can be read as a Zionist critique of Orthodox Judaism. But since the story is set in a country populated by Arabs, it may also satirize the quasi-messianic aspirations of Zionists in Palestine.

Kafka's most incisive contributions to the Zionist debates are, perhaps, the more general questions his texts raise about the nature of communal belonging. Many of his short prose texts depict communities in a state of disarray. The animal peoples in Kafka's late stories, including the pack of dogs in 'Forschungen eines Hundes' ('Investigations of a Dog') and the mouse folk in 'Josefine, die Sängerin oder Das Volk der Mäuse' ('Josefine, the Singer or The Mouse People'), evoke the Jewish diaspora. These animals live in isolation and are faced with outside forces – foreign precepts and faceless enemies – and it becomes increasingly unclear what kind of bond exists between them, and whether practices such as music, memory or the search for knowledge can create a communal consciousness and enable collective action. In 'Beim Bau der chinesischen Mauer' ('At the Building of the Great Wall of China', 1917), social fragmentation and communication gaps in the vast empire prevent the completion of the wall, the great national project. Indeed, in many of Kafka's stories communities are held together either by external threats or by a pervasive *uncertainty* about the institutions that supposedly govern them. Some texts, such as 'Gemeinschaft' ('Community', 1920) and 'Eine Gemeinschaft von Schurken' ('A Community of Scoundrels', 1917), depict more cohesive communities but at the same time expose the mechanisms that bring about social cohesion as arbitrary and potentially violent. As Vivian Liska sums up, Kafka remains torn between a longing for and an apprehension of communal identity: 'More intensely even than in solitude, Kafka lived in the difficult situation of one who recognizes the temptations and the terrors of saying "we"'.[4]

Tradition and Modernity

Kafka's relationship to Judaism has been subject to intense debate. Literary scholars have traced central motives, including the law, the court, the gatekeeper and the imperial message, back to Judaic texts and traditions. Although his Jewish education was by his own estimate scanty, Kafka was familiar with these traditions, and in particular their mystical strands, through his reading of Jewish folk tales. During the last years of his life, his intermittent study of Hebrew and the Talmud further exposed him to Jewish religious traditions.

The serious inquiry into Kafka's relationship to Judaism began with an epistolary debate between Walter Benjamin (1892–1940) and Gershom Scholem (1897–1982), both of whom rejected Max Brod's allegorical-theological readings of Kafka and instead focused on the relationship between revelation, text and commentary in his work. According to Benjamin, Kafka both evokes and suspends the Judaic tradition of commentary. He effectively emancipates the *aggadah* – the compilation of legends, anecdotes and practical advice in rabbinic literature – from the *halakha* – the legal materials in that same body of literature. Whereas traditional *aggadic* stories remain tethered to the *halakhic* laws they illustrate, Kafka's parables are severed from the search for truth and lacking in instruction: 'Kafka's real genius was that he tried something entirely new: he sacrificed truth for the sake of clinging to transmissibility, to its *aggadic* element.'[5] Rather than on the content of truth, Kafka focuses on the process of transmission, the mechanisms by which experience is relayed through parables, stories and novels.

As Robert Alter has argued, Benjamin and Scholem were the first to identify the peculiar 'textualisation of truth' that explains Kafka's affinity to the Hebrew tradition: 'The distinctive strength as well as the drastic limitation of the Hebrew orientation, with a belief in revelation as its point of departure, was its commitment to deriving everything from the text rather than from the circumambient world.'[6] Kafka's texts tend towards auto-exegesis, combining narration with a contemplation of the multiple meanings thus produced, most famously in the discussion of the parable told by the priest in *Der Process* (*The Trial*, 1914–15). In their ability to elicit a seemingly endless number of interpretations, these texts evoke the Judaic tradition of commentary, which is meant to unfold the infinite potential of meaning inherent in a sacred text. The status of this primordial text, however, is a point of dispute between Scholem and Benjamin. Benjamin argues that Kafka's figures have lost the Holy Writ; Scholem that they cannot decipher it. Benjamin holds that revelation is absent from Kafka's world;

Scholem that it is merely unfulfillable. Scholem explains what he means by
this 'nothingness of revelation':

> I understand by it a state in which revelation appears to be without meaning,
> in which it still asserts itself, in which it has *validity* but *no significance*. A
> state in which the wealth of meaning is lost and what is in the process of
> appearing (for revelation is such a process) still does not disappear, even
> though it is reduced to the zero point of its own content, so to speak.[7]

As Alter points out, the idea of a 'nothingness of revelation' allows Scholem
to read Kafka as a continuation of one strand of Jewish mysticism – the at
times nihilist and heretical messianic movements of the seventeenth and
eighteenth centuries – whereas Benjamin puts more emphasis on the disconnection between Jewish tradition and Kafka's secular modernity.

A brief look at two texts from the collection *Ein Landarzt* (*A Country Doctor*, 1920) suggests that Kafka can indeed be read in both of these
ways, and that he ultimately rethinks tradition as such. On the one hand,
'Der neue Advokat' ('The New Advocate', 1917) lends support to Scholem's
thesis that Kafka's figures are confronted with ancient texts they cannot
decipher. Bucephalus, the warhorse of Alexander the Great, has turned
from heroic deeds to the study of the law: 'Free, flanks unconfined by the
rider's thighs, in the quiet of the lamplight, far from the tumult of Alexander's battle, he reads and turns the pages of our ancient tomes' (*HA* 12/*DL*
252). While Bucephalus has access to the law books as the carriers of tradition, the rather grotesque image of the hoofed reader leafing through the
ancient books inspires little confidence that he will be able to make sense of
them. On the other hand, 'Eine kaiserliche Botschaft' ('A Message from the
Emperor', 1917) illustrates Benjamin's point that the message cannot even
reach its recipient – here, because of vast expanses stretching out in front
of the imperial messenger. Yet even in this text it is noteworthy that the
subject – 'you' – is not absolutely disconnected from the emperor and his
message. The concluding sentence reads: 'You, though, will sit at your window and conjure [that message] up for yourself in your dreams, as evening
falls' (*HA* 28/*DL* 282). If the imperial message is irretrievably lost in the act
of transmission, this in turn inspires a process of innovation and invention.
Rather than simply condemning the failure to pass on Jewish tradition –
as he appears to do in 'Letter to his Father' – Kafka here redefines tradition
as intrinsically dynamic and dialogical. Like Benjamin, Scholem and other
post-assimilatory German Jewish thinkers, Kafka promotes a new understanding of tradition as a vehicle of change and ongoing reflection rather
than a guarantor of stability.

NOTES

1 D. Miron, *From Continuity to Contiguity: Toward a New Jewish Literary Thinking* (Stanford University Press, 2010), p. 341.

2 For a longer interpretation of the speech, see K. Garloff, 'Kafka's Racial Melancholy' in S. Corngold and R. V. Gross (eds.), *Kafka for the Twenty-First Century* (Rochester, NY: Camden House, 2011), pp. 89–104.

3 M. Buber, *On Judaism*, ed. N. N. Glatzer (New York: Schocken, 1996), pp. 17 and 19.

4 V. Liska, *When Kafka Says We: Uncommon Communities in German-Jewish Literature* (Indiana University Press, 2009), p. 25.

5 *The Correspondence of Walter Benjamin and Gershom Scholem*, 1932–40, ed. G. Scholem, trans. G. Smith and A. Lefevre (New York: Schocken, 1989), p. 225.

6 R. Alter, *Necessary Angels: Tradition and Modernity in Kafka, Benjamin, and Scholem* (Cambridge, MA: Harvard University Press, 1991), p. 72.

7 *The Correspondence of Walter Benjamin and Gershom Scholem*, p. 142. Emphases by Scholem.

CHAPTER 24

Psychology and Psychoanalysis

Carolin Duttlinger

Modernism was a time of psychological exploration and Sigmund Freud (1856–1939) one of the towering figures of the age. His controversial theories – about the sexuality of adults and children, about hysteria, trauma and neurosis, about dreams and 'Freudian slips' – were omnipresent in cultural debates of the time and influenced writers and artists across different schools and movements. Kafka's earliest recorded reference to Freud can be found in a letter to Willy Haas, in which he calls Freud's ideas 'unprecedented' and professes 'a great, but empty respect' for him (19 July 1912; *B1* 162) – a suggestion that, at this point at least, he had not actually read any of Freud's texts. Even so, psychoanalysis was impossible to avoid. Its findings featured in the literary magazines Kafka read, and were discussed in Berta Fanta's philosophical salon and other reading groups he attended.[1] Unlike fellow modernist writers such Hermann Hesse (1877–1962), Robert Musil (1880–1942) and Arnold Zweig (1887–1962), Kafka never underwent psychotherapy and often expressed doubts about the validity, indeed the possibility, of analysing the mind. That said, one important access point to psychoanalysis was through his own writings. In September 1917 Kafka asked his friend Willy Haas to copy out a passage from *Onanie und Homosexualität* (*Masturbation and Homosexuality*, 1917), a study by the Freud pupil Wilhelm Stekel, in which *Die Verwandlung* (*The Metamorphosis*) is mentioned in passing (22 September 1917; *LFFE* 145/*B3* 328).

The earliest, and most frequently cited, psychoanalytic reading of Kafka's works, however, comes from the author himself. On 23 September 1912, having just finished his breakthrough story 'Das Urteil' ('The Judgement'), Kafka notes in his diary: 'Gedanken an Freud natürlich' ('thoughts about Freud, of course'; *D* 213/*TB* 461) – a remark as tantalizing as it is laconic. Like many of Kafka's texts, particularly those written between 1912 and 1915, 'The Judgement' evokes Freud's famous Oedipus conflict, based on Sophocles' *Oedipus Rex*, though it does so with several twists. In Kafka's story, the conflict between father and son ends with the death of the son rather than the father, while the mother – in Sophocles' drama the object of the son's fatally misdirected desire – has been dead for several years. There are two contenders for her place in Kafka's take on the Oedipal triangle: the protagonist Georg Bendemann's fiancée and his nameless male friend in Russia. Georg's father contests his son's relationship with both of them as he attacks, and eventually destroys, Georg's role as the head of the family. The word 'natürlich' ('naturally' or 'of course') in Kafka's diary entry thus has to be read as a warning. There is very little that is obvious, or 'natural', in Kafka's narratives with their sudden twists, unstable power dynamics and dark desires. Freud's influence looms large in Kafka's writings, though less as an uncontested authority than as a template – of life *and* writing – to be wrestled with and rewritten in the same way that Kafka rewrites other intertexts, from the Bible to mythology, from fairy tales to legal theory.

Psychoanalysis was only one strand within a wide and varied field of psychological theories. Having started out as a minor branch of philosophy, psychology in the early nineteenth century evolved into one of the pillars of German intellectual culture. Modelling itself on the neighbouring disciplines of physiology and medicine, psychological research strove to become more rigorous and scientific. One of the founding fathers of modern psychology was Gustav Theodor Fechner (1801–87). Fechner, a physicist by training, founded the new discipline of psychophysics, which analysed the relationship between physical sensory stimuli and sensation on the one hand, and between brain processes and mental processes on the other. By arguing that mental processes could be quantified using experimental methods, Fechner revolutionized the discipline and paved the way for other pioneering researchers such as Hermann von Helmholtz (1821–94) and Wilhelm Wundt (1832–1920). In 1879, Wundt set up the world's first laboratory to be exclusively devoted to psychological research at the University of Leipzig.

Psychology's evolution into an independent academic discipline was supported by education policy. In 1825, a Prussian decree ordered that psychology be taught at the *Gymnasium* (grammar school) as part of a programme of philosophical propaedeutics designed to prepare pupils for study at university. Austria and other German states soon followed suit. The syllabus included topics such as 'sensations from the outer senses, imaginative faculty, memory and other mental faculties, association of ideas, and the difference among ideas, thoughts, and concepts'.[2] Kafka's teacher, the Catholic priest and polymath Moritz Gschwindt, used Gustav Adolf Lindner's *Lehrbuch der empirischen Psychologie* (*Manual of Empirical Psychology*, 1880) as his textbook; Lindner (1828–87) had held the first chair in Psychology, Pedagogy and Ethics at the Charles University in Prague.

Lindner's textbook starts off with a physiological account of the brain and the different senses, before moving on to Fechner's model of the sensory threshold or *Reizschwelle*. To be discernible, a stimulus must exceed a certain threshold, which is in turn proportionate to the level of the pre-existing sensations. The higher the original noise level, the more additional volume is needed for a new sound to be discernible.[3] For sensory impressions to become conscious, however, they must be linked to pre-existing mental representations. Attention is key in this process: 'To turn one's attention towards an object is to sustain one's mental image of it on a level of maximal clarity.'[4] Attention can be deployed voluntarily (in a deliberate effort of concentration) or involuntarily, e.g. as a response to a loud noise or a bright light. It can have a clustering effect, drawing together the various impressions associated with its main object, or else moving from one point to another like a spotlight if the field of attention is more extensive.

These arguments hark back to the early modern philosopher Gottfried Wilhelm Leibniz (1646–1716), who distinguished between *perception* and *apperception*, that is, between purely sensory perception and conscious awareness. Apperceptions are 'perceptions of perceptions, which are combinations of infinitely many minute perceptions'.[5] In the first, more extensive edition of his textbook, Lindner echoes Leibniz by differentiating between 'dark' and 'light', or 'clear', consciousness ('dunkles und helles Bewußtsein'). As he writes, even 'opaque' impressions leave traces in the mind, forming a 'chorus . . . which, though it does not act in its own right, constantly gets involved in the drama of our inner life'.[6]

Kafka's engagement with psychology continued well beyond his school years. In 1903 he read Gustav Fechner's work,[7] and between 1903 and 1905 he attended a philosophical discussion group based at the Café Louvre. While at university he attended courses on recent philosophy and psychology taught by Anton Marty and Christian von Ehrenfels. Both were pupils of the philosopher Franz Brentano (1838–1917), author of *Psychologie vom empirischen Standpunkt* (*Psychology from an Empirical Standpoint*, 1874). His main focus was not on sensory perception as such but on the inner, mental processes to which such impressions are subjected; among Prague intellectuals, he was considered one the foremost thinkers of the age.

The theories of psychology which Kafka encountered at school, at university and later in life were extraordinarily rich and varied, their paradigms often at odds with each other. While a scientifically oriented, experimental psychology challenged the very categories – the self as a coherent and stable entity – that underpin narrative and storytelling, Freudian psychology is essentially a series of stories designed to explore questions of identity and psychological development. Brentano, in turn, saw his analysis of inner perception as a way of mediating between the humanities and the experimental sciences. Rather than trying to fuse or reconcile these contrasting models, Kafka's texts dramatize the tension between them: through characters whose attempts to sustain a coherent narrative of themselves is repeatedly undermined by the fluidity of perceptions and experiences, and through narratives which showcase the instability of attention and its far-reaching consequences.

Self-Observation: Putting Psychology into Practice

Self-observation was a key method of experimental psychology. In his early diaries, Kafka frequently emulates this approach as a source of creative inspiration. In an entry of 4 October 1911 he records his impressions while lying on his sofa at nightfall:

> Why does one take a rather long time to recognize a colour, but then, after the understanding has reached a decisive turning-point, quickly become all the more convinced of the colour... When the light in the ante-room is turned off and only the kitchen light remains, the pane nearer the kitchen becomes deep blue, the other whitish blue, so whitish that all the drawings on the frosted glass... dissolve. – The lights and shadows thrown on the wall and ceiling by the electric lights in the street and the bridge down below are distorted, partly spoiled, overlapping and hard to follow [schwer zu überprüfen]. (*D* 63/*TB* 55–6)

The observer is passive and immobile, taking in the changing colours and shapes. Perception is not a matter of direct contact with an objective, stable reality but the product of optical and perceptual distortions, creating impressions which are hard to grasp and harder to interpret. There is no explicit reference to a narrating 'I' here, though the final sentence shows the viewer trying to trace the shapes back to their source.

In another diary passage, a similar set-up sparks more negative emotions. Once again, Kafka is alone in his room, but this time it is morning and the room is invaded by noise as his parents and sisters are getting on with their routines. Unlike in the previous passage, the observer does not enjoy the stream of sensations but longs for quiet: 'I want to write, with a constant trembling on my forehead' (5 November 1911; *D* 104/*TB* 225). Indeed, despite all the distractions, he does precisely this: the resulting sketch is later published as a short story.[8]

Kafka's early diaries privilege the experience of sensations over the more conventional reflections of a self-aware subject. This openness can be a source of inspiration, but it can also leave the subject vulnerable, unable to fuse impressions into a coherent narrative:

> I don't need to make myself restless, I'm restless enough, but to what purpose, when will it come, how can one heart, one heart not entirely sound, bear so much discontent and the incessant tugging of so much desire? Distractedness, weak memory, stupidity! [Die Zerstreutheit, die Gedächtnisschwäche, die Dummheit!] (13 September 1915; *D* 341/ *TB* 751)

By linking distractedness ('Zerstreutheit') to forgetfulness and stupidity, Kafka echoes modernist pathologies of inattention, which is seen as symptomatic of conditions such as neurasthenia, hysteria and various forms of mental illness and 'degeneracy'. The modernist writer and doctor Alfred Döblin's article on 'Aufmerksamkeitsstörungen bei Hysterie' ('Disturbances of Attention in Hysteria', 1909) is one of countless scientific publications on this subject.[9]

Distracted Narratives – Narratives of Distraction

These anxieties surrounding attention are spectacularly expressed in *Der Process* (*The Trial*), whose entire plot can be traced back to one single moment of absentmindedness. In the opening chapter protagonist Josef K. muses:

> Someone, I can't remember who it was, once said to me, isn't it strange how when we wake up in the morning generally speaking everything is still in the same place as the night before. It seems that while sleeping and dreaming we were in a state that's fundamentally different from waking life, and it takes, as that man quite rightly said, a boundless presence of mind or, better, alertness [Schlagfertigkeit] to grasp things, as it were, in the place we'd let go of them the night before. That's why the moment of awakening is the riskiest moment in the day; once we've passed it without having been dragged away from our place to somewhere else, we can be calm for the rest of the day. What conclusions that man – by the way, I've remembered who it was, though the name of course doesn't matter – (*PA* 168–9)

This paragraph is one of Kafka's boldest and most original commentaries on the working of the mind. According to experimental psychology, previous experiences, recorded in memory, underpin a process of apperception, whereby new experiences are incorporated into our knowledge of the world. Most of the time, this process happens automatically and unconsciously. As Kafka argues, however, attention is vital at points of transition, for instance, in the moment of awakening. As his protagonist says, the challenge then is 'to grasp things, as it were, in the place we'd let go of them the night before', to 'fix' them in their usual place to prevent the subject from being 'dragged away' into unknown territory.

This idea is prefigured in Lindner's textbook: 'Apperception gives our mental life a certain continuity and stability by subordinating new impressions to older ones, and *by putting everything in its right place and into the right relation to the whole.*'[10] The similarities between his argument and Josef K.'s musings in *The Trial* are striking. Both conceive of habitual, ordered perception in spatial terms; relating new impressions to old, familiar ones is crucial in anchoring the perceiving subject in a familiar reality. A little later on, Lindner describes the tendency of the mind to subordinate the new to the familiar, seeing the world as if through a pane of glass tinted by prior experience.[11] Kafka in *The Trial* describes the reverse situation: not the power of prior apperceptions to colour and absorb everything new, but the capacity of new events to overrule this ordering, familiarizing process. In fact, Lindner also accounts for this possibility when he notes that 'it sometimes so happens that older clusters of apperceptions are shaken, destroyed, and even completely transformed by new ideas [Vorstellungen], so that the course of apperception is reversed'.[12]

This passage reads like a commentary on *The Trial*, where events do indeed shake, destroy and transform K.'s established understanding of the world around him. But whereas Lindner attributes this change to the sheer power of the new impressions, that is, to phenomena originating in the *outside* world, Kafka locates the cause of this upheaval *within* the perceiving subject, whose momentary inattention leaves him unable to incorporate new experiences into his habitual perception of the world.

For a reading of *The Trial*, the above passage has huge implications. It suggests that the reasons behind K.'s trial are not criminological or judicial but psychological – one fatal moment of absent-mindedness which leaves K. forever at the mercy of unfolding events. Read in this way, the double meaning of the German title – *Process* means both 'trial' and 'process' – takes on an added dimension, emphasizing reality not as a stable framework but as the product of cognitive processes unfolding according to their own opaque rules. The fact that Kafka subsequent deleted the passage from the manuscript suggests that it may have spelled out the logic behind the novel rather too clearly, detracting from its deliberate ambiguity.

Indeed, similar slippages of attention occur throughout the text and lend the narrative a disorienting character. Time and again, K. resolves to pay close attention, and time and again he fails to do so. His 'distracted glances' in the conversation with the Inspector (*T* 11/*P* 20) betray his more general state of absentmindedness, or rather, of misdirected attention. The narrative focalization is highly unstable, often zooming in on seemingly random details, their prominence within the narrative at odds with their apparent irrelevance for the plot. What is more, such focalization occludes what *is* important, as when, towards the end of the first chapter, K. fails to recognize three colleagues from his bank, who are present throughout the interrogation.

Here, a gulf opens up between looking and seeing, perception and apperception. When the identity of the three in the corner is pointed out to K., this comes as a huge blow, and yet soon afterwards he misses the departure of the guards and the inspector:

> It did not show great presence of mind, and K. resolved to keep a better eye on himself in this respect . . . He immediately turned back again, however, without even having attempted to look for anyone, and leant back comfortably in the corner of his seat. (*T* 16/*P* 29)

The adversative 'however', spoken by the omniscient narrator, stresses the discrepancy between K.'s intention and his actions. Rather than staying vigilant, K. literally and metaphorically settles back into his habitual way of seeing the world, which is easier and more comfortable.

Beyond Psychology

Texts such as *The Trial* show Kafka as an astute observer of human psychology, and yet he remained deeply sceptical of this undertaking:

> How pathetic is my self-knowledge, compared to my knowledge of my room. (Evening.) Why? There is no such thing as observation of the inner world, as there is of the outer world. Psychology is probably, taken as a whole, a form of anthropomorphism, a nibbling at our own limits [ein Annagen der Grenzen]. (*ON* 14/*NSII* 31–2)

An *objective* analysis of mental processes is impossible, for we cannot 'know' ourselves in the way we know the outside world. A curious detail here is Kafka's characterization of psychology as 'a form of anthropomorphism'; surely the mind *is* human? Perhaps Kafka is implying here that psychology is itself a cognitive construct: the use of social structures (the family, social hierarchies and institutions) or familiar narratives to explain processes that are ultimately unknowable. Once again, it is a subsequently deleted sentence which gets to the heart of the matter: 'The inner world can only be lived, it cannot be described' (*ON* 14/*NSII* 31–2). The workings of the mind cannot be captured through diagrams, formulas and experiments; they can only be experienced, or else related through narratives which closely trace a character's perspective.

The role of writing is addressed in another diary entry recorded when Kafka was about to embark on his final novel, *Das Schloss* (*The Castle*):

> The strange, mysterious, perhaps dangerous, perhaps saving comfort that there is in writing: it is a leap out of the lethal sequence action – observation, action – observation, for this creates a higher type of observation, a higher, not a keener type, and the higher it is and the less within the reach of the 'sequence', the more independent it becomes, the more it follows the laws of this movement, the more unpredictable, the more joyful, the more ascendant its course. (27 January 1922; *D* 406–7/ *TB* 892)

Here, Kafka modifies his own earlier claim that 'there is no such thing as observation of the inner world' by positing psychological (self-)observation as a constant of human experience. As his formulation of the 'lethal sequence' implies, however, this compulsion to analyse our every thought and action is neither freeing nor illuminating but paralysing, for it wrenches us out of the immediacy of lived experience into a vicious circle of self-consciousness. Writing, perhaps surprisingly, can offer a way out of this. As Kafka makes clear, the observation facilitated by writing is not 'keener' but 'higher', that is, somehow detached from the dynamics of self-observation – perhaps because it allows us an empathetic immersion in the lives of others. For all his reservations about the project of psychology, Kafka's writings enable both author and readers to reflect – not on the abstract 'laws' of psychology but on the richness of human experience with all its blind spots and contradictions.

NOTES

1 See T. Anz, 'Psychoanalyse' in M. Engel and B. Auerochs (eds.), *Kafka-Handbuch* (Stuttgart: Metzler, 2010), pp. 65–72: 65.
2 H. U. K. Gundlach, 'Germany' in D. D. Baker (ed.), *The Oxford Handbook of the History of Psychology: Global Perspectives* (Oxford University Press, 2012), pp. 255–88: 264.
3 G. A. Lindner and F. Lukas, *Lehrbuch der empirischen Psychologie: Für den Gebrauch an höheren Lehranstalten*, fourth edition (Vienna: Carl Gerolds Sohn, 1912), pp. 16–17. The fourth edition is identical to the third, 1900 edition used by Gschwindt. See P.-A. Alt, *Franz Kafka: Der ewige Sohn* (Munich: Beck, 2005), p. 79.
4 Lindner, *Lehrbuch*, p. 71.

5 Gundlach, 'Germany', p. 258.
6 G. A. Lindner, *Lehrbuch der empirischen Psychologie als induktiver Wissenschaft: Für den Gebrauch an höheren Lehranstalten* (Vienna: Carl Gerolds Sohn, 1880), p. 56.
7 9 November 1903; *LFFE* 10/*B1* 29; 401–2.
8 It appeared in 1912 under the title 'Großer Lärm' ('Great Noise') in the journal *Herder-Blätter* (*Herder Papers*).
9 A. Döblin, 'Aufmerksamkeitsstörungen bei Hysterie', *Archiv für Psychiatrie und Nervenkrankheiten*, 45 (1909), 464–88.
10 Lindner, *Lehrbuch*, p. 71 (my emphasis).
11 Lindner, *Lehrbuch*, p. 72.
12 Lindner, *Lehrbuch*, p. 70.

CHAPTER 25

Gender and Sexuality

Mark M. Anderson

Franz Kafka lived in a culture that both repressed the discussion of sexuality and subjected it to intense theorization and medicalization. His contemporary, the Viennese novelist Stefan Zweig (1881–1942), recalled in his memoir *Die Welt von Gestern* (*The World of Yesterday*, 1942) that even the word 'trousers' was considered 'unmentionable' in polite company.[1] And yet German-speaking medical and psychiatric researchers of the late nineteenth and early twentieth centuries, particularly in Austria, pioneered the clinical description of the full range of human sexuality, thus paving the way for an acknowledgement of non-normative sexual practices including homosexuality, voyeurism, fetishism and sadomasochism. Richard von Krafft-Ebing's *Psycopathia Sexualis*, published in 1886 (three years after Kafka's birth), catalogued an astonishing variety of sexual pathologies from his own patients, though he was careful to put the most explicit passages into Latin. Kafka's own diary entry right after finishing his breakthrough story 'Das Urteil' ('The Judgement') – 'thoughts about Freud, of course' (23 September 1912; *D* 213/ *TB* 461) – suggests just how prevalent psychoanalytic theory had become before the First World War, although Kafka later expressed reservations about the reductive nature of Freud's ideas.

Theories of Bi- And Homosexuality

More scandalous and popular than psychoanalysis, at the time, was Otto Weininger's theory that all humans contained differing proportions of female and male sexual identity. Despite its dense scholarly prose, his treatise on *Geschlecht und Charakter* (*Sex and Character*, 1903) became a runaway bestseller. His spectacular suicide in 1903 – Kafka was twenty at the time – only magnified public interest in his theories, which radiated far beyond Vienna to central Europe and beyond in the first two decades of the twentieth century. The trials of Oscar Wilde (1854–1900) and posthumous publication of his *De Profundis* in 1905 – well-covered in the Austrian press – increasingly pushed the love that dared not speak its name out of the closet.[2] Kafka attended a lecture on homosexuality in 1905 given by a school friend who would become a specialist in skin and venereal diseases (and who commented on Kafka's lack of interest in girls during their high school years together).[3] The Berlin sexologist Magnus Hirschfeld (1868–1935), the founder of the first political movement for homosexuality, sought to popularize the idea of a 'third gender' and decriminalize same-sex love between consenting adults.

Nor should one forget the special role of the 'Greek' tradition of homosexual love in German-speaking culture during Kafka's period. This tradition had already provided a socially acceptable cover for homoerotic attachments from Johann Winckelmann (1717–68) in the Enlightenment period to August von Platen (1776–1835) in the early nineteenth century. Around 1900 the Berlin magazine *Der Eigene: Ein Blatt für männliche Kultur* (*The Unique: A Journal for Male Culture*) began publishing suggestive photographs of adolescent boys in classicizing poses with articles on Greek love and the specifically German tradition of 'male culture' that would revitalize German youth, educational institutions and ultimately the state.[4] The popular *Wandervogel* movement, which brought adolescents, most of them male, together with a charismatic male leader, drew its energy, according to one notable participant and theorist, from the eroticized pedagogical bond. This same theorist, Hans Blüher, later wrote a treatise on *Die Rolle der Erotik in der männlichen Gesellschaft* (*The Role of Eroticism in Male Society*, 1917–19), which Kafka read attentively (as he did a few years later, to his dismay, Blüher's antisemitic pamphlet *Secessio Judaica*, 1922). Also noteworthy in this context is the classicizing 'system' of calisthenics developed by the Danish pedagogue J. P. Müller, which Kafka practised on a daily basis for much of his early adult life and which complemented his interest in the 'free body culture' or 'freie körperliche Kultur' of nude sun-bathing, swimming and open-air gymnastics. Kafka visited a variety of 'alternative' health spas during his lifetime, where homosexuality, the clothing reform movement for women and the redefinition of traditional gender roles were frequent topics of discussion.[5]

The Role of Literature in Exploring Alternative Sexuality

It was also literature, not just science, which provided groundbreaking descriptions of human sexuality, 'normal' and otherwise; indeed, literature and science often approached the topic hand in hand. The Austrian novelist Karl-Maria Kertbeny (1824–82) was apparently the first to coin the terms 'homosexual' and 'heterosexual', which were taken up by Krafft-Ebing in his treatise. The latter in turn referred to the Marquis de Sade (1740–1814) and Leopold von Sacher-Masoch (1836–95), whose 1870 novel *Venus im Pelz* (*Venus in Furs*) became an underground classic on male masochism and fetishism for an entire generation of modernists including James Joyce (1882–1941). Kafka pays open tribute to his Habsburg predecessor in the opening lines of *Die Verwandlung* (*The Metamorphosis*, 1912) with the picture of a fur-clad woman raising her muff-covered arm and fist towards the helpless Gregor Samsa, 'tied down' in his bed by his new insect body. Less explicit but no less potent references to Sacher-Masoch can be seen in the opening image of Lady Liberty holding a sword rather than a torch in *Der Verschollene* (*The Man who Disappeared*, 1912–14); in the dominatrix-like Klara and Brunelda in the same novel; or in the leather-clad, whip-wielding flogger in *Der Process* (*The Trial*, 1914–15) and the barmaid Pepi in *Das Schloss* (*The Castle*, 1922). Equally important literary explorations into these forbidden realms for Kafka's generation were Frank Wedekind's 'Lulu' plays[6] and the early novellas and stories of Thomas Mann with their depiction of homoerotic attachment – *Tonio Kröger* (1903) and *Der Tod in Venedig* (*Death in Venice*, 1912) – sadomasochism – 'Der kleine Herr Friedemann' ('Little Herr Friedemann', 1896) – incest and homosexuality – 'Wälsungenblut' ('Blood of the Volsungs', 1906) – and aesthetic-sexual narcissism ('Tristan', 1903).

We know almost nothing about Kafka's actual sexual practice. Relentlessly self-scrutinizing and explicit in his diaries and letters when it came to his identity as a writer, a son, a Jew, Kafka remained largely silent about his actual sex life. But it is clear that heterosexual love and marriage were always a struggle for him – the 'geographical area', he noted in his 'Brief an den Vater' ('Letter to the Father'), covered by Hermann Kafka and thus inaccessible to the son. Engaged three times to two different women, he never married; a torrid epistolary relationship with Milena Jesenská did not survive a few brief physical encounters. Nor is it clear how sexual his relationship was with Dora Diamant in the last year of his life; they lived together in Berlin for less than a year when Kafka was already severely ill. He formed his closest and longest relationships with Jewish men – Oskar Pollak, Max Brod, Franz Werfel, Oskar Baum, Felix Weltsch, Robert Klopstock, to name only the most prominent – some of whom inspired feelings of affection, jealousy and erotic attraction. 'If I go on to say that in a recent dream I gave Werfel a kiss', he wrote to Brod in mid-November 1917, 'I stumble right into the middle of Blüher's book [*The Role of Eroticism in Male Society*]. But more of that later. The book upset me [or "excited me", "es hat mich aufgeregt"]; I had to put it aside for two days' (mid-November 1917; *LFFE* 167/*B* 196).

What we do know is that Kafka was no prude when it came to sex, although Max Brod fostered this image when he excised from Kafka's diaries sexually explicit observations of the people around him – the bulging genitals of a man on a train; the sexual exploits and collection of pornographic photos of a passing acquaintance; the naked legs of two 'handsome Swedish boys' at the health spa 'Jungborn', which Kafka describes as so 'taut and well-formed that one could only properly travel over them with one's tongue' (9 July 1912; *D* 478/*TB* 1041). For a long time Kafka's reputation as an other-worldly, ascetic or neurotic writer helped mask his very active, physical engagement with the immediate environment. But in and outside his writings, the human body was always a centre of his attention.

In his texts Kafka proved himself every bit as capable and adventurous in exploring the range of human sexuality and changing gender identities of his culture as Daniel Defoe (1660–1731), de Sade, Honoré de Balzac (1799–1850), Sacher-Masoch, Oscar Wilde and Thomas Mann. Indeed, his writing seems linked from the very beginning with an interest in non-normative sexuality, rape, bondage and self-mutilation – sexuality as the site of power relations and violence. His first extended prose text, *Beschreibung eines Kampfes* (*Description of a Struggle*, 1904–10), concludes with a strong personal relationship between two male companions, which is threatened by an impending engagement; with varying degrees of explicitness this tension is also the subject of the unfinished 'Hochzeitsvorbereitungen auf dem Lande' ('Wedding Preparations in the Country', 1906–9), 'The Judgement' and 'Der Heizer' ('The Stoker'). His first novel, *The Man who Disappeared* (of which 'The Stoker' forms the first chapter) is set in motion by sexual trauma, specifically, the rape of the underage male protagonist, Karl Rossmann, by the family maid, an older, more experienced woman whose aggressive advances provoke the boy's disgust. Kafka does not shy away from a surprisingly explicit description of coitus:

> [she] pressed her naked belly against his body, fumbled with her hand between his legs in such a disgusting manner that Karl wriggled his head and neck out of the pillows, then thrust her belly against him several times, he felt as though she were part of himself and perhaps for this reason he was seized by a terrible sense of needing help. (*MD* 23/*V* 43)

Two aspects are worth noting about this scene. The first is the disgust that intimate heterosexual relations inspire in Karl – a trait we find at various points in Kafka's own diaries and letters: the disgust he feels for the sight of his parents' unmade bed, for instance, or even for a certain 'small gesture' and 'small word' made by the first woman he had sexual intercourse with. The tender physical affection he feels for the ship's stoker must be seen in contrast with this initial rape-like seduction. The second aspect is Karl's passive, victim role. Indeed, the trauma of the events that set the novel into motion – the violent sexual encounter plus the punitive gesture of the family casting him out – provides the blueprint for his subsequent adventures in America, where a temporary home is provided and then arbitrarily snatched away: a series of seductions and banishments mimicking the initial heterosexual violence and culminating in the sadomasochistic scenes of Brunelda's abuse of her male servants.

This passive, victim condition, suffused with the energy of illicit sexual violence, provided Kafka with the blueprint for many of his subsequent fictions. Terrible things happen to the unsuspecting, helpless male protagonist, and often they happen in bed. Gregor Samsa's metamorphosis takes place while he is sleeping; he awakens to find himself on his back, his legs waving helplessly, face to face with the picture of a dominating 'pin-up' female. Later in the story Gregor will attempt to rescue this eroticized picture from the housecleaning of his sister and mother, by crawling up the wall and pressing his hot body onto the image's cool glass in a bizarre sexualized coupling. At the beginning of *The Trial*, Josef K. is in bed, still in his nightclothes; his arrest begins with two officers of the Law 'penetrating' his intimate domestic sphere. Everything in his subsequent engagement with the Court confirms its rapaciously sexual nature, from the 'skirt-chasing' judges to the leather-clad whipper flogging delinquent officials and the dirty law books Josef K. discovers that are filled with crude pornographic drawings and a novel about marital sexual abuse. Here and elsewhere, Kafka's signature narrative device is to take the explicit scenarios of de Sade and Sacher-Masoch and infuse them into the margins and subtexts of his fictions. Potentially lifeless stories about the endless search for the law or the castle are galvanized by an undercurrent of illicit sexual violence. The device may be compared to that of the Gothic novel, whose stories of imprisonment in subterranean, dark, 'medieval' architectural sites derive their energy from the steady threat of sexual predation. Like the female protagonists of the Gothic novel, many of Kafka's heroes act by reacting to an external threat or violent act: pursued by a sexual predator, they must flee into a dark, labyrinthine, dangerous world. Their subjectivity is defensive, 'feminized'.

Punishment Fantasies in Kafka

Early commentators have described Kafka's fictions as 'punishment fantasies'[7]; one could go further and note that the punishment often seems to involve a sexualized father and homosexual rape. Note, for instance, the sexually charged encounter between Georg Bendemann and his father in 'The Judgement'

> 'Because she lifted her skirts', his father began to warble, 'because she lifted her skirts like this, the disgusting cow', and acting the part, he lifted his shirt so high that one could see the scar from his war-wound on his thigh, 'because she lifted her skirts like this and like this and like this, you went for her, and so that you that you could have it off with her undisturbed you dishonoured our mother's memory, betrayed your friend, and buried your father in bed so that he can't stir. But can he stir or can't he?' And he stood perfectly free and kicked up his legs. He radiated insight. (*M* 26/*DL* 57)

This moment in Kafka's breakthrough story 'The Judgement', where the simmering conflict between father and son suddenly breaks out into the open, is commonly interpreted as an example of German Expressionism's preoccupation with the Oedipal generational struggle. But the passage also provides proof of just how bizarre and original Kafka's depiction of patriarchal identity is, at once in dialogue with his time and singularly his own. Often overlooked is the performative, transgendered aspect of patriarchal authority: to defeat Georg the father impersonates his fiancée; the raised nightshirt reveals not the phallus but a feminized 'no-thing', an absence marked by a wound. The spectacle is at once grotesque and mesmerizing. Gregor is spellbound by the gender-bending spectacle of his father as both castrating patriarch and lascivious seductress.

The sexual fantasy undergirding *The Metamorphosis* is more classically Oedipal but no less bizarre. Each of the first two chapters involves Gregor venturing out from his bedroom into the family's living spaces, only to be thrust violently back by his father. At the end of the first section, Gregor's wide insect body gets stuck in the door, his legs painfully crushed and trembling: 'then his father gave him a vigorous kick from behind, which this time was truly a deliverance, and he flew, bleeding heavily, into the depths of his room' (*M* 43/*DL* 142). At the end of section two, his father bombards him with strangely electrified apples which pierce his stiff carapace back; rather than flee, Gregor succumbs to what seems to be exquisite pain, 'as if he were nailed fast', as he stretches himself out to watch the primal scene of his undressed mother 'in total union' with the father (*M* 59/*DL* 171). Christianity meets Freud and Sacher-Masoch in one of modern literature's decidedly most unusual climaxes.

The disturbing violence of these punishment fantasies only increased with the unhappy turn in Kafka's attempts to marry Felice Bauer and, simultaneously, with the outbreak of the First World War. A few months after the engagement was called off, in the autumn of 1914, he wrote 'In der Strafkolonie' ('In the Penal Colony'), where primitive rituals of adornment and mutilation combine with a high-tech (though dilapidated) execution apparatus that pierces the condemned man's body, tied down securely onto a 'bed', with ink-spurting glass needles and a giant iron stake. At the same time Kafka worked on 'Erinnerungen an die Kaldabahn' ('Memories of the Kalda Railway', which Brod half-suppressed by not publishing it as a separate story), an unfinished text that describes an explicit homosexual relationship against the backdrop of predatory giant rats clawing their way into the narrator's bedroom. And what are we to make of the odd short text 'The Bridge', in which the unnamed bridge protagonist is violated from behind by the iron tip of a man's walking stick? 'He came, he tapped me with the iron point of his stick, then he lifted my coattails with it . . . He plunged the point of his stick into my bush hair and let it lie there for a long time' (*CSS* 411/*NSI* 304–5). The sexual nature of this encounter is augmented by the first-person narrator's feminized identity: the gender for the German word for bridge is feminine, just as 'coat' could easily be translated as 'skirt' ('Rock', the same word used to describe the mother's petticoats in *The Metamorphosis*). Without warning, the unseen male intruder jumps with both feet onto the narrator's back, who shudders in 'wild pain', turns to see his aggressor, and then falls to his death, 'pierced by sharp rocks' (*CSS* 411/*NSI* 304–5).

For generations Kafka was read in isolation from his culture, as the lonely prophet of an abstract, bureaucratic modern world. All too often he himself was seen as asexual or neurotically incapable of heterosexual happiness. More recent commentators have emphasized the homoerotic, the Jewish or the conventionally heterosexual nature of his sexual identity.[8] But it is Kafka's writing, not his sex life, that ultimately is of interest. A full examination of all his writings – minor, unfinished stories as well as the more famous narratives; his uncensored letters and diaries (not all of which are available in English) – reveals an imagination that is much like the culture and society in which he lived: one that transgressed, expanded and explored the confines of an astonishing array of sexual identities, roles and practices. His narratives of the Law, punishment, guilt, bureaucracy and human versus animal identity engage us precisely because they are suffused with this sexual curiosity.

NOTES

1 S. Zweig, 'Eros Matutinus', *The World of Yesterday*, trans. H. Zohn (University of Nebraska Press, 1964), p. 74. The English translation actually leaves out the sentence where Zweig speaks of the 'hysterische Prüderie . . . dass eine Dame das Wort "Hose" damals überhaupt über die Lippen bringen dürfte' in *Die Welt von Gestern* (Berlin and Weimar: Aufbau-Verlag, 1981), p. 88.
2 S. L. Gilman, 'Karl Kraus's Oscar Wilde: Race, Sex, and Difference' in E. Timms and R. Robertson (eds.), *Vienna 1900: From Altenberg to Wittgenstein* (Edinburgh University Press, 1990), pp. 12–27.
3 R. Stach, *Kafka: Die frühen Jahre* (Frankfurt am Main: Fischer, 2014), p. 525.
4 M. M. Anderson, 'Kafka, Homosexuality and the Aesthetics of "Male Culture"' in R. Robertson and E. Timms (eds.), *Gender and Politics in Austrian Fiction* (Edinburgh University Press, 1996), p. 81.
5 M. M. Anderson, 'Body Culture' in *Kafka's Clothes: Ornament and Aestheticism in the Habsburg Fin de Siècle* (Oxford: Clarendon Press, 1992), pp. 74–97.
6 E. Boa, *Kafka: Gender, Class, and Race in the Letters and Fictions* (Oxford: Clarendon Press, 1996), p. 43.
7 W. Sokel, *Franz Kafka – Tragik und Ironie* (Munich: A. Langen, 1964), p. 107.
8 S. Friedländer, *Franz Kafka: The Poet of Shame and Guilt* (New Haven, CT: Yale University Press, 2013), esp. pp. 66–94; S. Gilman, *Kafka: The Jewish Patient* (New York: Routledge, 1995); R. Stach, *Kafka: The Early Years*, trans. S. Frisch (Princeton University Press, 2017), esp. pp. 325–34.

CHAPTER 26

The City

Andrew J. Webber

Certain of Kafka's best-known narratives are set in cities, albeit generally anonymous ones. They often turn on set-piece urban scenes and institutional arenas: the law courts and the cathedral in *Der Process* (*The Trial*, 1914–15); the railway station and the hospital in *Die Verwandlung* (*The Metamorphosis*, 1912); traffic flowing across the bridge in 'Das Urteil' ('The Judgement', 1912); or the grand hotel and the high-rise block in Kafka's first novel, *Der Verschollene* (*The Man who Disappeared*, 1912–14). Such scenes, set between urban place and non-place, inhabitation and transit, will be a central focus of this chapter. They will be discussed against the broader picture of Kafka's cities, as featured in both his fiction and his life-writing. The various unnamed cities, which might be seen as versions of an allegorical site of mass habitation, will be considered alongside a set of named cities – Prague, Vienna, Berlin, Paris and New York – as they feature in the travelling of Kafka's fictional, biographical and dream narratives.

Approaching the City

A first question for this chapter on Kafka and cities might be a more general one: how does he deal with space and place? Space is a fundamental experiential category in Kafka's writing, as most expressly figured in scenarios of acute corporeal constraint, where potential space is always hemmed in. As many of the titles of his works attest, he is certainly concerned with the placement of his narratives – with questions of setting. But it is also the case that space and place, like other key experiential categories, are subject to degrees of abstraction, cast between (sometimes excessive) attention to particularity and a sense of the generic and unlocatable. The preponderance of more or less abstract nouns relating to place in the titles of his narratives, with or without epithets, and with definite or indefinite articles attached, is indicative in this respect.

We could consider the opening scene of Kafka's most substantial work, *Das Schloss* (*The Castle*, 1922), the title of which appears to locate the text categorically. A castle may of course be an urban site (and indeed the Hradčany in Kafka's native Prague has often been seen as a model for this fictional one, transposed here to the country), but the key characteristic of the first encounter with this eponymous construction is how it eludes spatial categorization, an experience focalized through the protagonist, K., who claims to be a professional measurer of space and place. If there is some critical consensus that to be a 'Landvermesser', or land surveyor, in Kafka's fictional world is to be a mis-measurer ('Vermesser') of the dimensions of things, then this is indicative of a more general predicament regarding the measurement of the scale and disposition of human environments in that world. The castle as a singular construction also has the appearance of a more aggregated assemblage, and this creates a tension between the category of foreknowledge and that of phenomenal perception: 'If you hadn't known it was a castle you might have taken it for a small town' (*C* 11/*S* 17). And on closer approach, the castle is indeed seen as just a rather abject little town, assembled out of village houses. The castle, the small town and the village thus become confused in a network of slippages between environmental categories. The scene echoes with one of Kafka's fragments, where the first-person narrator makes out the outline of a city on the horizon, only to come to the conclusion that it is in fact a 'big village' (*NSII* 336), or with the narrative beginning 'Unser Städtchen liegt' ('Our little town lies...'), which, in locating 'our' little town, promptly becomes embroiled in the description of 'giant and narrow' cities (*NSII* 261). These forms of displacement through the categories of space and place are fundamental to Kafka's broader project. And, as the most imposing structure of human civilization, the city is also an exemplary figure of the sort of elusiveness of definition and coordination – the condition of unsettlement – that is at the core of Kafka's writing project.

Urban Knowledge

As the opening of *The Castle* illustrates, a key question in all of Kafka's writing is that of the subject's knowledge of where he or she is, and this extends in turn to the reader's knowledge of location. It is a question that is at once epistemological (asking how location may be knowable) and ontological (asking how being may be defined according to what may be known of location). And what applies to space and place in general certainly applies to representations of large-scale urban environments in particular. Cities are where human social life is most massed, dynamic and intensive, and for Kafka, knowing where you are in those conditions is never simply given. An exemplary short text might be 'Ein Kommentar' ('A Commentary', 1922), originally published as 'Gibs auf!' ('Give it up!'; *HA* 186–7/*NSII* 530). The subject of the narrative is on his way to the railway station, but is thrown by the fright of suddenly seeing the time on a clock tower against that on his watch. An urban monument that should be an instrument of orientation and coordination thus becomes one of disorientation and mismeasurement. The subject asks the way from a policeman ('Schutzmann', literally 'protection man'), whose advice, protective or otherwise, is to give up. The short text uses the unidentified urban setting in order to establish a paradigm for Kafka's writing: the subject who cannot find his or her way, an environment that causes confusion, and authority figures who compound that confusion. It casts that scene of radical – apparently, existential – disorientation in a narrative form that is as apparently clear as it is blank and reduced, also offering little sense of environmental orientation for the reader who might seek guidance in or through the narrative 'comment' or 'commentary'.

For pioneering urban theorists writing in Kafka's time, the city of modernity emerged at once as the acme of technical organization and orientation, and as a place of disorganization and disorientation, a site both of mass community and of atomic isolation and estrangement, an arena of sociocultural knowledge and of obscurity or fantasy. For the German sociologist Georg Simmel (1858–1918), in his landmark essay 'Die Großstädte und das Geistesleben' ('The Metropolis and Mental Life', 1903), the modern city's dynamic complexity represented a challenge to the capacity of the urban subject, a hyper-stimulating onslaught that could only be held in check by a kind of carapace of disengagement. And for the critics Siegfried Kracauer (1889–1966) and Walter Benjamin (1892–1940), writing in the wake of Simmel, the modern metropolis at once offered new forms of knowledge, resources for critical engagement with what it means to be human, and a set of illusory surfaces, tending to abstraction and distraction, a fetishist allure masking the reality of life in the city. For them, the city is not least a place of hyper-mediation, conditioned by technologies of communication, transportation, advertising and mass entertainment. It is a construction of utmost modernity, but also anachronistically shot through with archaic features.

Kafka's writings, caught between the ambiguous dynamics of the contemporary city and recurrent reference to the Babylonian model of archaic
urban catastrophe, as in the emblematic tale 'Das Stadtwappen' ('The City
Coat of Arms', 1920), can certainly be seen to chime with these contradictory views of urban life. In keeping with the thinking of those modernist
theorists, the cognitive and affective experience of the urban by the psyche
through the body – now heightened, now estranged – is a key theme for
Kafka. As critics have pointed out, that experience is not least mediated by
such technical apparatus as public transportation, photography, the *Kaiserpanorama* (Imperial Panorama) and the cinema, apparatus that at once
draws experience near and holds it at a distance.[1] Consider, for instance,
the short text 'Der Fahrgast' ('The Passenger', around 1907), where the
first-person narrator, borne along by a tram, and 'utterly uncertain' of his
place in the city, fixes his attention with an almost haptic intensity on a
girl who is about to alight (*M* 12/*DL* 27–8). The text is comparable in
its logic to the 'Denkbild', or thought-image, as developed by Benjamin
and Kracauer, not least in response to modern urban conditions. The tram
acts as another kind of urban visual medium, capturing experience in the
dialectical tension between mobility and fixation. And Kafka's urban writing can be understood as a second-order apparatus in these terms, reme-
diating the experience of the modern city, caught between fascination and
critical attention on the one hand and distanciation, avoidance and onward
propulsion on the other.

The ambivalent attachment to and evasion of the city is as significant
in Kafka's life writings as in his fictional texts. Kafka's epistolary writing is
characterized by a particular version of the condition that defines letters:
that they represent separation, often at remote distance. In Kafka's case,
they can also act as instruments of dislocation. His correspondence with
both Felice Bauer and Milena Jesenská constructs the cities in which his
addressees live (Berlin and Vienna, respectively) as spaces of separation. In
one letter to Milena, he describes a dream of Vienna, which represents it –
and this is a key topos for Kafka's cities – as a place of excessive 'traffic'
('Verkehr'; *LM* 49/*BM* 63), only in order for it to become a scene of displacement between the correspondents. The argument is now familiar that
the endless flow of urban traffic ('unendlicher Verkehr'; *M* 28/*DL* 61) that
passes over the bridge at the end of 'The Judgement' is in ironic tension
with the constantly blocked and diverted traffic or intercourse ('Verkehr')
between human subjects. As encapsulated in his dreams of Berlin, cities for
Kafka are typically places of impeded or misdirected motion and communication, or of (self-)exclusion.[2]

City of the Law

As we have begun to see, the condition of being out of the city, or unsettled within it, also pervades the fictional writing. If K.'s approach to the castle was a kind of false start for this chapter, for *The Castle* is surely not a city text, let us move on to another, more proximate scene of approach: that of *The Man who Disappeared*. This, too, is a title that, in its generic character, places the narrative in a space of uncertainty, one in which the subject has vanished. The initial potential site of disappearance is the emblematic city of early twentieth-century modernity: New York. And it is approached through a monumental, emblematic encounter, as the transatlantic ship passes by the Statue of Liberty. Here too, however, the sense of location is subject to subversive displacement, as the emblematic statue is recast in a travesty of its allegorical function, the torch replaced by a sword, the light of liberty by an instrument of existential combat.

If this chapter has started with two opening scenes of approach, and with one short text of urban disorientation, it is because such scenes are fundamental to an understanding of how Kafka's writing in general, and its negotiation of space in particular, works. These are scenes of uncertain definition, dimension and direction. And even where the subject is not arriving from outside, he or she is not at home in the territory of the narrative, 'not yet' knowing the city, as the first-person narrator of 'A Comment' has it (this, a subject who seems unable to find his way to leave the unknown city (*HA* 186/ *NSII* 530)).[3] In this sense, Kafka's urban subjects always come from somewhere else, retaining a share in the predicament depicted in one of his most familiar allegorical texts, 'Vor dem Gesetz' ('Before the Law'). This text, which may be freestanding, or embedded in the urban narrative of *The Trial*, where it forms part of the 'Cathedral' chapter, takes a protagonist from the country and places (one might say, displaces) him before the allegorical edifice of the Law. It is a construction, with its serial gates, that has to be understood as the antipode of the country. For the purposes of the judicial narrative *The Trial*, it is perhaps the city in which the broader narrative takes place, or its *mise-en-abyme* (the parable is indeed constructed as a set of structures within structures). We might think of the representation of the Trocadéro in Paris in one of Kafka's notes, where the gargantuan building in the great capital, unthinkable from the perspective of the little town, is cast as a super-scaled space entirely occupied by the activities of 'a large trial' (*NSIA* 281).

By indicating that the city is, implicitly, the site of the Law, Kafka installs it as the key arena for the questions of political and judicial organization – what contemporary political science would call governmentality – that preoccupy his writing. If there is a common thread that runs through the social structures of Kafka's writing, it is the enactment of power relations. And while the form that these take may be familial, interpersonal, communal or managerial, they all ultimately refer to the model of state and its governmental and judicial authority. In one of the variations excised from *The Trial*, Josef K. imagines the state intervening in his case through the figure of the policeman on the street, so that the action against him will be transferred to the level of 'laws of state' ('Staatsgesetz[e]'; *PA* 322). As the archaic figure of the policeman, with bushy moustache and the sabre 'vested in him by the state' (*PA* 322) in his hand, indicates, the state in question is of an archaic, patriarchal character.

It is the feudal model of empire, and of the imperial capital at its core, that underlies the different iterations of fundamental power relations here. While Kafka spent most of his life as the subject of a modern version of the imperial sovereign (also moustachioed and sabre-bearing), the archaic model of empire preoccupies much of his writing. The imperial capital is, it seems, the ultimate location of absolute sovereignty, and so the ultimate model for relationships of power and subjection. Its authority as such is installed in texts like 'Beim Bau der chinesischen Mauer' ('At the Building of the Great Wall of China', 1917), with Peking as an inescapable Chinese box of urban structures within structures. And the regulation of those relationships of power in Kafka's writings is fundamentally biopolitical in character; that is, it is exacted upon the body, which is subject to macro- and microsystems of control and constraint. The 'Before the Law' parable is a model case. The subject who is placed in waiting outside the gate of the Law is implicitly a kind of foreign body, to be held at bay. And his deferment is enacted through an elaborate process of bodily interaction, following a principle of metonymic displacement. Rather than giving his attention to the gates that might lead him into the city of the Law, the man from the country examines the fleas on the collar on the fur coat of the guard who stands bodily before the first of that flight of gates. And, as such, the man adopts the biopolitical status of the parasitic body, mortally attached to the epistructural surface of the city that is the Law.

City Limits

The gate to the city, the point of access in the epistructure, through which the body of the subject has – or would have – to pass in order to be incorporated into the civic space, is a key emblematic structure for Kafka's writing. It is typically guarded (the Statue of Liberty with sword in hand is such a guardian figure), and there is no guarantee that the subject seeking entry will be allowed to pass, rather than being held (or holding him- or herself) at bay, like the man from the country. One of Kafka's fragments has the subject from outside taking advantage of a deserted city gate in order to pass without identity papers (*NSII* 542). Another has the narrator 'over-running' (*NSII* 343), that is, illicitly passing, the first guardian of the gate(s). He realizes his transgression with a fright that is described as 'nachträglich', a term that might well be understood in its psychoanalytic sense, so that the apparently unwitting passing of the gate is retroactively invested with the fright in question. In these terms, entry to the city is inherently traumatic. When the over-running subject returns to confess his transgression, his admission is met with enigmatic silence, which may or may not mean that he can indeed now pass into the gated community. Such innocents from the country, masquerading as city-dwellers, are haunted by a lack of civic legitimacy. They are the sort of subjects who are liable to fall prey to, and so be unmasked by, the urban trickster of 'Entlarvung eines Bauernfängers' ('Unmasking of a Confidence Man' [literally, 'Peasant Hunter'], 1910–12).

In such examples of the gate-scene, it remains profoundly uncertain whether the subject has, or ever could have, what urban theorist Henri Lefebvre (1901–91) has called the right to the city.[4] And this sense of having inadequate licence to be in the city is a constant condition of Kafka's urban subjects, from Josef K. (apprehended by guards at the point of entry – the gate, one might say – to his narrative), to Karl Rossmann, challenged and pursued by policemen on the streets of Ramses and then kept in a kind of house-arrest in a high-rise block, removed from the spectacle of life on the city streets, or Gregor Samsa, in another kind of house-arrest in the quiet, but 'completely urban' Charlottenstraße (*M* 50/*DL* 156). At the end of his narrative, Josef K. is brought to his place of execution beyond the city limits, but the scene is also witnessed by, or from, an apparently displaced house, which is 'still' urban (*T* 163/*P* 310). The scene echoes a fragment of Kafka's in which a subject lost in a forest encounters a city house, the landscape around it cast as a scene of 'städtischer Verkehr', where the 'city traffic' in question is, however, frozen in place (*NSII* 518). As K. cannot know what kind of settlement the castle he has been called to at the start of his narrative really is – a castle indeed, or a small town, a mere assemblage of village houses, or perhaps even a city – so Josef K. at the end of his is still within the scenography of the city that is his trial, even as he has apparently been expelled from it. The city, it seems, is a paradigmatic place of displacement for Kafka, one that his writing is always at once within and without.

NOTES

1 C. Duttlinger, *Kafka and Photography* (Oxford University Press, 2007), pp. 62–81; P.-A. Alt, *Kafka und der Film: Über kinematographisches Erzählen* (Munich: C. H. Beck, 2009), pp. 48–100.
2 A. J. Webber, *Berlin in the Twentieth Century: A Cultural Topography* (Cambridge University Press, 2008), pp. 6–10.
3 The English translation misses this 'not yet'.
4 H. Lefebvre, 'The Right to the City' in E. Kofman and E. Lebas (eds. and trans.), *Writings on Cities* (Oxford: Wiley-Blackwell, 1996), pp. 147–59.

CHAPTER 27

Childhood, Pedagogy and Education

Katharina Laszlo

Dangerous Parents

When Kafka's oldest sister, Elli, pondered the question of whether to send her nine-year-old son Felix to boarding school in the autumn of 1921, she consulted Kafka, who was taking an active interest in the development of his nephew and nieces. In a series of letters, Kafka unreservedly supports the idea of Felix's early departure from home, and pronounces himself in favour of the progressive school Hellerau near Dresden. The school's prospectus, which Kafka ordered, presents the institution as a kind of substitute family, which crucially sets itself apart from the nuclear family by allowing children to choose their family members: 'The children make their own choices when they align themselves with educators with whom they also live, thereby creating closer circles of human community, which we call pedagogical families.'[1] In a 1947 letter Kafka's niece, Gerti, told Max Brod about her uncle's recommendation that she too be sent to Hellerau:

> I remember that he advised my mother, when I was ten or twelve years old, to send me away from home, to a dancing school at Hellerau. He must have experienced a very unhappy childhood, for I still remember his exclamation to 'take the children away from home'.[2]

To persuade his sister of the damage done by living with one's family, Kafka cites a passage from Jonathan Swift's *Gulliver's Travels* (1726) which depicts the child-rearing practices amongst the inhabitants of Lilliput, and singles out its memorable conclusion that 'Parents are the last of all others to be trusted with the Education of their own Children.'[3] According to the view Kafka attributes – with no suspicion of irony – to Swift, it is not their selfless care for any future children which leads two adults to procreate, but the selfish desire for sexual gratification. Kafka contrasts parental education, which he defines as a 'striving for equilibrium between parents and children', with 'true education', which he describes as 'the quiet, unselfish, loving development of potentialities of a growing human being or merely the calm toleration of the child's independent development' (autumn 1921; *LFFE* 294/*B* 344). And he concludes with Swift that it is not unconditional love which is the defining emotion in the family unit, but 'all gradations of tyranny and slavery' (*LFFE* 296/*B* 346). To believe that children are in good hands with their parents is to fall for a long-perpetuated myth; as long as their children live with them – as long as they are free to exercise their 'monstrous superiority in power' – parents should be considered essentially dangerous relations (*LFFE* 294–5/*B* 344).

Kafka's interest in pedagogy was certainly not unrelated to his own experience of an unhappy childhood, which he describes and analyses in the 'Brief an den Vater' ('Letter to his Father', 1919). The critique of parental education he voices in the letters to his sister, however, transcends the purely personal. His complex and radical view of child-rearing, which also emerges in other fictional and non-fictional texts, is social-scientific and literary, not pathological nor abstract. When considered alongside contemporary pedagogical thinkers crusading for an improvement of the living conditions of children, Kafka emerges in an unexpected light: as a devoted champion of children.

Kafka and progressive educational thinkers are united in their rejection of corporal punishment and those tyrannical, psychologically abusive means of child-rearing which would later be referred to as *Black Pedagogy*.[4] In the late nineteenth century, physical violence against children had significantly subsided in favour of educational techniques which, although they left the child's body unharmed, allowed parents to manipulate their children's mental life. For example, the physician Daniel Gottlob Moritz Schreber (1808–61), one of the most successful writers of child-rearing pamphlets of the mid-nineteenth century, recommends 'moderate, intermittent, bodily admonishments' merely as a means to an end.[5] As soon as a child has experienced beating once, Schreber claims, a look or a threatening gesture will be sufficient to uphold the kind of master–slave relationship between parents and children he postulates as not only acceptable but desirable.

The lives of Kafka's child characters are especially defined by this notion that threats are more effective than their execution; as the pedagogue Tuiskon Ziller (1817–82) advised in 1857, adults could 'more potently affect the mind of the child' if they do not allow the child to purge his/her conscience via punishment.[6] Indeed, the formulation of empty threats against children is such an integral part of Kafka's texts that in *Der Process* (*The Trial*, 1914–15) Josef K. receives 'empty exhortations, such as one gives to children' (*T* 80/*P* 150). In the 'Letter to his Father', Kafka provides a genealogy of his internalized guilt in response to the experience of threats of physical punishment which are not executed. 'I'll tear you into little bits – like a fish!', Hermann Kafka exclaims, exhibiting the kind of parenting championed by Schreber and Ziller that cements the child's feelings of nullity without ever raising a hand (*M* 109/*NSII* 161). It is difficult to determine which of Kafka's child figures wins the macabre contest to have the most menacing guardian. Whether this credit belongs to the young trainees in 'Blumfeld, ein älterer Junggeselle' ('Blumfeld, An Elderly Bachelor', 1915), who owe the dubious pleasure of staying alive to the eponymous protagonist's mercy ('[T]hey were children, and Blumfeld couldn't beat children to death, could he?' (*HA* 96/*NSI* 259)), or to Karl Rossmann in *Der Verschollene* (*The Man who Disappeared*, 1912–14), whom the head porter threatens with sexual violence ('I'm going to enjoy you' (*MD* 133/*V* 262)), their shared fate demonstrates that if one wants to severely damage a child, there are more effective ways than corporal punishment.

The Century of the Child?

In 1900, animated with combative spirit and optimism, the Swedish feminist and educational theorist Ellen Key (1849–1926) invoked a new, child-friendly era. In her pamphlet *Barnets Århundrade* (*The Century of the Child*), which was first translated into German as *Das Jahrhundert des Kindes* in 1902 and proved so popular that it had reached its thirteenth edition by 1905, she anticipates 'increasing limitations of the rights of parents over children' in the twentieth century.[7] By this she refers not only to physical punishment but more broadly to the often intangible ways adults mistreat children, urging prospective parents to respect their children's individual needs, and not to subject them to emotional manipulation. After centuries of adults abusing their power over children, Key was hopeful that, as Lloyd DeMause would later put it, society was slowly beginning to awaken from the 'nightmare' that was 'the history of childhood'.[8]

While Key's name does not feature in Kafka's notes, his letters contain numerous references to Friedrich Wilhelm Foerster (1869–1966) – in many respects a Keyan pedagogue. Foerster's handbook, *Jugendlehre* (*Youth Manual*, 1904), was required reading at the *Jüdisches Volksheim* (Jewish People's Home) in Berlin, where Felice Bauer worked in the summer and early autumn of 1916 caring for eleven- to fourteen-year-old girls. In his letters to Felice, Kafka referred to the book time and time again; he even sent her an extensive summary of the chapter 'Ethical viewpoints on various academic subjects'. Foerster argues that parents should 'not only criticise and

punish, warn and preach, command and forbid, but, during a trusting conversation, afford children the means to recognise that they not only should
[be good], but that they themselves want to [be good] – that they have to
want to'.[9] Foerster devises short scenarios to educate children by encouraging them to fulfil their own potential to be 'good'. In the case of a child
who slams doors behind himself, for example, he suggests that instead of
rebuking him, adults should calmly discuss the matter and, when the child
does as he is told, praise him with words like 'Bravo . . . you are becoming a
nobleman.'[10]

Although the non-threatening nature of this child-rearing technique
might have appealed to Kafka, he is clear that it does not constitute 'the
calm toleration of the child's independent development' he theorizes about
in his letters to Elli – perhaps the best summary of Kafka's educational
ideal. For this reason he judges Foerster's 'education to self-mastery' to fos-
ter consolidated *parental* mastery, not self-mastery in the child. Indeed, the
pedagogue's remark that children will not only want to behave well, but also
realize that they 'have to want to', exhibits undertones of the kind of emotional violence Kafka critiques in a diary entry of 8 October 1916. He terms
Foerster's concept of education a 'conspiracy on the part of adults', and
notes that adhering to such techniques means luring children 'from their
unconstrained romping into our narrow dwelling by pretences in which we
perhaps believe, but not in the sense we pretend. (Who would not like to be
a nobleman? Shut the door'); D 370/ *TB* 804). Foerster himself comments
that the parent in his door-closing example 'tied . . . the quiet and gentle
opening and closing of doors to the boy's desire for knightliness', but he
praises this technique for its effectiveness and tenderness in comparison
with a slap or reprimand.[11] Kafka's diary entry, in contrast, denounces it
for being based on false foundations: one does not become a nobleman
by closing doors quietly, nor are such manners acquired voluntarily. Above
all, it is the parental appeal to the child's perception of him- or herself
which Kafka views as depriving the child of freedom. When he elaborates
on these reflections in a letter to Max Brod more than a year later, his
rejection of latent coercion is still prevalent: 'I would be utterly at a loss if
I had to [train a child to close doors]', he writes in December 1917, 'but
then I consider being at a loss toward that sort of thing as right' ('[D]ie
Fähigkeit des Türschließens zu erkitzeln . . . ist eine Aufgabe, der gegenüber
ich . . . Ratlosigkeit für richtig halte'; *LFFE* 177/ *B3* 379). Since slamming
doors is not morally reprehensible, he continues, it is at best pointless to
stop children from doing so. At worst, as the reference to tickling suggests, making children believe they choose to close doors quietly is like

forcing someone to laugh: it constitutes a manipulation of their thoughts and actions.

Flashbacks to two early childhoods in *The Man who Disappeared* exemplify the way in which the mere presence – or absence – of parents can leave children with emotional scars. Karl Rossmann, who is abandoned and expelled by parents and parent figures throughout the novel, remembers a subtle yet severe manifestation of parental indifference:

> And he always felt that his mother, standing behind him, was not following all the events closely enough, he had pulled her towards him till he could feel her at his back, and spent so long drawing her attention . . . that she finally put her hand over his mouth and probably relapsed into her previous state of inattention. (*MD* 31/ *V* 58)

In Karl's memory, the image of the mother's hand, usually a signifier of protection and care, comes to connote rejection and carelessness. This is also true in the self-contained narrative the young typist Therese tells Karl about her mother's death. Therese recalls walking through a blizzard with her mother as a five-year-old girl:

> [H]er mother at first led her by the hand . . . until her hand became numb and without looking round she let go of Therese, who now had to make an effort to keep hold of her mother's skirts. Therese often stumbled and even fell, but her mother seemed to be obsessed and wouldn't stop. (*MD* 100/ *V* 199)

Therese's separation anxiety is not misguided, for her mother subsequently abandons her in the most radical way: death. Although the text never fully discloses whether this death is an act of desperation or an accident, Therese's inference that if she had herself been 'a bit smarter – she was still such a little child – [her mother] wouldn't have suffered such a miserable death' reveals her internalized guilt (*MD* 100/ *V* 197). As a child in Kafka's universe, Therese develops this mentality as naturally as other child characters intimidated by empty threats – with the difference that her sense of guilt does not stem from some specific misdeed but from the very essence of her identity: her *being a child*. Kafka's theoretical objection to a manipulation of children's self-image, which he detects even in Foerster's apparently good-natured educational approach, is hence underlined in his fiction. While Foerster and Key consider the parent–child relationship a bond worth redefining and protecting, Karl's and Therese's present-yet-absent mothers personify Kafka's conviction that the exposure even to

well-meaning parents can harm a child. His critique of parental education is uncompromising: as he phrases it in autumn 1921, 'selfishness' is the
essence of parenthood, not love (*LFFE* 295/*B* 345).

More than a decade before Kafka advocated the effective abolition of
the family, the publicist Karl Hauer (1875–1919) made a similar point. As
he argued in an article published in the Austrian journal *Die Fackel*, children and mothers would be best protected if they were separated.[12] Like
Kafka, Hauer judged the 'protection of children in the "age of childhood"
to be wholly unsatisfactory'.[13] However, whereas Kafka, after he has elaborated how children should not be treated, was 'at a loss' about how children
should be treated, Hauer put forward instructions for what he considers a
truly child-friendly education. While Hauer's plea not to constrain children's true nature ('I . . . believe that one should let the child's nature – the
way it really is – unfold itself') recalls Kafka's definition of 'true education', he was much more specific about what he understood this to mean:
educators should not confuse children by confronting them with abstract
subject matter, but should allow them to learn on their own terms. At the
same time, they should be firm with children, and not hope that they will
somehow miraculously develop a virtuous character on their own.[14]

Amidst the Children

Hauer's normative statements thus bring to light the ambiguity that underpins Kafka's reflections on education. Kafka was undoubtedly 'very interested' in pedagogy, as his niece Gerti reported to Max Brod, yet his engagement with it was non-pedagogical.[15] The only aspect of education about
which Kafka was prescriptive is literature. He enthusiastically provided
family and friends with lists of books he believed their children should
read, plays they should watch and stories they should be told. In his letters to Felice of autumn of 1916, and alongside his dissection of Foerster,
he recommends books for the girls at the Jewish People's Home: 'Under
your guidance, the children's library cannot remain so poorly stocked', he
writes on 31 October, urging Felice to introduce the children to Adelbert
von Chamisso's *Peter Schlemihls wundersame Geschichte* (*Peter Schlemihl's
Miraculous Story*, 1813), folk tales by Johann Peter Hebel and Leo Tolstoy,
Gotthold Ephraim Lessing's *Minna von Barnhelm* (1767) and Hans Christian Andersen's fairy tales, especially 'The Shoes of Fortune' (10 October
1916, *B3* 252). Kafka was simultaneously conscientious and self-conscious
about the task of guiding the children's reading, enquiring multiple times
about the whereabouts of a puzzle book he had sent to Berlin, even though
he deemed it not 'substantial' enough for his liking (13 October 1916, *B3*

256). Similarly, he posted a book as a present for Felice's four-year-old niece Muzzi in late December 1915 but regretted his 'mediocre selection' by January (18 January 1916; *B3* 150–1).

Kafka's involvement in young people's mental nourishment did not stem simply from a heightened sense of responsibility for children. Rather, it was also a matter of empathy. When he chose books for children, it seems that Kafka not only selected those which he imagined would be suitable or enjoyable for them: he imagined what it would be like to read them *as a child.* Of course, one does not have to be a child to take pleasure in adventure stories and fairy tales. At the age of thirty-three, Kafka would still describe *Schaffsteins Grüne Bändchen*, a series of booklets containing mainly adventure stories, as his 'favourite books' – notably without the addition 'for children' (31 October 1916; *B3* 270–1). Occasionally, he even seems to have carried these books with him: 'I am interested in Red Indians', the Prague Zionist Klara Thein remembers Kafka telling her one day, when accompanying her home. According to Thein, he then showed her the small book he was holding in his hand, the illustrated *Schaffstein* booklet 'Bei den Indianern am Shingu' ('At the Shingu with the Red Indians'), and gave it to her as a present.[16] A poem jotted down on the second page of Ludwig Bechstein's *Selected Fairy Tales*, a gift for Gerti's birthday, shows that Kafka, willing to bestow children's books on adults, was also not averse to 'borrowing' books from children:

> 'Uncle Franz's Monologue'
> Is it not a shame
> to present Gerti
> with such a beautiful book on her birthday?
> No, it is not, because first of all
> she is a magnificent girl, and second,
> she will leave the book
> behind sometime
> and then one can take it back[17]

Determined to uncover and combat the 'conspiracy on the part of the adults', Kafka's ardent advocacy of children's physical and mental integrity was not that of a detached theorist. On 21 June 1916 he noted in his diary: '[A]s a grown person, I walked amidst the children' (*TB* 651).

NOTES

1 Prospectus cited in R. Stach, *Kafka: Die Jahre der Erkenntnis* (Frankfurt am Main: Fischer, 2008), pp. 334–6. Except where otherwise stated, translations are mine.

2 H. G. Koch, 'Als Kafka mir entgegenkam . . . ': Erinnerungen an Franz Kafka (Frankfurt am Main: Fischer, 2000), p. 225.

3 J. Swift, Gulliver's Travels, ed. C. J. Rawson and I. Higgins (Oxford University Press, 2005), p. 54.

4 The concept was first introduced by Katharina Rutschky in her collection of extracts from eighteenth- and nineteenth-century educational manuals. See K. Rutschky, Schwarze Pädagogik: Quellen zur Naturgeschichte der bürgerlichen Erziehung (Berlin: Ullstein, 1997).

5 D. G. M. Schreber, Kallipädie oder Erziehung zur Schönheit durch naturgetreue und gleichmässige Förderung normaler Körperbildung (Leipzig: Fleischer, 1858), pp. 60–1. Quoted in M. Schatzman, Soul Murder: Persecution in the Family (London: Allen Lane, 1973), p. 26.

6 T. Ziller, Die Regierung der Kinder: Für gebildete Eltern, Lehrer und Studierende (Leipzig: Teubner, 1857), pp. 84. Quoted in Rutschky, Schwarze Pädagogik, pp. 421–3.

7 E. Key, The Century of the Child, trans. F. Maro (New York and London: G. P. Putnam's Sons, 1909), p. 317.

8 L. DeMause, The History of Childhood (London: Bellew Publishing, 1974), p. 1.

9 F. W. Foerster, Jugendlehre (Berlin: Georg Reimer, 1907), p. 89.

10 Foerster, Jugendlehre, p. 91.

11 Foerster, Jugendlehre, p. 92.

12 K. Hauer, 'Das Kind', Die Fackel, 227 (1907), 10–20: 19.

13 Hauer, 'Das Kind', 16–17.

14 Hauer, 'Das Kind', 16.

15 Koch, 'Als Kafka mir entgegenkam . . . ', p. 225.

16 Thein discloses these memories in letters to the Kafka scholar Hartmut Binder. See H. Binder, 'Frauen in Kafkas Lebenskreis', Sudetenland, 40 (1998), 25.

17 J. Born, Kafkas Bibliothek: Ein beschreibendes Verzeichnis (Frankfurt am Main: Fischer, 1990), pp. 69, 71.

CHAPTER 28

Ethnography and Anthropology

Nicola Gess

The Discourse of the 'Primitive' around 1900

'They *are* what we *were*.' Friedrich Schiller's famous dictum, in his poetological treatise 'On Naïve and Sentimental Poetry' (1795), summarizes a view that is prominent across European history: a primordial condition of human existence can be found among peoples elsewhere on the globe, and often this state is deemed to include children, animals, and parts of the natural world. '[P]lants, minerals, animals, and landscapes, as well as . . . children . . . the customs of country folk, and . . . the primitive world', Schiller writes, 'we were nature just as they.'[1] This figure of thought transfers the foreign of the present to the past of the familiar; the category of the 'foreign' can be filled in any number of ways, but it always lies outside history: it is either undeveloped or stands at the very beginning of such a process. Its 'proper' place is at the point of origin; inasmuch as it persists in the present, it proves an anachronistic remainder. Such a view readily translates into the opposition between nature and culture. The foreign is conceived as nature; in contrast, the familiar is understood as culture.[2]

Notwithstanding its long existence, this figure of thought varies according to historical and scientific circumstances. In medieval times the precultural state was seen not as the starting point for evolution but as lying outside historical space. Until the late eighteenth century a clear demarcation between nature/the state of nature and culture/history was maintained, but around 1800 occurred the onset of a way of thinking, according to Michel Foucault (1926–84) marking the 'age of history',[3] when the 'source' or 'origin' of human civilization was no longer located outside, but inside the sphere of historical development.[4] Friedrich Schiller (1759–1805) took an interest in the foreign because it promised to reveal something about the familiar, i.e. about the present: the study of faraway peoples now furthered self-understanding. But at the same time, this self-understanding destabilized identity for it incorporated matters that ultimately remained alien – and alienating. The modern conception of origins is deeply ambiguous. On the one hand, foreign peoples epitomize the opposite of Europeans' self-image as 'mature', reasonable, self-disciplined, socialized and cultivated, and yet these foreign 'children of nature' – irrational, governed by emotion and drives, and potentially antisocial – formed part of European culture inasmuch as they are supposed to represent Europe's own point of departure. And so, encounters with 'others' meant to affirm European identity by revealing its origins actually unsettle its native sense of self.

This version of 'they are what we were' pervades nineteenth- and early-twentieth-century cultural history. However, it took on a new form in the context of the human sciences and their historical and developmental focus. Around 1800, equating humanity's origins with the way non-European peoples still lived was often just an analogical gesture. But over the course of the century, it came to stand as a matter of positive fact. Anthropology and ethnography (and, later, developmental psychology and psychopathology) now declared that so-called 'primitive' peoples offered empirical proof of how mankind had existed in its primal state. Behaviour and thinking from prehistoric times were thought to have endured among indigenous peoples, which had not progressed and therefore had no history. By the same token, the development of children was thought to cycle through the evolution of the species. Finally, the mentally ill – especially schizophrenics – were supposed to suffer from having fallen back into earlier stages of development archived in the unconscious mind and primitive organs. And so, enlisting these figures as examples, the human sciences followed either a genealogical orientation (in other words, they sought to retrace the development of the human species) or an ontological one (in other words, they sought to understand the 'true' – and timeless – essence of mankind).

Around 1900, the 'primitive' emerged as a key paradigm in the fields of anthropology, developmental psychology and psychopathology for explaining the thinking and behaviour of modern society's 'others'. Whether applied to indigenous peoples, children or the mentally ill, the term referred to a supposedly distinct, prelogical way of thinking based on relational networks determining perception and worldview. The ethnographer Karl von den Steinen (1855–1929), for instance, claimed that members of the Amazon tribe he studied thought they *were* red parrots; Ernst Kretschmer (1888–1964), a psychologist, held that schizophrenics believed magical, telekinetic powers were influencing them; and according to developmental psychologist Jean Piaget (1896–1980), children believed they could talk to animals, control the sun's course and transform one object into another. By turns, 'primitive' thinking qualified as magical (Piaget,

Karl Theodor Preuss, Kretschmer), mythical (Ernst Cassirer, Wilhelm Wundt), or prelogical and mystical (Lucien Lévy-Bruhl). Commonly, a direct connection was posited between this form of thought and the essence of creativity. In *Genius in the Child* (1922), the educator Gustav Friedrich Hartlaub wrote: 'this general imaginative power of the child . . . is preserved only in the poet and the artist . . . The "artist" alone knows how to retain a greater or lesser degree of access to the gigantic and monstrous inner life of childhood.'[5] Kretschmer thought Expressionism might be explained in terms of schizophrenia and the mental processes of prehistoric humans, which such art brought (back) to life.[6] And according to the ethnologist Edward B. Tylor, the primitive mentality could unlock the mysteries of poetic language: 'In so far as myth is the subject of poetry, and in so far as it is couched in language whose characteristic is that wild and rambling metaphor which represents the habitual expression of savage thought, the mental condition of the lower races is the key to poetry.'[7]

If the human sciences in general took an interest in connections between artistic/creative processes and the ways indigenous peoples, children and the mentally ill supposedly think, scholars of art and literature expressly looked to develop new aesthetic concepts. In *Philosophie des Metaphorischen* (*Philosophy of the Metaphorical*, 1893), Alfred Biese argued that figurative usage is primary and underlies language; indeed, poetry promises privileged access to 'true reality'.[8] By enlisting anthropology, ethnography, developmental psychology and psychopathology, scholars of art and literature found new ways to classify and justify their objects of study. Writers did much the same. By turns, they styled themselves as the inheritors of 'primitive' cultures, as the heirs of an animal- or even plant-like existence (Gottfried Benn), or as childlike beings (Rainer Maria Rilke); others trumpeted how close they stood to madness (Robert Müller). Artists renewed their creative vision by taking primitive works as models. Paul Klee's declaration is representative:

> There are also primitive beginnings [Uranfänge] of art, such as one is more likely to find in ethnographic collections or at home in the nursery . . . parallel phenomena are the drawings of the mentally ill . . . All that, in truth, must be taken far more seriously than all the museums when it's a matter of reforming contemporary art.[9]

Literary Primitivism in the Works of Franz Kafka

By the time that Robert Goldwater's *Primitivism in Modern Painting* appeared in 1938, the concept of 'primitivism' was firmly established. William Rubin's authoritative exhibition catalogue, *Primitivism in*

Twentieth Century Art (1984), presents 'primitivism' as a school of art that took artefacts from tribal cultures in West Africa and the Pacific Islands as models, mainly for formal inspiration. Nothing comparable could be realized in literature. European observers deemed objects to be directly accessible, but linguistic barriers prevented them from understanding foreign, non-Western literature. Few authors knew the relevant languages, and translations were scarce; those that did exist paid little attention to particularities of style.[10] There are, however, other models of primitivism that fed into literature, for the 'primitive' could also be found closer to home: in folk art, drawings by children or the mentally ill, and in works dating from earlier periods, such as the Middle Ages. As Colin Rhodes observes, 'there is a large body of Primitivist art, particularly among Dadaists and Surrealists, which bears no direct relationship to primitive art – its Primitivism lies in the artists' interest in the primitive mind and it is usually marked by attempts to gain access to what are considered to be more fundamental modes of thinking and seeing'.[11]

This broadened definition makes it easier to incorporate the concept of primitivism into the history of literature, where the model of intellectual primitivism – that is, one related to 'primitive thought' – found entry into the works of modernist writers such as Franz Kafka. Kafka's texts exhibit what contemporary discourse called 'primitive thinking' in multiple ways: animate objects (for example, Odradek, the spool of thread), the possibility of being two things at once (Gregor Samsa is both a man and a beetle) and of reality and dream becoming fused (for instance the bailiffs' punishment in the storage room of K.'s office building). Yet at the same time, the texts do not assign this way of thinking to figures marked as 'alien'; as a rule, it belongs to the narration itself, which prompts the reader to perceive his or her own life as strange.

Searching for an affinity between this mode of thought and the three figures mentioned above, for Kafka the figure of the child proves especially relevant. Even though Kafka's protagonists are rarely children, they often realize childish fantasies – for example, of riding on an inanimate object, as in 'Der Kübelreiter' ('The Rider on the Coal-Scuttle', 1917). Also, childishness is often associated with another 'primitive' group of characters: Kafka's animals. The protagonist of 'Josefine, die Sängerin oder Das Volk der Mäuse' ('Josefine, the Singer or The Mouse People', 1924) is described as a 'frail, vulnerable creature', for whom her people 'care . . . as a father does, accepting a child who stretches out her little hand towards him' (*HA* 70/*NSII* 660); she is seen acting 'the way children behave and show their gratitude' (*HA* 70/*NSII* 661); indeed, her song cannot be distinguished from 'childish peeping' (*HA* 68/*NSII* 656). The dog-narrator in 'Forschungen eines Hundes' ('Investigations of a Dog', 1922) describes his inquisitiveness as something left over from younger years (*HA* 127/*NSII* 434–5), adding: 'perhaps in my old age there beckons to me, as the reward earned by a hard life, more childlike happiness than a real child would have the strength to bear' (*HA* 128/*NSII* 436). While Kafka also invests childhood with a negative charge – most famously, the dominion wielded by fathers over sons – his recourse to 'childish thinking' at the same time has utopian connotations, suggesting a discursive bridge between the child and the artist. Both 'Investigations of a Dog' and 'Josefine, the Singer' describe the search to grasp the mystery of art, a search driven by a 'yearning for happiness which, it may be, flows from music' (*HA* 65/*NSII* 651). Josefine not only 'loves music' (*HA* 65/*NSII* 651) but knows how to bestow this gift onto her people as the joy of a community: 'We too immerse ourselves in the feelings of the crowd, fervently listening, bodies packed close, hardly daring to breathe' (*HA* 69/*NSII* 658).

If many of Kafka's works, then, are drawn to the notion of 'primitive thought', two groups of texts bear directly on questions concerning anthropology and ethnography. The first comprises texts in which the narrator investigates a foreign culture – as in 'Schakale und Araber' ('Jackals and Arabs', 1917), 'Beim Bau der chinesischen Mauer' ('At the Building of the Great Wall of China', 1917), 'In der Strafkolonie' ('In the Penal Colony', 1914) and 'Ein altes Blatt' ('An Ancient Manuscript', 1917). The second consists of works that reverse the ethnographic gaze and direct it at familiar cultures and institutions. Here, animal narratives again prove especially relevant, as in 'Ein Bericht für eine Akademie', ('A Report to an Academy', 1917), 'Der Bau' ('The Burrow', 1923–4), and *Die Verwandlung* (*The Metamorphosis*, 1912).

As John Zilcosky has demonstrated, Kafka avidly read popular accounts of colonial expeditions, a fascination reflected in the numerous traveller and explorer figures in his texts. Even though the author devoted little attention to anthropological writings in the narrower sense, his works bear the imprint of contemporary encounters with foreign cultures: colonialism, a fascination with the exotic and ethnographic observation. The latter project in particular is cast in a critical light, for instance in 'At the Building of the Great Wall of China', whose protagonist is an amateur ethnographer 'interested . . . almost exclusively, in comparing the history of different nations' (*HA* 107/*NSI* 348). In the course of his narrative, he reflects on the riddle of the Great Wall's incompleteness, the enigma the Emperor represents, and the people's relation to their ruler. While some of the country's institutions are 'uniquely lucid', others are 'uniquely obscure' (*HA* 107/*NSI* 348), making his task so difficult that he finally breaks off his investigation. The text underlines the unsteady relation between the ethnographer and his object. First, he takes the stage as a chronicler, speaking at a distance, but then increasingly becomes a 'participant observer' (Bronislaw Malinowski, 1884–1942) – and finally the subject of his own report, which surreptitiously turns into an autobiographical narrative. Kafka's text thus thematizes the fundamental problem of ethnography, namely 'the implication of the observer in the observed' and, as a consequence, 'the transformation, the deformation, of the object of observation through the figure of the isolated observer'.[12]

The narrative also communicates the fascination the foreign exercises on the ethnographer, which prompts him to seek its utopian potential: 'to some extent a free life without the constraints of government' prevails among the country people, 'a life governed by no laws of the present day, [which] obeys only the decree and direction that come down to us from ancient times' – even if this means 'arbitrarily' raising up an Emperor who, long dead, 'only survives in song' to be the 'lord' of the village (*HA* 109–10/*NSI* 352–4). Here, the text articulates the same insight proposed by French anthropologists at the time (such as Emile Durkheim, Marcel Mauss, Henri Hubert and Lucien Lévy-Bruhl), who described how collective ascriptions of meaning confer magical power upon objects in indigenous societies. Once again, the narrator's ethnographic pursuits relate back to his childhood; he recalls his father telling him about the wall's construction: 'Of course, I have no exact memory of his words, but their meaning sank in deeply because the circumstances were so extraordinary, compelling even the child, so that I can nevertheless still trust myself to repeat the gist, more or less' (*HA* 112/*NSI* 357). But instead of repeating what he has been told, he falls into silence; the narrative stops abruptly.

Encounters with the foreign, be it as part of another culture or through one's own childhood, remain enigmatic and difficult to grasp by means of language. This is also the case in narratives where a foreigner suddenly appears in a familiar setting. One example is the undead huntsman Gracchus – who might be read as a figure for ethnography inasmuch as he is constantly forced to look at the 'picture' of a 'bushman' (*HA* 116/*NSI* 312) – who is condemned to sail the seas after his ship took a wrong turn on its way to the underworld. Another, similarly mysterious figure is the hunter Hans Schlag featured in an untitled fragment (*ON* 123/*NSI* 272–3), who is discovered in an attic by a group of children. His speech only becomes understandable 'retrospectively' and his story remains untold; also, his introduction conjures up the promises of childhood once again ('The children had a secret', *ON* 123/*NSI* 272) as well as the defamiliarization of familiar environments, the child Hans suddenly encountering another, utterly strange Hans (*ON* 124/*NSI* 273).

The defamiliarizing inversion of perspective at work in such ethnographic (or childhood) narratives is intensified in Kafka's animal stories. Animals occupy an interesting position in the modernist discourse of 'primitive thinking' insofar as they often represent the apex of regressive yearning; they stand for a state *before* all thinking, when the animal-human has not yet been estranged from the world and lives in the eternal present of gratified drives. In contrast, Kafka's animals do not embody a sense of renewed intimacy with the world, but rather a sense of profound alienation, in turn generating estrangement in the reader. Here, the ethnographic perspective turns into a critical view of social institutions and the ways modern societies erect borders (for example, between human beings and animals) for the purpose of exclusion. In 'A Report to an Academy', the trained ape Rotpeter tells his life story, from the moment he was captured until he became a celebrated performer at the circus. In the process, he lays bare the illusory notion of freedom, with which 'all too often humans deceive themselves' (*HA* 40/*DL* 304). After his capture the ape can no longer experience an animal's 'great feeling of [true] freedom on all sides' (*HA* 40/*DL* 304); in a painful process, he adopts human behaviour, which he exposes as forced and self-destructive (such as smoking and drinking). Animal stories that do not present direct encounters with the human world also allow reflection on cultural paradigms by way of parable. 'Josefine', for instance, simultaneously foreshadows and subverts an aesthetic ideology and political practice gaining in currency when Kafka wrote: the fabrication, by way of (musical) performances, of a *völkisch* ('folkish') identity that is centred on a leader seeking to orchestrate the nation as a 'total work of art'.[13]

Within the modernist discourse on 'primitive' thought, Kafka warrants special notice because his works not only take up the magical thinking characteristic of children and their 'functional equivalents', but also feature traveller and explorer figures and their proto-ethnographic perspective on foreign cultures. What is more, they also add a fourth figure already implicit in contemporary discourse: the animal. Kafka's animal texts display a different kind of relation from, and understanding of, the 'primitive'. Instead of promising renewed intimacy with the world, they express an intense feeling of estrangement. They turn ethnography on its head in order to direct curiosity and manifest bewilderment at the institutions of modern European life.

NOTES

1 F. Schiller, 'On Naïve and Sentimental Poetry' in H. S. Nisbet (ed.), *German Aesthetic and Literary Criticism: Winckelmann, Lessing, Hamann, Herder, Schiller, and Goethe* (Cambridge University Press, 1985), pp. 177–232: 180, 181.

2 The first part of this chapter draws on research presented in N. Gess, 'Sie sind, was wir waren: Literarische Reflexionen einer biologischen Träumerei von Schiller bis Benn', *Jahrbuch der deutschen Schillergesellschaft*, 56 (2012), 107–25. See also N. Gess, *Primitives Denken: Kinder, Wilde und Wahnsinnige in der literarischen Moderne* (Munich: Fink, 2013).

3 M. Foucault, *The Order of Things: An Archaeology of the Human Sciences* (New York: Vintage, 1994), p. 217.

4 This paragraph and the next draw on the reflections of S. Werkmeister, *Kulturen jenseits der Schrift: Zur Figur des Primitiven in Ethnologie, Kulturtheorie und Literatur um 1900* (Munich: Fink, 2010), pp. 57–70.

5 G. F. Hartlaub, *Der Genius im Kinde: Zeichnungen und Malversuche begabter Kinder* (Breslau: Hirt, 1922), p. 30.

6 E. Kretschmer, *Medizinische Psychologie* (Stuttgart: Thieme, 1922), pp. 137ff.

7 E. B. Tylor, *Primitive Culture: Researches into the Development of Mythology, Philosophy, Religion, Art, and Custom* (London: Murray, 1871), vol. II, p. 404.

8 A. Biese, *Die Philosophie des Metaphorischen: In Grundlinien dargestellt* (Leipzig: Voss, 1893).

9 Quoted in A. Hueneke (ed.), *Der blaue Reiter: Dokumente einer geistigen Bewegung* (Leipzig: Reclam, 1989), p. 170.

10 See E. Schüttpelz, *Die Moderne im Spiegel des Primitiven: Weltliteratur und Ethnologie (1870–1960)* (Munich: Fink, 2005), p. 360.

11 C. Rhodes, *Primitivism and Modern Art* (London: Thames & Hudson, 1994), p. 7.

12 G. Neumann, 'Kafka als Ethnologe' in H. Bay and C. Hamann (eds.), *Odradeks Lachen: Fremdheit bei Kafka* (Freiburg: Rombach, 2006), pp. 325–46: 325.

13 See N. Gess, 'The Politics of Listening: The "Power of Song" in Kafka's "Josefine the Singer"' in S. Corngold (ed.), *Kafka's Selected Stories* (New York: Norton & Company, 2007), pp. 275–88: 288.

PART IV

Reception and Influence

CHAPTER 29

Early Critical Reception

Ruth V. Gross

Kafka criticism dates back to the time of his very first book publication: the small volume *Betrachtung* (*Meditation*), which appeared in November 1912. This collection of short prose texts engendered a rash of critical responses, beginning a tide that has not stopped, and probably will never stop as long as Kafka continues to be read. Indeed, Kafka's writing immediately made a strong impact on its readers and quickly became a topic of discussion. His life and texts were subjected to a wide variety of approaches and critical methods during his lifetime and in the years after his death. This chapter will provide an overview of Kafka's reception during his lifetime, placing him in the context of his era. It will then look at the way perspectives changed in the early years after his death, highlighting the predominant and often conflicting ways of interpreting this literary phenomenon and demonstrating their importance as foundations for subsequent scholarship.

Kafka's Reception during his Lifetime

Initially, it was the Prague Circle that picked up on Kafka's publications; Max Brod (whom I will discuss in more detail below), Otto Pick, Felix Weltsch and Ernst Weiss, among others, pushed Kafka's name out into the world. Kafka was quick to dismiss these early responses, since they were written by friends. In February 1913 he writes to Felice Bauer:

> A few reviews have already appeared, needless to say all of them by friends, valueless in their exaggerated praise, valueless in their comments, and explicable only as a sign of misguided friendship, an overrating of the printed word, a misunderstanding of the general public's attitude to literature. (14/15 February 1913; *LF* 194/*B2* 92)

Like any new author, Kafka was in these early reviews and articles either directly compared to more established writers or at least juxtaposed to them in order to place him in a recognizable context.

Perhaps the very first review of an actual work of Kafka's appeared in 1912 in *Selbstwehr* (*Self-Defence*), a periodical focused on Jewish literature and culture. Its author, Hans Kohn, considers Kafka's short prose collection *Meditation* in conjunction with books by three other Prague authors. In discussing the book, Kohn notes the difference in Kafka's writing from anything that had come before.[1] Other early reviewers likewise noted Kafka's unusual style, although some also recognized important influences. Thus Kohn, in another piece written a few months later, was the first to recognize a Dickensian quality in 'Der Heizer' ('The Stoker', 1912),[2] while Alfred Ehrenstein compares the pieces of *Meditation* to 'intellectual dreams'.[3] It is interesting to note that even without yet having an established discourse to talk about the Kafkan experience, these early reviewers perspicaciously – and not just because they were his friends – understood the unique and enigmatic style they encountered in Kafka's work, a quality that has prompted Kafka scholars in subsequent generations to continue plumbing his texts for meanings and connections.

Any review of Kafka's reception during his lifetime must, however, focus on Max Brod (1884–1968), Kafka's closest friend, literary colleague and ultimately the executor of Kafka's literary estate, who served as the writer's most fervent champion. Without Brod, Kafka might have been just one more name and eventually, as he says of his creation Josefine, the mouse, 'lost [him]self happily . . . redeemed and transfigured' and been 'forgotten, like all [his] brethren' (*HA* 80/*DL* 294). Even before Kafka had published a word, Brod promoted the young writer in a Berlin monthly, praising Kafka's style in conjunction with three already established authors – Heinrich Mann (1871–1950), Frank Wedekind (1864–1918) and Gustav Meyrink (1868–1932).[4] Brod also reviewed *Meditation* and was soon publishing pieces on Kafka and his work wherever and whenever possible. In his investigation of the history of Kafka criticism, Peter Beicken highlights a gradual change in Brod's focus. At first Brod singled out Kafka's attention to elements of style and form, for instance the way his texts shift from the representation of an external reality to the construction of new, 'unique' realities, emphasizing the 'dialectic movement' and 'sovereignty' of Kafka's prose.[5] In later articles, in contrast, Brod started to focus on the content of Kafka's texts rather than on his style. In October 1916, he published the essay 'Unsere Literaten und die Gemeinschaft' ('Our Writers and the Community') in Martin Buber's monthly *Der Jude* (*The Jew*), in which he suggests that Kafka's texts illustrate the essence of the modern Jew in his feeling of being isolated from everything, including himself. Unlike other writers, who consider this separateness as a painful but necessary condition,

Brod argues, Kafka sees it as actually sinful, and his characters are burdened by the guilt they carry around with them. In this way, Brod concludes, although the word 'Jewish' never appears in them, Kafka's texts are among 'the most thoroughly Jewish documents of our [their] day'.[6] With this pronouncement, Brod was to set a religious-allegorical agenda and context for reading Kafka that would endure for many years.

Brod was also responsible for one of the most important pieces published on Kafka during his lifetime – a 1921 article entitled 'Der Dichter Franz Kafka' ('The Poet Franz Kafka'), which appeared in *Die neue Rundschau*, one of the most highly regarded literary and cultural journals in the German language. Brod's effusive portrait of Kafka, so different from any kind of literary review published today, declares that among all modernist writers, 'truth and nothing but truth' is to be found '*only* in Kafka',[7] describing Kafka's prose with words such as 'healthy' and 'crystal clear', and as 'having a sweetness that you've never before experienced'.[8] According to Brod, 'If the angels in heaven told jokes, it would have to be in the language of Franz Kafka.'[9] What might seem like hyperbole in Brod's words bears some discussion. After all, it was Brod who, by his own admission, 'exacted almost everything that Kafka published by cunning and armtwisting'.[10] The very fact that the article is called 'Der *Dichter* Franz Kafka' shows Brod's reverence; he is talking about no mere 'Schriftsteller' (writer) or 'Autor' (author). Whatever else the subsequent world of Kafka scholarship ultimately thought of Brod either as an editor of Kafka's works or as a critic, his unshakeable belief in Kafka's uniqueness and artistry was essential in securing Kafka's status in world literature today. Some critics have surmised that Brod was driven by such love and admiration for Kafka that he may have unconsciously been trying to compensate for the relatively small total page output by giving Kafka's works 'a religious meaning they were never intended to have'.[11]

Until Kafka's death in 1924, the writer and his works were seen as one. For the most part, those who discussed the texts, if they did not know him directly, knew of him, and Kafka's personal attributes would often be applied to interpretations of the texts. Franz Blei's (1871–1942) humorous *Große[s] Bestiarium der modernen Literatur* (*Big Bestiary of Modern Literature*, 1920), which describes famous authors as exotic animals, contains a beautifully ambiguous definition of Kafka that alludes to two prevalent perspectives on Kafka during his lifetime – the fantastic enigmatic and the Jewish writer: 'The Kafka: The Kafka is a very seldom seen splendid mouse of lunar blue that does not eat meat, but rather nourishes itself with bitter herbs. Its looks are fascinating for it has the eyes of a human being.'[12]

After Kafka's Death: Max Brod and his Critics

In the first few years following Kafka's death, questions arose as to whether his texts could be described as symbolic, allegorical or parabolic. As early as 1926, the writer and critic Siegfried Kracauer (1889–1966) discussed the fairy-tale elements in *Das Schloss* (*The Castle*, 1922), turning away from Brod's religious reading; Brod himself, however, continued to read both *Der Process* (*The Trial*, 1914–15) and *The Castle* as exemplifying the theme of divine judgement and mercy, while others, like Felix Weltsch (1884–1964), pursued a similar direction by emphasizing Zionism and moral guilt as subtexts in the Kafka novels.

In 1937 Brod, further pursuing the reading of Kafka as a Jewish allegorist, published a biography of the author in which he portrays him as a kind of Zionist saint. He understands Kafka's protagonists, especially in the novels, as individuals who seek integration not only into society but into the realm of God, and uses Kafka's aphorisms to substantiate his ideas about the allegorical nature of the texts. Brod's insistence that Kafka's work was rooted in Jewish tradition gave rise to a plethora of Jewish readings of the Kafkan corpus. Because of his status as Kafka's editor and friend, his religious allegorical readings gained widespread popularity and determined the direction of Kafka criticism in the decades after Kafka's death.[13]

And yet there were some critics even in these early years who diverged from Brod. Some approached the texts from a totally non-theological perspective while others chose different kinds of Jewish readings. There was a critical strand that emphasized Kafka's radical stylistic break from tradition; Walter Muschg (1898–1965) belonged to this group, seeing Kafka as the voice of an entire post-Great War generation and proposing that his works could be understood on more than one level. In his 1929 essay 'Über Franz Kafka' ('On Franz Kafka') he describes *The Trial* as a tragic satire of the justice system and *The Castle* as a cry for help against the imperial power of bureaucracy.[14] Here he also introduces the possibility of reading Kafka from a psychological perspective, relating the way Kafka portrays dreams to Freudian dream theory. Though Kafka's views towards psychoanalysis were ambiguous, Muschg's essay was the foundation for subsequent, more in-depth psychological and psychoanalytical readings.[15]

Another example of a diverging point of view was Willy Haas's 1934 Berlin radio address delivered in commemoration of the tenth anniversary of Kafka's death. Seemingly echoing Brod, Haas (1891–1973), editor of the influential journal *Die literarische Welt* (*The Literary World*), spoke about the metaphysical punishment meted out in *The Trial* and interpreted *The*

Castle as the seat of Grace; but there was a difference in Haas's discussion. He read Kafka in the light of Søren Kierkegaard's existential philosophy, emphasizing Kafka's religious scepticism and positing that Kafka's motifs reach back into a pre-Biblical world. For Haas, it was not Kafka's Jewishness but his religiosity per se that was central.[16] This was, indeed, a different approach from Brod's and paved the path for critics such as Walter Benjamin (1892–1940), who understood Kafka's texts as suffused with the opaque remnants of a pre-modern, even a prehistoric world.

Benjamin's 1931 radio lecture 'Franz Kafka: Beim Bau der chinesischen Mauer' ('At the Building of the Great Wall of China') and his commemorative essay 'Franz Kafka: On the Tenth Anniversary of His Death' (1934) are brilliant texts that did not become widely known until after the Second World War. They have exerted huge influence on the direction of Kafka criticism. In his lecture, Benjamin avows that Kafka took every possible precaution in order to thwart interpretation of his texts and would probably be horrified at what had been written about them under Brod's influence. He dismisses Brod's critical hegemony and argues that his approach 'amounts to a particular way of evading – or, one might almost say, of dismissing – Franz Kafka's world'.[17] In his 1934 essay, Benjamin disparages the two schools of criticism that, he believes, totally misunderstand Kafka – the psychoanalytic and the theological. His is a reading of Kafka that grows out of close reading, a focus on the inner workings of his texts. Going beyond the customary focus on *The Trial* and *The Castle* by including *Der Verschollene* (*The Man who Disappeared*, 1912–14) and various short stories, Benjamin shows how Kafka, in illustrating the human's alienation from him- or herself, actually reaches back to an alienated, mythical, prehistoric world. Here, Benjamin introduces a significant critical concept for future Kafka criticism: the *Gestus* (gesture). He argues that for Kafka certain things are graspable not in language but only through pre-linguistic gestures, which remain incomprehensible to the characters and even to the author himself, and thus contribute to the indecipherability of his texts. For Benjamin, modernity has lost its understanding of traditional myths and epic texts and can merely transform and re-express the traces of these older collective experiences; thus Kafka's texts are necessarily products of decline, and, as such, 'remainders of an epic wisdom'.[18]

Benjamin's readings gave rise to a wave of text-immanent Kafka criticism after the Second World War. Critics such as Theodor W. Adorno (1903–69), Gilles Deleuze (1925–95) and Jacques Derrida (1930–2004), though very different in their theoretical outlook, would all draw on aspects of Benjamin's essays.[19] Benjamin was also one of the first to discuss aspects of humour in Kafka's works, an element that was noted by readers early on but that only became an explicit focus of interpretation several decades later.[20]

Early Jewish Readings

After Kafka's death, various Jewish readings developed out of, but took a turn away from, Brod's religious allegorical readings. When Kafka's works were translated into English and became topics of discussion in the English-speaking world in the late 1930s and early 40s, the religious aspect of Kafka's works remained central, although some critics, as Haas had earlier, found ways to approach the works from alternative perspectives. There were three primary directions for Jewish criticism of Kafka. Focusing on Jewish religious questions and themes, some critics searched for lost Jewish origins and Jewish authenticity: the law, issues of purity and the like. Many based their arguments on Kafka's fascination with Yiddish theatre and other elements of his biography. Others, like Gershom Scholem (1897–1982), dealt with Kafka's interest in Jewish mysticism, Kabbalah, Chassidism and Messianism, connecting Kafka's texts to Jewish scriptural teachings through *halakha* (religious law), the Torah and the Talmud.[21] And Zionist readings became a third 'Jewish' direction for Kafka criticism. These dealt with the concepts of Jewish *Volk* and concentrated on the differences between Eastern and Western Jewry that may be indicated in Kafka's texts without actually being called Jewish or Zionist. These readings also brought up the topic of antisemitism. The first publication of parts of Kafka's diaries in 1937 fed into this interpretation of his prose writing as a response to his Jewish identity. It is not surprising that when Kafka's works started gaining real notice in the United States shortly after the end of the Second World War, the Jewish perspective was foremost.

In 1955 Clement Greenberg (1909–94), who had translated some Kafka short stories, published his essay 'The Jewishness of Franz Kafka', in which he opined that Kafka's vision could not be dissociated from his religious background, especially the tradition derived from the *halakha*; furthermore, according to Greenberg, because Kafka's texts 'exclude moral issues . . . no moral choices are made'.[22] Greenberg's Kafka is based on obedience to law, not moral choice. And his essay sparked a literary dispute with British critic and Cambridge academic F. R. Leavis (1895–1978), who argued for Kafka's 'universality' and, contrary to Greenberg, found that, like all 'good' writers, Kafka engaged with ethical issues and had something to teach us. Greenberg's ultimate response, after more exchanges, was to insist upon the beauty and aesthetic values of Kafka's works, seeing them as perfect examples of modernism, powerful precisely because they forgo an ethical mode.[23]

As these discussions unfolded in the English-speaking world, Kafka also became a major topic in France. The two most important existentialists, Albert Camus (1913–60) and Jean-Paul Sartre (1905–80), were drawn to what they saw in Kafka's works – that is, the absurdity of the world, angst, the death of God, nothingness and revulsion. For them, Kafka was the writer of the void.

After the Second World War, Kafka truly became a world author. It is no exaggeration to say that his popularity was due, in large part, to the exiles from Hitler's Europe who had taken Kafka with them or discovered him during the 1940s and 50s. Wherever he was read after the war, however, Kafka was situated in one particular (and universal) context: he quickly became the paradigmatic modernist author; and it is there he remains as we begin a second century of Kafka criticism.

NOTES

1 H. Kohn, 'Prager Dichter' in *Selbstwehr*, Prague, 20 December 1912, cited in J. Born (ed.), *Franz Kafka: Kritik und Rezeption zu seinen Lebzeiten 1912–1924* (Frankfurt am Main: Fischer, 1979), pp. 17–19.

2 H. Kohn, 'Prager Dichter' in *Selbstwehr*, Prague, 6 June 1913, cited in Born (ed.), *Franz Kafka: Kritik und Rezeption*, p. 41.

3 A. Ehrenstein, 'Franz Kafka, Betrachtung' in *Berliner Tageblatt*, 6 April 1913, cited in Born (ed.), *Franz Kafka: Kritik und Rezeption*, pp. 28–9.

4 P. U. Beicken, *Franz Kafka: Eine kritische Einführung in die Forschung* (Frankfurt am Main: Atheneion, 1974), p. 22.

5 M. Brod, quoted in Beicken, *Franz Kafka*, p. 22.

6 M. Brod, 'Unsere Literaten und die Gemeinschaft', *Der Jude*, Berlin and Vienna, October 1916, cited in Born (ed.), *Franz Kafka: Kritik und Rezeption*, pp. 148–50.

7 M. Brod, 'Der Dichter Franz Kafka', *Die neue Rundschau*, 32, no. 2, November 1921, p. 1210 (my emphasis).

8 Ibid., p. 1211.

9 Ibid.

10 Beicken, *Franz Kafka*, p. 23.

11 M. Spann, *Franz Kafka* (Boston, MA: Twayne Publishers, 1976), p. 175.

12 F. Blei, *Das große Bestiarium der modernen Literatur* (Berlin: Rowohlt, 1922), p. 42.

13 Beicken, *Franz Kafka*, p. 25.

14 Beicken, *Franz Kafka*, pp. 27–8.

15 For a more detailed discussion of the early psychoanalytic direction in Kafka criticism, see Beicken, *Franz Kafka*, p. 32, where he discusses Wilhelm Stekel and Hellmuth Kaiser.

16 W. Haas, 'Über Franz Kafka' in W. Haas, *Gestalten der Zeit* (Berlin: Kiepenhauer, 1930), p. 212.

17 W. Benjamin, 'Franz Kafka: Beim Bau der chinesischen Mauer' in M. W. Jennings, H. Eiland and G. Smith (eds.), R. Livingstone (trans.), *Walter Benjamin: Selected Writings 1931–1934* (Cambridge, MA: Belknap Press of Harvard University Press, 1999), vol. II.2, pp. 494–500: 495.

18 B. Hanssen, 'Kafka's Animals' in B. Hanssen, *Walter Benjamin's Other History: Of Stones, Animals, Human Beings, and Angels* (Berkeley, CA: University of California Press, 1998), p. 141.

19 D. Kremer, *Kafka, die Erotik des Schreibens* (Frankfurt am Main: Athenäum, 1989), p. 340.

20 W. Fromm, 'Kafka-Rezeption' in M. Engel and B. Auerochs (eds.), *Kafka-Handbuch* (Stuttgart: Metzler, 2010), pp. 255–6, and Kremer, *Kafka, die Erotik des Schreibens*, p. 341.

21 D. Biale, 'A Letter from Gershom Scholem to Zalman Schocken, 1937' in D. Biale, *Gershom Scholem: Kabbalah and Counter History* (Cambridge, MA: Harvard University Press, 1979), p. 32.

22 C. Greenberg, quoted in J. M. Rabate, 'Universalism and its Limits – the Reasons of the Absurd' in J. M. Rabate, *Crimes of the Future: Theory and its Global Reproduction* (New York and London: Bloomsbury, 2014), p. 172.

23 Rabate, 'Universalism and its Limits', pp. 171–5.

CHAPTER 30

Critical Theory

Anthony Phelan

Critical Theory is the name given to a body of writing, engaged with a philosophical investigation of contemporary society, through a development of Marx's leading ideas. It emerged in the framework of the Frankfurt Institut für Sozialforschung (Institute for Social Research), founded in 1924. For critics associated with the Institute, Kafka's stories and unfinished novels became the touchstone for a discussion of modernity. Instead of adopting a religious interpretation by reading the texts allegorically, these left-wing intellectuals attempted to place Kafka in a historical context, and to investigate the forms of representation Kafka finds for the phenomena of the modern world. The key essays are by Walter Benjamin (1892–1940) and Theodor Adorno (1903–69); but an early and sustained reflection on the representation of modernity is also evident in the work of Siegfried Kracauer (1889–1966), who anticipated and influenced the methods and critical posture of critical theory.

Siegfried Kracauer

The critic, writer and journalist Siegfried Kracauer was a close friend of Benjamin and Adorno, though he was never formally a member of the Institute. In a review essay for the newspaper *Frankfurter Zeitung*, Kracauer wrote about *Das Schloss* (*The Castle*, 1922) when it appeared in 1926. His key insight is that Kafka's work represents his world as the stencil ('Matrize') of a fairy tale. A stencil, rather like a photographic negative, achieves the desired image negatively, by what it cuts out. Thus in *Der Process* (*The Trial*, 1914–15), the nature of the court as an institution, of the judges and even of the accusation remain utterly obscure; all that is visible is the detailed legal process; and in *The Castle* all the institutions that supposedly exist for the preservation and transmission of authority (filing systems, officials, messengers, letters) are repeatedly frustrated or delegitimized. Kracauer concludes that, in *The Castle*, all human access to truth is irrecoverably blocked, and this is sufficient reason to reject any attempt to read Kafka's novels in theological terms. Kafka's matrix excises the restitution of truth and reality we expect at the end of a fairy tale in order to reveal dialectically the distortion to which a world bereft of truth is now subject.

Kracauer returned to Kafka in a 1931 review. He links the texts of 'Beim Bau der chinesischen Mauer' ('At the Building of the Great Wall of China', 1917) to the period in which they were written. The First World War and its consequences, he suggests, enabled Kafka to get the measure of 'the confusion in the world'. This review was included in Kracauer's collection *Ornament der Masse* (*The Mass Ornament*, 1927), in which he shows how cultural and intellectual forms can reveal the underlying pressures and tendencies in the 'mass society' that emerged after the war.[1]

In a changing social and economic order, Kracauer finds the self-defeating logic of capitalist rationality exposed in Kafka's work, in stories such as 'Forschungen eines Hundes' ('Investigations of a Dog', 1922) through a canine parody of the human pursuit of knowledge and in 'Der Bau' ('The Burrow', 1923–4) through the image of a building project that, as a desperate attempt to maintain individual security, in reality subjects its architect, the animal building its labyrinthine burrow, to endless constraints and anxiety. The same logic appears in the development of scientific knowledge and technical expertise that celebrated its greatest triumphs in the trenches and barbed wire of the First World War, and in projects of financial management that ended in massive inflation. This reading of Kafka's resistance to ideas of human progress achieved through the application of reason foreshadows the argument of *Dialektik der Aufklärung* (*Dialectic of Enlightenment*, 1944/47) by Adorno and Max Horkheimer, the Institute's first director: 'In the most general sense of progressive thought, the Enlightenment has always aimed at liberating men from fear and establishing their sovereignty. Yet the fully enlightened earth radiates disaster triumphant.'[2]

Walter Benjamin

Before *Dialectic of Enlightenment* formulated the paradoxes and contradictions inherent in the systematic application of reason through technology for exploitative ends, Walter Benjamin developed a critical reading of Kafka which explored further the quizzical relation of his writing to Jewish religious traditions, and laid bare the primordial origins of humanity that could be glimpsed through and beyond mythology. Benjamin's interest in Kafka went back to the appearance of the volume *Ein Landarzt* (*A Country Doctor*) in 1920; and in January 1927 he told Kracauer that he would not read the review of *The Castle* that Kracauer had sent until he had read the novel for himself. Four years later Benjamin's radio talk 'Franz Kafka: At the Building of the Great Wall of China' was broadcast. In it he insists that attempts to decipher Kafka's fictions biographically are misconceived; like Kracauer, he prefers a more direct account of Kafka's work than the theological schemes to which it had been subjected. In reading from the centre of Kafka's image-world, Benjamin thinks of Kafka's text as a mirror. Things the text represents are like the objects seen in a mirror, at a certain distance from its surface. And then Benjamin introduces time into this optical set-up: we look into Kafka's mirror and see images from the deep past as 'the actual unconscious object' of his writing: 'In that case, the interpreter would have to look for its reflection at precisely the same distance from the mirror as the reflected model, only in the opposite direction. In other words it would have to be sought in the future.'[3] Although Kafka's fictions may seem to evoke historical worlds, when the reflection is produced in a geometrically 'opposite direction' this unconscious model will point to something beyond us, yet to be encountered.

This brings Benjamin's reading of Kafka close to what he had discussed with the playwright Bertolt Brecht (1898–1956) during one of his visits to Denmark, where Brecht was in exile. Kafka's writing, they judged, has *prophetic* force because it already registers the shifts in all social relations in modernity, yet without being able to accommodate fully the new (social, economic or political) structures that are coming into being. For Benjamin, Kafka's detailed dwelling on human alienation, predatory sexuality, and all the distortions of existence is like the endless rabbinical stories and lore (*aggadah*) in Judaism. In Kafka, instead of expounding the pure doctrine of religious law (*halakha*), on Benjamin's reading, this body of tales is no longer the ornament of the law; its infinite delays and deferrals of meaning become the threadbare world generated by pointless hierarchies and labyrinthine bureaucracies for Kafka's protagonists. If such is the anxious world of the modern, it continues to be a projection of its unconscious 'model' – beyond and behind the reflecting surface and its optical space. The fear that it generates is also fear of the primordial, the immemorial, as the repressed violent origin of human civilization. If this fear is fundamental to the condition of modernity, reflecting on Kafka can provide (as Benjamin wrote to Werner Kraft) a compass 'on unchartered terrain'.[4]

Benjamin's major essay 'Franz Kafka: On the Tenth Anniversary of His Death' (1934) is again organized from the centre of Kafka's 'image-world', around four scenes or images either associated directly with Kafka or otherwise reminiscent of his work. The first is Pushkin's depressive statesman

Potemkin, who provokes the frustration encountered by Kafka's protagonists in the face of so many down-at-heel representatives of unaccountable
authority. Beyond such impenetrable autocratic behaviour, Kafka's subal-
tern figures confront ancient forces: the primal conflict between father and
son; irrational guilt; and the unfathomable logic of an original sin of which
only the son can be guilty precisely because he must accuse the father of
committing or communicating it. The laws that might govern such fundamental guilt belong to a deep prehistory, and even myth is a temporally
more recent phenomenon than Kafka's primal world. His writing yields
some orientation in a trajectory that has seen the successful happy ending of
fairy tale provide emancipation from a world of (organized) mythical powers, as Kracauer had already suggested in 1927. Yet for Benjamin modernity is structured by the prehistoric that he calls Kafka's 'secret present': in
this way Kafka can yield a 'historical-philosophical index' of the modern
condition.[5]

Benjamin's essay focuses next on the famous studio photograph of Kafka
as a child. The sadness of his eyes, Benjamin suggests, could have been
assuaged by the fulfilment of a 'wish to be a Red Indian' (the title of a short
text by Kafka), which leads Benjamin into a discussion of *Amerika*, or *Der
Verschollene* (*The Man who Disappeared*, 1912–14), and its hero, Karl Rossmann. The 'Theatre of Oklahama', which Max Brod's edition suggested
was the final section of the novel, is used to introduce a discussion of gestures in Kafka's stories, those seemingly significant actions that stop short
of meaning – just as the actors in Kafka's imaginary theatre represent only
themselves, and the message or doctrine that his parable-like texts might be
trying to illustrate is never clarified. The part of the parables that remains
unclear – 'cloudy', the essay calls it – is this unfathomable gesture, which
invites understanding but in its prelinguistic simplicity also withholds it.[6]
Far from preserving some higher mystical sense, however, Kafka's parables
are trapped in the backward immobility of a village world, 'permeated with
all the aborted and overripe elements that form such a putrid mixture'.[7]

In the third section of Benjamin's essay, the 'Little Hunchback', an
uncanny figure from a German nursery rhyme, dispatches theological readings, particularly those derived from the Zürau aphorisms, that see the
Castle as a seat of divine grace, the Trial as a site of judgement and damna-
tion, and America as an earthly destiny. Neither religious nor psychological accounts of Kafka are tenable because they reduce Kafka's motifs
to manageable concepts. Benjamin returns to the mirror model: the primordial forces that lay claim to Kafka's literary work remain unknown,
but the archaic world holds up a mirror 'in the form of guilt' – and in

this mirror the future emerges 'in the form of judgement'. Guilt, shame, 'untrammelled' and 'dirty kinds of lust' that Benjamin cites from the classical anthropologist Johann Jakob Bachofen (1815–87) – all these archaic forces take precedence over the rational unfolding of a legal or bureaucratic process, as Kafka 'move[s] cosmic ages in his writing'.[8] His human protagonists have forgotten the archaic, while Kafka for his part seeks it out among his animal figures. But it is above all present in the sheer physicality of the body: through distortion and disability, the mute presence of the body, charged with archaic power, is brought to consciousness but remains beyond the reach of understanding in Kafka's hybrids and crossbreeds, and we might include his transgressive apes and dogs alongside the thing-creature Odradek and the cat-lamb hybrid of 'Eine Kreuzung' ('A Crossbreed', 1917).

In a final swirl of stories and quotations – from Kafka, from Chassidic tradition, from Plutarch via Bachofen – the possibility that the distortions of time might be set to rights is pursued with regard to those half-formed beings that appear as Kafka's assistant-figures ('Gehilfen') and as his students – Karl Rossmann and the student he encounters. Study and the attention it demands can overcome the risk of forgetfulness, but this takes Benjamin back to the Nature Theatre 'at the end' of *The Man who Disappeared*. Studying their part when 'the role is their earlier life',[9] its actors can open up a tiny margin between themselves and the part they play; Benjamin quotes Kafka's 1920 diary entry: 'Truly for them "hammering is real hammering and at the same time nothing".'[10] Short of that, fragments of existence caught in the gestures of Kafka's figures could be misrecognized, just as an individual might not recognize his own recorded voice or her own gait on film.

When Benjamin asserts, in reference to the story 'Der neue Advokat' ('The New Advocate', 1917), that 'reversal is the direction of study which transforms existence into script',[11] there seems a chance that writing itself might overcome forgetfulness through a re-ordering of time. Kafka's 'assistants', Benjamin argues, are lowly servants of the Jewish community ('Gemeindediener') whose task it was to call the faithful to Sabbath prayers: but their synagogue has gone astray; and the students of Torah have lost their Scripture. Only Kafka's tale of 'Sancho Panza' (1917) offers a glimmer of freedom. His 'existence is exemplary', as Benjamin wrote to Gershom Scholem on 11 August 1934, 'because it actually consists in rereading one's own existence – however buffoonish and quixotic'.[12] This rewriting of Cervantes concludes Benjamin's 'Kafka' essay: Sancho Panza's antics derail the demonic forces of myth that weigh on modernity. For Kracauer, perhaps anticipating Benjamin, Kafka-Sancho distracts the project of reason, embodied by Don Quixote and rendered impotent in spite of its logical power, and now accompanies this defeated *ratio* through the undergrowth of human life. Kafka's fictions stage the defeat of reasoned and realistic insights and intentions.[13] In each case Kafka's texts and their world of gesture give the coordinates of modernity in the cosmic epochs that haunt and disrupt the utopia of reason.

Theodor W. Adorno

Adorno read Benjamin's essay in 1934 and agreed, in a letter of 17 December, that the relationship of primal history to modernity in Kafka had not yet been properly conceptualized, though any successful interpretation would depend on it. His own engagement with Kafka between 1942 and 1953 produced a major essay, 'Notes on Kafka' (1953), a sequence of nine extended readings that follow the slippages and blind spots of Kafka's texts. Adorno too seeks to reclaim Kafka's work from current misinterpretations: 'most is existentialism'.[14] Echoing Benjamin, Adorno sees Kafka's works as parables whose interpretative key has been purloined, so that they resist understanding while inviting interpretation. But understanding that fact does not in itself yield a controlling meaning: instead it enforces the need to attend to all the incomprehensible detail and its *literal* sense. As in Benjamin, gesture yields the opaque, 'sedimented' substratum of experience, before language and interpretation. Resisting the idea that these enigmatic expressions could be decoded like dream-symptoms, Adorno nevertheless identifies common ground in Freud and Kafka in the exclusion of the 'soul', that is, of a substantial and accountable human subject. Like Sigmund Freud (1856–1939) in his attention to the fragments of the unconscious that are the psychic detritus of the ego, Kafka in Adorno's view can only extract the possibility of an authentic form of life from the 'waste products' of the 'perishing present'.[15]

Like neurotic symptoms, gestures in Kafka immobilize the ephemeral like a snap-shot. But the pregnancy of its meaning turns out to be an experience of *déjà-vu*, now rendered permanent and universal – a seemingly private memory from which the individual is unaccountably separated. Thus the unique moment becomes a site of repetition. Kafka's predilection for doubles and series (K.'s assistants in *The Castle*; Sortini and Sordini; Titorelli's identical landscapes in *The Trial*) is deciphered by Adorno as reflecting a Fordist technique of industrial mass-production. Adorno traces the evocation of a socio-economic framework here, arguing that Kafka confronts and disempowers the rational approach to knowledge that has led to the technologization of society and the distractions of popular culture. This lines him up with Adorno's other heroes of modernist resistance to mass culture – the satirist Karl Kraus (1874–1936) and the composer Arnold Schönberg (1874–1951). Kafka's readers and critics, and even his own writing, confront the overwhelming forces of modern alienation, and beyond it the horrors of the concentration camps.

The central fifth section of the essay explores ways of resolving the problems posed by Kafka's texts in terms of social questions: the parasitism of power; human reproduction as subordinate to industrial production; the social psychosis of the petty-bourgeoisie; and even the coal shortages of the First World War and the Weimar Republic – in 'Der Kübelreiter' ('The Bucket Rider', 1917) – or the Oklahoma dustbowl and the depopulation it brought. Stanley Corngold has offered a critique of 'the main complex of themes in Adorno's essay: Kafka's world is a cryptogram of a decaying capitalist social order' – 'a vast fable, told in Freudian and demonic terms, of the capitalist reification of human consciousness'.[16] Conversely for Adorno, the threadbare world of Kafka's stories allows a glimpse of the future that surpasses it – as revolution[17] or, with equal plausibility, as 'forms of fascist organisation'.[18] Adorno re-imagines the Nazis conspiring in attics like those of *The Trial*, and Gisa, the blonde schoolmistress of *The Castle*, as a primordial antisemite. This reading is less an exposition of Kafka's powers of 'prophecy' than a deployment of his writing and his 'method' to reflect the political world Adorno had found himself in between 1942 and 1953. The point would not be that this was what Kafka had really intended all along; rather, the 'foreshortening' of experience as myth in his texts 'reveals the trend of society'.[19]

Having sited Kafka between myth and history, Adorno returns his work to its point of origin, in literary Expressionism: 'the torments of bureaucracy, the bloodthirstiness of the family, the neurasthenia of the outcast self'.[20] Beyond such stock themes, however, Kafka is said to create prose that 'functions like music' – one of Adorno's mainstays against the appropriative power of capitalism. Finally, Kafka can therefore be seen in an alternative literary tradition that includes adventure serials, de Sade, and the theologically liberal parables of the eighteenth-century writer Gotthold Ephraim Lessing (1729–81). In such a context, Kafka emerges as the remorseless opponent of all those forces that continue to exert mythical or 'divine' power.

Adorno's essay is as alert to the social implications of Kafka's work as Kracauer had been more than twenty years previously. And he is as keen to scotch over-prompt psychological, theological and existentialist interpretations. By demonstrating that the mythical powers discerned by Benjamin, in human gestures and physical objects, can be decrypted by the Marxian commentator as the stuff of damaged parables, Adorno's essay illuminates the continuing engagement of Kafka's texts with the abjection and reification of the human subject.

NOTES

1 S. Kracauer, *The Mass Ornament: Weimar essays*, trans. T. Y. Levin (Cambridge, MA: Harvard University Press, 1995), p. 15.

2 T. W. Adorno and M. Horkheimer, *Dialectic of Enlightenment*, trans. J. Cumming (London: Verso, 1997), p. 3.

3 *Walter Benjamin: Selected Writings 1927–1934*, ed. M. W. Jennings, H. Eiland and G. Smith, trans. R. Livingstone (Cambridge, MA: Harvard University Press, 1999), vol. II p. 496.

4 Letter of 12 November 1934: *The Correspondence of Walter Benjamin 1910–1940*, ed. and annot. G. Scholem and T. W. Adorno, trans. M. R. Jacobson and E. M. Jacobson (University of Chicago Press, 2012), p. 462.

5 Letter to Gershom Scholem of 11 August 1934: *The Correspondence of Walter Benjamin and Gershom Scholem 1932–1940*, ed. G. Scholem, trans. G. Smith and A. Lefevere (New York: Schocken, 1989), p. 135.

6 See Benjamin, *Selected Writings*, vol. II, p. 808.

7 Ibid., p. 806.

8 Ibid., p. 808.

9 Ibid., p. 814.

10 Ibid., p. 813–14.

11 Ibid., p. 815.

12 Letter to Gershom Scholem of 11 August 1934: *The Correspondence of Walter Benjamin and Gershom Scholem 1932–1940*, ed. Scholem, p. 135.

13 Kracauer, *The Mass Ornament*, p. 273.

14 T. W. Adorno, *Prisms*, trans. S. Weber and S. Weber (Cambridge, MA: MIT Press, 1981), p. 243.

15 Ibid., pp. 251–2.

16 S. Corngold, 'Adorno's "Notes on Kafka": A Critical Reconstruction' in S. Corngold, *Lambent Traces: Franz Kafka* (Princeton University Press, 2004), pp. 162, 160.

17 Adorno, *Prisms*, pp. 257–8.

18 Ibid., p. 259.

19 Ibid., p. 260.

20 S. Corngold, *The Fate of the Self* (New York: Columbia University Press, 1986), p. 168.

CHAPTER 31

Deconstruction

Stanley Corngold

There is no consensus about the definition of the deconstruction of a literary work. Accounts vary, depending on the favourable or unfavourable bias
of the definition-giver and on whether the method derives from the work
of Jacques Derrida (1930–2004) or Paul de Man (1919–1983), both rivals for
the distinction of progenitor. Derrida performs his readings on the strength
of a philosophical tradition including, importantly, Friedrich Nietzsche's
genealogical method of disabusing pure origins; Edmund Husserl's phenomenological *epoché* or 'bracketing', in which the real existence of the
contemplated object is set aside to enable a description of its perceptual
qualities; and Martin Heidegger's so-called *Destruktion* ('destructuring') of
metaphysics – the philosophical tradition that considers theoretical knowledge to supply a foundational relation to being. De Man is well acquainted
with these thinkers but, as he claims, his approach is chiefly motivated by
the American New Criticism. In other respects, it appears to have been
inspired by the literary criticism of Walter Benjamin (1892–1940), especially in viewing modern literature as fraught with allegories in which the
relation of figure to meaning is lost in time. De Man aims to align his
own readings with the work of deconstruction that every text possessing a
certain rhetorical complexity performs on itself.

Derrida's often-cited reading of Kafka's story 'Vor dem Gesetz' ('Before
the Law'), originally part of the 'Cathedral' chapter of *Der Process* (*The
Trial*, 1914–15), sees this text undermining every conventional determinant
of 'literature', including the thoroughgoing distinction between the author
and his work: there is no accessible law that establishes this distinction.[1]
For de Man, on the other hand, the literary character of complex texts can
be taken for granted as can the absolute separation between the empirical
personality of the author and the iron cage of the work. Derrida brings
a measure of witty wordplay into his critical diction; de Man, in his late
work, rarely, not at all – or to ill effect: he takes little patience with his
translation of German words. Both types of reading, however, may safely be

said to focus on what is called the self-reflexive character of complex texts, based on the presence of traces of the process by which they come about. This perspective will undermine any supposed unitary meaning of the text, so that the literary work appears as an unstable allegory of the forever-elusive act of writing or reading literature in mooted conformity with its putative 'essence'. Many – if not all – of Kafka's texts have answered to this description and generated vividly deconstructive readings by Derrida, his students, and students of Paul de Man.

Deconstructing Kafka's Texts

At their best, such readings explore with rigour and acuity the recipro-cally mediating internal elements of Kafka's texts, so that they constitute a 'world' of their own. (The French word *récit* means 'story' or 'narrative' as well as 'relation'.) At the same time, deconstructive critics will identify echoes of the many other texts that resonate within them. Both perspectives answer to Derrida's protocol that reads: 'Il n'y a pas de hors-texte' ('there is nothing outside the text'), which can mean at once that literary works – such as Kafka's – are preoccupied entirely with themselves as worlds con-stituted by relations founded on acts of writing or, as Derrida intended the phrase, the due opposite: there is nothing in the world of texts that is alien to the text at hand.[2] The context of the work is everywhere present and past: the features of all other texts, in the widest sense, resonate near or from afar in the text at hand. Within this matrix the alert critic detects inconspicuous details, often figures of speech, which, when tugged on, can unravel the apparent architectonic, semiotic and semantic coherence of the whole. The outcome, for the reader, is a vertiginous sense of undecidability as to the meaning of the work. The critic's attempt to stabilize his reading by an appeal to authorial intention is, in the words of Derrida in his read-ing of 'Before the Law', both 'inevitable and pointless', since intentions are available only as they are set down in other texts, which then in turn call for deconstruction.[3] In the case of Kafka, his authorial intentions are present only in his confessional *writings* – his notebooks and his letters – or in the reports of others (as, for example, Max Brod's assertion that in writing the conclusion to his breakthrough story, 'Das Urteil' ('The Judge-ment'), Kafka 'was thinking of a strong ejaculation').[4] All such statements regarding intentions, especially where a figure is involved whose 'real' or metaphorical status is undetermined – here, 'a strong ejaculation' – invite deconstruction.

Let us look at some of these propositions in slower motion. Deconstruc-tive readings will tease out the account that stories give of themselves as acts of writing. For more than half a century, Kafka's work has attracted such readings, since many of his stories and novels exhibit textual trace markers of their own production. A passage in *The Trial*, for example, describes Josef K.'s effort to give a full, written account of his predicament while wondering how, with the burden of his office responsibilities, he can ever advance in his narrative. In her pioneering study of 'neostructural' (read: post-structuralist) approaches to Kafka, the narratologist Dorrit Cohn emphasized this 'conception of writing as an end in itself', adding, as well, literature's facility in 'making signs opaque, shaping signifiers without signifieds, and referring to no world beyond itself: this conception is singularly applicable to Kafka'. She adduces a reading that interprets the figure of Gregor Samsa in *Die Verwandlung* (*The Metamorphosis*, 1912) as 'a word broken loose from the context of language', become 'an opaque sign'. 'Read in this fashion', Cohn continues, 'Kafka comes to stand at that limit point of literature where the verb "to write" becomes, as in the title of one of [Roland] Barthes' essays, "an intransitive verb".'[5] It is not so much that one writes something, that writing takes an object; rather, like being or breathing or becoming, writing, for some, is a human condition. Indeed, Kafka wrote to his fiancée, Felice Bauer, 'I have no literary interests, but am made of literature, I am nothing else . . .' (14 August 1913; *LF* 341/*B2* 261).

Deconstructive readings in English mainly follow de Man in stressing the disparity between the empirical life of the author and the literary text, though they too waver in the degree of finality that they give to this distinction. For de Man purists, this disparity is absolute and arises from literature's primordial 'separation from empirical reality, its divergence, as a sign, from a meaning that depends for its existence on the constitutive activity of this sign'.[6] This customary 'activity' of daily language is interrupted in literary works; literature's fabled power to represent intelligible, 'living', fully present things and produce paraphrasable 'meanings' is subverted by literary language, which may be said to enjoy its own deconstructive power, as it plays off its rhetoric (its 'tropes', its figurative language) against the constraints of grammar, or the cognitive dimension of tropes against the text's performative aspect, as in the case, for example, of Kafka's accusatory 'Brief an den Vater' ('Letter to his Father', 1919). In this field of serious play, literature enacts what Derrida calls *différance*, which is to say, internal difference and a perpetual deferring of a primordial origin, an activity producing unfulfilled desire and a sort of excruciating enjoyment of a tension termed *jouissance*. Kafka's diaries, for one, constitute a field of incessant metaphorical exchange, where beginning metaphors spawn new metaphors in a movement spiralling on through endless reversals that defer the meaning of each single figure. Indeed, on several occasions, Kafka confesses to an irrational enjoyment of this 'whole orchestration of changes' on the theme of his sufferings (19 September 1917; *D* 384/ *TB* 834).

This vertigo can prompt the deconstructive critic to summon up a variety of references to stabilize the meaning of complex texts, but only in order to show that that effort will not lead to a final conclusion. Derrida's idea is referentiality without reference. Kafka memorably referred to 'the commentators' despair' with the words: 'It is only in a chorus [of lies] that a certain truth may be present' ('Erst im Chor mag eine gewisse Wahrheit liegen'; *NSII* 348). For him, as in the deconstructive perspective, all synthetic propositions are to some extent 'choristers of lies'; a certain truth might be present in this multiplication of zero, but no single reading can reach it. Post-structuralist readings will show why it cannot. Cohn locates several additional obstacles in 'the special features Kafka critics have so insistently reserved for their subject: unstable and ambiguous narrative voices, reversible and open-ended actional sequences, enigmas of plot that remain unresolved, flickers of meaning that resist consistent interpretation, contradictory symbolic hints, unstable cultural references'.[7]

An Exemplary Deconstruction

It might be useful to proceed with one sustained example of a deconstructive reading. Consider an essay by J. Hillis Miller, an eminent devotee of the work of Paul de Man and Jacques Derrida. Miller's essay, which associates Kafka and Derrida, cites a famous letter Kafka wrote to his lover Milena Jesenská, in which Kafka informs Milena that he 'hates' letter-writing. He then justifies his passion by summoning up the image of insatiable ghosts who drink the kisses mailed to the beloved before they arrive at their destination. 'Writing letters', Kafka says, 'means exposing oneself to the ghosts, who are greedily waiting precisely for that. Written kisses never arrive at their destination; the ghosts drink them up along the way' (*LM* 183/*BM* 302).

For these haunting images to be meaningful, we need some additional context from Kafka's letter. He continues:

> Writing letters is actually a communication with ghosts and by no means just with the ghost of the addressee but also with one's own ghost, which secretly evolves inside the letter one is writing or even in a whole series of letters, where one letter corroborates another and can refer to it as a witness. (*LM* 183/*BM* 302)

At this point Miller finds in Kafka's prose a key deconstructive thesis:

> The ghosts in question here are the distorted spectres or phantoms of the sender and receiver of the letter, *generated by the words of the letter*. The letter is an invocation of ghosts, but these are not to be identified with the sender and receiver of the letter as such. The letter itself deflects the letter and the written kisses it contains away from its intended message and its goal, its destination. The letter is deflected toward the ghosts of sender and recipient *that the letter itself raises*, by a powerful incantation or conjuration.[8]

In this example, Kafka's own imagination of the ghostly 'poetic self' seems to fly into the waiting arms of the deconstructive critic, who is glad to see the point made – once again – of the disparity between Kafka's empirical self and his life-concerns, on the one hand, and the poetic self, such as it is, generated by his texts. Weight goes to the work of the letter of the text as the sole begetter of this elusive personality; 'the sender and the receiver of the letter as such' are out of court.

This point will briefly occupy us. In the parlance of Paul de Man, the 'poetic self' appears as 'the transcendental poetic consciousness', but no rigorous phenomenology of this second self is attempted or encouraged. The famous analogy recurring in *fin-de-siècle* modernist literature between the self and a written text (James Joyce's *Ulysses* cites Mallarmé's Hamlet 'reading in the book of himself') is unbalanced in the deconstructive reading. Generative power goes to the text: the personal self vanishes from behind its ghostly veils. Post-structuralist critics in sympathy with deconstruction speak of the death of the author, though he may live on as a ghostly murmuring of the rumour of his death.

Kafka's letter, quoted above, would certainly seem to produce this key deconstructive thesis – the disparity between an empirical author and his text. And if the point should not be explicit enough, Kafka makes it beautifully once more: in a letter to Max Brod dated 'beginning of 1918', Kafka wrote: 'When we write something, we have not coughed up the moon, whose origins might then be investigated. Rather, we have moved to the moon with everything we have . . . The only separation that can be made, the separation from the homeland, has already taken place' (beginning of April 1918; *LFFE* 204/*B4* 39). These images suggest the radical character of the act of writing for Kafka: in its very inception it 'breaks' with the person said to be at home in 'the homeland' of ordinary experience. The written 'something' represents an unrecoverable journey into the uncanny, moon-like world of writing. Deconstructionist critics of Kafka have been assailed for seeing Kafka as a deconstructionist *avant la lettre*.

A passage like the one above, however, would make this claim very nearly irrefutable.

Deconstruction, however, is a never-ending process: this conclusion as to Kafka's postmodernity calls for further deconstruction. The critic, *pace* de Man, observes what, in the last resort, is the *incomplete* separation of the empirical person from the poetic apparition – their entanglement, a falling back from absolute separation – an unstoppable but productive error. This complexity is generated by the rhetoric of the passage, the trope of 'coughing up' the moon, since 'coughing up' is not, so to speak, a free, 'transcendental' rhetorical choice; it is determined, though with no discernible intention on Kafka's part, by his own predicament as a tubercular patient. And so what we have called the radical separation of the empirical person from his text would seem to be a beleaguered truth, a truth that, to come to light over time, requires a perpetually renewed activity of deconstruction. As if in confirmation of this thesis, Kafka then proceeds, in the passage quoted above, to make the point explicitly: 'The earth, which has shaken off the moon, has since held itself more firmly, but we have lost ourselves for the sake of a homeland on the moon. *Not finally, there is nothing final here*, but still we're lost.'[9] In a gesture of modesty and also of frustration that recurs throughout his work, Kafka 'takes back' any claim to the completeness of the journey from the homeland of – let us call it Prague – to the 'moon' of the accomplished literary work. For this would amount to a definitive loss of the personal self. He wavers in between these worlds in a way that leaves even the conclusion of being lost uncertain; in this sense he is lost once more. At the same time this very uncertainty provokes the deconstruction of these sentences, for this mode of reading must now proceed to question further the figure of 'a homeland on the moon' and complicate the apparently straightforward identification of the moon with Kafka's literary production.

Kafka's taste for astronomical effects is well-documented: in a famous early diary entry in 1910, he wrote, 'Every day at least, one line should be trained on me, the way they now train telescopes on comets' (*D* 12/*TB* 14). Halley's comet, which had been forecast to appear in the skies over Prague during the morning hours of 19 May 1910, gives Kafka a brilliant image for the writing process. The comet interests him not as an object of scientific investigation but as a fiery sign, a warrant of writing. The comet trails fire through the night sky, with all of Prague's eyes on it, but this phenomenon matters to Kafka chiefly as it corresponds to a moment of fiery *disappearance*. The empirical world is interesting for the intensity of its literary dissolution; no less interesting is the viewpoint that it is its astral embodiment that disappears.[10]

For Kafka, such astronomical figures point over and beyond their immediate visible character. A read image can be attached to the invented or experienced one; the *discourse* of literary alienation precedes the immediate experience of alienation. We return now to the image of the moon, the writer's 'homeland' – though not in any final sense. Kafka cannot have been ignorant of the *Somnium* of Johannes Kepler (1571–1630), the astronomer from Prague, a work in which Kepler describes a visit to the moon, *his* new homeland. Kafka's closest friend Max Brod wrote a novel, *Tycho Brahes Weg zu Gott* (*Tycho Brahe's Search for God*, 1915); in this novel, Kepler, who works with Brahe, as he did in life, has salient traits of Kafka. In Brahe's gamut of feelings, ranging from adoration of Kepler's purity to a kind of hatred of his unworldliness, we have Brod's expression and avowal of his feelings for Kafka. Kepler's imagination of the earth from the viewpoint of an observer on the moon gives a further spin to Kafka's poetics.[11] Because such allusions upon allusions cannot be stopped, one will feel the force of Derrida's precept 'il n'y a pas de hors-texte' in the way that Derrida said he intended it: the text at hand cannot exclude any trace of its context.

Conclusion: Deconstructive Hierarchies

Deconstructive theory amounts essentially to a denial of authorial agency and control. One expert critic puts this claim succinctly, 'It is not we who use language, it is language that uses us.'[12] Another critic, the philosopher Judith Butler, offers a more moderate view: Derrida's notion of 'reading' 'presupposes that signs come to signify in ways that no particular author or speaker can constrain in advance through intention. This does not mean that language always confounds our intentions, but only that our intentions do not fully govern everything we end up meaning by what we say and write.'[13]

Because deconstruction will not *rest* with polar oppositions, specious hierarchies, and determinate endings, it must be kept rigorously active. The severity of the diction describing its practice is striking. 'Technically correct' rhetorical readings, writes de Man, 'may be boring, monotonous, predictable and unpleasant, but they are irrefutable. They are also totalizing (and potentially totalitarian) . . . consistently defective models of language's impossibility to be a model language.'[14]

At the same time, the deconstructive tendency to give hierarchical superiority to effects entirely constituted by acts of writing literature by no means finds Kafka always meeting it halfway as in the passages cited above. It is not for lack of evidence in Kafka's work that critics like Jeremy Adler will insist on reversing the hierarchy. 'What was it about Kafka that enabled him to depict modern life more tellingly than his contemporaries?' It is, he writes, 'the *identity* of his personality and his writing, and of his writing with a modern impersonal world'.[15] Hence, there will be points where the text's resistance to the claim as to its hierarchical superiority to the living person can be felt – a resistance enticing for the deconstructive critic to erase and at the same time suggesting to the reader that, in the grip of deconstruction, Kafka's text may have fallen prey to an ideologically driven, critical appropriation.

NOTES

1 J. Derrida, 'Before the Law' in D. Attridge (ed.), *Jacques Derrida: Acts of Literature* (New York: Routledge, 1992), pp. 181–220.
2 J. Derrida, *Of Grammatology* (Baltimore, MD: Johns Hopkins University Press, 1976), p. 173.
3 Derrida, 'Before the Law', p. 199.
4 M. Brod, *Franz Kafka: A Biography*, trans. G. Humphreys Roberts (New York: Schocken, 1947), p. 129.
5 D. Cohn, 'Trends in Literary Criticism: Some Structuralist Approaches to Kafka', *The German Quarterly*, 51, no. 2 (March 1978), 182–8: 184.
6 P. de Man, *Blindness and Insight* (Minneapolis, MN: University of Minnesota Press, 1983), p. 17.
7 Cohn, 'Trends in Literary Criticism', p. 184.
8 J. Hillis Miller, 'Derrida's Destinerrance', *Modern Language Notes*, 121, no. 4 (2006), 893–910: 901–2 (emphasis added).
9 Ibid. (emphasis added).
10 S. Corngold, *Lambent Traces: Franz Kafka* (Princeton University Press, 2005), p. 22.
11 M. Brod, *Tycho Brahe's Path to God: A Novel* (Evanston, IL: Northwestern University Press, 2007), translated by Felix Warren Crosse, with an informative introduction by P. Fenves.
12 D. Bromwich, 'Slow Deconstruction', *London Review of Books*, 15, no. 19 (7 October 1993), p. 22.
13 J. Butler, 'Jacques Derrida', *London Review of Books*, 26, no. 21 (4 November 2004), p. 32.
14 P. de Man, *Resistance to Theory* (Minneapolis, MN: University of Minnesota Press, 2002), p. 19.
15 J. Adler, *Franz Kafka* (New York: Overlook, 2001), p. 4 (emphasis added).

CHAPTER 32

Reading Kafka

Emily T. Troscianko

A Short History of Kafka's Readers

Reading is what we do with literature, but twentieth-century literary criticism doesn't always make this clear. Critical readings of literary texts over the past century or so have often been more concerned with imposing complex theoretical frameworks than exploring the reading experience in which all interpretive efforts originate. Overblown theory enjoyed a particularly long field day with Kafka. But a closer look at the history of Kafka studies reveals a consistent concern with the fundamental question of how specific texts guide the reading process, a concern that begins with Kafka's very first critical readers, the reviewers of his early publications in literary periodicals from around 1910, and continues right up to the present, in twenty-first-century cognitive approaches to his fiction.

Teaching Kafka is always a rewarding experience, because students love reading him. A recurring theme in their initial responses, though, is that they have raced pleasurably through the short stories and the novels, but are left with the feeling that they have missed something crucial, that in some profound but elusive way they 'haven't got it'. This response probably owes something to the tenacious Kafka myth that insists on his preternatural powers of prophecy, but it also derives directly from one particular element of his writing style: its simplicity.

From the very beginning, reviewers have invoked 'the blossoming simplicities of his language' and the way 'his simplicity is so sublime it resonates'[1] as a key to understanding how Kafka's texts work. The funny thing about Kafka's particular way of writing simply is that the simplicity is not sterile: it does blossom, or resonate; it manages to hint constantly at details or complexities it does not articulate. His four-line story 'Die Bäume' ('Trees', 1907), which begins 'For we are like tree-trunks in the snow' (*M* 15/*DL* 33), has elicited reams of critical commentary from every conceivable conceptual standpoint. More recent critical responses have linked this complexity-within-simplicity with the shift in Kafka from a realist to a modernist style of description: because Kafka's writing achieves precision without the surfeit of concrete descriptive detail typical of nineteenth-century realism, it has the effect of 'present[ing] the reader with the paradox of extremely precise outlines in the absence of the precise qualities for which the realist canon had prepared him'.[2] This linguistic simplicity has even had a parodic function attributed to it: through his 'seductive intelligibility and simplicity' and the 'economy of his unpretentious style', Kafka may trick us into expecting something straightforwardly realist, before then giving us something altogether more complicated.[3]

This odd mixture of complexity in simplicity, or of opacity despite transparency, remarked on by students and professional critics of Kafka, is one instance of a broader phenomenon in the reading and reception of Kafka: a feeling of internal contradictions. This feeling provides an explanatory basis for the ubiquitous notion of paradox in Kafka studies, from Heinz Politzer's *Parable and Paradox* (1961)[4] to more specific concepts like Gerhard Neumann's 'sliding paradox'.[5] The sense of contradictory dualities also structures Kafka's best-known bequest to humanity: the word 'Kafkaesque'. Analysis of dictionary definitions and colloquial usage shows that the unifying feature of its many disparate uses is the combination of something compelling with something unsettling, or something that is hard to understand with a need to try to understand.[6] The idea of the Kafkaesque has achieved the feat of escaping from the literary sphere out into the real world of bureaucratic nightmares because Kafka's writing gave early readers so strong a sense of opposites colliding that the term stuck – and now you do not even have to have read Kafka, or have more than a vague sense of who he was, to have it at your fingertips when describing your experiences renewing a driving licence or having sex.[7]

The memetic success of the term and concept 'Kafkaesque' makes clear that if we want to get to grips with what Kafka's texts are, do and mean, we need to take seriously the experiences they make possible – starting with the reading experiences they elicit. Amidst all the critics who have let themselves be carried away by the ease of attributing self-sufficiently dazzling meanings to Kafka's texts without acknowledging the route by which that attribution happened, there are many others who have tried, from rather different starting points, to pin down what happens in the time and space between the words on the page and the reader's mind. I will consider three strands of this collective but largely uncoordinated effort to ask and answer questions about the reading process and its interpretive consequences: the analysis of narrative perspective, of psychology as textually thematized, and of reading as a cognitive act.

Reading Kafka's Narrative Perspectives

It would be easy to think of narrative perspective as a technical back-alley of Kafka studies, but in fact it is a surprisingly good way of getting right to the heart of the field. Friedrich Beissner is probably Kafka's most famous critic, and his most infamous. He coined the term *Einsinnigkeit*, usually translated as 'monopolized perspective', to encapsulate what seemed to him the most striking effect of Kafka's fiction: that as readers we do not see, or know, any more than the protagonist does, because the narrator doesn't either. Not only does Beissner claim that narrator and protagonist are united in texts like *Der Process* (*The Trial*, 1914–15) and *Das Schloss* (*The Castle*, 1922) – an innovative effect given the third- rather than first-person perspective; he also suggests that the narrator and the narration actually become identical with what is narrated. Beissner's ostensible subject matter here is narrative perspective, but the point of his analysis is to answer questions about the relation between author, narrator, character and reader; about what Kafka's reader 'feels' or 'detects'; about 'the feeling of inevitability, of magical captivation by the totally absorbing, apparently absurd events, and hence the oft-attested effect of oppressiveness'; about the fact that Kafka and the reader are both transformed into the protagonist, and that Kafka 'does not let [the reader] go'.[8]

Even though its details did not ultimately stand the test of time or more careful analysis (the relationship between protagonist and narration is more complicated than complete identity), Beissner's thesis of monopolized perspective made critics think more carefully about how Kafka's narratives are constructed. Ritchie Robertson built on this tradition in arguing that perspective is the means by which, in *The Trial*, Kafka 'provides for the reader's partial distancing from K.', and gives the reader 'a perspective congruent with but superior to K.'s'.[9] The suggestion that in the novel 'there is virtually no narrative voice other than Josef K.'s' represents a tentative but distinct distancing from Beissner, and leads to an assertion of opposites colliding in readerly experience which harks back to the contradictory dualities of the Kafkaesque: 'Kafka's achievement as a narrator, here [in *The Metamorphosis*] and elsewhere, is to make the reader share intimately in the hero's feelings, despite having superior knowledge.'[10] This leads, Robertson suggests, to an at once 'compelling' and 'uncomfortable' simultaneity of 'sympathetic identification' with 'the ironic form of identification in which one comprehends the character's situation from the vantage-point of superior knowledge'.[11]

Reading Kafka's Psychologies

If our question is what reading Kafka is like and why, another way of approaching it is to consider psychology as a theme of the texts, and analyse it to draw conclusions about how the reader's own psychology is engaged. The earliest and still most common angle from which to approach textual evocations of psychology is a psychoanalytic, and specifically Freudian, one. Certain stories, like 'Das Urteil' ('The Judgement', 1912) and 'Ein Landarzt' ('A Country Doctor', 1917), lend themselves to this more than others, and with these two stories, as more widely, the notion of the dream is used to mediate between text-centred observations and the question of readers' responses. Edward Timms, for example, remarks that 'A Country Doctor' 'is by general consent one of the most dreamlike of Kafka's narratives, and its surrealistic imagery has sometimes seemed to defy comprehension'.[12] Freudian analysis is Timms's way of trying to show that the story *is* coherently structured after all; he can rescue Kafka from charges of incomprehensibility by rescuing the dream from the realm of the unnarrativized incoherence that without Freud it might seem to inhabit. Again, the point is less the thematic analysis in itself than its pay-off for a certain view of how we read Kafka.

Psychoanalytic approaches raise all kinds of problems relating to the dubious claims of the theory itself and the simplistic readings of literature it tends to yield, but the theme of psychology has also figured in Kafka studies from other, less fraught perspectives. Anniken Greve's discussion of *Die Verwandlung* (*The Metamorphosis*, 1912), for instance, explores embodiment, self and human nature in the story as a way to better understand the difficulties confronting Kafka's readers, in particular with regard to Gregor's transformation into some kind of vermin: if we accept the problems with drawing neat allegorical equations between what is given in the text and meta-abstractions of one kind or another, none of which seems adequate, what do we do instead? 'Is there a way of responding to [features of the text that resist face-value readings] without resorting to an allegorical reading?'[13] Greve concludes that the reader will take most from the text if he or she does not simply abandon the face-value approach in despair, but follows it to its limit, seeking to recognize and optimize the significance of this limit, specifically by accepting the invitation to '*experience* the connection between the thesis of dualism and the ontological-existential anguish of the Samsa family'.[14] In Greve's argument, the discussion of cognition as evoked in the text and as engaged in the reader dovetail tightly, and Kafka's great achievement is, Greve suggests, that the narrative form 'helps us reconnect the thesis with the anguish'[15] – something of both philosophical and experiential significance. Reading Kafka does not give us a detachable self-sufficient theory of self, but offers us one that is made meaningful through the reading experience; the experience – of recalibrating our conceptual frameworks as we read – is inherent to the idea, and not subservient to it.

Critics who apply the principles of reader-response theory to Kafka's works make the reading experience more explicitly central. Focusing again on Gregor's bafflingly concrete transformation, Richard Murphy uses Wolfgang Iser's well-known remarks on the expansion of textual indeterminacy in modern literature and how this changes the relationship between reader and text as a point of departure for an investigation of how *The Metamorphosis* 'resists closure but simultaneously attracts unending semantic determinations and interpretations by the reader'.[16] Thinking about indeterminacy in another of Kafka's most elusive texts, 'The Judgement', James Phelan elaborates a rhetorical approach which bears similarity to one of the major tenets of Iser's thesis of the implied reader – that all texts are full of gaps that the reader has to fill – but diverges from it by showing how Kafka's story beautifully illustrates the fact that different kinds of gaps manifest different degrees of 'stubbornness', to the extent that some can never be filled at all, and are not meant to be.[17] Phelan's analysis centres on this story's unfillable gap, one just as tantalizing as Gregor's night-time transformation: the gap between Georg's father getting angry and condemning his son to death by drowning, and Georg's immediate capitulation to his father's judgement by running out to the bridge and throwing himself off it. There is simply no adequate explanation for why Georg does this. Phelan argues that here Kafka 'has discovered something remarkable: a way to make a significant interpretive gap surrounding the climax of a narrative enhance rather than detract from an audience's interpretive, ethical, and aesthetic experience'.[18] The apparent simplicity of the narrative description creates an indeterminacy that compels as much as it unsettles.

Reading Kafka Psychologically

In all the examples I have discussed so far, we see Kafka's professional readers converging, from different starting points, on a question that goes to the heart of Kafka studies and literary studies as a whole: what makes reading (Kafka) feel like this? The latest academic addition to the long line of reader-critics who have asked and answered this question tackles it with a new epistemological toolkit. Drawing on methods and findings from current cognitive science, including experimental psychology, cognitive neuroscience, cognitive linguistics and philosophy of mind, cognitive approaches to Kafka have begun to yield insights into how the relationship between Kafka's texts and their readers is configured. In fact, the history of this way of approaching Kafka is longer than one might expect, going back at least to the late 1970s. The earliest example I have come across, an article by Christine Sizemore, begins, as do so many attempts to grapple with Kafka, with that now familiar structure of Kafkaesque opposition: 'One of the most fascinating and yet discomforting aspects of Franz Kafka's fiction lies in its attack on the reader's sense of reality. Kafka's work reflects simultaneously a realistic and yet a dreamlike situation.'[19] Sizemore argues that the unexpected shift from the realistic to the unrealistic, without any change in the matter-of-fact tone, makes Kafka's reader uneasy, and that this uneasiness grows as the 'two irreconcilable interpretations of reality remain'. She suggests that our unease can be understood as an example of the phenomenon of cognitive dissonance. According to the theory developed by Leon Festinger in the late 1950s, cognitive dissonance is the discomfort we feel when we hold two conflicting opinions at once, which we typically try to reduce either by revising the first-held opinion or by somehow rationalizing away the new, conflicting information. Both strategies for resolution are, she argues, withheld by Kafka's writing in works like *The Trial* and *The Metamorphosis*, including by the common Kafkaesque tactic of holding out to us the possibility that it is all just a dream, but then making it clear that even if it is, this is not the kind of dream that can be woken up from, so it offers no comfort after all. The psychological theory gives Sizemore a way to 'delineate the stages through which the reader progresses' when reading Kafka's work, which are comparable to those passed through in confrontation with drastic change, illness or death.[20]

A few decades later, my own research has aimed to do something similar: to create hypotheses about what the reading experience may be like for real readers of Kafka based on the connections that specific qualities of the text establish with facets of readers' minds. In particular, this line of research has uncovered what seems a powerful correspondence between how Kafka's texts evoke key areas of cognition (like vision and emotion) as inherently embodied and enactive, and how current cognitive science understands these faculties as operating. This correspondence, a form of 'cognitive realism', may account for some of the compelling characteristics

Figure 6 'Of the castle hill there was nothing to be seen.' A reader's Kafkaesque imagining.

of Kafka's prose (because it evokes cognition as it really is) and also its unsettling qualities (because in both cases our folk-psychological intuitions tell us that our minds work otherwise, as separable from our bodies). This kind of inquiry can therefore start to explain the ubiquitous dualities of response that contribute to what it feels like to read Kafka.[21]

Empirical work can take this research one step further, going beyond the critic's own experiences and preconceptions by investigating how other, often non-expert, readers respond to specific texts. In an experiment on reading *The Castle*, readers were asked to draw what they imagined when they read the opening paragraph of the novel (in English translation). Although the only thing the text says about the eponymous castle is that it cannot be seen – 'of the castle hill there was nothing to be seen, not even the faintest gleam of light hinted at the great castle' (my translation; see *C* 5/*S* 7) – just over 50 per cent of readers (where n = 81) drew the castle, many in quite some detail (ivy, crenellations, big wooden door with round handle, etc.).[22] Around 10 per cent also remarked on the paradox that they imagined what was meant to be invisible (see Figure 6). This tells us something we may perhaps have intuited: the strange capacity of Kafka's prose to make us richly but uncomfortably imagine things it does not even need to describe. Such experiments also allow us to give substance and detail to the critical hunch, with reference to readers who are, crucially, not ourselves.

Investigating the process of reading Kafka can also tell us important things about reading and cognition beyond Kafka. Another of my experiments on Kafka has uncovered potential weaknesses of standard measures of mental imagery in psychology, the Vividness of Visual Imagery Questionnaire: readers who scored zero on all the imaging tasks in the questionnaire (for example visualize a rising sun, and then a rainbow appearing) nonetheless reported rich imaginative experiences in response to Kafka's short story about a European traveller in a desert, 'Schakale und Araber' ('Jackals and Arabs', 1917).[23] Another use of Kafka's texts to contribute to empirical research on the human mind involved asking people to read 'A Country Doctor' before taking a test involving identifying patterns in long strings of letters.[24] The group who had read Kafka performed better on the task than a control group who had read a simple, specially constructed story without any of Kafka's strangenesses, brilliantly titled 'A Country Dentist'. The researchers interpreted this result as indicating that the threat to cognitive frameworks of meaning caused by Kafka's story increased participants' motivation and ability in their efforts at maintaining meaning through pattern detection. Experiments like these pave the way for future explorations of what reading Kafka might reveal about the human mind.

In Conclusion

Underlying all these varied approaches to trying to understand what it means to read Kafka are the questions of what is meant by 'the reader' or 'readers', and what is meant by the process of 'interpretation' in which those readers supposedly engage. These questions are among the greatest challenges facing literary studies in the twenty-first century. The complexity of Kafka's fiction, not to mention its intriguingly indeterminate simplicities, make it a great candidate for helping us tackle them, from both the textual and the cognitive perspectives and the points where they converge.

Kafka is so suitable an object for the question of how we read precisely because it is so difficult to come up with satisfactory 'readings' of his texts, which is in turn part of why he is so compellingly readable in the first place. Thematic interpretive readings easily end up glaringly simplistic with Kafka, so considering *ways of reading* him, rather than insisting on singular *results of reading*, is all the more rewarding. In all literature the cognitive context is the most immediate and the most encompassing of all – and consequently as hard to appreciate as the earth's atmosphere. But Kafka often makes the air feel thinner and headier, and so forces us to think as we breathe.

NOTES

1 In J. Born (ed.), *Franz Kafka: Kritik und Rezeption: 1924–1938* (Frankfurt am Main: Fischer, 1983), pp. 173, 121.

2 R. A. Berman, 'Producing the Reader: Kafka and the Modernist Organization of Reception', *Newsletter of the Kafka Society of America*, 6 (1982), 14–18: 16.

3 S. D. Dowden, *Sympathy for the Abyss: A Study in the Novel of German Modernism: Kafka, Broch, Musil, and Thomas Mann* (Tübingen: Niemeyer, 1986), pp. 102–4.

4 H. Politzer, *Franz Kafka: Parable and Paradox* (Ithaca, NY: Cornell University Press, 1962).

5 G. Neumann, 'Umkehrung und Ablenkung: Franz Kafkas "Gleitendes Paradox"', *Deutsche Vierteljahrsschrift für Literaturwissenschaft und Geistesgeschichte*, 42 (1968), 702–44.

6 E. T. Troscianko, *Kafka's Cognitive Realism* (New York: Routledge, 2014), pp. 35–6.

7 www.usabilityviews.com/uvoo8824.html; *Annie Hall*, 1977, directed by Woody Allen (USA: Rollins Joffe).

8 F. Beissner, *Der Erzähler Franz Kafka: Ein Vortrag* (Stuttgart: Kohlhammer, 1952), pp. 40–2.

9 R. Robertson, *Kafka: Judaism, Politics and Literature* (Oxford: Clarendon, 1985), pp. 91, 101–2.

10 Ibid., p. 75.

11 Ibid.

12 E. Timms, 'Kafka's Expanded Metaphors: A Freudian Approach to *Ein Landarzt*' in J. P. Stern and J. J. White (eds.), *Paths and Labyrinths* (Institute of Germanic Studies, University of London, 1985), pp. 66–79: p. 71.

13 A. Greve, 'The Human Body and the Human Being in "Die Verwandlung"' in J. Lothe, B. Sandberg and R. Speirs (eds.), *Franz Kafka: Narration, Rhetoric, and Reading* (Columbus, OH: Ohio State University Press, 2011), pp. 40–57: 40.

14 Ibid., p. 55 (original emphasis).

15 Ibid.

16 R. Murphy, *Theorizing the Avant-Garde: Modernism, Expressionism, and the Problem of Postmodernity* (Cambridge University Press, 1999), p. 199.

17 J. Phelan, 'Progression, Speed, and Judgment in "Das Urteil"' in Lothe, Sandberg and Speirs (eds.), *Franz Kafka: Narration, Rhetoric, and Reading*, pp. 22–39.

18 Ibid., p. 29.

19 C. W. Sizemore, 'Anxiety in Kafka: A Function of Cognitive Dissonance', *Journal of Modern Literature*, 6 (1977), 380–8: 380.

20 Ibid., p. 388.

21 Troscianko, *Kafka's Cognitive Realism*.

22 Troscianko, *Kafka's Cognitive Realism*, pp. 220–1.

23 'Reading Imaginatively: The Imagination in Cognitive Science and Cognitive Literary Studies' in M. Burke and E. T. Troscianko (eds.), *Explorations in Cognitive Literary Science*, special issue, *Journal of Literary Semantics*, 42 (2013), 181–98. See also http://socrates.berkeley.edu/~kihlstrm/MarksVVIQ.htm.

24 T. Proulx and S. J. Heine, 'Connections from Kafka: Exposure to Meaning Threats Improves Implicit Learning of Artificial Grammar', *Psychological Science*, 20 (2009), 1125–31.

CHAPTER 33

Editions

Clayton Koelb

No complete critical edition exists as yet for all Kafka's writings, although substantial progress towards that goal has been made over the past two decades. Two very important editorial projects are currently in progress that aim to offer the original German-language corpus as a whole: the multi-volume Fischer critical edition produced by a distinguished team of experts; and the 'historisch-kritische Ausgabe' published by Stroemfeld Verlag under the leadership of Roland Reuß. In addition, texts of individual works are widely available in great profusion, both in German and in translation.

Both the scholar and the general reader face a daunting task in selecting from that profusion. The difficulties result not only from the sheer volume of material available but also from the sometimes radically different approaches taken by editors and from the peculiar circumstances of Kafka's literary life. Although Kafka wrote a great deal, he published very little of what he wrote and was often unsatisfied even with what appeared in print. He wrote at work, in his capacity as an employee of the Arbeiter-Unfall-Versicherungs-Anstalt (Workers' Accident Insurance Institute); and he wrote at home, in what he thought of as his true calling as a literary artist. He regularly used notebooks for everything he wrote outside the office, making no clear generic distinctions. Diaristic observations mingle with drafts of letters and stories in a manner that makes it sometimes impossible to distinguish one from the other. It is therefore surprisingly difficult to say for certain what should count as Kafka's 'fiction'.

Initial Considerations

One preliminary step is to divide his writings into two broad categories: first, works published as fiction by Kafka during his lifetime; and second, everything else he wrote. The small compass of the first category may come as a surprise. It totals all in all under 500 pages printed in large format and includes only the following:

A. Seven publications in book form
   1. *Betrachtung* (*Meditation*, a collection of eighteen short pieces)
   2. *Das Urteil* (*The Judgement*)
   3. *Der Heizer* (*The Stoker*, part of a manuscript fragment Max Brod would later publish as the novel *Amerika*, today more commonly known under Kafka's own title *Der Verschollene* (*The Man who Disappeared*))
   4. *Die Verwandlung* (*The Metamorphosis*)
   5. *In der Strafkolonie* (*In the Penal Colony*)
   6. *Ein Landarzt* (*A Country Doctor*, fourteen stories, including the one from which the volume takes its title)
   7. *Ein Hungerkünstler* (*A Hunger Artist*, four stories, including the one named in the title)
B. Ten items, all relatively brief, that appeared in various periodicals (among these are such things as the 'Gespräch mit dem Beter' ('Conversation with the Supplicant') and the 'Gespräch mit dem Betrunkenen' ('Conversation with the Drunk') that Kafka excerpted from larger projects he never completed to his satisfaction).

For both the scholar and the general reader, these works published in Kafka's lifetime offer a certain security: one can safely assume that the author meant these works to be read in the form in which he published them. Like the works of any important and widely studied writer, the published texts can be compared to the manuscript materials available to us, and we can make note of changes and occasional errors. Such investigations can uncover interesting details about the process of composition, but they do not (and in principle could not) detract significantly from the authority of the published material. In some cases, the materials from Kafka's literary estate offer a larger context in which these published texts can perhaps be better understood. Even so, the texts Kafka authorized for printing set a safe norm against which we can read the variants revealed by study of archival materials and can reasonably be taken to represent a firm authorial intention. Many editions of this material exist in both English and German, but scholars will generally wish to consult the authoritative two-volume *Drucke zu Lebzeiten* (*DL* and *DLA*) of the Fischer critical edition.

The second category comprises everything Kafka wrote but did not publish, and it presents a very different picture. Here we are on far less secure ground. We can divide this 'unpublished' material into three broad areas:

1. Business reports, memos, letters and so on, produced as part of Kafka's career in insurance (published post mortem as Kafka's *Amtliche Schriften* – *O* and *A*)
2. Letters to diverse friends, associates, lovers, and relatives (edited and published after Kafka's death by various hands – e.g. *LF* or *BF*, *LM* or *BM*, *LFFE* and *BE*)
3. The literary *Nachlass* or literary estate, placed in the care of Max Brod by Kafka's will and containing a large variety of material, some of it, including the three unfinished novels, clearly drafts of fictional works-in-progress, some of it diary-like notes, some of it of an indeterminate kind (e.g. *ON*, *TB*, *NSI* and *NSII*).

The first class of material is that which Kafka produced in his capacity as an employee at the Insurance Institute. There was a time when it could be assumed that only specialists and the extraordinary Kafka enthusiast would be interested in the business writings (twenty-seven items, as presented by the editors of the German edition (*A*)), since they play no role in Kafka's reputation as a giant of modern literature. That assumption is no longer tenable. The appearance of an English-language version (*O*, a selection of eighteen of the items in the German edition, some in abbreviated form) demonstrates that a powerful appetite exists among a broad audience for even the most esoteric Kafka material.

For two decades at the end of the twentieth century, the only edition of the office writings available was that published in 1984 by the Akademie Verlag, Berlin, in the former German Democratic Republic, under the editorship of Klaus Hermsdorf. In 2004 a newer edition (*A*, edited by Hermsdorf and Benno Wagner and complemented by a DVD of related textual material) appeared as part of the Fischer Kritische Ausgabe and is now the standard consulted by all scholars. The English version (*O*), edited by Stanley Corngold, Jack Greenberg and Benno Wagner, is based on the Hermsdorf–Wagner material but does not reproduce it entirely.

The second, very large class of writing, the letters, was never intended for public consumption but has won a readership nearly equal in enthusiasm to that of the fiction. That popularity started relatively early on in Kafka's post-mortem career. Long before the business-related materials appeared, collections of Kafka's letters were published (by various editors) and avidly consulted. The letters, especially those to his fiancée Felice Bauer and his close friend (and sometime lover) Milena Jesenská, have gained a wide following beyond the scholarly community, securing a special place of their own in the Kafka canon. Though some material was long withheld from publication, a complete critical edition in German is well under way. Four volumes of a projected five-volume edition edited by Hans-Gerd Koch are now in print (*B1*, *B2*, *B3* and *B4*). When complete, the Koch edition is likely to remain the standard for a long time to come.

For the English-speaking reader, there is currently nothing comparable. The following collections are available (the dates refer to the publication of the most recent English edition):

- *Letters to Milena* (1953; revised edition including Milena's letters to Max Brod, 1992)
- *Letter to his Father* (many editions, one as recent as 2014)
- *Letters to Felice* (includes letters to Grete Bloch and a few letters from Kafka's relatives concerning Kafka's engagement to Felice, 1992)
- *Letters to Friends, Family, and Editors* (2011)
- *Letters to Ottla and the Family* (reprints some letters from *LFFE* but adds others, 2013).

A note of caution is in order. No matter how highly we value this material, it is useful to recall the reservations Kafka had concerning all epistolary activity. Although he wrote hundreds of letters, his diligence and skill as a letter-writer was by no means an unconditional endorsement of any letter's value. His doubts are evident in a letter to Milena of March 1922: '[Y]ou know how much I hate letters. All my misfortune in life . . . derives, one might say, from letters or from the possibility of writing letters' (*LM* 223/*BM* 198).

The third category of material left unpublished at the time of Kafka's death (generally referred to as his *Nachlass*, or literary estate) is heterogeneous in the extreme, although this fact was obscured by Max Brod's first efforts at publication and remains somewhat obscured even by the Fischer critical edition. It has only recently become clear to the community of Kafka scholarship just how complex, disorganized and downright confusing this mass of manuscript pages really was when Brod got possession of it.[1] These were products of his intense, though sporadic, after-hours labour. Most of it is fiction, but he tended to write his fiction in notebooks that also contain a kind of writing that resembles nothing so much as diary entries. The notebooks also include miscellaneous jottings, such as drafts of letters, and other material that defies generic categorization. While the publication of the three novel manuscripts as self-contained volumes is entirely understandable, the division of the rest of the literary estate into diaries (*TB*, *TBA*, *TBK*) and 'Nachgelassene Schriften und Fragmente' (*NSI*, *NSIA*, *NSII*, *NSIIA*) suggests quite wrongly that some of these notebooks are of a fundamentally different generic character from the others. The fact that Kafka occasionally called some of his notebooks 'Tagebücher' means only that he was using a convenient mode of reference for volumes that did indeed often contain diaristic material.

In addition to the notebooks are various bundles of paper and stray single sheets. Some of the bundles contain many pages, some only a few. Some are clearly related to other bundles, while others have no obvious connection to the rest. The material found in bundles and stray sheets is often very similar to what we find in the notebooks and 'diaries' and in some cases shows clear signs of having been ripped out of notebooks.

After studying the manuscripts from the literary estate, one must conclude that much of their complexity, disorganization and confusion constitutes an essential element of their nature. One of Kafka's goals as a writer of fiction was to set his compositions loose from conscious control. Successful stories would therefore be those that emerged directly from the depths of the author's psyche with only the most minimal authorial oversight. He called this mode of writing 'being in the grip' ('im Ergriffensein', 30 August 1914; *D* 313/ *TB* 675–6), a notion reminiscent of the classical conception of inspiration by the muse. What gripped him, however, was not a supernatural power but rather what he called the 'tremendous' (or 'monstrous' – 'ungeheuer') world inside his own head.

Kafka regularly engaged in a process that we might call (after Roland Reuß) 'continuous drafting'.[2] He never made outlines or preliminary sketches. When he started on a story he often had no notion of where it was going or how it would end. In fact, the great majority of his fictions do not end. They just stop where the author lost contact with whatever had held him 'in the grip'. He would work over a literary idea without ever bringing it to what he felt was a satisfactory conclusion. Sometimes he would produce multiple versions of the same idea, and even when he did complete a text, he was often unhappy with it. Only in the rarest moments did he achieve what he felt was literary success.

Problems of Editing the Literary Estate

The peculiar nature of Kafka's writing process precludes the possibility of determining a 'final' intention for much of what he wrote and renders most editorial decisions permanently provisional. No German edition of

Kafka's works can therefore be taken as absolutely authoritative. The same obviously goes for readers who approach Kafka through English translations – complicated further, however, by the fact that decisions made by the editors of the underlying German texts are inevitably supplemented (and sometimes obscured) by the translation process.

Another complication arises because Kafka's literary executor, Max Brod, did everything he could to transform the difficulty and obscurity of the material in Kafka's estate into clarity and simplicity. This was unquestionably a well-intentioned and perhaps even a laudable misrepresentation. Brod's goal, after all, was to make a place in the world for his dead friend's work, thus building on the enthusiastic but very limited readership Kafka had acquired in his lifetime. Brod believed that Kafka was a literary giant and that his duty as executor lay in bringing this giant before the widest possible public. In this endeavour he was stunningly successful. It is entirely probable that without Brod's efforts, Kafka's reputation would never have spread as far or as fast as it did.

It was Brod's Kafka that everyone read, and Brod's Kafka that became an international literary phenomenon. Brod's editions must remain the baseline from which one must begin, in spite of the fact that we now know how heavily Brod intervened in some of this material. Nowhere is this more evident than in his edition of *Der Prozeß* (*The Trial*; I cite the title here as Brod published it, which diverges from Kafka's own spelling, *Der Process*), first published in 1925, one of the clearest examples of Brod's willingness to recast the materials he found in his friend's legacy. An examination of the materials Kafka actually wrote shows that the projected novel had never reached a form even remotely ready for publication; that Kafka had not yet formed a clearly discernible conception of the narrative as a whole; and that much of what he had been working on had been produced as disjointed fragments, each having only the sketchiest relation to the others. The only clear elements were the beginning and the end, which Kafka had evidently produced in the first hot enthusiasm of his inspiration.

Brod took this unwieldy and often obscure pile of papers and turned it into one of the most important novels of the twentieth century. It was in reality a collaboration between a living novelist and a dead one, with Brod supplying the narrative line missing in the manuscript by a quite intelligent paste-up job. All the words, all the sentences were Kafka's, but the actual story those sentences told was largely created by Brod's arrangement. So what are we to do with this distinctly impure text? The first impulse of the literary scholar is to reject the enterprise as an impermissible intervention by Brod, since it is Kafka's work we want to read, Kafka's work we thought we were reading before we realized how far Brod's hand had reached into the text.

This would be an unfortunate and ultimately counterproductive rejection. Brod's edition of *Der Process* is the one which was translated and read around the world, the one which influenced several generations of writers and readers, and indeed the one which changed the course of modern literary history. It is now an indisputable part of that history, which no scholarly denunciation, no matter how loud and no matter how well documented, can expect to dislodge. It is possible that future generations of readers will come to know this text in the form Kafka left it, which is the intention behind the Historisch-Kritische Ausgabe headed by Roland Reuß – though it remains uncertain that such readers will really wish to do so – but the past will not be changed. Literary historians will always have to use Brod's editions of this and other major texts as the basis on which to understand the Kafka of the twentieth century.

It does not follow from this that the Brod editions should be considered only as historical artefacts. If we accept the fact that a book like *The Trial* was indeed a collaborative effort, we might accept further that it is actually quite a good book indeed. And it may not even be the terrible twisting of Kafka's real intentions that we might surmise. After all, Kafka had wanted to collaborate with Brod – not on this project, to be sure, but on others we know about, most notably a proposed novel called *Richard and Samuel*. And he did give the manuscript of *The Trial* to Brod in a very deliberate act of sharing his most intimate artistic self with another. Of course it was an ambivalent act, since in the giving he also in effect took it back by instructing that it be burned. But Brod – correctly, one has to think – assumed that Kafka's act of entrusting the manuscript to the very person *least likely* to destroy it overrode any other intention. Brod acted on the belief that his friend wanted him to take proper care of the book, which indeed he tried to do. Proper care, however, required a great deal of input on Brod's part – indeed to such a degree that he became a co-creator of the work as we know it. The Kafka–Brod collaboration needs not only to be acknowledged; it needs to be given our informed consent.

The Current State of the Editorial Enterprise

That said, however, it remains essential for us to look elsewhere, at the editions that have emerged from the critical and historical-critical editions, for a better sense of what, and how, Kafka actually wrote and left behind in the papers entrusted to Brod. We should do this, not necessarily in the hope of getting a 'better' text to read, but rather out of a desire to understand the precise origins of the texts we have read and have come to care about. There are two important critical projects that can help us in that effort.

The first is the Fischer critical edition project referred to in the discussion above, nearly all of which has already appeared. These volumes present reliable texts with carefully prepared apparatus that both scholars and general readers will find useful. No serious student of Kafka can afford to ignore this edition. But it has to be conceded that the editors of the Fischer volumes have not necessarily broken with the precedent set by Brod in his first editorial interventions. Again, the example of *Der Process* (the form of the title used in Kafka's manuscript) is instructive. The Fischer volume, edited by Malcolm Pasley, presents some material not present in the Brod edition, and it slightly rearranges the order of some of it. But the basic narrative framework proposed by the Brod version remains unaltered.

A stark contrast is offered by another critical project, the facsimile edition that we find in the Historisch-Kritische Ausgabe of Roland Reuß. Here we see clearly the great value to scholarship of an editorial enterprise (still in progress) intended to give us the texts of the *Nachlass* exactly as Kafka left them at his death. In the case of *The Trial*, for example, there is no effort to put together the various fragments into a coherent narrative, and the 'novel' we have come to know from the Brod version is nowhere to be seen. Instead, there are sixteen sheaves of loose leaves, each save one with a cover sheet on which Kafka had written a notation of the contents. There is only one indication of the order in which these sheaves might be arranged, and that is the sheaf called 'End'. Brod decided that some of these sheaves constituted 'chapters', while others were merely 'fragments', but that distinction has no basis in the manuscript Kafka left at his death.

The work of Reuß and his colleagues is of inestimable value to scholarship even in the incomplete state in which it now exists. It allows us to see Kafka's works as he actually wrote them, as drafts that will always remain drafts. We can hope that such an important project will not only come to completion in its present form but also form the basis for a future electronic edition that will allow readers searchable access on a variety of platforms.

NOTES

1 The condition of the manuscript of *Der Process* is especially revealing. See R. Reuß, 'Zur kritischen Edition von "Der Process" im Rahmen der Historischen-Kritischen Franz-Kafka Ausgabe' in R. Reuß und P. Staengle (eds.), *Franz*

Kafka. Der Process: Historisch-Kritische Ausgabe sämtlicher Handschriften, Drucke, und Typoskripte (Basel and Frankfurt am Main: Stroemfeld/Roter Stern, 1997), pp. 3–25.

2 See R. Reuß, 'Running Texts, Stunning Drafts' in S. Corngold and R. V. Gross (eds.), *Kafka for the Twenty-First Century* (Rochester, NY: Camden House, 2011), pp. 24–47.

CHAPTER 34

Translation

Mark Harman

Kafka and translation could mean two things: the art and craft of translating Kafka or the relevance of translation to his writing in the fraught context of early-twentieth-century Prague. In addressing those two issues, I shall broach the significance of Kafka's affinity for languages such as Czech and Yiddish; certain parallels between his linguistic in-betweenness and that of another polyglot modernist, James Joyce (1882–1941); his astute understanding of the necessary give and take in literary translation; and his awareness of the need for translators to render not merely his surface meaning, but also his underlying 'music'.

Kafka, who wrote exclusively in his native German, straddles cultural boundaries and can even be considered a kind of cultural translator. For instance, when a reviewer calls *Die Verwandlung* (*The Metamorphosis*, 1912) a decidedly German story and Max Brod characterizes it as a quintessentially Jewish tale Kafka asks himself whether he isn't 'a circus rider on 2 horses' (7 October 1916; *LF* 630/*B3* 250) Although that metaphor is characteristically ambiguous, it reveals both his awareness of the way his writing bestrides Jewish as well as German traditions and his ambivalence about writing in German. While smuggling traces of his intense absorption in Jewish history, language, religion and folklore into his German, he remains smitten with Czech, for, as he puts it in a letter to Milena Jesenská: 'I have never lived among German people. German is my mother tongue, and therefore natural to me, but I find Czech much more heartfelt [herzlich]' (*LM* 26/*BM* 17). The same is even truer of his relationship to Yiddish and, to a lesser extent, Hebrew.

Just as Stephen Dedalus's encounter in Joyce's *Portrait of the Artist as a Young Man* (1916) with the English-born Dean of Studies at University College Dublin galvanizes him into reconsidering his relationship to English, Kafka's discovery of the power of Yiddish through his immersion in Yiddish theatre in 1911–12 makes him reassess his relationship to German. Whereas Joyce firmly establishes his hold on the language of Shakespeare, Kafka never quite shakes off the originally antisemitic notion that his mother tongue (*Muttersprache*) belongs to ethnic Germans alone. His adherence to this prejudice as well as the influence of the withering attacks by Karl Kraus on so-called *mauscheln* – talking in Yiddish but also with antisemitic innuendo fiddling or wheeling and dealing – of writers such as Franz Werfel underlie his famously bleak diagnosis of the difficulties that writing in German posed for Jews. In a letter to Max Brod in June 1921, he invokes multiple quandaries facing German-Jewish writers, which he tentatively identifies as 'linguistic impossibilities': 'The impossibility of not writing, the impossibility of writing German, the impossibility of writing differently. One might also add a fourth impossibility, the impossibility of writing' (June 1921; *LFFE* 289/*B* 337–8) Yet, just as Joyce transforms his Irish uncertainty about English into a creative asset, Kafka in his letter is well aware that the despair of German-Jewish writers was their inspiration.

Kafka's Covert Multilingualism and Elusive 'Music'

In a pioneering talk on the Yiddish language on 18 February 1912 Kafka claims that attempts to translate Yiddish into German would 'annihilate' Yiddish. Yet he also suggests, in a letter to Max Brod in September 1917, that it might be possible to translate into High German an essay for Martin Buber's journal *Der Jude* (*The Jew*) by his Yiddish actor friend Jizchak Löwy, which was written in Yiddish-inflected German, although the task would call for an exceptionally 'delicate hand'. As an example he cites a phrase in which Löwy contrasts the audience for Jewish drama with the audience in Polish theatres, comprising 'tuxedoed men and ballgowned ladies' (end of September 1917; *LFFE* 148/*B* 173). Although Kafka admires the vitality of such Yiddish neologisms, he does not believe that they are acceptable in German: 'Excellently put, but the German language baulks. And there is a great deal like that; his highlights are the more effective since his language veers between Yiddish and German, inclining a bit toward the German' (*LFFE* 148/*B* 173) Then, with characteristic modesty, and possibly also in the hope that Brod will take over this 'impossible' task, Kafka adds: 'If only I had your powers of translation!'

Kafka has an unusually fine understanding of the balancing act required in literary translation, as one can see from his comments to Milena Jesenská about her Czech version of 'Der Heizer' ('The Stoker', 1912) – the first ever Kafka translation into any language: 'I am moved by your faithfulness toward every little sentence, a faithfulness I would not have thought possible to achieve in Czech, let alone with the beautiful natural authority

you attain' (*LM* 21/ *BM* 9). Yet, although he undoubtedly wants to strike
a gallant tone with a translator who doubles as his (occasional) lover, he is
too honest to suppress his suspicion that she may have pushed her Czech
too close to his German: 'I just don't know whether Czechs won't hold its
very faithfulness against you . . . my feeling for Czech – I have one too –
is fully satisfied, but it is extremely biased' (*LM* 25/*BM* 17). Here Kafka is
describing the inevitable tension between what theorists call foreignizing
and domesticating approaches to translation. Upon reading Milena's translation of 'Das Urteil' ('The Judgement', 1912) Kafka praises not just how
she recreates individual phrases and sentences, but also how she captures
his music:

> Every sentence, every word, every – if I may say so – music in that story
> is connected with that 'fear'. It was then, during one long night, that the
> wound broke open for the first time, and in my opinion the translation
> catches this association exactly, with that magic hand which is yours. (*LM*
> 152/*BM* 235)

The fear and the wound refer both to his tormented relationship with Felice
Bauer and to what, by the early 1920s, had become severe tuberculosis.

Kafka, who confessed to having little appreciation of music, uses the
term metaphorically to describe the sound, rhythm and visceral quality of
his prose. In a diary entry of 19 September 1917, written just a few weeks
after receiving the official diagnosis of tuberculosis, he invokes another
musical metaphor to explain the relationship between his suffering and
his compulsion to write:

> Have never understood how it is possible for almost everyone who writes
> to objectify his sufferings in the very midst of undergoing them . . . I can
> even go beyond that and with as many flourishes as I have the talent for,
> all of which seem to have nothing to do with my unhappiness, ring sim-
> ple, or contrapuntal, or a whole orchestration of changes on my theme. (19
> September 1917; *D* 384/ *TB* 834)

The attempt to transpose this 'music' to a different linguistic medium is a
great – and perhaps the truly insuperable – challenge facing translators. Of
course, the sound of the music we hear partly depends on the context in
which we read Kafka, which has changed considerably since he first became
known outside German-speaking literary circles in the 1930s.

Changing Paradigms in Translating Kafka

Rather than attempting to sketch the history of Kafka translation, I shall
focus on a few salient issues raised by changing interpretations of Kafka and

their impact on how translators tackle his work. As Edwin Muir observed in his introductory note to the first English-language edition of *Das Schloss* (*The Castle*, 1922) in 1930, Kafka was at the time almost unknown to English readers. Willa and Edwin Muir's rapid success in establishing his reputation in English-speaking countries and beyond stemmed both from the elegance and inventiveness of their translations – Willa appears to have done the lion's share of the work – and the persuasive force of Edwin's writing about Kafka, which portrayed him as a modern religious allegorist, even a latter-day John Bunyan.

Edwin Muir's interpretation of Kafka, partly inspired by Brod, was so influential that nobody paid any attention when in 1949 he expressed doubts about his allegorical reading.[1] Also, in spite of widespread misgivings about the adequacy of the Muirs' versions, articulated especially by Ronald Gray and S. S. Prawer, their translations remained the well-nigh canonized 'Kafka' until after the publication of the Fischer critical editions, beginning with Malcolm Pasley's 1982 edition of *Das Schloss*. It and subsequent Fischer Kafka editions, as well as the facsimile versions of the manuscripts with facing typescripts produced by the Stroemfeld Verlag, brought about a new understanding of the fluidity of Kafka's texts. It became clear that the manuscripts contain not securely delimited individual texts but a stream of fragments, diary-like entries and stories, the precise boundaries of which are often open to interpretation. The fact that both the Fischer and the Stroemfeld editions have been criticized for not being entirely 'faithful' – the very charge so often levelled against translators! – and for making unacknowledged editorial interventions raises the question of whether there can ever be a definitive Kafka edition. Translations are inherently less stable than the originals; in the case of Kafka, they are also dependent on the somewhat provisional decisions made by the German editors.

The wave of new Kafka translations in recent decades can be considered part of a broader movement in literary studies, which stresses cultural and historical contexts. It also mirrors a decisive turn in Kafka scholarship against the allegorical readings which prevailed when the Muirs first brought Kafka to the attention of English-speaking readers. Just as Kafka continued to write in spite of the perceived 'impossibility' of his endeavour, the fundamental difficulty of translation ought not to deter us from attempting fresh renditions of this great but elusive writer. Most of us undertaking new translations in this 'post-critical-edition' context subscribe to a conception of the task which allows less freedom for a translator's discretion than the Muirs could permit themselves. The essence of this new paradigm for translating Kafka was captured as early as 1978 in an article by Ronald Gray with the eye-catching, if finger-pointing, title, 'But Kafka wrote in German':

> translating Kafka is not a matter of making a daring fling, or of taking the whole meaning of a sentence into one's 'English' consciousness to refashion it entirely anew, with such faithfulness as one language can accord to another, but rather of a patient attention to the resonance of each word, the rhythm of each sentence, with only occasionally the challenge of retreating out of a totally foreign medium.[2]

Translator's Crux: Recreating Meaning(s) and Style

Forging a plausible analogue for an author's style is one of the chief tasks of the translator. But how best to describe Kafka's style? Perceptive readers noticed early on that his prose has a classical ring to it. Kurt Tucholsky (1890–1935), who was the first to overhear echoes of Heinrich von Kleist (1777–1811), describes Kafka's prose as 'the best classical German of our time',[3] a perception shared by Hermann Hesse (1877–1962) and Thomas Mann (1875–1955). If Kafka's style is classical, it is so in a low key, since he usually opts for the least striking phrasing, favouring understated rather than vivid or expressive diction. The resulting tonal neutrality is central to the effect of his prose, which juxtaposes the even-keel demeanour of his central figures, whose consciousness is the prism through which the story is mostly told, with the extraordinary events that befall them.

Kafka's style is also unobtrusively subversive. As Milan Kundera rightly insists, we are dealing with a writer who deliberately offends against 'good German', and an important task facing translators of Kafka is to replicate this offence in their own languages. In *Testaments Betrayed*, his polemic against literary and musical go-betweens, Kundera uses a punning injunction to convey his indignation at French translators who embroider upon Kafka's style by resorting to synonyms: 'O ye translators, do not sodonymize [*sic*] us!'[4] However, his broadside against all previous French translators of *The Castle* says less about the deficiencies of those alleged 'betrayers' than it does about Kundera's literalist and Nabokovian conception of translation, which contrasts markedly with Kafka's sophisticated understanding of the inevitable compromises that the craft entails.

There has to be some give and take between the goal of offering a close reading of Kafka and the attempt to create a prose style that does at least some justice to the 'music' of his prose. As a general rule, translations are wordier than the source text, for as Walter Benjamin (1892–1940) famously put it, the language of a translation wraps itself around 'its content like a royal robe with ample folds'.[5] At times, Kafka's prose has ample folds, as when he parodies the prolixity of the Austro-Hungarian bureaucracy, with which he was, of course, intimately familiar from his day job as an accident-insurance lawyer. But more often than not he is remarkably succinct. Syntax mirrors content. Each word serves one or more functions; this is true, I believe, even of those pesky qualifiers and modal particles with which he strews his sentences. The variable meanings in mid-sentence of otherwise simple German words like 'ja', 'aber' and 'doch' play a significant role in creating the underlying melody. Take, for instance, the triple use in *Der Verschollene* (*The Man who Disappeared*, 1912–14) within two consecutive sentences of the word 'ja' during an exchange between the hero Karl and a ship's stoker: "'Die amerikanischen Universitäten sind *ja* unvergleichlich besser." "Das ist *ja* möglich", sagte Karl, "aber ich habe *ja* fast kein Geld zum Studieren'" (*V* 12 [italics mine]). In my rendering of that passage in *Der Verschollene* I translated each 'ja' differently: "'The American universities are, of course, incomparably better." "That may well be so," said Karl, "but I've barely any money to pay for my studies."'[6] Some critics regard such flavouring particles as verbal tics and even advocate excising them in translation. Others criticize his prose for its allegedly awkward and repetitive phrasing. The problem with editing out such supposedly irritating features of his style is that it would alter the timbre of his characteristically diffident voice. A self-assured Kafka might sound more 'classical', but would not tilt in quite the same way against 'good German'. Kafka hints as much when he calls the prose of German-Jewish writers an 'organic compound' of 'officialese' ('Papierdeutsch') and 'mime' ('Gebärdensprache') – the latter term may also allude to the Yiddish substratum in his own writing (June 1921; *LFFE* 288/*B* 336).

If carried to an extreme, however, a translator's fidelity to the meaning of each little phrase can fail to capture expressive features of his style such as rhythm and repetition. Often, in translations of James Joyce, 'the music is switched off in favour of the literal meaning',[7] as the Swiss critic Fritz Senn puts it. The difficulty of rendering Kafka's underlying 'music' is just as acute as it is with Joyce's – Malcolm Pasley even likens the manuscript of *The Castle* to a 'musical score'.[8] Moreover, Kafka's notorious talent for ambiguity creates further challenges. Even the titles of works such as *Das Schloss* ('the castle' or 'the lock') and *Der Process* ('the trial' or 'the process') defy translators' best efforts. Kafka often draws on the multiple possible meanings of seemingly straightforward German words. English does not always offer comparable opportunities for ambiguity, and the poor translator must choose one meaning over the other. One solution to this and comparable dilemmas is for the translator to supply footnotes or marginal annotations, if perhaps not quite so industriously as does the Kafka scholar Claude David, who revised Alexandre Vialatte's first French translation of *The Castle* by adding 210 pages of notes at the back of the Pléiade edition.

While an argument can be made against furnishing translations with extensive explanatory notes, there are moments when such notes can not only alert readers to the translator's rationale for a certain solution but also point out ironic or humorous undertones that might otherwise get lost. For instance, in the second chapter of *The Castle*, an obscure Castle official named Oswald calls K. 'der ewige Landvermesser' ('the eternal land surveyor').[9] Lurking behind Oswald's annoyance over K.'s pestering of the authorities is an allusion to the myth of the 'ewige Jude' (wandering Jew). Since there is no way to introduce this allusion in English while retaining the tone of the exchange, a note about the double meaning of the term would be helpful to the reader. Even if this is not possible, translators can include prefaces, which are often well worth reading. A single example will have to suffice: Joyce Crick's description of Kafka's sentences as 'a vehicle for the way his figures think, as these conduct their seeming-rational arguments with themselves, which so often, after great expenditure of energy, conclude a paragraph or even a page later with the proposition' with which they began.[10]

Kafka, who relished the oral qualities of his literary favourites, frequently read his own prose aloud to family and friends, often to much laughter. As a diary entry inspired by Rudolf Steiner's Prague lectures on anthroposophy in March 1911 indicates, he was keenly aware of the relationship between punctuation, breathing and the flow of a sentence:

> Omission of the full stop. In general, the spoken sentence starts off from the speaker with its initial capital letter, curves in its course, as far as it can, out to the audience, and returns with the full stop to the speaker. But if the full stop is omitted then the sentence, no longer held in check, blows directly with full breath at the listener. (26 March 1911; *D* 45/*TB* 125)

Given the attention that Kafka paid to the sound of his prose, it seems reasonable to expect that translations of his writing should work for the ear. Only thus can his subterranean irony and humour find halfway adequate expression.

As I prepared my translation of *The Castle*, I was fortunate enough to have a group of friends to whom I read it aloud, chapter by chapter. Attempting to capture the oral quality of Kafka's prose enabled me to hear the novel afresh and to recognize how – especially in the eerily comic dialogue between the self-described land surveyor K. and his two ostensible assistants – it anticipates such masters of drily humorous, surreal repartee as Samuel Beckett, Harold Pinter and the Stoppard of *Rosencrantz and Guildenstern Are Dead* (1966).

NOTES

1 W. Binder (ed.), *Kafka-Handbuch* (Stuttgart: Kröner, 1979), vol. II, p. 669.
2 R. Gray, 'But Kafka wrote in German' in A. Flores (ed.), *The Kafka Debate* (New York: Gordian Press, 1977), p. 251.
3 K. Tucholsky, *Ausgewählte Briefe 1913–1935* (Frankfurt am Main: Büchergilde Gutenberg, 1962), p. 473.
4 M. Kundera, *Testaments Betrayed: An Essay in Nine Parts*, trans. L. Asher (New York: Harper Collins, 1995), p. 109.
5 W. Benjamin, 'The Task of the Translator' in L. Venuti (ed.), H. Zohn (trans.), *The Translation Studies Reader* (New York and London: Routledge, 2000), p. 79.
6 F. Kafka, *Amerika: The Missing Person*, trans. M. Harman (New York: Schocken, 2008).
7 F. Senn, *Joyce's Dislocutions: Essays on Reading as Translation*, ed. J. P. Riquelme (Baltimore, MD: Johns Hopkins University Press, 1984), p. 30.
8 'Nachbemerkung' (Postscript) to *Das Schloß* (Frankfurt am Main: Fischer Taschenbuch Verlag, 1994), p. 390.
9 F. Kafka, *The Castle*, trans. M. Harman (New York: Schocken Books, 1998), p. 21; *The Castle*, trans. M. Harman, introduced by J. Sutherland, illustrated by B. Bragg (London: Folio Society, 2011), p. 21.
10 'Note on the Translation' in *The Metamorphosis and Other Stories*, trans. J. Crick, introduction and notes by R. Robertson (Oxford University Press, 2009), p. xxv.

CHAPTER 35

Film Adaptations

Dora Osborne

Scholarship has shown that Kafka had an ambivalent relationship with visual media and technology. We know that he was a cinema-goer and that these encounters with film shaped his writing.[1] However, we also know that he reacted with horror to the suggestion that an illustrator depict the insect protagonist of *Die Verwandlung* (*The Metamorphosis*, 1912), Gregor Samsa (25 October 1915; *LFFE* 115/*DLA* 189). Kafka's response is hardly surprising, since he uses Samsa's metamorphosis to probe the limits of representation, to confront his reader with what cannot be shown in any literal sense. When Gregor's mother sees her insect-son, he appears only as a brown stain in her field of vision (*M* 56/*DL* 166). Yet Kafka's texts are strikingly visual: in their sober realism, they include vivid details, and in their theatricality, they focus on the gestures of protagonists. Indeed Walter Benjamin (1892–1940) noted how 'Kafka's entire work constitutes a code of gestures', and Theodor W. Adorno (1903–69) stressed the affinity of Kafka's work with silent cinema.[2] Such observations suggest why film directors have taken on the challenge of adapting Kafka for the screen, even if several attempts have hardly grabbed attention and even the more memorable have met with mixed responses. In a kind of caveat to any evaluation, commentators have noted the difficulties of filming Kafka, even suggesting that his work defies adaptation. Pitfalls surely exist, for although Kafka's visual language seems to invite its rendering as image, his narratives strain constantly and resolutely at the limits of representability.

Whilst the number of explicit adaptations of Kafka is relatively small, there are many films that reveal the influence of the author, or at least elements of the Kafkaesque, for example, work by Czech director Jan Švankmajer and the Brothers Quay, or Martin Scorsese's cult comedy *After Hours* (1985), which includes a reference to the parable 'Vor dem Gesetz' ('Before the Law'). In 1995, Peter Capaldi won an Oscar for his short film *Franz Kafka's It's a Wonderful Life*. In this surreal, Monty Python-inspired tale, literature meets film via a slip made by Capaldi's wife: referring to Frank Capra's Christmas classic, *It's a Wonderful Life* (1946), she mistakenly called the director Kafka, which gave Capaldi an idea. The film imagines the scene in which Kafka, trying to finish the first, notorious sentence of *The Metamorphosis*, struggles to imagine what exactly Gregor Samsa might have turned into. Reflecting Kafka's own concern with the hybrid, genre-defying nature of 'minor literature',[3] Capaldi's off-beat comedy is quite unrestricted by conventional boundaries; rather it revels in the hybrid premise of Kafka's beetle-man, mixing high modernism with popular culture, a Prague Jew with a Christmas carol, and a German-language source with Scottish accents. Capaldi used the transcultural appeal and currency of Kafka's story to produce a film which intriguingly became the subject of nationalistic debates: the status of the film as Oscar-winner raised questions about whether this was a victory for British culture or a 'local hero'.[4]

An adaptation does more than reference a source text, however. Adaptation can be understood as a kind of translation, here, of Kafka's texts to the medium of film, or as a form of intermediality, whereby the textual medium is brought into dialogue with the visual medium of film. Yet, precisely because adaptation implies a further act of re-presentation, it is beset by problems: how close can or should it remain to the original, and what kind of losses does the transition between media entail? David Jones's *The Trial* (1993), for example, is a very faithful adaptation, but, little more than a costume drama, does not add much to Kafka's text. By contrast, Jean-Marie Straub's and Danièle Huillet's *Klassenverhältnisse* (*Class Relations*, 1984) is a very challenging adaptation of *Der Verschollene* (*The Man who Disappeared*, 1912–14). However, it engages only one very specific aspect of Kafka's text, namely the social roles and power structures indicated in the title. Shot in Hamburg, it seems to elide Kafka's descriptions of New York, which are considered to be overtly cinematic, focusing instead on performance and gesture. Scholarly assessments of Kafka adaptations have tended to focus on the relative success or failure of his complex and challenging texts to the medium of film, but this approach limits what can be said about these projects, not least because, in the majority of cases, critics have concluded that they did not particularly succeed. Following the lead given by directors themselves, the more interesting assessments of Kafka film adaptations have focused on how these works use his 'cinematic' literary texts to reflect on, or even critique, the filmic medium and the cinematic traditions of the twentieth century.

Orson Welles, *The Trial*

The most iconic Kafka adaptation is Orson Welles's *The Trial* (1962), which is considered a landmark production for cinema and for Kafka reception. Whilst most of the characters and action follow the original, Welles's *Trial* is a Cold War, *noir* remake: it features men in trench coats, post-war architecture, a giant computer and a reference to atomic warfare. It is not only the shift in style and technology that updates Kafka's story for the nuclear age, however. *The Trial* is emphatically a film made after Auschwitz, including a scene with dishevelled prisoners (apparently also victims of the court) carrying number cards round their necks, redolent of those deported under the Nazi regime. At the end of the film, as K. is taken to his execution, this desolate space – a kind of transit camp – is empty; we must assume that these numbered victims have met their fate. Crucially, Welles's K. defies his own destiny, refusing to take the knife from his executioners to perform the deed himself and tossing the stick of dynamite they ignite back at them. For the director, this was the only possible way to end Kafka's story after 1945.

Perhaps the most significant intervention Welles makes in Kafka's text is his repositioning of the priest's parable – published separately under the title 'Vor dem Gesetz' ('Before the Law') – which he uses to frame not only the narrative but also his project as film adaptation. A series of eighteen specially made illustrations tell the story as a pre-photographic slide-show, accompanied by Welles's own voiceover; a cut to a sleeping Anthony Perkins suggests this is K.'s dream. The sequence returns at the end, shown to K. as a slide-show, not by the prison chaplain, but the advocate Hastler (Kafka's Huld), played by none other than Welles. As Hastler's exposition of the parable gives way to Welles's explanation of its relation to Kafka's text and thus his own adaptation, the line between diegetic and extra-diegetic voices blurs. Welles's approach has been criticized because, by positioning 'Before the Law' before the *Trial*, it confers on the parable a rationalizing or explanatory function withheld in the novel, and because it uses the parable to subordinate the authority of Kafka's enigmatic text to that of the film director. 'Before the Law' is used not only as part of the narrative, part of Josef K.'s trial, but as a device that, playing with the medium and technology of film, allows Welles to demonstrate absolute control over the narrative through its adaptation, manipulation and projection.

Steven Soderbergh, *Kafka*

In making his 1991 film *Kafka*, Steven Soderbergh claims not to have been drawn to the author, but rather to Lem Dobbs's innovative screenplay, which seemed to avoid the pitfalls of both a biopic and textual adaptation by attempting neither. Set in Prague and focusing on a writer protagonist with obvious affinities to the author, *Kafka* weaves characters and scenarios from his life and work into a fantasy fiction. Following the mysterious death of a colleague, who, it transpires, was an anarchist after dark, Soderbergh's Kafka discovers inhumane experiments being carried out at the ominous and anonymous castle and attempts to stop this work with a bomb. *Kafka* is thus both a kind of palimpsest, layering different stories over each other (*The Castle*, *The Trial*, 'In the Penal Colony'), and a network, making and creating connections across literature, film and history. Soderbergh gives his characters names we recognize. Gabriela Rossmann, for example, an anarchist who vanishes when she becomes a victim of the castle's medical experiments, is a reference to Kafka's 'man who disappeared', Karl Rossmann. The thriller is also triggered by a disappearance, that of Eduard Raban, who shares his name with one of Kafka's early protagonists in 'Hochzeitsvorbereitungen auf dem Lande' ('Wedding Preparations in the Country', 1906–9), and who the audience knows has been murdered. Whilst in Kafka's story, Raban imagines he has turned into a beetle and sends out a 'clothed body' in his stead, in Soderbergh's film, it is the protagonist Kafka who must go out into the world in place – and in search – of Raban, who lies, not in bed, but in a morgue. Other familiar names, but with less textual resonance, are those of Kafka's superior, Burgel, and Grubach, the inspector charged with investigating and ultimately covering up two mysterious deaths. Familiar figures include Max Brod, who appears as a sculptor and grave-digger (both a creative and a morbid presence), and the two clumsy assistants from *The Castle*, who later transform into more threatening guards, Soderbergh's version of the amateur actors who, in *The Trial*, escort Josef K. to the scene of his execution.

The response to *Kafka* was mixed: whilst some critics praised the film, others were more sceptical, agreeing with audiences that Soderbergh had taken liberties with a revered literary figure. However, Soderbergh claimed his project was principally about cinema and, despite his choice of title, not the author Kafka. And he can hardly have been drawn to the cinematic quality of Kafka's writing, since, for him, it has 'certain faults as cinema material'.[5] Thus, *Kafka* should not be viewed as a straight adaptation of Kafka, or even as concerned with his work, but rather as a film that uses a network of associations constructed around the author – most significantly, Expressionist cinema – for a 'postmodern pastiche'.[6] *Kafka* does engage with the author Kafka in one important regard, however; it questions the construction of a cultural icon, dramatizing the slippage between reality and fiction which is at work in the shift from the historical and literary figure of Kafka to the ubiquitous notion of the Kafkaesque. If Soderbergh's film, in its playful use of Kafka's texts, seems to offend a dominant image of the revered author, it also asks how this image came about in the first place and how much it in fact relates to any reality or truth about Kafka and his work. Moreover, in so doing, Soderbergh's film does manage to convey one characteristic of Kafka's writing often omitted from the reverential cultural image of the author, namely its humour: the clownish behaviour of the assistants references the element of slapstick in Kafka's writing; the protagonist's lover makes a wry reference to Kafka's excessive correspondence, telling him that now she has come to Prague he can save on postage; and the protagonist's sarcastic retort to his superior, 'I'll write that down', signals how the author's ironic gaze on bureaucratic institutions was readily incorporated into his writing. Wittiest of all is the remark made by Armin Mueller-Stahl's chain-smoking inspector: 'Kafka . . . Kafka . . . Kafka . . . Is that your real name?'

Michael Haneke, *Das Schloss*

Of the examples discussed, *Das Schloss* (*The Castle*, 1997) by Austrian director Michael Haneke is the most faithful adaptation of a single Kafka text, but, made for television (and with a national television audience in mind), it focuses on its subject rather differently from big screen adaptations. Whilst the film adds little that is not in the original (it adheres to the story using extracts read out from the novel as voiceover), Haneke necessarily had to omit material in order to reduce the long novel fragment to a format suitable for television. Critical responses to *The Castle* have been reserved, mainly because, in its literal, 'straight' approach to the text, it is rather flat and thus lacking Haneke's characteristic emotional intensity. The director is also reticent about the work, insisting on its genesis and status as television project – he would never have dared to make a Kafka adaptation for the cinema.[7] Nevertheless, of the directors discussed, Haneke seems to have the greatest regard for and understanding of Kafka and the legacy of modernism. For instance, Haneke is attentive to the way the novel is both a fragment (it stops mid-sentence) and fragmentary, and seeks ways to convey this through film. His most distinctive device is his frequent use of cuts to black, which serve to break up, and ultimately break off, the narrative. The duration of these interruptions means Haneke does more than announce a scene change: he arrests the temporal flow of narrative in a way that parallels the freezing of the harsh, snowy winter landscape of the village.

In these empty spaces, we are made aware both of the construction of narrative and the absence of structural integrity. We thus become conscious of ourselves watching, in a way that undermines the passive consumption of images.

Haneke also understands that providing visual correlates for textual description would limit the possibility of active engagement with the narrative. A crucial feature of his adaptation is the absence of any shot of the castle itself. In Kafka's text the structure remains obscure and seemingly multifaceted, but is nevertheless perceived by K. In Haneke's film, however, the camera remains fixed on images of the village, and the only visualization of the castle is the black and white image (possibly a reproduction of an old drawing or print) of a fortress town inadequately attached to the back of the inn door. Even this image is obscured as a table of statistics falls down over it, symbolizing how bureaucracy dominates and refuses K. access to any kind of truth about the castle. For Haneke, Kafka's strategic use of the castle as metaphor prohibits its literalization through the medium of film. Beyond this key example, Haneke is also keen to avoid the imperative that, in television productions, sound should mirror or double images (thereby avoiding any ambiguity for the viewers).[8] Thus, at several points in *The Castle*, most noticeably the (open) end, the images we see do not correspond to – in the sense of simply illustrating – the words we hear. Haneke achieves this disjuncture through his strategic use of voice-over. Throughout the film, a narrator (notably, unlike in Welles's *Trial*, the voice is not the director's) speaks text taken directly from Kafka. This might function as a conventional device to underpin a faithful adaptation, but in fact is used to more complex ends. Haneke has the voice of Kafka's narrator overlap with the spoken dialogue of his actors, which serves to heighten the staged nature of their speech, as well as the hybrid nature of adaptation: the written word and moving image do not merge seamlessly but are made conspicuous in their medial and stylistic differences.

Stan Douglas, *Vidéo*

Adapting Kafka for the screen is obviously no mean feat and leaves anyone willing to take up the gauntlet open to criticism. And yet, like any challenge, it seems to invite renewed attempts. A German production of *Der Bau* (*The Burrow*, directed by Jochen Alexander Freydank), played in cinemas in 2015, and Soderbergh, apparently undeterred, even spurred on, by criticism, has announced plans to re-cut *Kafka*, this time with German dubbing.[9] With his video installation *Vidéo* (2007), Canadian artist Stan

Douglas has not simply taken on the challenge of adapting Kafka (here *The Trial*), but reflects on the author's work using other, cinematic intertexts (Welles's *The Trial* and Samuel Beckett's *Film* (1965) and Jean-Luc Godard's *Two or Three Things I Know About Her* (1967)). Made for gallery viewing and often shown on loop, installation invites a very different experience from films made for cinema or television. In his work, Douglas is interested in the re-mediation of the past and uses visual media to mark the temporal gap in acts of re-presentation.[10] *Vidéo* uses colour film, but the lighting in fact creates a monochrome effect, thereby re-creating the black-and-white aesthetic of *film noir* referenced by Welles. Douglas emphasizes the sense of surveillance in *The Trial* by having his camera pursue the protagonist, K, from behind, moving only to the side, and never showing us a face (a reference to Beckett's *Film*). Crucially, Douglas's protagonist is a Senegalese woman. Here, the act of showing papers to officials updates both Kafka's novel and Welles's Cold War adaptation, suggesting how, in the twenty-first century, it is migrant women who are especially threatened by inaccessible and indifferent authorities. The spoken language is French, but *Vidéo* includes no audio recording of this dialogue. Here the silent cinema to which Kafka's work has been likened has become silenced cinema; the operations of power and (in)justice remain frustratingly incomprehensible. Ultimately, like Kafka's and Welles's protagonists, Douglas's K is executed (we hear a shot being fired). She is dragged across a desolate lot in front of a modern apartment block – both a reference to Welles and to the sites of the 2005 Paris riots. Yet, shown on a loop, *Vidéo* rejects the use of Welles's framing device, which allows him to anticipate the power of the law in K.'s trial and inscribe himself in, indeed over, Kafka's narrative. Instead Douglas re-inscribes an important element of Kafka's *Der Process*, namely the way the process (both as narrative and as trial) is subject to repetition. As the film replays without any kind of break to indicate beginning or end, there is no sense of narrative trajectory or resolution. K's trial, like Josef K.'s, does not follow any clear moral or ethical logic, but, in its obscurity, is relentless.

NOTES

1 See H. Zischler, *Kafka Goes to the Movies*, trans. S. H. Gillespie (Chicago University Press, 2003) and S. Horstkotte's chapter on film in this volume.

2 W. Benjamin, 'Franz Kafka: On the Tenth Anniversary of His Death' in M. W. Jennings, H. Eiland and G. Smith (eds.), R. Livingstone (trans.), *Walter Benjamin: Selected Writings*, 4 vols. (Cambridge, MA: The Belknap Press of Harvard University Press, 2002–6), vol. ii.2, pp. 794–818: 801; T. W. Adorno and

W. Benjamin, *The Complete Correspondence 1928–1940*, ed. H. Lonitz, trans. N. Walker (Cambridge, MA: Harvard University Press, 2001), p. 70.

3 See G. Deleuze and F. Guattari, *Kafka: Toward a Minor Literature*, trans. D. Polan (Minneapolis, MN: University of Minnesota Press, 1986).

4 See M. Woods, 'Adapting Kafka' in Woods, *Kafka Translated: How Translators Have Shaped Our Reading of Kafka* (London: Bloomsbury, 2014), pp. 191–239: 233–9.

5 A. Kaufman (ed.), *Steven Soderbergh: Interviews* (Jackson, MS: University Press of Mississippi, 2002), p. 48.

6 I. Ritzer, 'Philosophical Reflections on Steven Soderbergh's *Kafka*', in R. B. Palmer and S. M. Sanders (eds.), *The Philosophy of Steven Soderbergh* (Lexington, KY: University Press of Kentucky, 2011), pp. 145–58: 150.

7 S. Foundas, 'Michael Haneke: The Bearded Prophet of *Code Inconnu* and *The Piano Teacher*', *indiewire*, 4 December 2001, https://tinyurl.com/kjedvxe.

8 Interview with Michael Haneke, DVD extras, Haneke (dir.), *Das Schloss* (Absolut Medien, 1996).

9 P. de Semlyen, 'Steven Soderbergh on His Kafka Recut and Hints at a Lem Dobbs Commentary', *Empire*, 29 May 2013, https://tinyurl.com/k3hswkn.

10 See M. Bal, 'Re-: Killing Time' in H. D. Christ and I. Dressler (eds.), *Stan Douglas: Past Imperfect – Works 1986–2007* (Ostfildern: Hatje Cantz, 2008), pp. 65–93.

Further Reading

1 FAMILY

Alt, P.-A., *Franz Kafka: Der ewige Sohn* (Munich: C. H. Beck, 2005)

Brod, M., *Franz Kafka: A Biography*, trans. G. H. Roberts and R. Winston, second enlarged edition (New York: Schocken Books, 1960)

Binder, H., *Kafkas Welt: Eine Lebenschronik in Bildern* (Reinbek: Rowohlt Verlag, 2008)

Koch, H.-G. (ed.), *'Als Kafka mir entgegen kam . . . ': Erinnerungen an Franz Kafka* (Berlin: Wagenbach, 2013)

Northey, A., *Kafka's Relatives: Their Lives and His Writing* (New Haven, CT and London: Yale University Press, 1991)

Stach, R., *Kafka: The Decisive Years*, trans. S. Frisch (Princeton University Press, 2013)

Kafka: The Years of Insight, trans. S. Frisch (Princeton University Press, 2015)

Kafka: The Early Years, trans. S. Frisch (Princeton University Press, 2017)

Wagenbach, K., *Kafka*, trans. E. Osers (Cambridge, MA: Harvard University Press, 2003)

2 FRIENDSHIP

Alt, P.-A., *Franz Kafka: Der ewige Sohn* (Munich: C. H. Beck, 2005)

Stach, R., *Kafka: The Decisive Years*, trans. S. Frisch (Princeton University Press, 2013)

Kafka: The Years of Insight, trans. S. Frisch (Princeton University Press, 2015)

Kafka: The Early Years, trans. S. Frisch (Princeton University Press, 2017)

3 WOMEN

Buber-Neumann, M., *Milena*, trans. R. Manheim (London: Collins-Harvill, 1988)

Diamant, K., *Kafka's Last Love: The Mystery of Dora Diamant* (London: Secker and Warburg, 2003)

Hayes, K. (ed.), *The Journalism of Milena Jesenská: A Critical Voice in Interwar Central Europe* (Oxford: Berghahn, 2001)

Jesenká, M., *Ich hätte zu antworten tage- und nächtelang: Die Briefe von Milena*, ed. A. Wagnerova (Frankfurt am Main: Fischer, 1999)

Kotlandova Koenig, D., 'Moderate and Sensible: Higher Education and the Czech Women's Rights Movement', *Central European Review*, 1, no. 14 (1999), www.ce-review.org/99/14/koenig14art.html

Pawel, E., *The Nightmare of Reason: A Life of Franz Kafka* (London: Collins Harvill, 1988)

4 WORK

Corngold, S., 'Kafka and the Ministry of Writing' in S. Corngold, J. Greenberg and B. Wagner (eds.), *The Office Writings*, trans. E. Patton with R. Hein (Princeton University Press, 2008), pp. 1–18

Posner, R. A., 'Kafka: The Writer as Lawyer', *Columbia Law Review*, 207 (2010), 207–15

Wagner, B., 'Kafkas Poetik des Unfalls' in C. Kassung (ed.), *Die Unordung der Dinge: Eine Wissens- und Mediengeschichte des Unfalls* (Bielefeld: Transcript, 2009), pp. 421–54

Wolf, B., 'Die Nacht des Bürokraten: F. K.s statistische Schreibweise', *Deutsche Vierteljahrsschrift für Literaturwissenschaft und Geistesgeschichte*, 80 (2006), 97–127

Zilcosky, J., '"Samsa war Reisender": Trains, Trauma, and the Unreadable Body' in S. Corngold and R. V. Gross (eds.), *Kafka for the Twenty-First Century* (Rochester, NY: Camden House, 2011), pp. 179–206

5 HEALTH AND ILLNESS

Anderson, M. M., *Kafka's Clothes: Ornament and Aestheticism in the Habsburg Fin de Siècle* (Oxford: Clarendon Press, 1992)

Barton, S., *Healthy Living in the Alps: The Origins of Winter Tourism Switzerland, 1860–1914* (Manchester University Press, 2008)

Gilman, S., 'Kafka und Krankheit' in B. von Jagow and O. Jahraus (eds.), *Kafka Handbuch* (Göttingen: Vandenhoeck & Ruprecht, 2008), pp. 114–20

Gradman, C., 'Robert Koch and the Pressures of Scientific Research: Tuberculosis and Tuberculin', *Medical History*, 45, no. 1 (2001), 1–32

Türk, J., *Die Immunität der Literatur* (Frankfurt am Main: Fischer, 2011)

Zadoff, M., *Next Year in Marienbad: The Lost Worlds of Jewish Spa Culture* (Philadelphia, PA: University of Pennsylvania Press, 2012)

6 WRITING

Binder, H., *Kafka: Der Schaffensprozeß* (Frankfurt am Main: Suhrkamp, 1983)

Fromm, W., 'Schaffensprozess' in M. Engel and B. Auerochs (eds.), *Kafka-Handbuch* (Stuttgart: Metzler, 2010), pp. 428–37

Harmann, M., 'Die Ästhetik der Andeutung: K.s Streichungen im Schreibprozeß', *Neue Rundschau*, 112, no. 2 (2001), 104–23

Neumann, G., 'Der verschleppte Prozeß: Literarisches Schaffen zwischen Schreib-strom und Werkidol', *Poetica*, 14 (1982), 92–111

Pasley, M., 'Der Schreibakt und das Geschriebene: Zur Frage der Entstehung von Kafkas Texten' in C. David (ed.), *Franz Kafka: Themen und Probleme* (Göttingen: Vandenhoeck & Ruprecht, 1980), pp. 9–25

Reuß, R., 'Running Texts, Stunning Drafts' in S. Corngold and R. V. Gross (eds.), *Kafka for the Twenty-First Century* (Rochester, NY: Camden House, 2011), pp. 24–47

Schuster, M., *Franz Kafkas Handschrift zum 'Schloss'* (Heidelberg: Winter, 2012)

7 STYLE

Coetzee, J. M., 'Kafka: Translators on Trial' (review of *The Castle*, trans. M. Harman), *New York Review of Books*, 14 May 1998, 14–17

Cohn, D., 'Kafka's Eternal Present: Narrative Tense in "Ein Landarzt" and other First-Person Stories', *Publications of the Modern Languages Association of America*, 83 (1968), 144–50

Koelb, C., *Kafka's Rhetoric: The Passion of Reading* (Ithaca, NY and London: Cornell University Press, 1989)

Müller-Seidel, W., 'Kafkas Begriff des Schreibens und die moderne Literatur', *Zeitschrift für Literaturwissenschaft und Linguistik*, 17, no. 68 (1987), 104–21

White, J. J., 'Endings and Non-Endings in Kafka's Fiction' in F. Kuna (ed.), *Franz Kafka: Semi-Centenary Perspectives* (London: Elek, 1976), pp. 146–66

8 LITERARY MODERNISM

Anderson, M. M., *Kafka's Clothes: Ornament and Aestheticism in the Habsburg Fin de Siècle* (Oxford: Clarendon Press, 1992)

Corngold, S., *Lambent Traces: Franz Kafka* (Princeton University Press, 2004)

Engel, M. and Auerochs, B. (eds.), *Kafka-Handbuch* (Stuttgart: Metzler, 2010)

Huyssen, A., *Miniature Metropolis: Literature in an Age of Photography and Film* (Harvard University Press, 2015)

Sokel, W. H., *The Myth of Power and the Self: Essays on Franz Kafka* (Detroit, MI: Wayne State University Press, 2002)

9 KAFKA'S READING

Dodd, W. J., *Kafka and Dostoyevsky: The Shaping of Influence* (London: Macmillan, 1992)

Engel, M. and Lamping, D. (eds.), *Franz Kafka und die Weltliteratur* (Göttingen: Vandenhoeck & Ruprecht, 2006)

Peters, F. G., 'Kafka and Kleist: A Literary Relationship', *Oxford German Studies*, 1 (1966), 114–62

Rohde, B., *'Und blätterte ein wenig in der Bibel': Studien zu Franz Kafkas Bibellektüre und ihren Auswirkungen auf sein Werk* (Würzburg: Königshausen & Neumann, 2002)

Tedlock, E. W., 'Kafka's Imitation of David Copperfield', *Comparative Literature*, 7 (1955), 52–62

10 GESTURE

Agamben, G., 'Notes on Gesture', in G. Agamben, *Means Without End: Notes on Politics* (Minneapolis, MN: University of Minnesota Press, 2000), pp. 49–60

Benjamin, W., 'Franz Kafka: On the Tenth Anniversary of His Death', in M. W. Jennings, H. Eiland and G. Smith (eds.), R. Livingstone (trans.), *Walter Benjamin: Selected Writings*, 4 vols. (Cambridge, MA: The Belknap Press of Harvard University Press, 2002–6), vol. II.2, pp. 794–818

Klages, L., *Ausdrucksbewegung und Gestaltungskraft: Grundlegung der Wissenschaft vom Ausdruck* (Leipzig: Barth, 1923)

Lack, E., *Kafkas bewegte Körper: Die Tagebücher und Briefe als Laboratorien von Bewegung* (Munich: Fink, 2009)

Nitschke, C., 'Evidenz und Verrätselung: Gesten und Logical Turn in Kafkas *Betrachtung*' in C. Duttlinger (ed.), *Kafkas 'Betrachtung': Neue Lektüren* (Freiburg: Rombach, 2014), pp. 141–64

Puchner, M., 'Kafka's Antitheatrical Gestures', *The Germanic Review: Literature, Culture, Theory*, 78, no. 3 (2003), 177–93

Schiffermüller, I., *Franz Kafkas Gesten: Studien zur Entstellung der menschlichen Sprache* (Tübingen: Francke, 2011)

Warburg, A., *The Renewal of Pagan Antiquity: Contributions to the Cultural History of the European Renaissance* (Los Angeles, CA: Getty Research Institute for the History of Art and the Humanities, 1999)

Weber, S., 'Going Along for the Ride. Violence and Gesture: Agamben Reading Benjamin Reading Kafka Reading Cervantes', *The Germanic Review: Literature, Culture, Theory*, 81, no. 1 (2006), 65–83

Wundt, W., *Elements of Folk Psychology: Outlines of a Psychological History of the Development of Mankind* (London: G. Allen & Unwin, Macmillan, 1916)

11 PERFORMANCE AND RECITATION

Beck, E. T., *Kafka and the Yiddish Theater: Its Impact on his Work* (Madison, WI: University of Wisconsin Press, 1971)

Massino, G., *Franz Kafka, Jizchak Löwy und das jiddische Theater* (Frankfurt am Main: Stroemfeld/Nexus, 2007)

Müller, L., 'Die Unruhe eines Westjuden: Franz Kafka, das jiddische Theater und die Unübersetzbarkeit des Jargons', *brücken. Germanistisches Jahrbuch Tschechien – Slowakei*, 15 (2007), 149–80

Die zweite Stimme: Vortragskunst von Goethe bis Kafka (Berlin: Wagenbach, 2007)

Puchner, M., 'Kafka and the Theater', *The Germanic Review*, 78, no. 3 (2003), 163–5

12 FILM

Alt, P.-A., *Kafka und der Film: Über kinematographisches Erzählen* (Munich: C. H. Beck, 2009)

Duttlinger, C., *Kafka and Photography* (Oxford University Press, 2007)

Gunning, T., 'The Cinema of Attraction: Early Film, its Spectator, and the Avant-garde' in T. Elsaesser (ed.), *Early Cinema: Space, Frame, Narrative* (London: BFI Publishing, 1990), pp. 229–35

Kreimeier, K., *Traum und Exzess: Die Kulturgeschichte des frühen Kinos* (Wien: Zsolnay, 2011)

Zischler, H., *Kafka geht ins Kino* (Reinbek: Rowohlt, 1996); *Kafka Goes to the Movies*, trans. S. H. Gillespie (University of Chicago Press, 2003)

13 PHOTOGRAPHY

Duttlinger, C., *Kafka and Photography* (Oxford University Press, 2007)

Milne, E., *Letters, Postcards, Email: Technologies of Presence* (New York: Routledge, 2010)

Skopec, R., 'Bohemia, Moravia and Slovakia', *History of Photography*, 2 (1978), 141–53

Wagenbach, K., *Kafka: Bilder aus seinem Leben*, second edition (Berlin: Wagenbach, 1994)

Witkovsky, M. (ed.), *Foto: Modernity in Central Europe, 1918–1945* (Washington, DC: National Gallery of Art, 2007)

Zischler, H., *Kafka geht ins Kino* (Reinbek: Rowohlt, 1996); *Kafka Goes to the Movies*, trans. S. H. Gillespie (University of Chicago Press, 2003)

14 MUSIC

Caduff, C., 'Der gottverlorene Ton: Musik in Texten von Kleist, Kafka und Anne Duden' in R. Sorg and B. Würffel (eds.), *Gott und Götze in der Literatur der Moderne* (Munich: Fink, 1999), pp. 245–57

Daiber, J., *Kafka und der Lärm: Klanglandschaften der frühen Moderne* (Münster: Mentis, 2015)

Kafka and Music. Special issue of *Journal of the Kafka Society of America: New International Series*, 28, nos. 1–2 (2004)

Kittler, W., 'His Master's Voice: Zur Funktion der Musik im Werk Franz Kafkas' in W. Kittler and G. Neumann (eds.), *Franz Kafka: Schriftverkehr* (Freiburg: Rombach, 1990), pp. 383–91

Lubkoll, C., 'Dies ist kein Pfeifen: Musik und Negation in Franz Kafkas Erzählung "Josefine, die Sängerin oder Das Volk der Mäuse"', *Deutsche Vierteljahrsschrift für Literaturwissenschaft und Geistesgeschichte*, 66 (1992), 748–64

Neumann, G., 'Kafka und die Musik' in W. Kittler and G. Neumann (eds.). *Franz Kafka: Schriftverkehr* (Freiburg: Rombach, 1990), pp. 391–9

15 ARCHITECTURE

Eisenman P., *Eisenman Inside Out: Selected Writings 1963–1988* (New Haven, CT: Yale University Press, 2004)

Lefebvre, H., *The Production of Space*, fourteenth edition (Oxford and Cambridge, MA: Blackwell, 2001)

Mallgrave, H. F., *Gottfried Semper: Architect of the Nineteenth Century* (New Haven, CT and London: Yale University Press, 1996)

Mühlmann, H., *The Nature of Cultures: A Blueprint for a Theory of Culture Genetics* (Heidelberg: Springer, 1996)

Neumeyer, F. (ed.), *Quellentexte zur Architekturtheorie* (Munich: Prestel, 2002)

Rahmani, A. B., *Kafka's Architectures: Doors, Rooms and Windows of an Intricate Edifice* (Jefferson, NC: McFarland & Company, 2015)

Thiel, R., *Anarchitektur: Lektüren zur Architektur-Kritik bei Franz Kafka* (Berlin: Vorwerk 8, 2011)

16 PRAGUE: HISTORY AND CULTURE

Čapková, K., *Czechs, Germans, Jews? National Identity and the Jews of Bohemia* (New York: Berghahn Books, 2012)

Cohen, G. B., *The Politics of Ethnic Survival: Germans in Prague 1861–1914* (Princeton University Press, 1981)

Kieval, H. J., *The Making of Czech Jewry: National Conflict and Jewish Society in Bohemia, 1870–1918* (Oxford University Press, 1988)

Languages of Community: The Jewish Experience in the Czech Lands (Berkeley, CA: University of California Press, 2000)

Nekula, M., *Franz Kafka and his Prague Contexts: Studies in Language and Literature* (Prague: Karolinum, 2016)

Spector, S., *Prague Territories: National Conflict and Cultural Innovation in Franz Kafka's Fin de Siècle* (Berkeley, CA: University of California Press, 2000)

17 CZECH LANGUAGE AND LITERATURE

Čermák, J., 'Die Kafka-Rezeption in Böhmen (1913–1949)' in K. Krolop and H.-D. Zimmermann (eds.), *Kafka und Prag* (Berlin and New York: De Gruyter, 1994), pp. 217–37

Chitnis, R. A., 'Putting Granny in a Home: Czech Writers and the Village in Kafka's Lifetime' in M. Engel and R. Robertson (eds.), *Kafka: Prag und der erste Weltkrieg/Prague and the First World War*, Oxford Kafka Studies (Würzburg: Königshausen & Neumann, 2013), vol. II, pp. 107–25

Kosík, K., 'Hašek and Kafka, 1883–1922/23', in L. Matejka and B. Stolz (eds.), *Cross Currents: A Yearbook of Central European Culture* (Ann Arbor, MI: Michigan Slavic Publications, 1983), vol. II, pp. 127–36

Wutsdorff, I., 'Dá se mluvit o pražské moderně? Poznámky ke komparaci česko- a německojazyčné literatury' in T. Kubiček and J. Wiendl (eds.), *Moderna/moderny* (Olomouc: Palacký University, 2013), pp. 23–35

Zusi, P., 'States of Shock: Kafka and Richard Weiner' in M. Engel and R. Robertson (eds.), *Kafka: Prag und der erste Weltkrieg/Prague and the First World War*, Oxford Kafka Studies (Würzburg: Königshausen & Neumann, 2015), vol. II, pp. 127–42

18 THE FIRST WORLD WAR

Engel, M. and Robertson, R. (eds.), *Kafka: Prag und der erste Weltkrieg/Prague and the First World War*, Oxford Kafka Studies (Würzburg: Königshausen & Neumann, 2015)

Kieval, H. J., *The Making of Czech Jewry: National Conflict and Jewish Society in Bohemia 1870–1918* (Oxford University Press, 1988)

Kučera R., *Rationed Life: Science, Everyday Life, and Working-Class Politics in the Bohemian Lands, 1914–1918* (New York: Berghahn 2016)

Mommsen, H., Kováč, D., Malíř, J. and Marková, M. (eds.), *První světová válka a vztahy mezi Čechy, Slováky a Němci [The First World War and Relations between the Czechs, Slovaks and Germans]* (Brno: Matice moravská, 2000)

Robertson, R., *Kafka: Judaism, Politics and Literature* (Oxford: Clarendon Press 1985)

Šedivy, I., *Češi, české země a velká válka 1914–1918 [The Czechs, the Bohemian Lands and the Great War 1914–1918]* (Prague: NLN, 2001)

19 TRAVEL, COLONIALISM AND EXOTICISM

Dunker, A., 'Kolonialismus in der Literatur des 20. Jahrhunderts: Am Beispiel von Hugo von Hofmannsthal, Gottfried Benn, Franz Kafka, Friedrich Glauser, Hermann Hesse, Arno Schmidt und Hubert Fichte' in G. Dürbeck and A. Dunker (eds.), *Postkoloniale Germanistik: Bestandsaufnahme, theoretische Perspektiven, Lektüren* (Bielefeld: Aisthesis, 2014), pp. 271–327 (pp. 289–98 on Kafka)

Goebel, R. J., 'Kafka and Postcolonial Critique: *Der Verschollene*, "In der Strafkolonie", "Beim Bau der chinesischen Mauer"' in J. Rolleston (ed.), *A Companion to the Works of Franz Kafka* (Rochester, NY: Camden House, 2006), pp. 187–212

Honold, A. 'Berichte von der Menschenschau: Kafka und die Ausstellung des Fremden' in H. Bay and C. Hamann (eds.), *Odradeks Lachen: Fremdheit bei Kafka* (Freiburg: Rombach, 2006), pp. 305–24

Patrut, I.-K., 'Kafkas "Poetik des Anderen", kolonialer Diskurs und postkolonialer Kanon in Europa' in H. Uerlings and I.-K. Patrut (eds.), *Postkolonialismus und Kanon* (Bielefeld: Aisthesis, 2012), pp. 261–88

Zilcosky, J., *Kafka's Travels: Exoticism, Colonialism, and the Traffic of Writing* (New York: Palgrave Macmillan, 2003)

20 LAW

Emmel, H., *Das Gericht in der deutschen Literatur des 20. Jahrhunderts* (Bern and Munich: Francke, 1963)

Heidsieck, A., *The Intellectual Contexts of Kafka's Fiction: Philosophy, Law, Religion* (Columbia, SC: Camden House, 1994)

Kirchberger, L., *Franz Kafka's Use of Law in Fiction: A New Interpretation of 'In der Strafkolonie', 'Der Prozess', and 'Das Schloss'* (New York: Peter Lang, 1993)

Lloyd, D., *The Idea of Law* (Baltimore, MD: Penguin, 1964)

Strejcek, G., *Franz Kafka und die Unfallversicherung: Grenzgänger des Rechts und der Weltliteratur* (Vienna: Wiener Universitätsverlag, 2006)

21 PHILOSOPHY

Born, J., *Kafkas Bibliothek: Ein beschreibendes Verzeichnis.* (Frankfurt am Main: Fischer, 1990)

Bridgwater, P., *Kafka and Nietzsche* (Bonn: Bouvier, 1974)

Bukdahl, J., *Søren Kierkegaard and the Common Man*, trans. B. H. Kirmmse (Grand Rapids, MI: Eerdmans, 2001)

Haecker, Th., 'F. Blei und Kierkegaard', *Der Brenner*, 4, no. 10 (1914), 457–65

Heidler, I., *Der Verleger Eugen Diederichs und seine Welt (1896–1930)* (Wiesbaden: Harrassowitz, 1998)

Irina, N., 'Franz Kafka: Reading Kierkegaard' in J. Stewart (ed.), *Kierkegaard's Influence on Literature, Criticism and Art. Volume I: The Germanophone World* (Farnham: Ashgate, 2013), pp. 115–39

Kierkegaard, S., *Buch des Richters: Seine Tagebücher 1833–1855*, ed. H. Gottsched (Leipzig: Eugen Diederichs, 1905)

Fear and Trembling. Kierkegaard's Writings, ed. H. V. Hong and E. H. Hong (Princeton University Press, 1983), vol. VI

Morgan, B., 'Kierkegaard in the German-Speaking World During the Early 20th-Century' in M. Engel and R. Robertson (eds.), *Kafka und die Religion in der Moderne/Kafka, Religion, and Modernity* (Würzburg: Königshausen & Neumann, 2014), pp. 71–92

Oschmann, D., 'Philosophie' in M. Engel and B. Auerochs (eds.), *Kafka-Handbuch* (Stuttgart: Metzler, 2010), pp. 59–64

22 RELIGION

Agamben, G., *Homo Sacer: Sovereign Power and Bare Life* (Stanford University Press, 1998)

Alter, R., *Necessary Angels: Tradition and Modernity in Kafka, Benjamin, and Scholem* (Cambridge, MA: Harvard University Press, 1991)

Benjamin, W., 'Franz Kafka: On the Tenth Anniversary of His Death' in M. W. Jennings, H. Eiland and G. Smith (eds.), R. Livingstone (trans.), *Walter Benjamin: Selected Writings, 1927–1934* (Cambridge, MA: Harvard University Press, 1999), vol. II, pp. 794–818

Brod, M. and Schopeps, H. J., *Im Streit um Kafka und das Judentum* (Königstein/Ts: Jüdischer Verlag bei Athenäum, 1985)

Engel, M. and Robertson, R. (eds.), *Kafka und die Religion in der Moderne/Kafka, Religion, and Modernity* (Würzburg: Königshausen & Neumann, 2014)

Neumann, G., 'Umkehrung und Ablenkung: Franz Kafkas "gleitendes Paradox"', *Deutsche Vierteljahrsschrift für Literaturwissenschaft und Geistesgeschichte*, 42 (1968), 702–44; reprinted in Politzer, H. (ed.), *Franz Kafka* (Darmstadt: Wissenschaftliche Buchgesellschaft, 1973), pp. 459–515

23 JUDAISM AND ZIONISM

Alter, R., *Necessary Angels: Tradition and Modernity in Kafka, Benjamin, and Scholem* (Cambridge, MA: Harvard University Press, 1991)

Bruce, I., *Kafka and Cultural Zionism: Dates in Palestine* (Madison, WI: University of Wisconsin Press, 2007)

Gelber, M. H. (ed.), *Kafka, Zionism, and Beyond* (Tübingen: Max Niemeyer, 2004)

Liska, V., *When Kafka Says We: Uncommon Communities in German-Jewish Literature* (Bloomington, IN: Indiana University Press, 2009)

Miron, D., *From Continuity to Contiguity: Toward a New Jewish Literary Thinking* (Stanford University Press, 2010)

24 PSYCHOLOGY AND PSYCHOANALYSIS

Alt, P.-A., *Franz Kafka: Der ewige Sohn* (Munich: Beck, 2005)

Anz, T., 'Psychoanalyse' in M. Engel and B. Auerochs (eds.), *Kafka-Handbuch* (Stuttgart: Metzler, 2010), pp. 65–72

Bell, M., *The German Tradition of Psychology in Literature and Thought, 1700–1840* (Cambridge University Press, 2005)

Gundlach, H. U. K., 'Germany' in D. D. Baker (ed.), *The Oxford Handbook of the History of Psychology: Global Perspectives* (Oxford University Press, 2012), pp. 255–88

Ryan, J., *The Vanishing Subject: Early Psychology and Literary Modernism* (University of Chicago Press, 1991)

Smith, B., 'Brentano and Kafka', *Axiomathes*, 8 (1997), 83–104

25 GENDER AND SEXUALITY

Boa, E., *Kafka: Gender, Class, and Race in the Letters and Fictions* (Oxford: Clarendon Press, 1996)

Friedländer, S., *Franz Kafka: The Poet of Shame and Guilt* (New Haven and London: Yale University Press, 2013)

Gilman, S. L., *Franz Kafka: The Jewish Patient* (New York: Routledge, 1995)

Mosse, G. L., *Nationalism and Sexuality: Respectability and Abnormal Sexuality in Modern Europe* (New York: Fertig, 1985)

Stach, R., 'Kafka's Egoless Woman: Otto Weininger's "Sex and Character"' in M. M. Anderson (ed.), *Reading Kafka: Prague, Politics and the Fin de Siècle* (New York: Schocken Books, 1989), pp. 149–69

Stach, R., *Kafka: The Early Years*, trans. S. Frisch (Princeton University Press, 2017)

26 THE CITY

Alter, R., *Imagined Cities and the Language of the Novel* (New Haven, CT and London: Yale University Press, 2005)

Frisby, D., *Fragments of Modernity: Theories of Modernity in the Work of Simmel, Kracauer and Benjamin* (London: Routledge, 2013)

Goebel, R. J., 'The Exploration of the Modern City in The Trial' in J. Preece (ed.), *Cambridge Companion to Franz Kafka* (Cambridge University Press, 2002), pp. 42–60

Spector, S., *Prague Territories: National Conflict and Cultural Innovation in Franz Kafka's Fin de Siècle* (Berkeley, CA: California University Press, 2000)

Tambing, J., *Lost in the American City: Dickens, James and Kafka* (Basingstoke: Palgrave Macmillan, 2001)

27 CHILDHOOD, PEDAGOGY AND EDUCATION

Key, E., *The Century of the Child*, trans. F. Maro (New York and London: G. P. Putnam's Sons, 1909)

Robertson, R., 'Children and Childhood in Kafka's Work', in C. Duttlinger (ed.), *Kafkas 'Betrachtung': Neue Lektüren* (Freiburg: Rombach, 2014), pp. 179–99

Rutschky, K. (ed.), *Schwarze Pädagogik: Quellen zur Naturgeschichte der bürgerlichen Erziehung* (Berlin: Ullstein, 1997)

Schatzman, M., *Soul Murder: Persecution in the Family* (London: Allen Lane, 1973)

Stach, R., *Kafka: The Early Years*, trans. S. Frisch (Princeton University Press, 2017)

28 ETHNOGRAPHY AND ANTHROPOLOGY

Gess, N., *Primitives Denken: Kinder und Wahnsinnige in der literarischen Moderne (Müller, Musil, Benn, Benjamin)* (Munich: Fink, 2013)

Gess, N. (ed.), *Literarischer Primitivismus* (Berlin: De Gruyter, 2012)

Goebel, R. J., *Constructing China: Kafka's Orientalist Discourse* (Columbia, SC: Camden Hause, 1997)

Kohn, M., 'Kafka's Critique of Colonialism', *Theory & Event*, 8, no. 3 (2005)

Pan, D., *Primitive Renaissance: Rethinking German Expressionism* (Lincoln, NE: University of Nebraska Press, 2001)

Zilcoskcy, J., *Kafka's Travels: Exoticism, Colonialism, and the Traffic of Writing* (New York: Palgrave Macmillan, 2003)

Zink, J., 'Rotpeter als Bororo: Drei Erzählungen Franz Kafkas vor dem Hintergrund eines "Literarischen Primitivismus" um 1900' (PhD dissertation, University of Würzburg, 2005)

29 EARLY CRITICAL RECEPTION

Beicken, P., *Franz Kafka: Eine kritische Einführung in die Forschung* (Frankfurt am Main: Atheneion, 1974)

Born, J. (ed.), *Franz Kafka: Kritik und Rezeption zu seinen Lebzeiten, 1912–1924* (Frankfurt am Main: Fischer, 1979)

Ermath, M. (ed.), *Kurt Wolff: A Portrait in Essays and Letters*, trans. D. Schneider (University of Chicago Press, 1991)

Fromm, W., 'Kafka-Rezeption' in B. von Jagow and O. Jahraus (eds.), *Kafka Handbuch* (Göttingen: Vandenhoeck & Ruprecht, 2008), pp. 250–72

Karl, F. R., 'Early Years of Achievement in an Age of Hostility' in *Franz Kafka: Representative Man* (New York: Ticknor and Fields, 1991), pp. 234–308

Rubin, A. A., 'Kafka's German-Jewish Reception as Mirror of Modernity' (PhD dissertation, City University of New York, 2014), CUNY Academic Works. http://academicworks.cuny.edu/gc_etds/376/

30 CRITICAL THEORY

Adorno, T. W., 'Notes on Kafka' in T. W. Adorno, *Prisms*, trans. S. Weber and S. Weber (Cambridge, MA: MIT Press, 1981), pp. 243–71

Benjamin, W., 'Franz Kafka: "Beim Bau der chinesischen Mauer"' in M. W. Jennings, H. Eiland and G. Smith (eds.), R. Livingstone (trans.), *Walter Benjamin: Selected Writings 1927–1934* (Cambridge, MA: Harvard University Press, 1999), vol. II, pp. 494–500

'Franz Kafka: On the Tenth Anniversary of His Death' in M. W. Jennings, H. Eiland and G. Smith (eds.), R. Livingstone (trans.), *Walter Benjamin: Selected Writings, 1927–1934* (Cambridge, MA: Harvard University Press, 1999), vol. II, pp. 794–818

Corngold, S., 'Adorno's "Notes on Kafka": A Critical Reconstruction' in S. Corngold, *Lambent Traces: Franz Kafka* (Princeton University Press, 2004), pp. 158–75

Frisby, D., *Fragments of Modernity: Theories of Modernity in the Work of Simmel, Kracauer, and Benjamin* (Cambridge, MA: MIT Press, 1986)

Hamacher, W., 'The Gesture in the Name: On Benjamin and Kafka' in W. Hamacher, *Premises: Essays on Philosophy and Literature from Kant to Celan*, trans. P. Fenves (Stanford University Press, 1996), pp. 294–336

Kracauer, S., 'Franz Kafka' in S. Kracauer, *The Mass Ornament: Weimar Essays*, trans. T. Y. Levin (Cambridge, MA: Harvard University Press, 1995), pp. 267–78

31 DECONSTRUCTION

Bernheimer, C., *Flaubert and Kafka: Studies in Psychopoetic Structure* (New Haven, CT and London: Yale University Press, 1982)

Corngold, S., 'Ritardando in *Das Schloß* (*The Castle*)' in S. Wilke (ed.), *From Kafka to Sebald: Modernism and Narrative Form* (London: Continuum, 2012), pp. 11–26

Culler, J., *On Deconstruction: Theory and Criticism after Structuralism* (Ithaca, NY: Cornell University Press, 1982)

Derrida, J., 'Before the Law' in D. Attridge (ed.), *Jacques Derrida: Acts of Literature* (New York: Routledge, 1992), pp. 181–220

Hamacher, W., 'The Gesture in the Name: On Benjamin and Kafka' in W. Hamacher, *Premises: Essays on Philosophy and Literature from Kant to Celan*, trans. P. Fenves (Stanford University Press, 1996), pp. 294–336

Sussman, H., *Franz Kafka: Geometrician of Metaphor* (Madison, WI: Coda Press, 1979)

32 READING KAFKA

Greve, A., 'The Human Body and the Human Being in "Die Verwandlung"' in J. Lothe, B. Sandberg and R. Speirs (eds.), *Franz Kafka: Narration, Rhetoric, and Reading* (Columbus, OH: Ohio State University Press, 2011), pp. 40–57

Phelan, J., 'Progression, Speed, and Judgment in "Das Urteil"' in J. Lothe, B. Sandberg and R. Speirs (eds.), *Franz Kafka: Narration, Rhetoric, and Reading* (Columbus, OH: Ohio State University Press, 2011), pp. 22–39

Proulx, T. and Heine, S. J., 'Connections from Kafka: Exposure to Meaning Threats Improves Implicit Learning of Artificial Grammar', *Psychological Science*, 20 (2009), 1125–31

Troscianko, E. T., 'First-Person and Second-Generation Perspectives on Starvation in Kafka's "Ein Hungerkünstler"', *Style*, 48 (2013), 331–48

'Reading Kafka Enactively', *Paragraph*, 37 (2014), 37–51

33 EDITIONS

Corngold, S., and Gross, R. V. (eds.), *Kafka for the Twenty-First Century* (Rochester, NY: Camden House, 2011)

Gray, R. T., et al. *A Franz Kafka Encyclopedia* (Westport, CT: Greenwood, 2005)

Koelb, C., *Kafka: A Guide for the Perplexed* (London: Continuum, 2010)

Robertson, R., *Kafka: A Very Short Introduction* (Oxford University Press, 2004)

Rolleston, J. (ed.), *A Companion to the Works of Franz Kafka* (Rochester, NY: Camden House, 2002)

Stach, R., *Kafka: The Decisive Years*, trans. S. Frisch (Princeton University Press, 2013)

34 TRANSLATION

Coetzee, J. M., 'Translating Kafka', in J. M. Coetzee, *Stranger Shores: Literary Essays 1986–1999* (New York and London: Viking, 2001), pp. 74–87

Damrosch, D., 'Kafka Comes Home', in D. Damrosch, *What is World Literature?* (Princeton University Press, 2003), pp. 187–208

Durrani, O., 'Editions, Translations, Adaptations' in J. Preece (ed.), *The Cambridge Companion to Kafka* (Cambridge University Press, 2002), pp. 206–25

Gray, R., 'But Kafka Wrote in German' in A. Flores (ed.), *The Kafka Debate* (New York: Gordian Press, 1977), pp. 242–52

Harman, M., 'Digging the Pit of Babel: Retranslating Franz Kafka's *Castle*', *New Literary History*, 27 (1996), 291–311

Kundera, M., 'A Sentence' in M. Kundera, *Testaments Betrayed: An Essay in Nine Parts*, trans. L. Asher (New York: Harper Collins, 1995), pp. 101–20

Woods, M., *Kafka Translated: How Translators have Shaped our Reading of Kafka* (London: Bloomsbury, 2014)

35 FILM ADAPTATIONS

Jeffrey A., 'Soderbergh's *Kafka*: In Retrospect', *Post Script*, 31, no. 1 (2011), 26–39

Brady, M. and Hughes, H., 'Kafka Adapted to Film' in J. Preece (ed.), *The Cambridge Companion to Kafka* (Cambridge University Press, 2002), pp. 226–41

Holmes, D., 'Literature on the Small Screen: Michael Haneke's Television Adaptations of Josef Roth's *Die Rebellion* and Kafka's *Das Schloß* in J. Preece, F. Finlay and R. J. Owen (eds.), *New German Literature: Life-Writing and Dialogue with the Arts* (Bern: Peter Lang, 2007), pp. 107–22

Pohland, V., 'Trains of Traffic: Kafka's Novels into Film', *Journal of the Kafka Society of America*, 24, no. 1–2 (2000), 54–74

Vatulescu, C., 'The Medium on Trial: Orson Welles Takes on Kafka and Cinema', *Literature Film Quarterly*, 41, no. 1 (2013), 52–66

Index